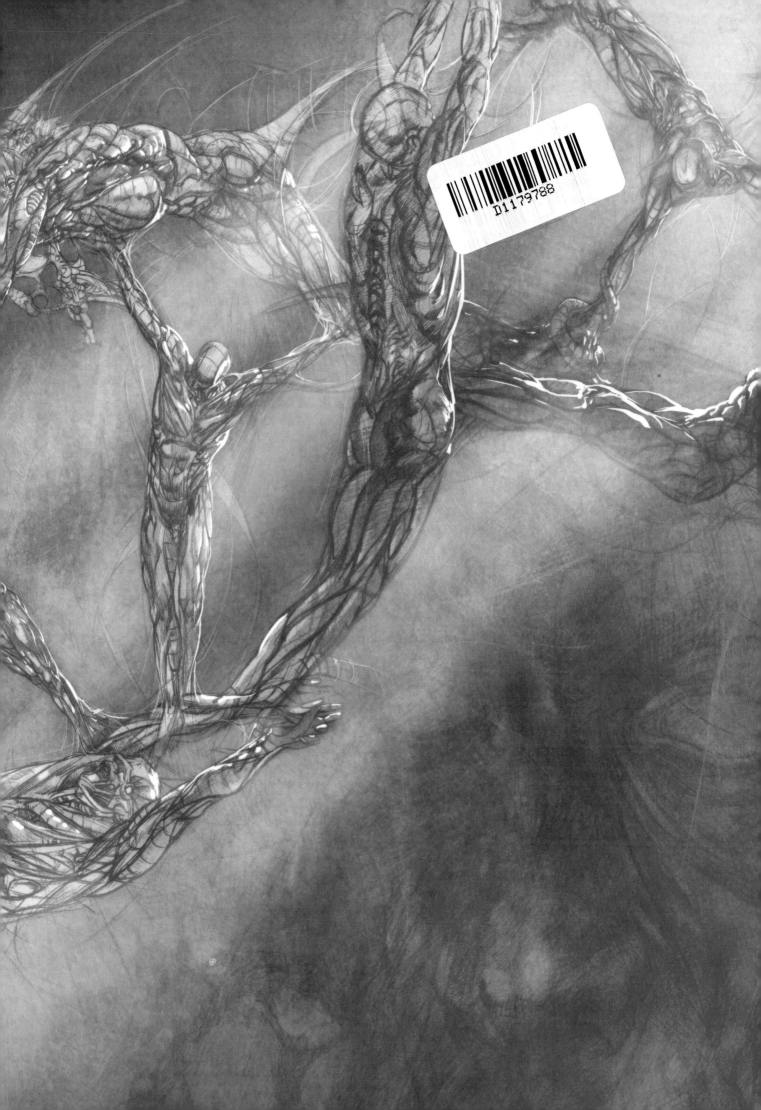

SHOCK ™

AFTERSHOCK ™

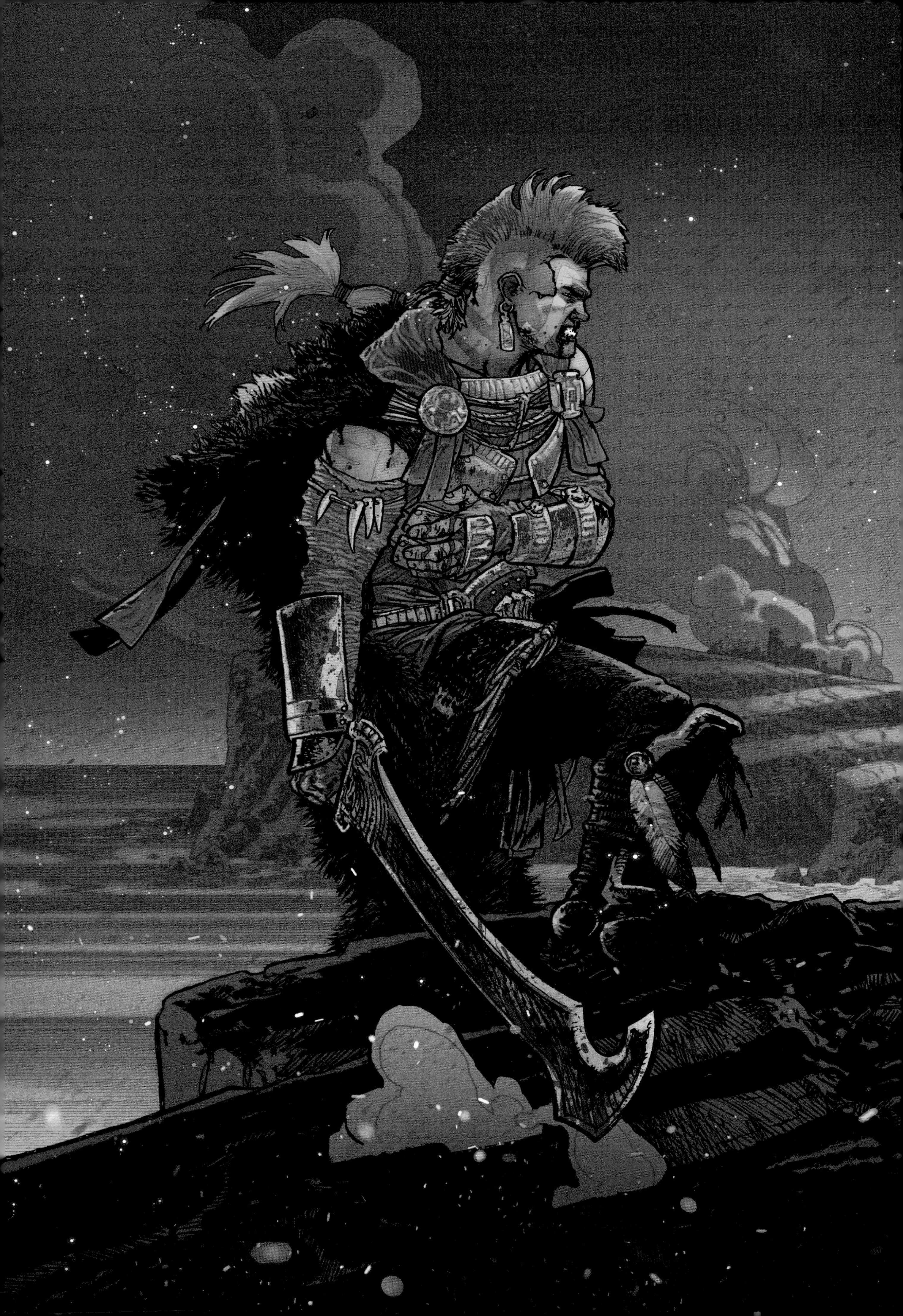

CONTENTS

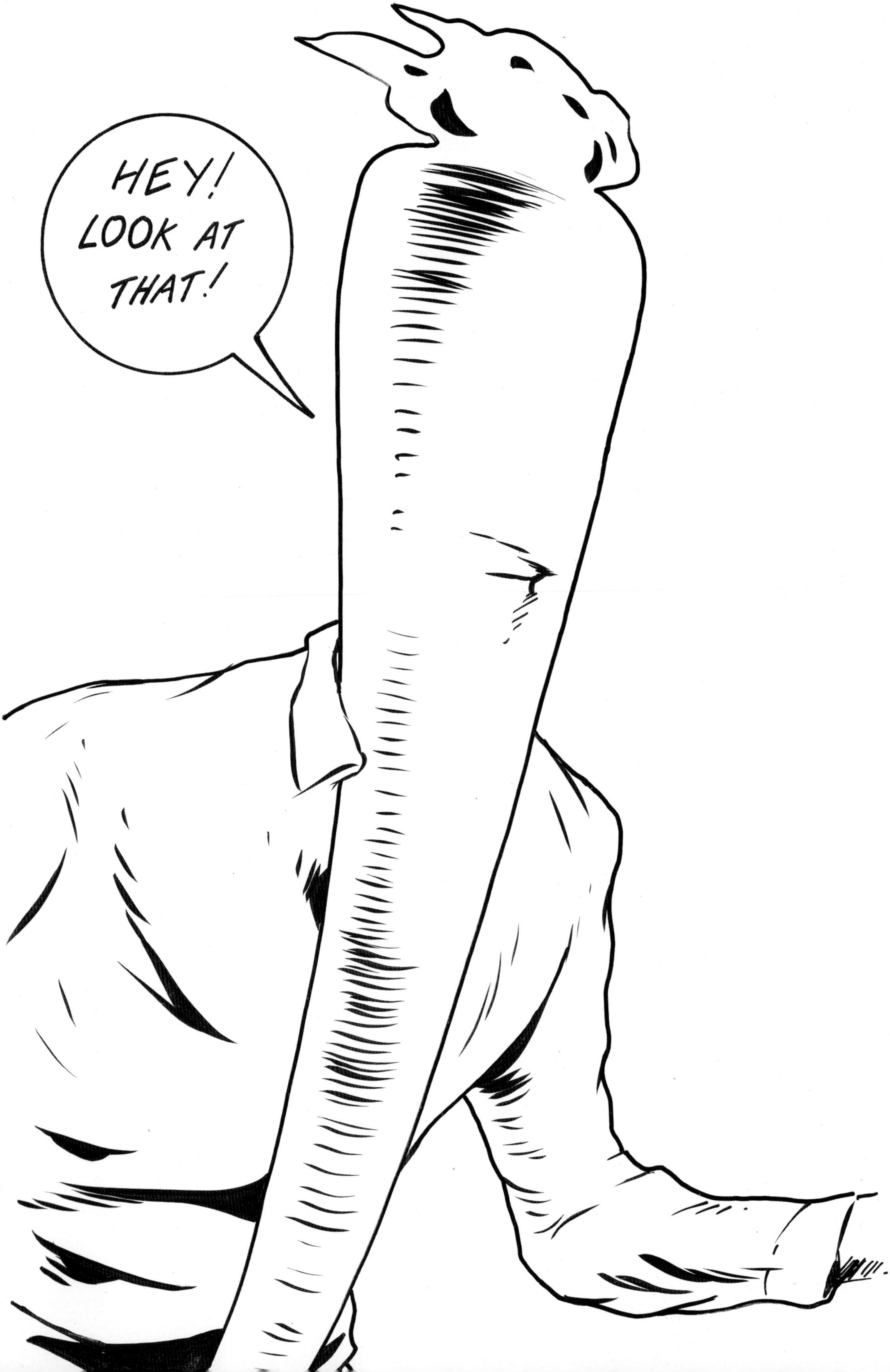
HEY! LOOK AT THAT!

FRONT COVER ART
TIM BRADSTREET

BACK COVER ART
SAM KIETH

INSIDE COVER ART
SZYMON KUDRANSKI

TABLE OF CONTENTS PAGE ART
ANDREI BRESSAN

CREDITS PAGE ART
BOB BURDEN

LOGO DESIGN
JOHN J. HILL

BOOK DESIGN
JOE PRUETT

PRODUCTION
MARSHALL DILLON

EDITOR
JOE PRUETT

FIRST EDITION
13 12 11 10 1 2 3 4

ISBN
978-1-949028-10-2

AFTERSHOCK COMICS
MIKE MARTS - Editor-in-Chief • JOE PRUETT - Publisher/CCO • LEE KRAMER - President • JON KRAMER - Chief Executive Officer
STEVE ROTTERDAM - SVP, Sales & Marketing • DAN SHIRES - VP, Film & Television UK • CHRISTINA HARRINGTON - Managing Editor
MARC HAMMOND - Sr. Retail Sales Development Manager • RUTHANN THOMPSON - Sr. Retailer Relations Manager • BLAKE STOCKER - CFO
AARON MARION - Publicist • LISA MOODY - Finance • RYAN CARROLL - Development Coordinator
CHARLES PRITCHETT - Comics Production • COREY BREEN - Collections Production
TEDDY LEO - Editorial Assistant • STEPHANIE CASEBIER & SARAH PRUETT Publishing Assistants

AfterShock Logo Design by COMICRAFT
Publicity: contact AARON MARION (aaron@publichausagency.com) & RYAN CROY (ryan@publichausagency.com) at PUBLICHAUS
Special Thanks to: MARINE KSADZHIKYAN, IRA KURGAN, ANTONIA LIANOS, STEPHAN NILSON & JULIE PIFHER

Follow us on social media

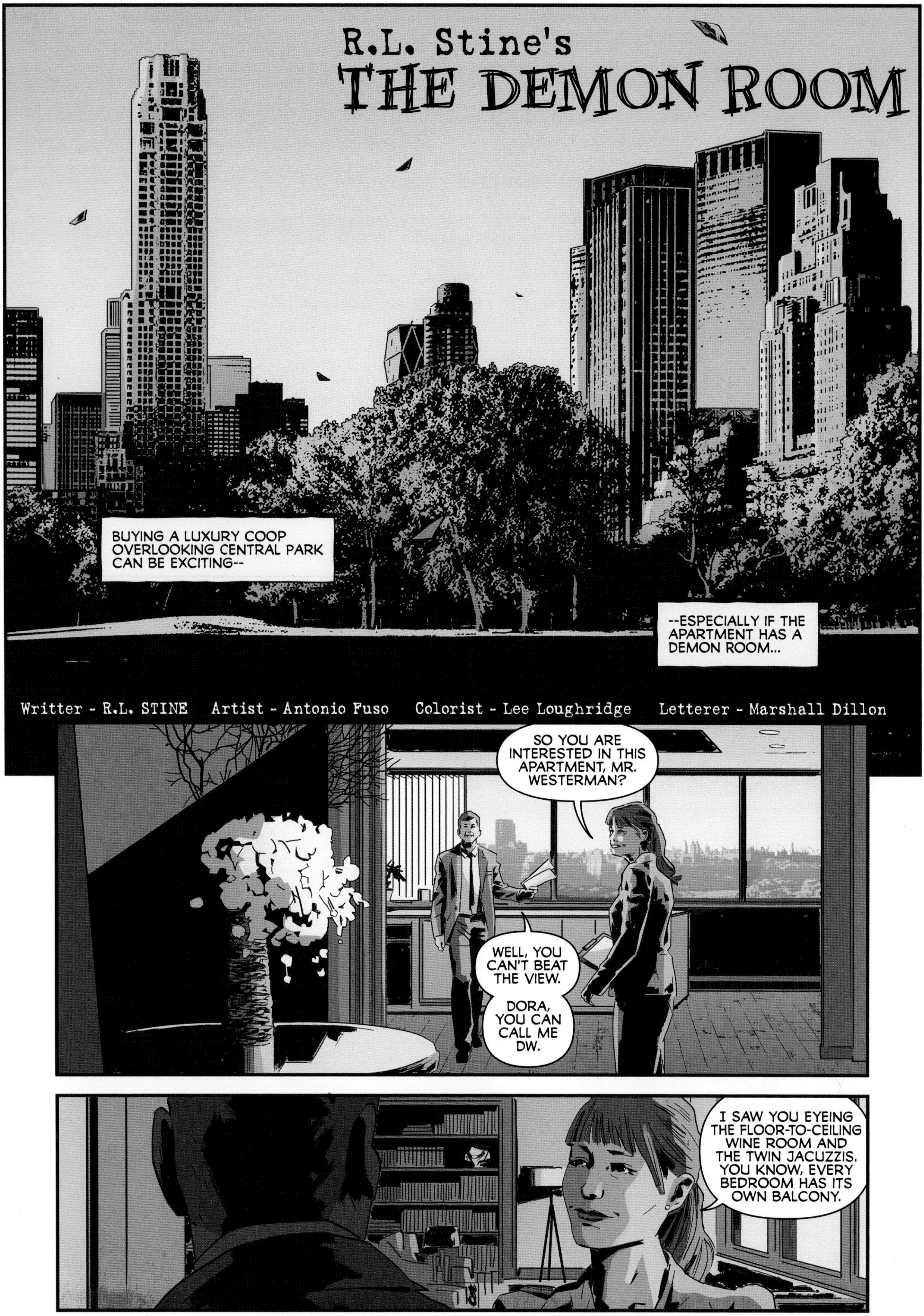
R.L. Stine's
THE DEMON ROOM
BUYING A LUXURY COOP OVERLOOKING CENTRAL PARK CAN BE EXCITING--
--ESPECIALLY IF THE APARTMENT HAS A DEMON ROOM...
Writter - R.L. STINE Artist - Antonio Fuso Colorist - Lee Loughridge Letterer - Marshall Dillon
SO YOU ARE INTERESTED IN THIS APARTMENT, MR. WESTERMAN?
WELL, YOU CAN'T BEAT THE VIEW.
DORA, YOU CAN CALL ME DW.
I SAW YOU EYEING THE FLOOR-TO-CEILING WINE ROOM AND THE TWIN JACUZZIS. YOU KNOW, EVERY BEDROOM HAS ITS OWN BALCONY.

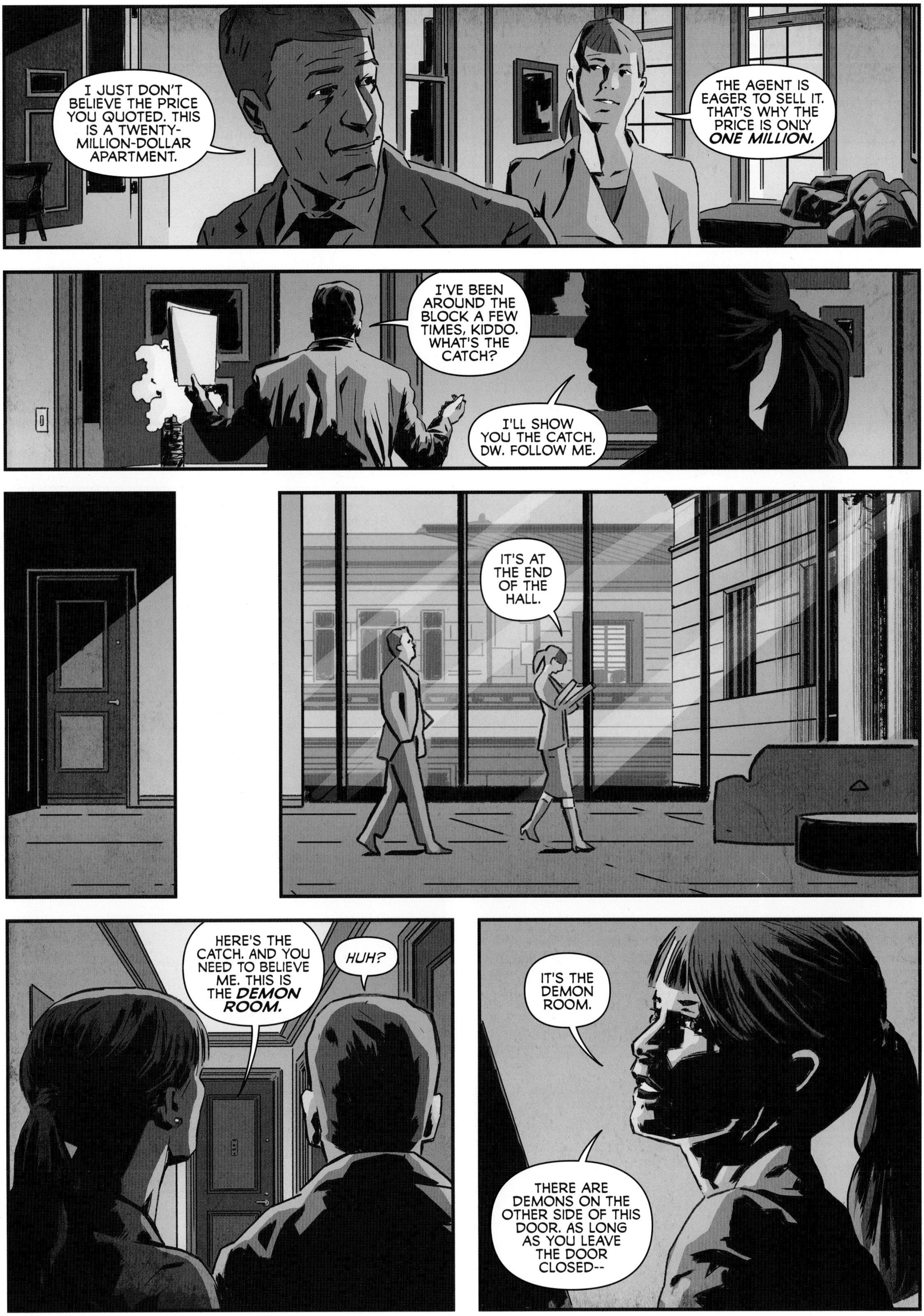

I JUST DON'T BELIEVE THE PRICE YOU QUOTED. THIS IS A TWENTY-MILLION-DOLLAR APARTMENT.
THE AGENT IS EAGER TO SELL IT. THAT'S WHY THE PRICE IS ONLY ***ONE MILLION.***
I'VE BEEN AROUND THE BLOCK A FEW TIMES, KIDDO. WHAT'S THE CATCH?
I'LL SHOW YOU THE CATCH, DW. FOLLOW ME.
IT'S AT THE END OF THE HALL.
HERE'S THE CATCH. AND YOU NEED TO BELIEVE ME. THIS IS THE ***DEMON ROOM.***
HUH?
IT'S THE DEMON ROOM.
THERE ARE DEMONS ON THE OTHER SIDE OF THIS DOOR. AS LONG AS YOU LEAVE THE DOOR CLOSED--

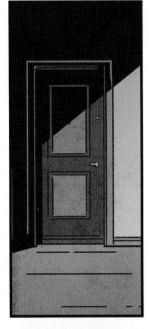

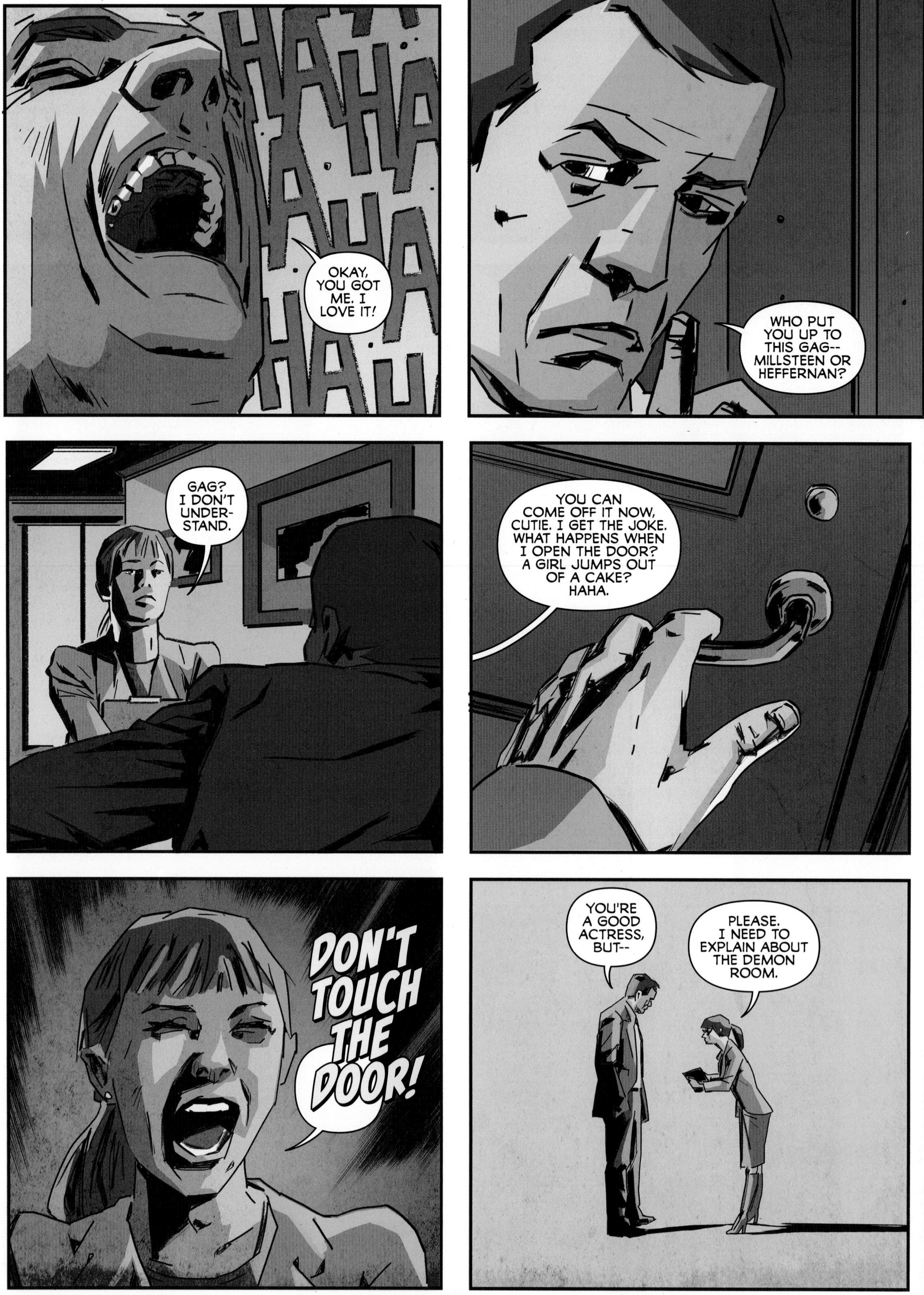
HAHAHAHA
OKAY, YOU GOT ME. I LOVE IT!
WHO PUT YOU UP TO THIS GAG-- MILLSTEEN OR HEFFERNAN?
GAG? I DON'T UNDER-STAND.
YOU CAN COME OFF IT NOW, CUTIE. I GET THE JOKE. WHAT HAPPENS WHEN I OPEN THE DOOR? A GIRL JUMPS OUT OF A CAKE? HAHA.
DON'T TOUCH THE DOOR!
YOU'RE A GOOD ACTRESS, BUT--
PLEASE. I NEED TO EXPLAIN ABOUT THE DEMON ROOM.

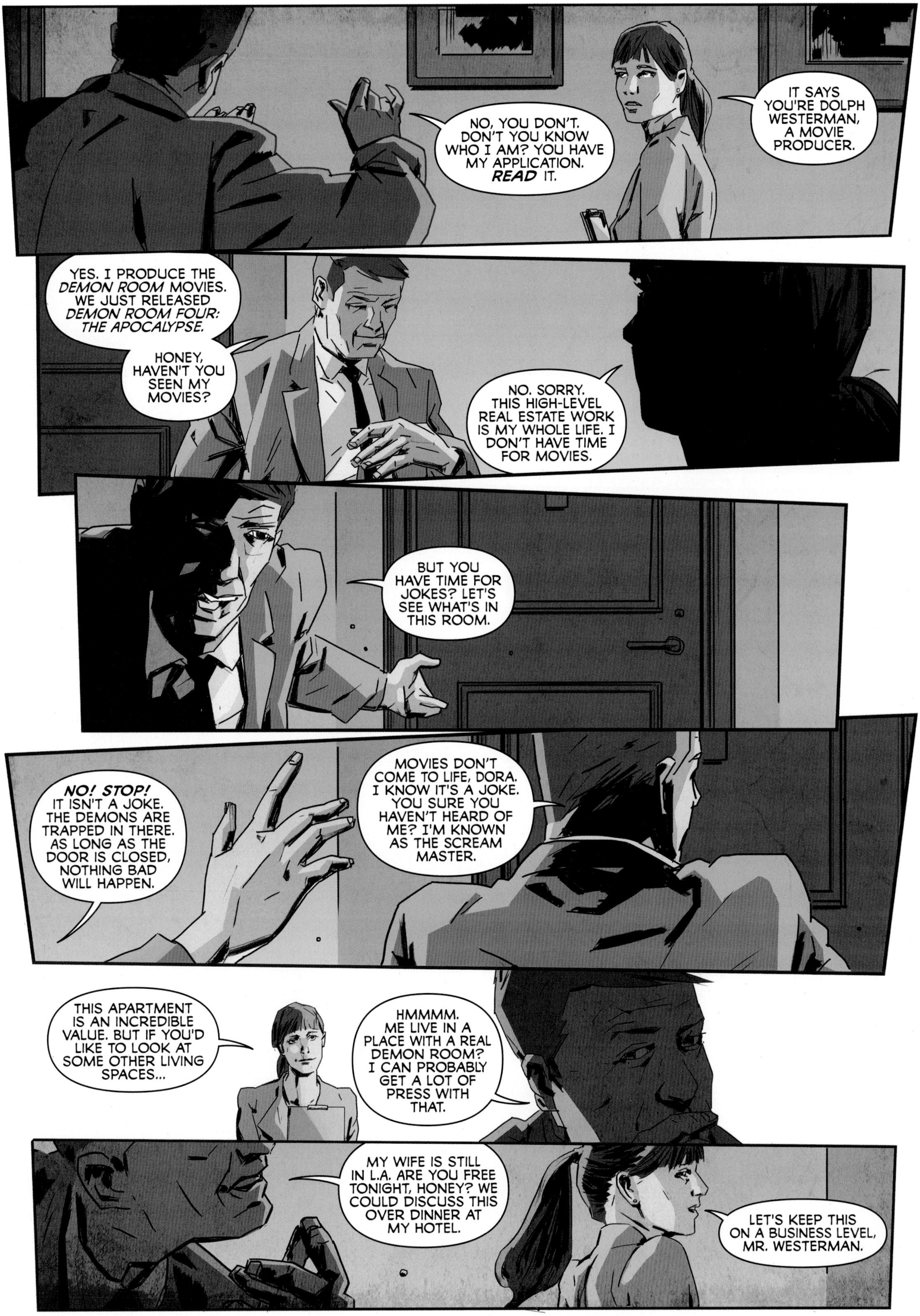
NO, YOU DON'T. DON'T YOU KNOW WHO I AM? YOU HAVE MY APPLICATION. *READ* IT.
IT SAYS YOU'RE DOLPH WESTERMAN, A MOVIE PRODUCER.
YES. I PRODUCE THE *DEMON ROOM* MOVIES. WE JUST RELEASED *DEMON ROOM FOUR: THE APOCALYPSE.*
HONEY, HAVEN'T YOU SEEN MY MOVIES?
NO. SORRY. THIS HIGH-LEVEL REAL ESTATE WORK IS MY WHOLE LIFE. I DON'T HAVE TIME FOR MOVIES.
BUT YOU HAVE TIME FOR JOKES? LET'S SEE WHAT'S IN THIS ROOM.
NO! STOP! IT ISN'T A JOKE. THE DEMONS ARE TRAPPED IN THERE. AS LONG AS THE DOOR IS CLOSED, NOTHING BAD WILL HAPPEN.
MOVIES DON'T COME TO LIFE, DORA. I KNOW IT'S A JOKE. YOU SURE YOU HAVEN'T HEARD OF ME? I'M KNOWN AS THE SCREAM MASTER.
THIS APARTMENT IS AN INCREDIBLE VALUE. BUT IF YOU'D LIKE TO LOOK AT SOME OTHER LIVING SPACES...
HMMMM. ME LIVE IN A PLACE WITH A REAL DEMON ROOM? I CAN PROBABLY GET A LOT OF PRESS WITH THAT.
MY WIFE IS STILL IN L.A. ARE YOU FREE TONIGHT, HONEY? WE COULD DISCUSS THIS OVER DINNER AT MY HOTEL.
LET'S KEEP THIS ON A BUSINESS LEVEL, MR. WESTERMAN.

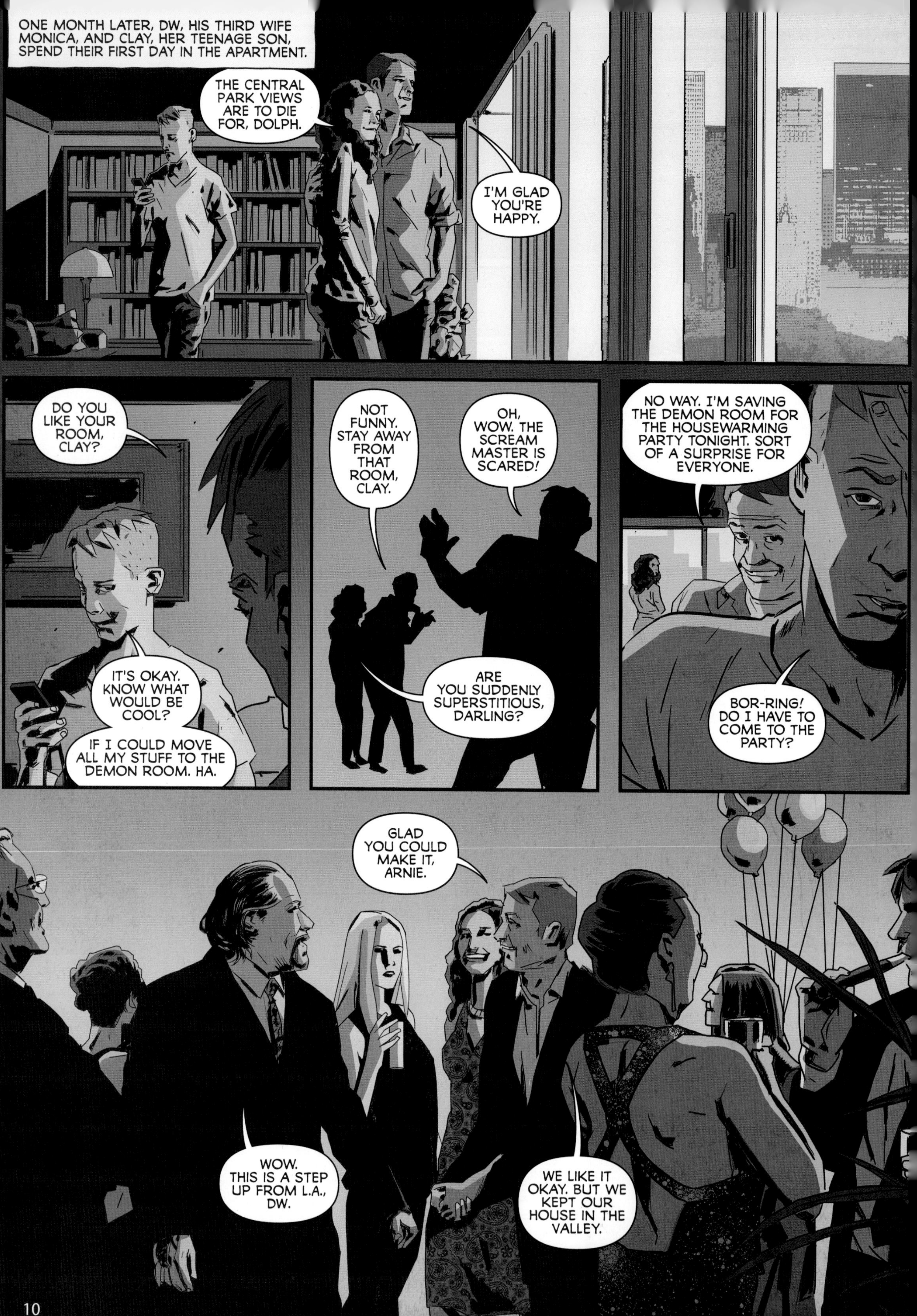
ONE MONTH LATER, DW, HIS THIRD WIFE MONICA, AND CLAY, HER TEENAGE SON, SPEND THEIR FIRST DAY IN THE APARTMENT.
THE CENTRAL PARK VIEWS ARE TO DIE FOR, DOLPH.
I'M GLAD YOU'RE HAPPY.
DO YOU LIKE YOUR ROOM, CLAY?
IT'S OKAY. KNOW WHAT WOULD BE COOL?
IF I COULD MOVE ALL MY STUFF TO THE DEMON ROOM. HA.
NOT FUNNY. STAY AWAY FROM THAT ROOM, CLAY.
OH, WOW. THE SCREAM MASTER IS SCARED!
ARE YOU SUDDENLY SUPERSTITIOUS, DARLING?
NO WAY. I'M SAVING THE DEMON ROOM FOR THE HOUSEWARMING PARTY TONIGHT. SORT OF A SURPRISE FOR EVERYONE.
BOR-RING! DO I HAVE TO COME TO THE PARTY?
GLAD YOU COULD MAKE IT, ARNIE.
WOW. THIS IS A STEP UP FROM L.A., DW.
WE LIKE IT OKAY. BUT WE KEPT OUR HOUSE IN THE VALLEY.

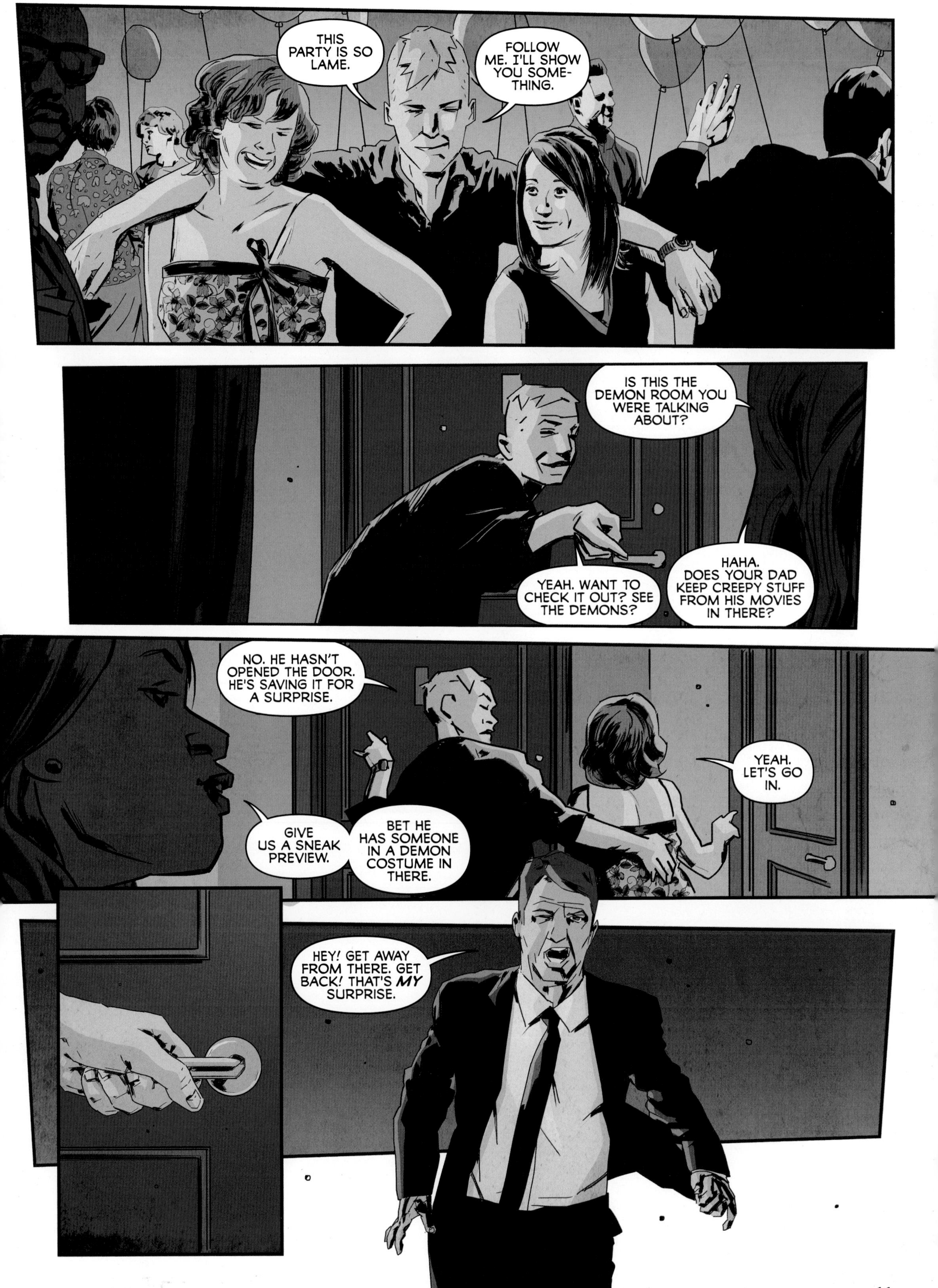
THIS PARTY IS SO LAME.
FOLLOW ME. I'LL SHOW YOU SOME-THING.
IS THIS THE DEMON ROOM YOU WERE TALKING ABOUT?
YEAH. WANT TO CHECK IT OUT? SEE THE DEMONS?
HAHA. DOES YOUR DAD KEEP CREEPY STUFF FROM HIS MOVIES IN THERE?
NO. HE HASN'T OPENED THE DOOR. HE'S SAVING IT FOR A SURPRISE.
YEAH. LET'S GO IN.
GIVE US A SNEAK PREVIEW.
BET HE HAS SOMEONE IN A DEMON COSTUME IN THERE.
HEY! GET AWAY FROM THERE. GET BACK! THAT'S *MY* SURPRISE.

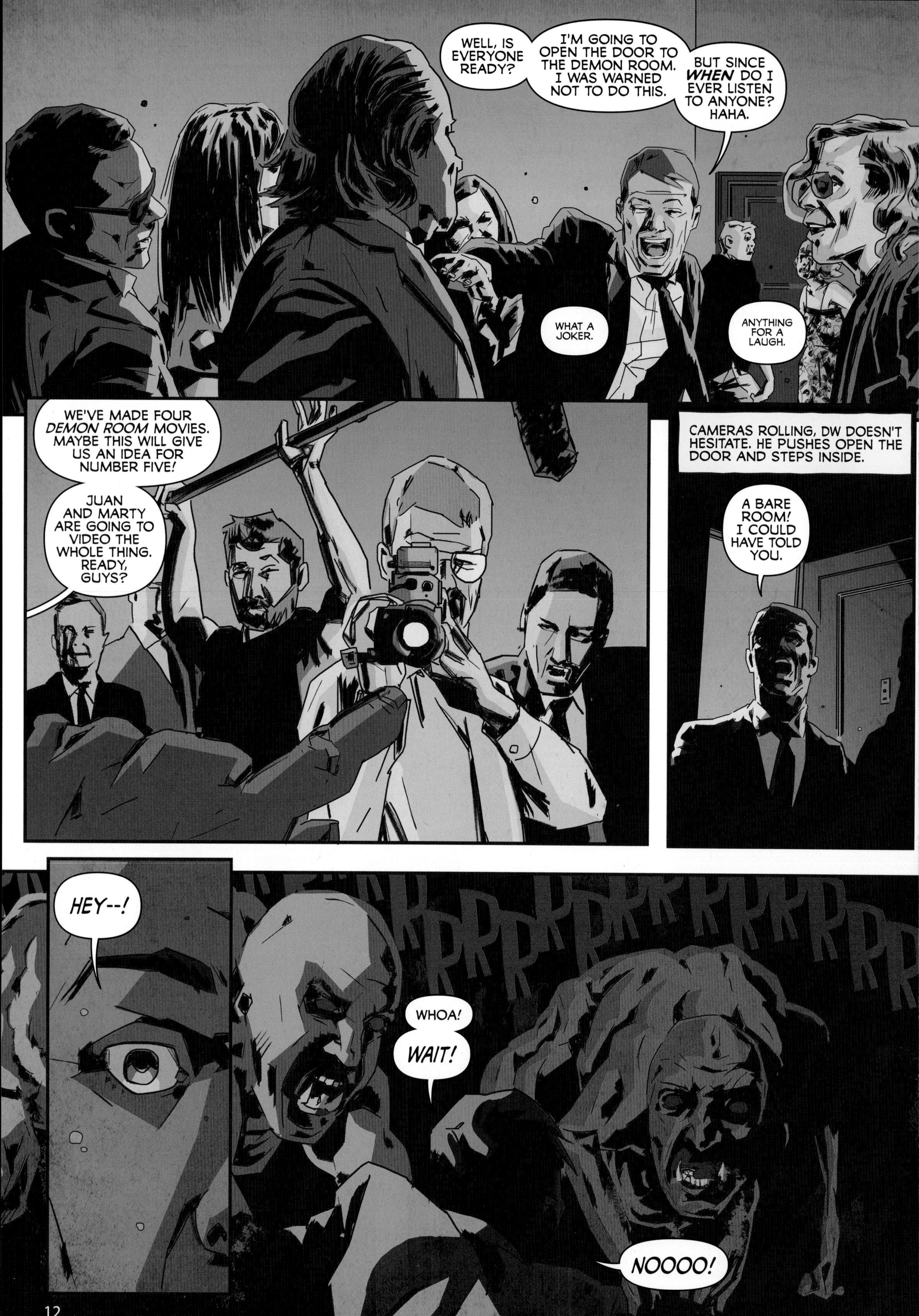
WELL, IS EVERYONE READY?
I'M GOING TO OPEN THE DOOR TO THE DEMON ROOM. I WAS WARNED NOT TO DO THIS.
BUT SINCE *WHEN* DO I EVER LISTEN TO ANYONE? HAHA.
WHAT A JOKER.
ANYTHING FOR A LAUGH.
WE'VE MADE FOUR *DEMON ROOM* MOVIES. MAYBE THIS WILL GIVE US AN IDEA FOR NUMBER FIVE!
JUAN AND MARTY ARE GOING TO VIDEO THE WHOLE THING. READY, GUYS?
CAMERAS ROLLING, DW DOESN'T HESITATE. HE PUSHES OPEN THE DOOR AND STEPS INSIDE.
A BARE ROOM! I COULD HAVE TOLD YOU.
HEY--!
RRRRRRRRRRRRRR
WHOA!
WAIT!
NOOOO!

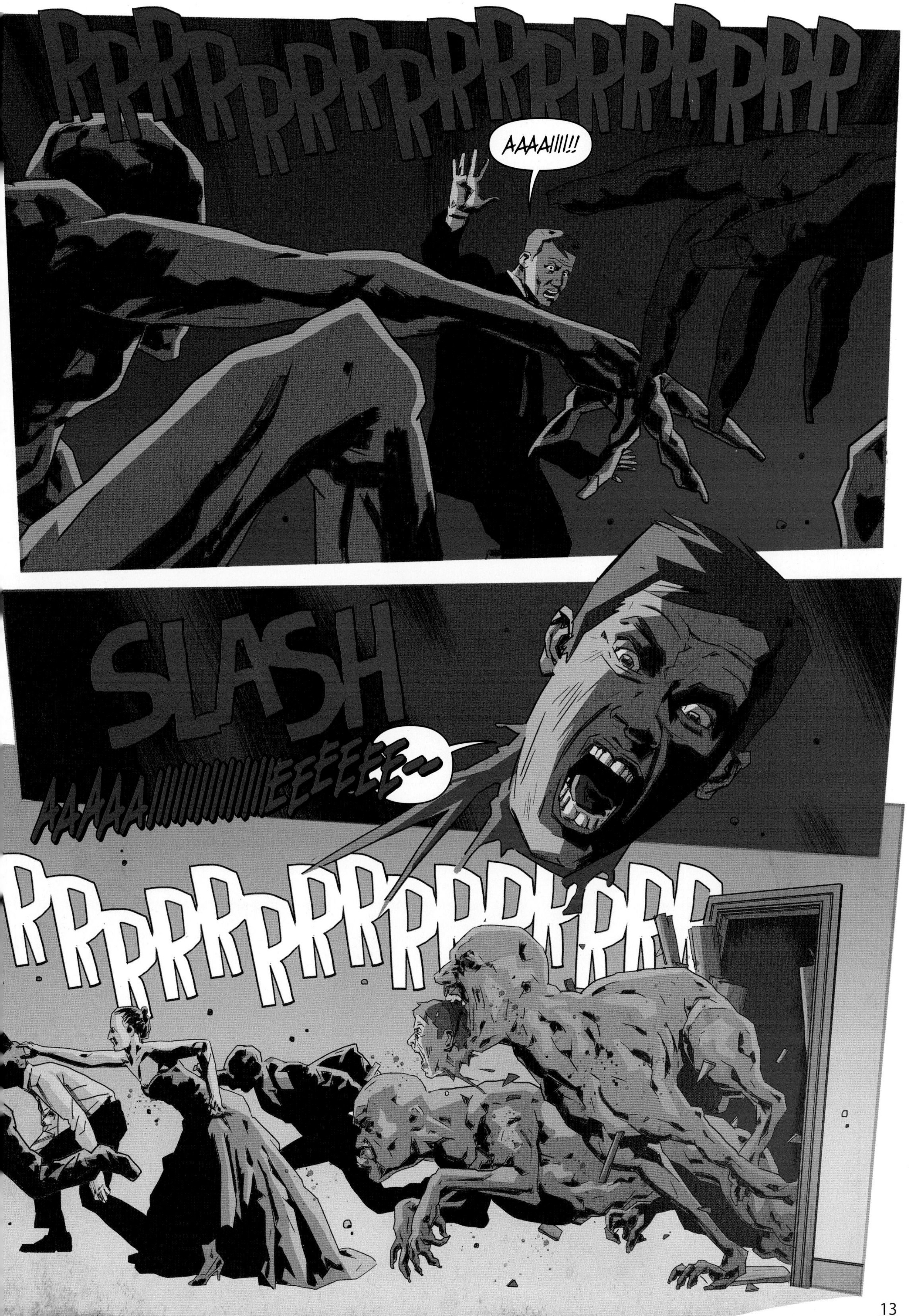
RRRRRRRRRRRRRRRRRRRRRR
AAAAIIII!!
SLASH
AAAAAIIIIIIIIIIIIIIIIEEEEEEE~~
RRRRRRRRRRRRRRRRRKRRR

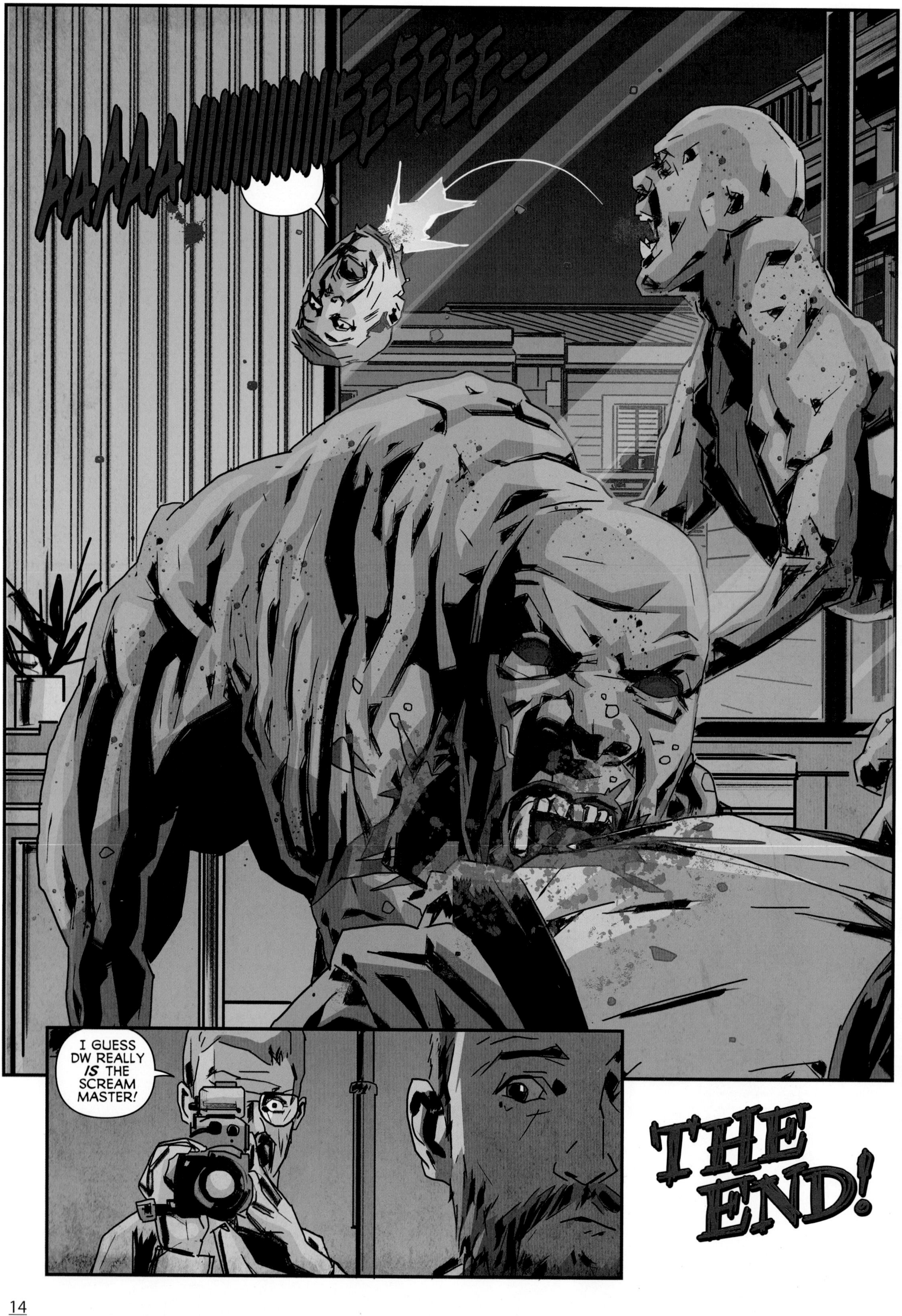
AAAAA!!!!!!!!!!!!!!!!!!!!!EEEEEE--
I GUESS DW REALLY *IS* THE SCREAM MASTER!
THE END!

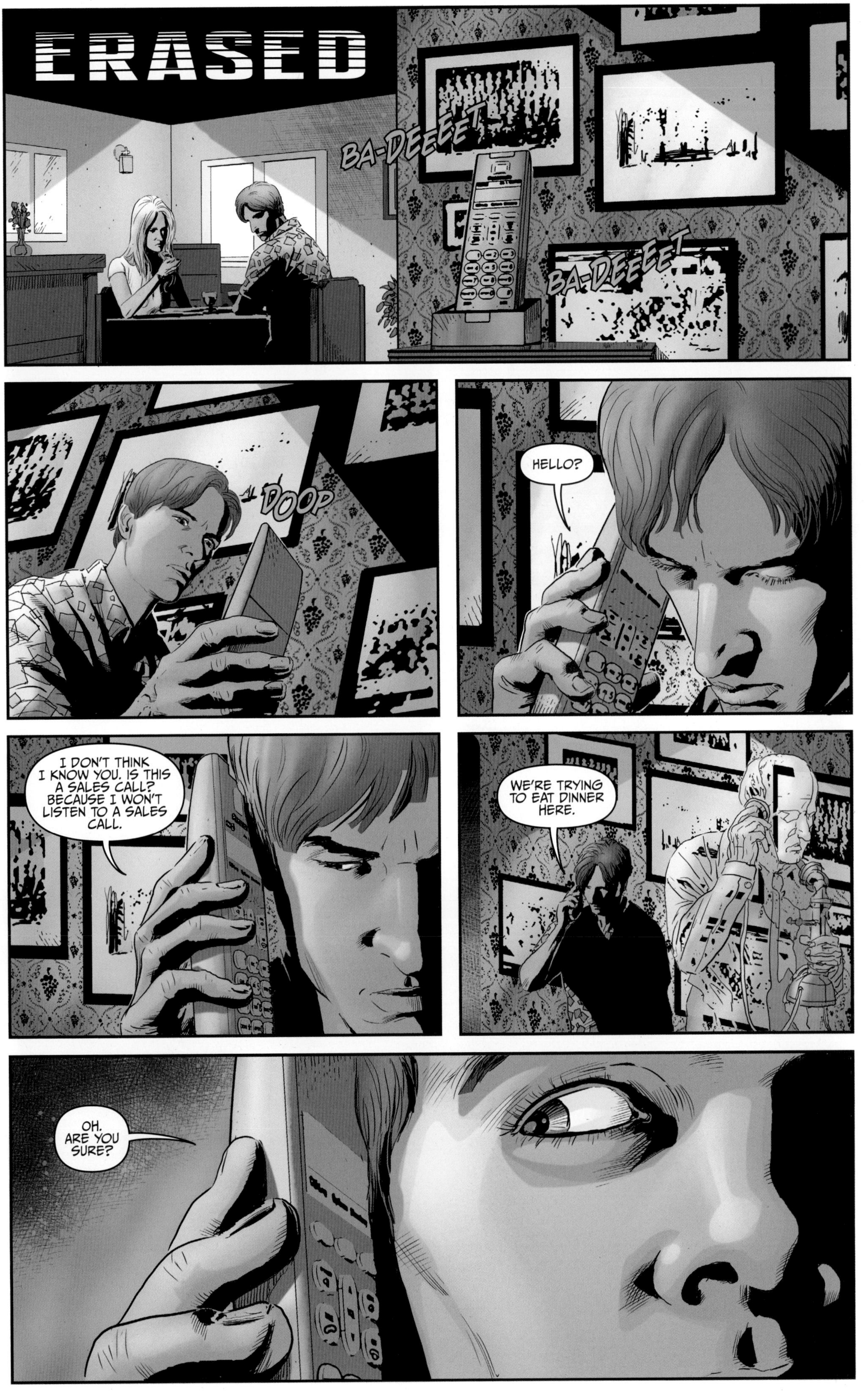
ERASED
BA-DEEEET
BA-DEEEET
DOOP
HELLO?
I DON'T THINK I KNOW YOU. IS THIS A SALES CALL? BECAUSE I WON'T LISTEN TO A SALES CALL.
WE'RE TRYING TO EAT DINNER HERE.
OH. ARE YOU SURE?

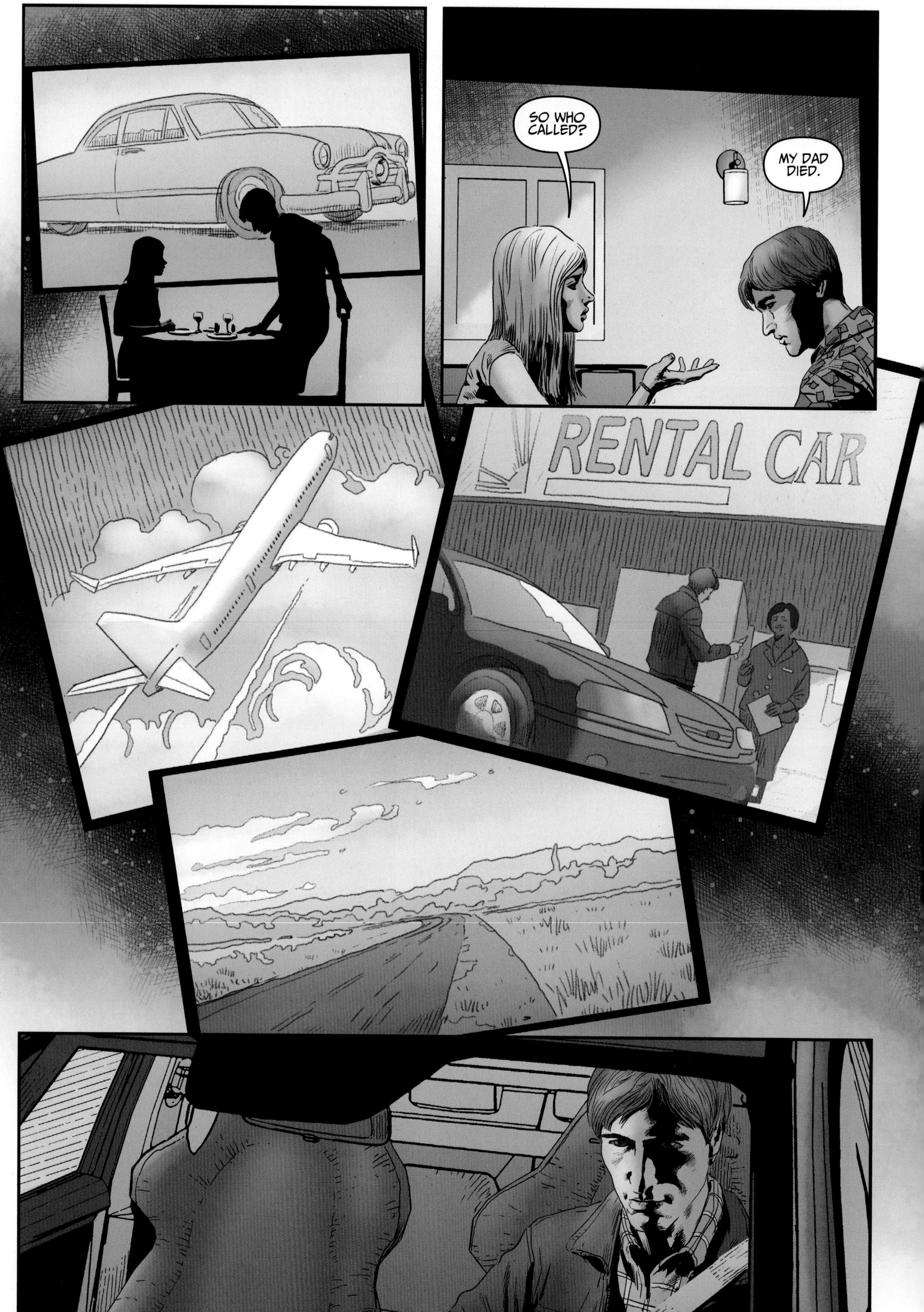
SO WHO CALLED?
MY DAD DIED.
RENTAL CAR

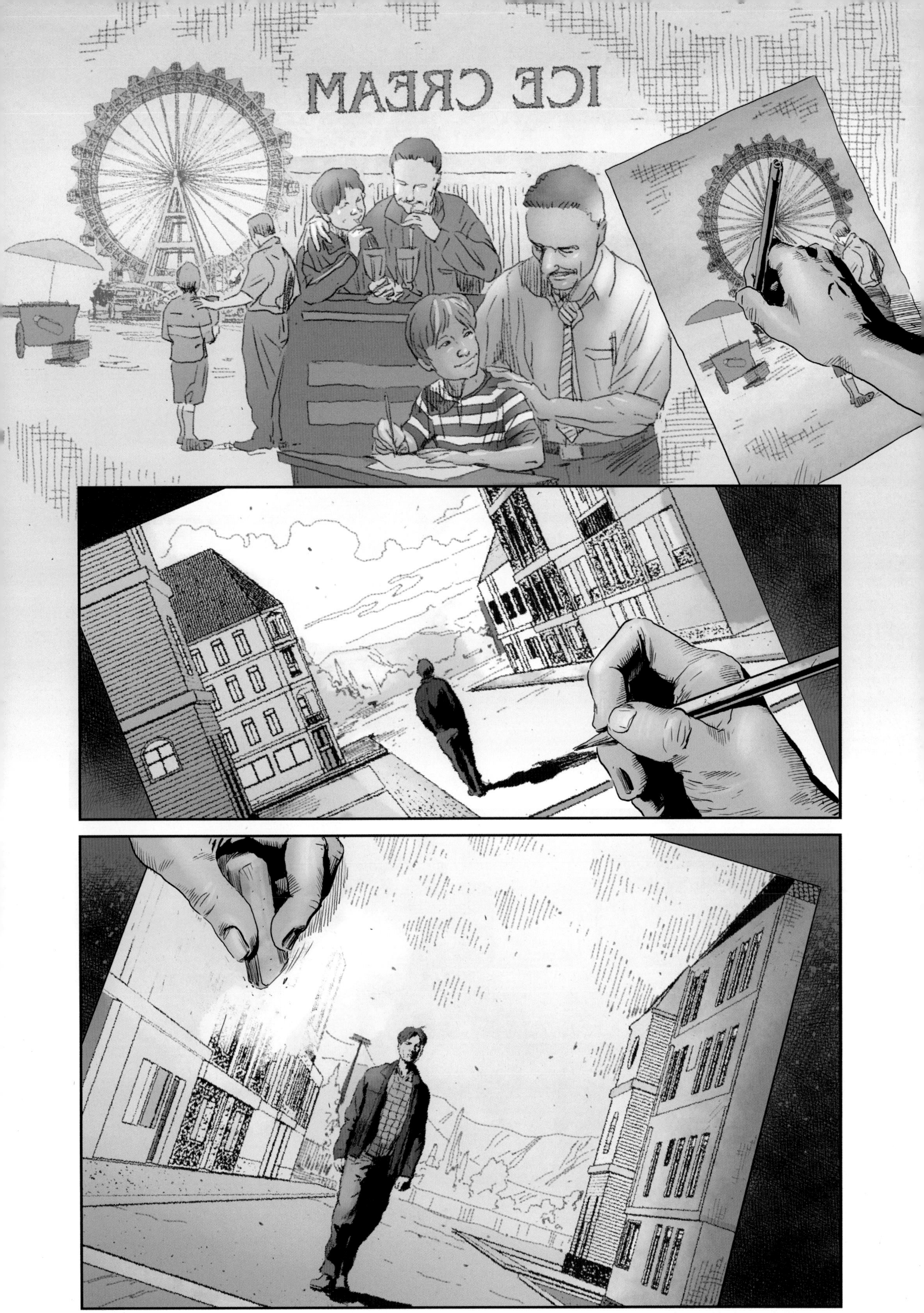
ICE CREAM

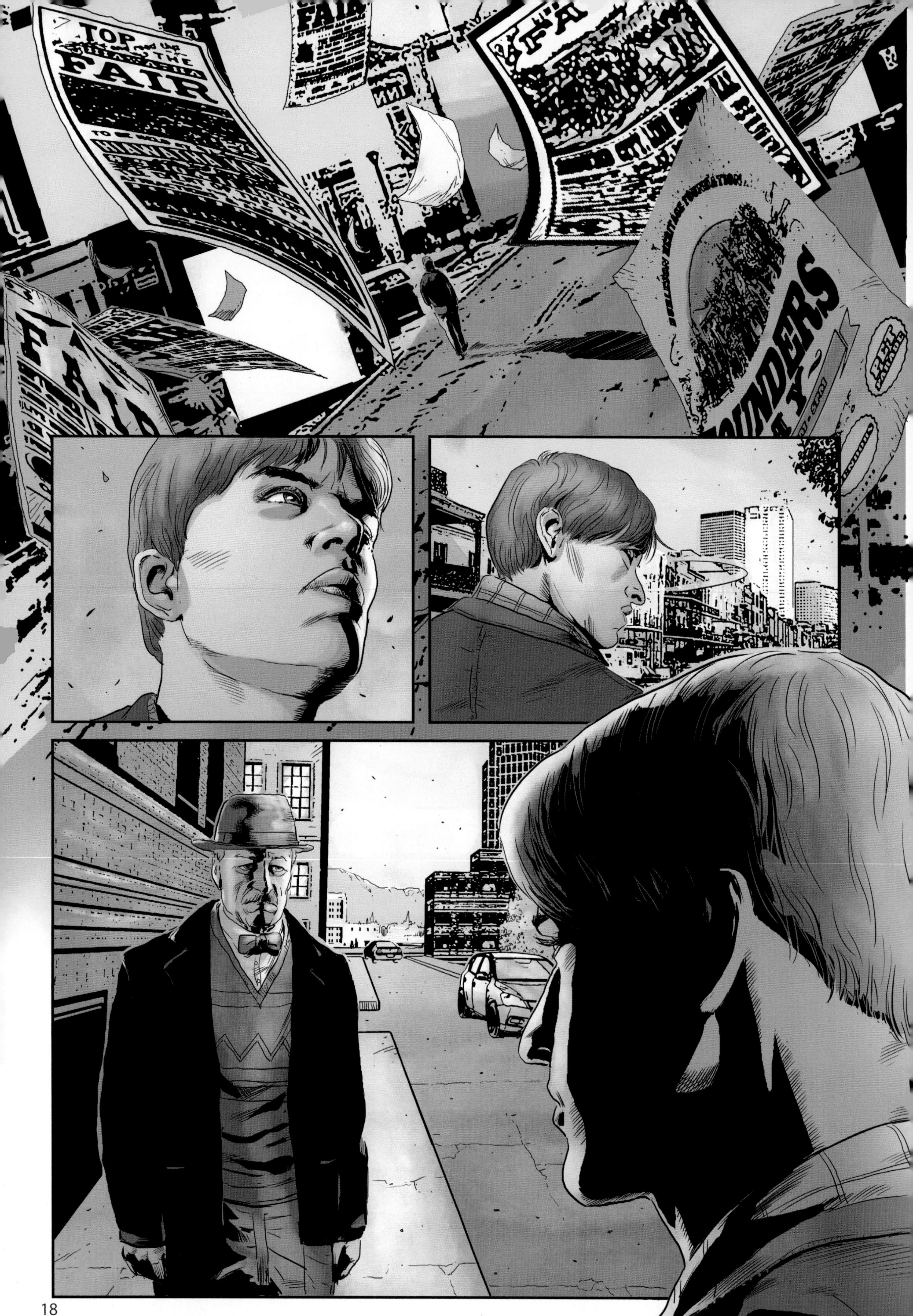
TOP
FAIR

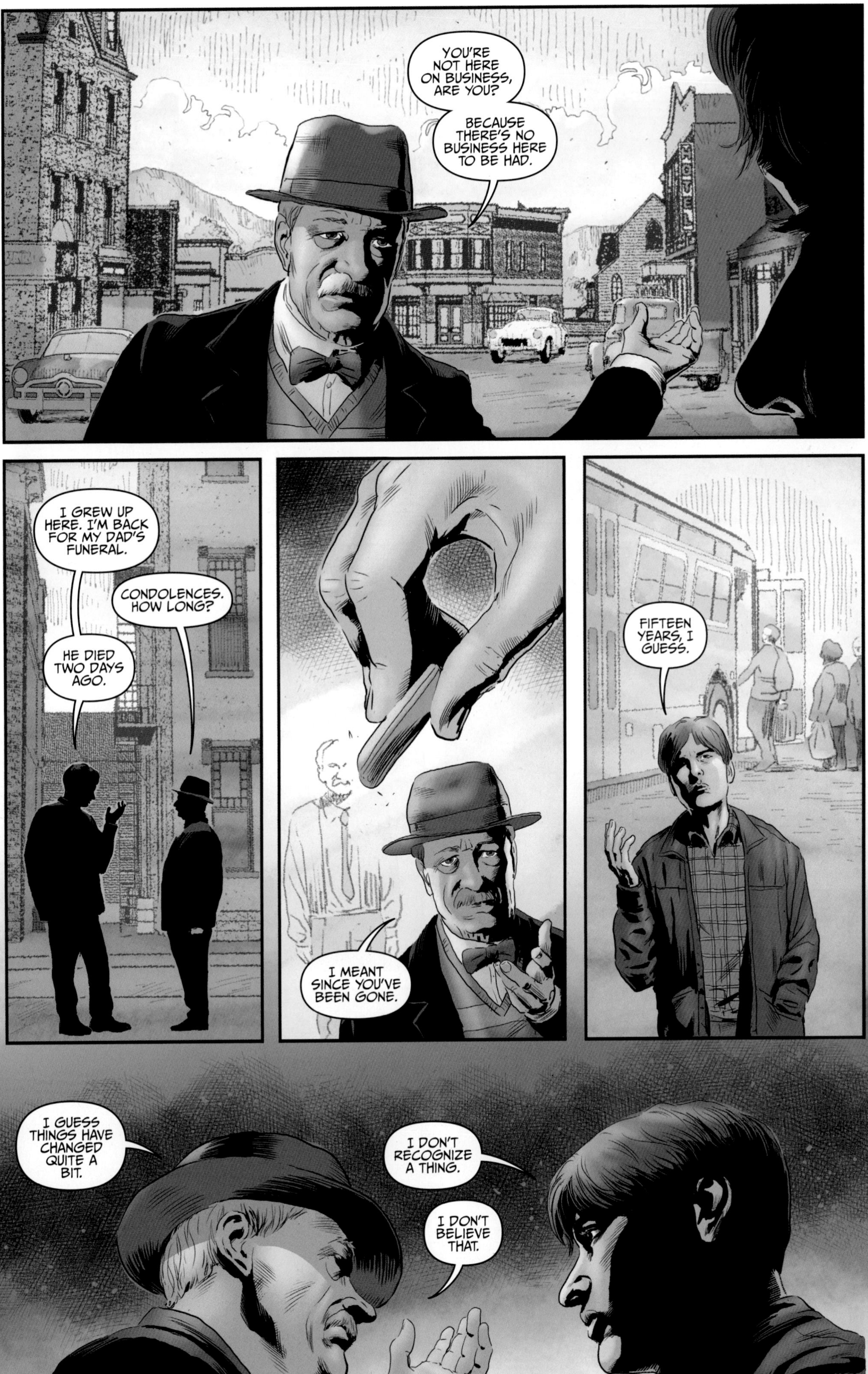
YOU'RE NOT HERE ON BUSINESS, ARE YOU?
BECAUSE THERE'S NO BUSINESS HERE TO BE HAD.
I GREW UP HERE. I'M BACK FOR MY DAD'S FUNERAL.
CONDOLENCES. HOW LONG?
HE DIED TWO DAYS AGO.
I MEANT SINCE YOU'VE BEEN GONE.
FIFTEEN YEARS, I GUESS.
I GUESS THINGS HAVE CHANGED QUITE A BIT.
I DON'T RECOGNIZE A THING.
I DON'T BELIEVE THAT.

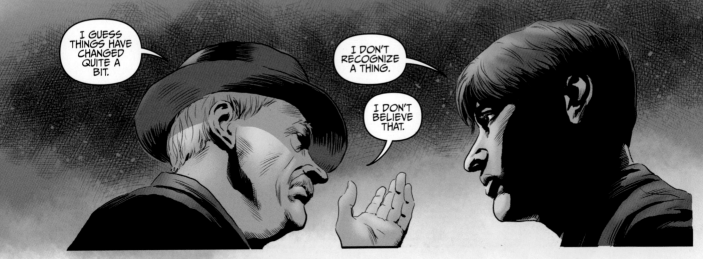

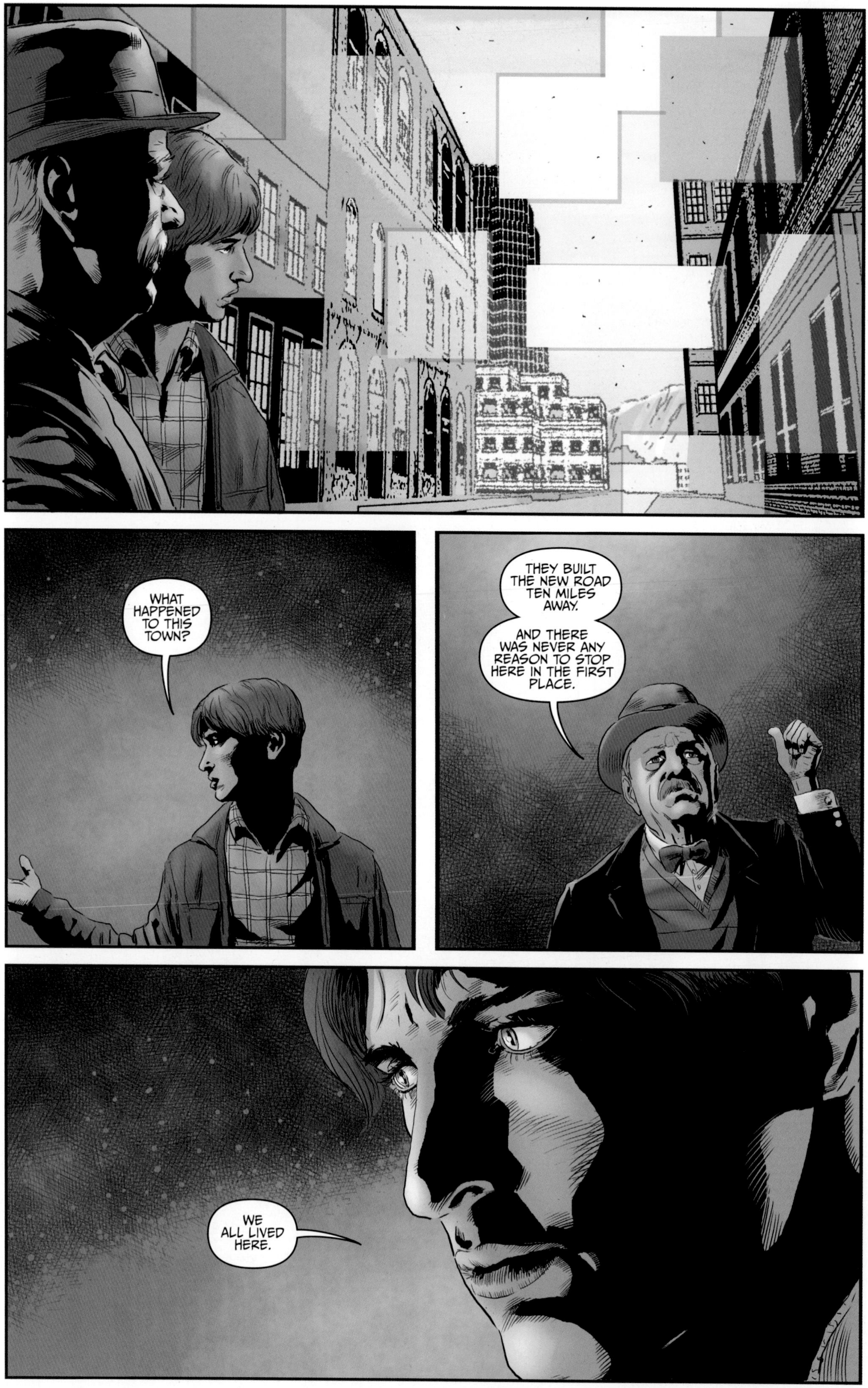

WHAT HAPPENED TO THIS TOWN?
THEY BUILT THE NEW ROAD TEN MILES AWAY.
AND THERE WAS NEVER ANY REASON TO STOP HERE IN THE FIRST PLACE.
WE ALL LIVED HERE.

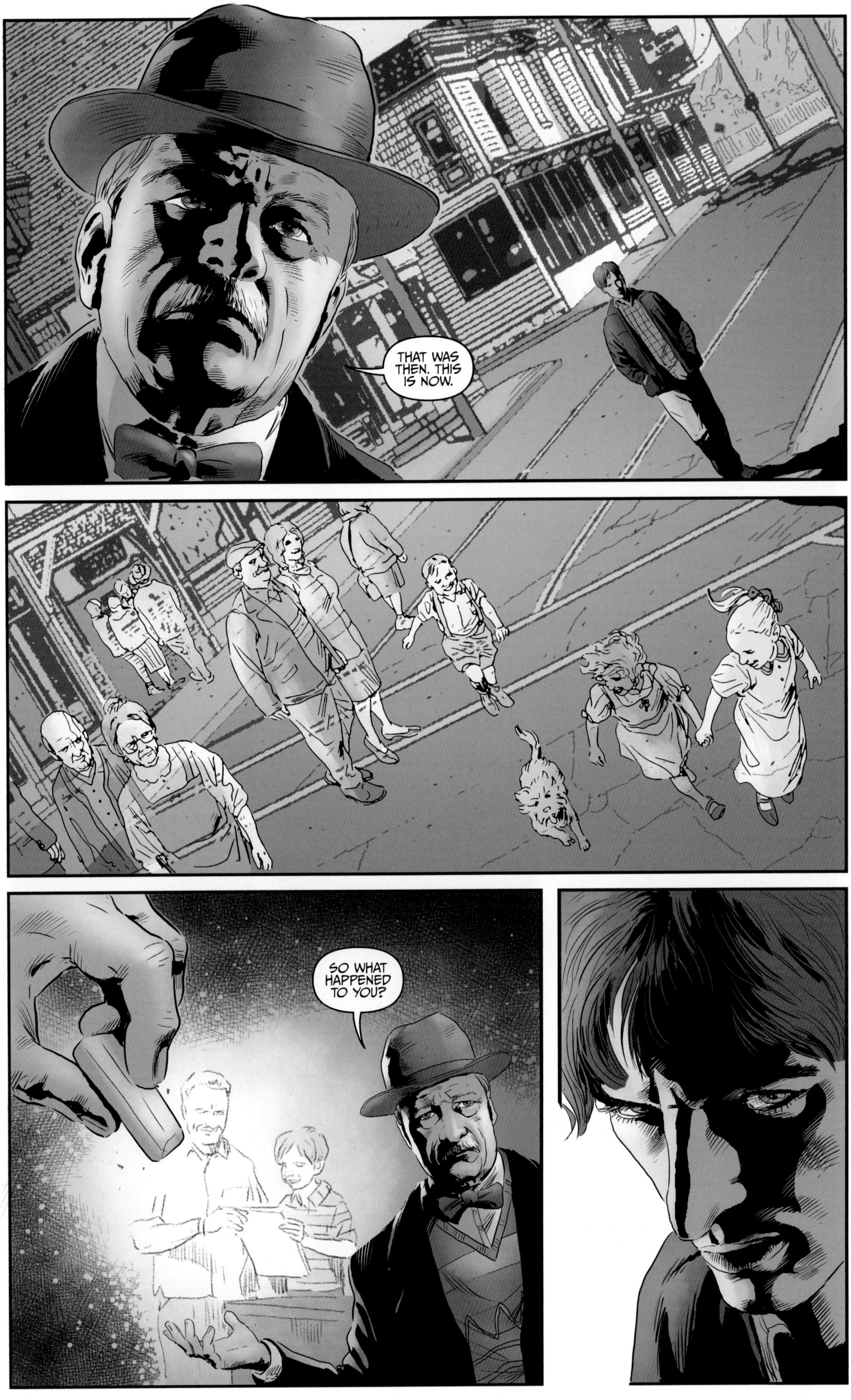
THAT WAS THEN. THIS IS NOW.
SO WHAT HAPPENED TO YOU?

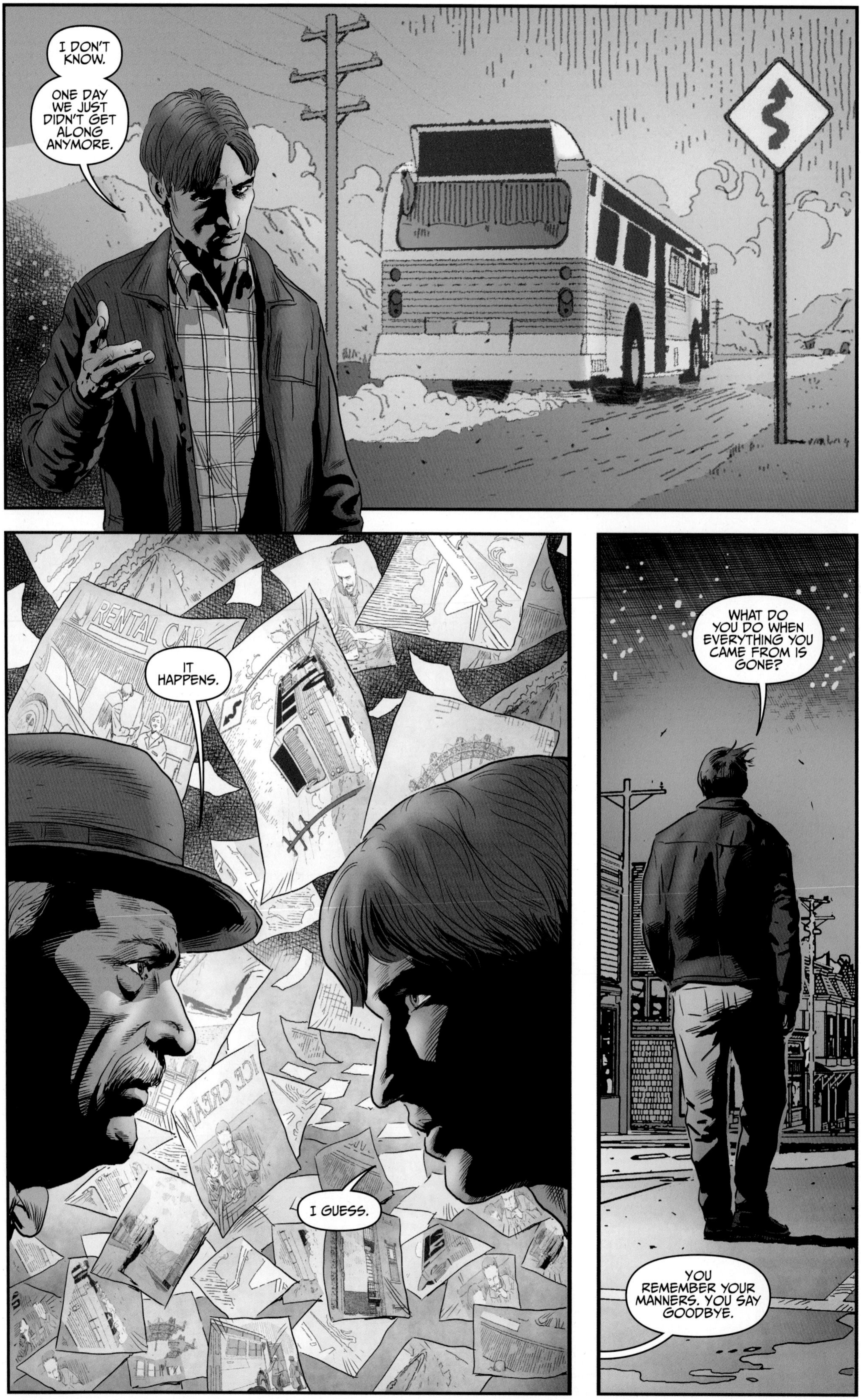
I DON'T KNOW.
ONE DAY WE JUST DIDN'T GET ALONG ANYMORE.
RENTAL CAR
IT HAPPENS.
ICE CREAM
I GUESS.
WHAT DO YOU DO WHEN EVERYTHING YOU CAME FROM IS GONE?
YOU REMEMBER YOUR MANNERS. YOU SAY GOODBYE.

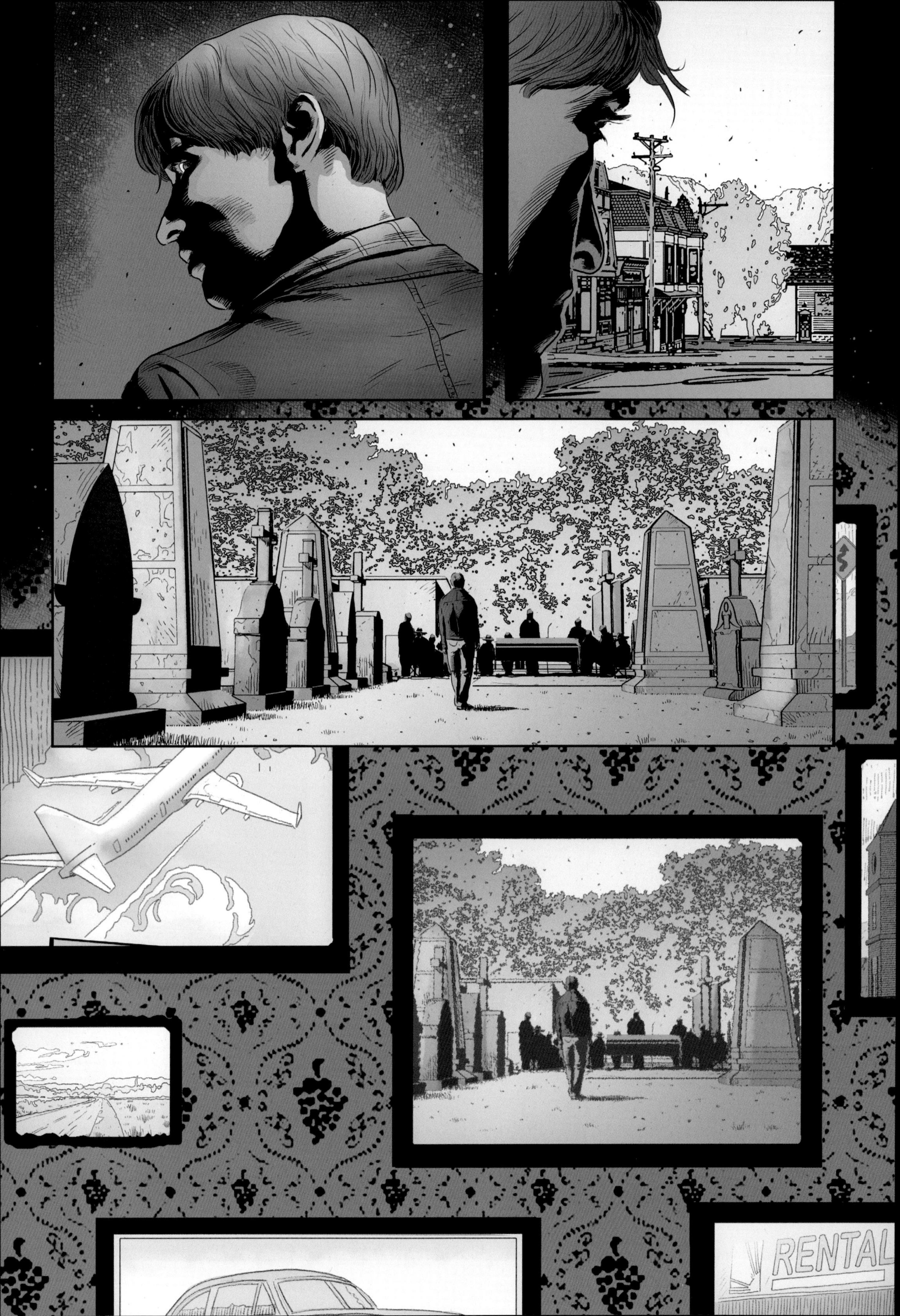
RENTAL

FAME!

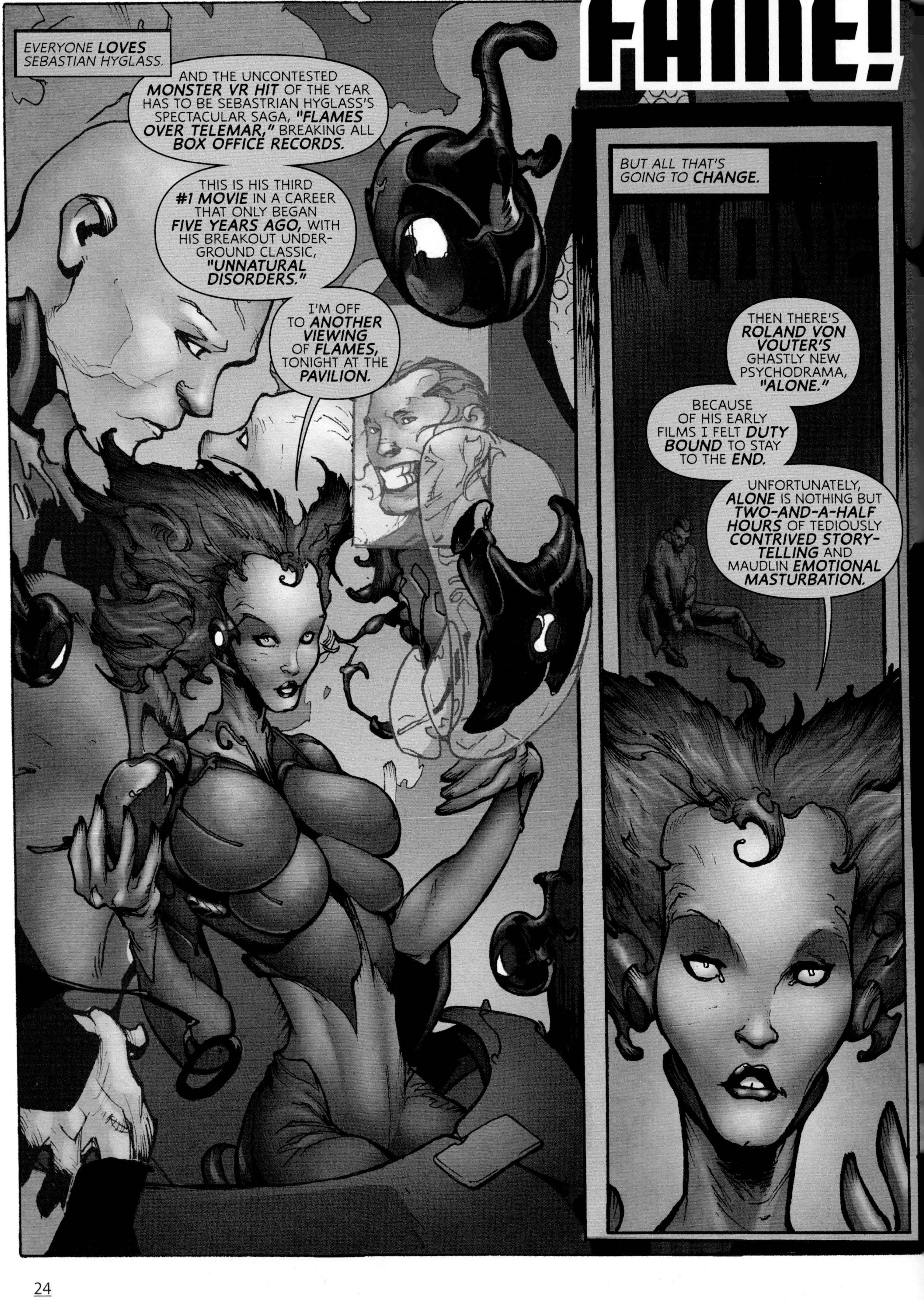
EVERYONE LOVES SEBASTIAN HYGLASS.
AND THE UNCONTESTED MONSTER VR HIT OF THE YEAR HAS TO BE SEBASTRIAN HYGLASS'S SPECTACULAR SAGA, "FLAMES OVER TELEMAR," BREAKING ALL BOX OFFICE RECORDS.
THIS IS HIS THIRD #1 MOVIE IN A CAREER THAT ONLY BEGAN FIVE YEARS AGO, WITH HIS BREAKOUT UNDER-GROUND CLASSIC, "UNNATURAL DISORDERS."
I'M OFF TO ANOTHER VIEWING OF FLAMES, TONIGHT AT THE PAVILION.
BUT ALL THAT'S GOING TO CHANGE.
ALONE
THEN THERE'S ROLAND VON VOUTER'S GHASTLY NEW PSYCHODRAMA, "ALONE."
BECAUSE OF HIS EARLY FILMS I FELT DUTY BOUND TO STAY TO THE END.
UNFORTUNATELY, ALONE IS NOTHING BUT TWO-AND-A-HALF HOURS OF TEDIOUSLY CONTRIVED STORY-TELLING AND MAUDLIN EMOTIONAL MASTURBATION.

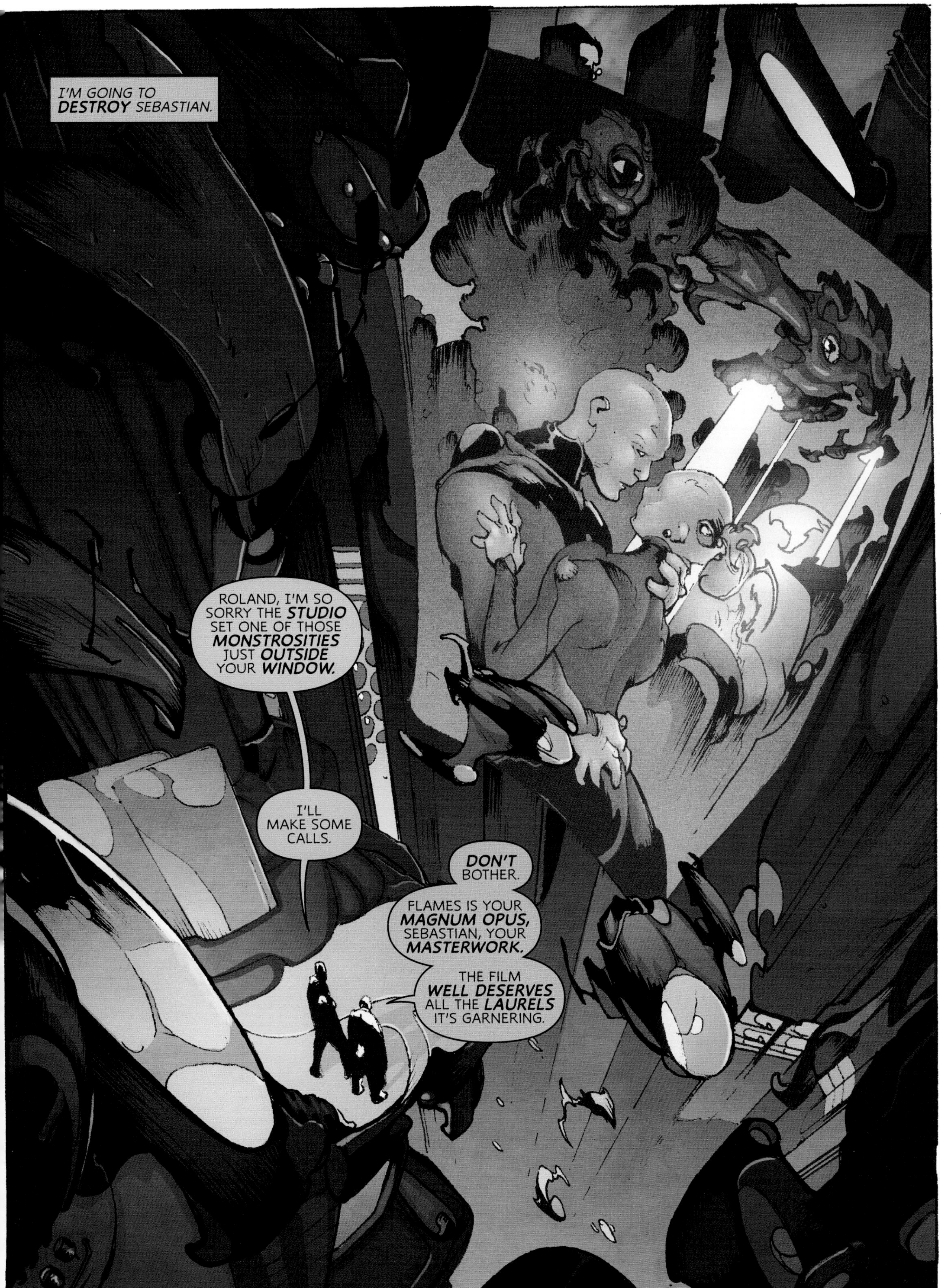
I'M GOING TO DESTROY SEBASTIAN.
ROLAND, I'M SO SORRY THE STUDIO SET ONE OF THOSE MONSTROSITIES JUST OUTSIDE YOUR WINDOW.
I'LL MAKE SOME CALLS.
DON'T BOTHER.
FLAMES IS YOUR MAGNUM OPUS, SEBASTIAN, YOUR MASTERWORK.
THE FILM WELL DESERVES ALL THE LAURELS IT'S GARNERING.

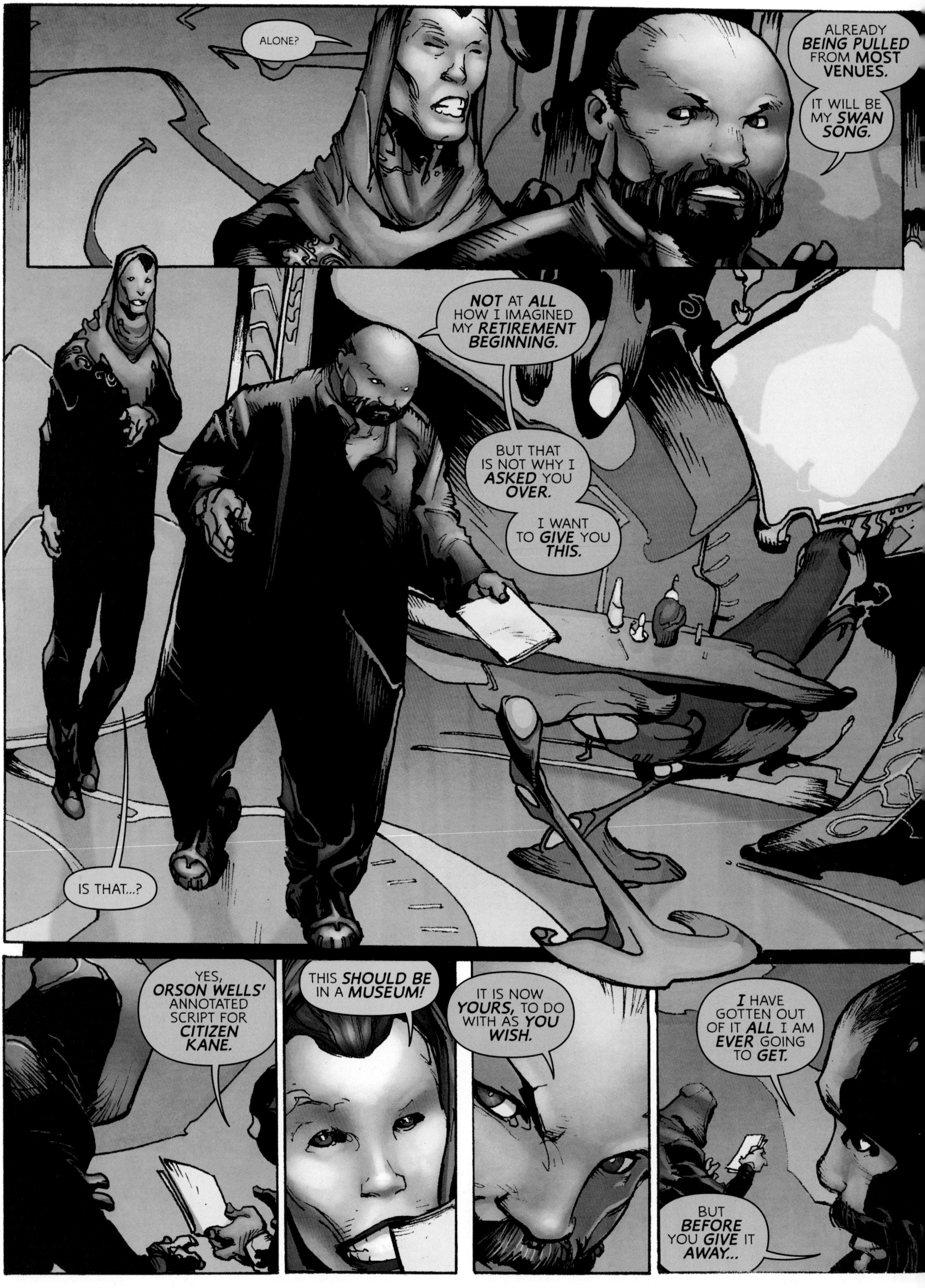
ALONE?
ALREADY BEING PULLED FROM MOST VENUES.
IT WILL BE MY SWAN SONG.
NOT AT ALL HOW I IMAGINED MY RETIREMENT BEGINNING.
BUT THAT IS NOT WHY I ASKED YOU OVER.
I WANT TO GIVE YOU THIS.
IS THAT...?
YES, ORSON WELLS' ANNOTATED SCRIPT FOR CITIZEN KANE.
THIS SHOULD BE IN A MUSEUM!
IT IS NOW YOURS, TO DO WITH AS YOU WISH.
I HAVE GOTTEN OUT OF IT ALL I AM EVER GOING TO GET.
BUT BEFORE YOU GIVE IT AWAY...

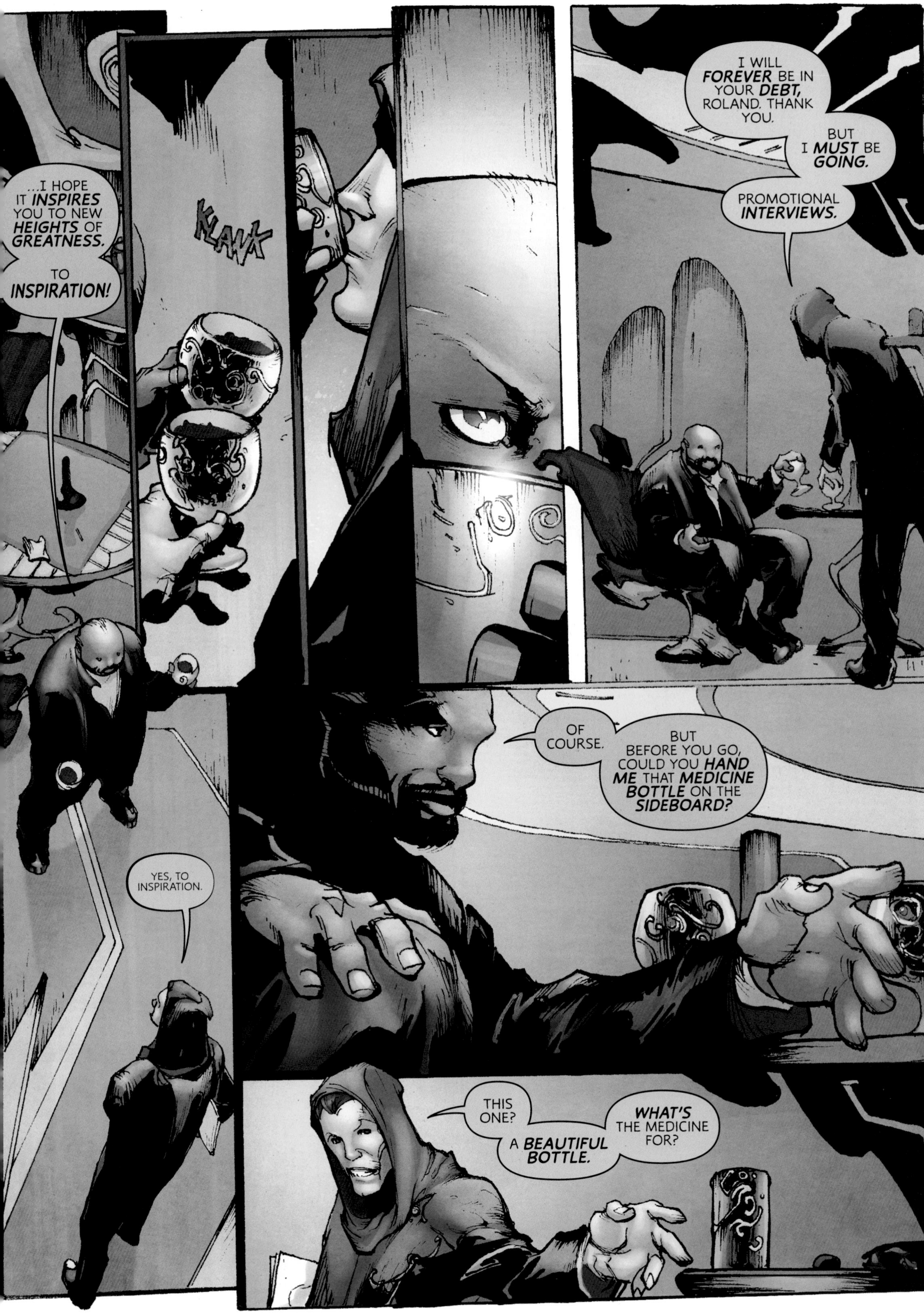

...I HOPE IT INSPIRES YOU TO NEW HEIGHTS OF GREATNESS.
TO INSPIRATION!
KLANK
I WILL FOREVER BE IN YOUR DEBT, ROLAND. THANK YOU.
BUT I MUST BE GOING.
PROMOTIONAL INTERVIEWS.
YES, TO INSPIRATION.
OF COURSE.
BUT BEFORE YOU GO, COULD YOU HAND ME THAT MEDICINE BOTTLE ON THE SIDEBOARD?
THIS ONE?
A BEAUTIFUL BOTTLE.
WHAT'S THE MEDICINE FOR?

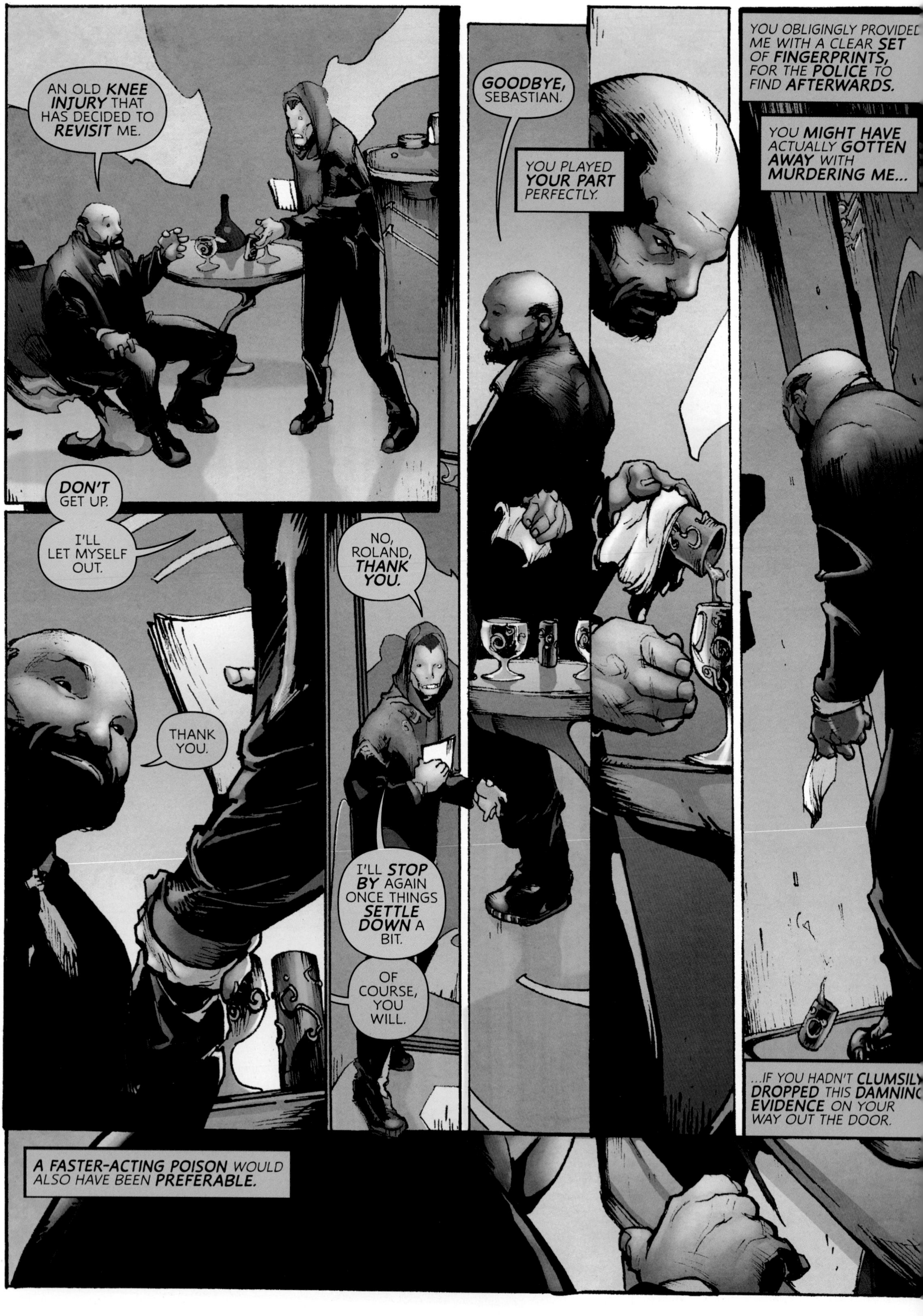
AN OLD KNEE INJURY THAT HAS DECIDED TO REVISIT ME.
GOODBYE, SEBASTIAN.
YOU PLAYED YOUR PART PERFECTLY.
YOU OBLIGINGLY PROVIDED ME WITH A CLEAR SET OF FINGERPRINTS, FOR THE POLICE TO FIND AFTERWARDS.
YOU MIGHT HAVE ACTUALLY GOTTEN AWAY WITH MURDERING ME...
DON'T GET UP.
I'LL LET MYSELF OUT.
THANK YOU.
NO, ROLAND, THANK YOU.
I'LL STOP BY AGAIN ONCE THINGS SETTLE DOWN A BIT.
OF COURSE, YOU WILL.
...IF YOU HADN'T CLUMSILY DROPPED THIS DAMNING EVIDENCE ON YOUR WAY OUT THE DOOR.
A FASTER-ACTING POISON WOULD ALSO HAVE BEEN PREFERABLE.

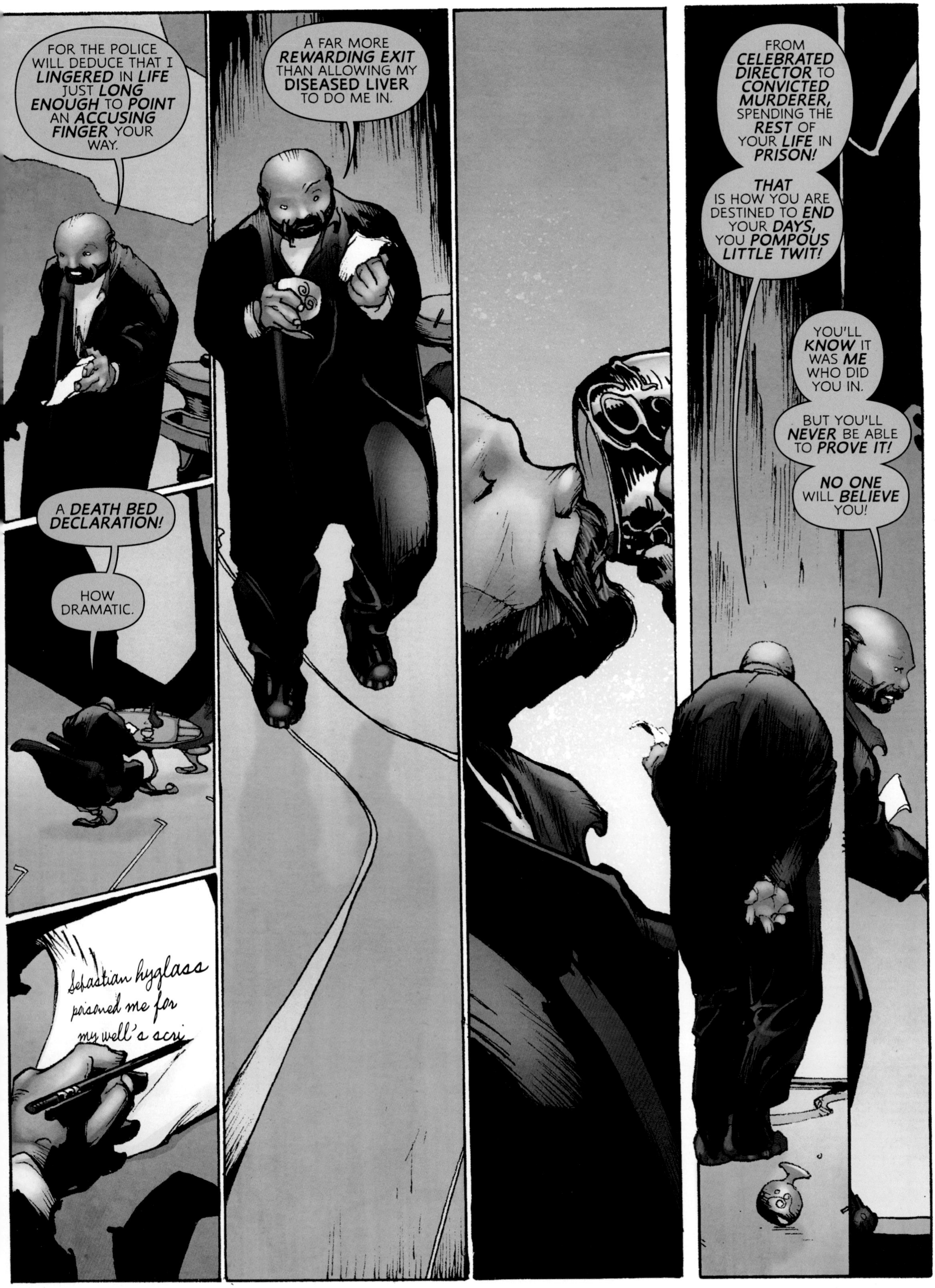
FOR THE POLICE WILL DEDUCE THAT I LINGERED IN LIFE JUST LONG ENOUGH TO POINT AN ACCUSING FINGER YOUR WAY.
A DEATH BED DECLARATION!
HOW DRAMATIC.
Sebastian hyglass poisoned me for my well's scri
A FAR MORE REWARDING EXIT THAN ALLOWING MY DISEASED LIVER TO DO ME IN.
FROM CELEBRATED DIRECTOR TO CONVICTED MURDERER, SPENDING THE REST OF YOUR LIFE IN PRISON!
THAT IS HOW YOU ARE DESTINED TO END YOUR DAYS, YOU POMPOUS LITTLE TWIT!
YOU'LL KNOW IT WAS ME WHO DID YOU IN.
BUT YOU'LL NEVER BE ABLE TO PROVE IT!
NO ONE WILL BELIEVE YOU!

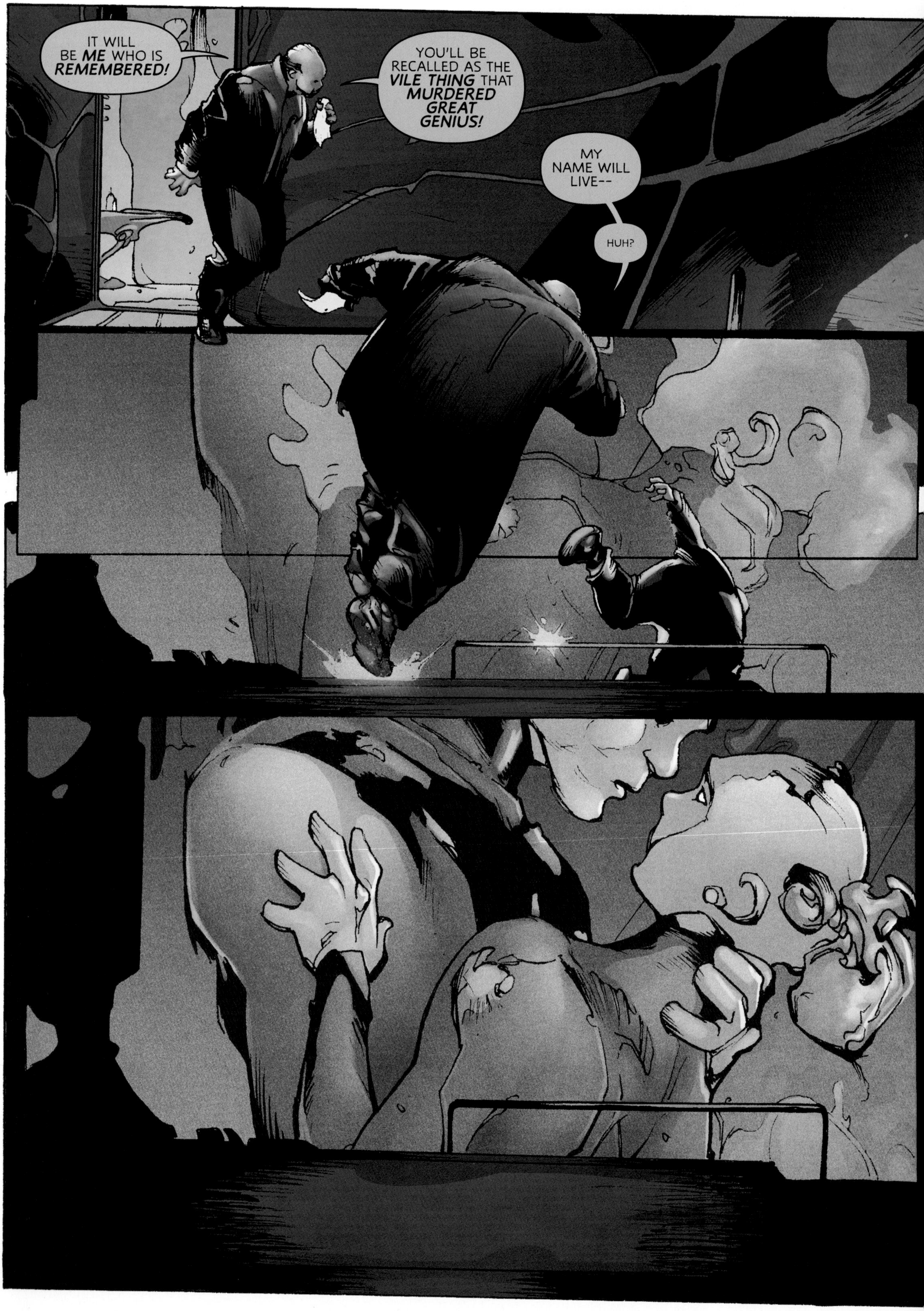
IT WILL BE ME WHO IS REMEMBERED!
YOU'LL BE RECALLED AS THE VILE THING THAT MURDERED GREAT GENIUS!
MY NAME WILL LIVE--
HUH?

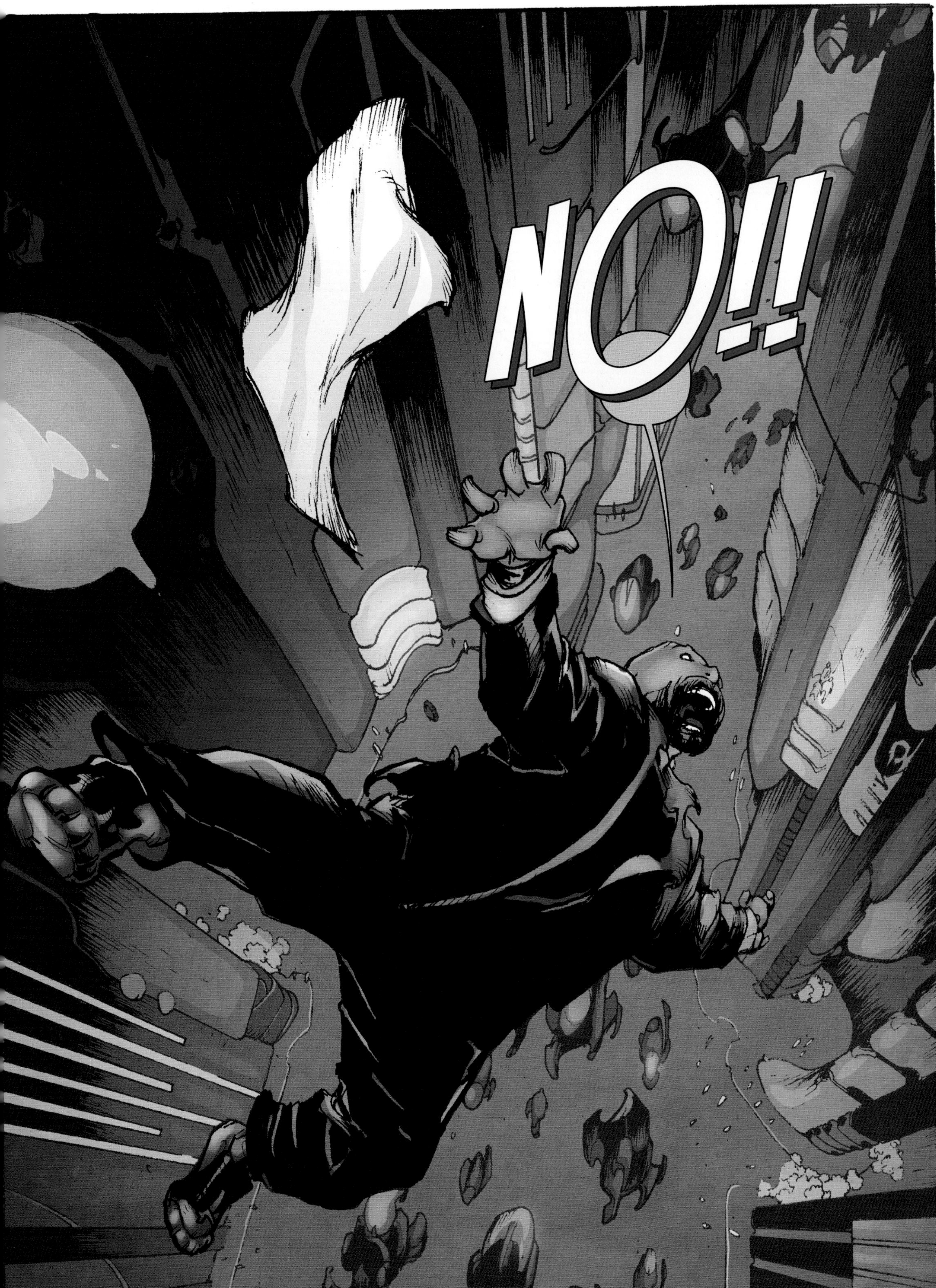
NO!!!

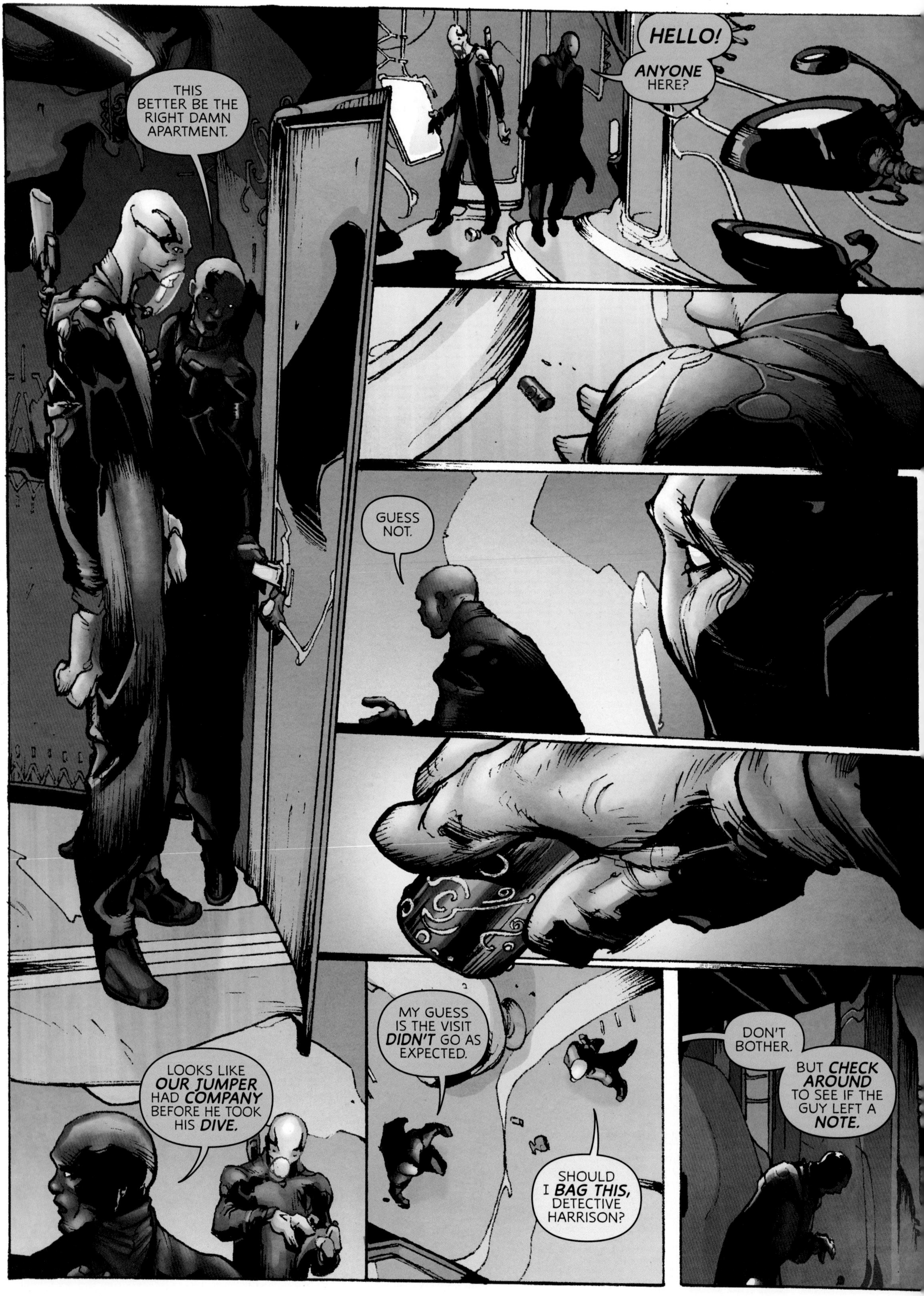
THIS BETTER BE THE RIGHT DAMN APARTMENT.
HELLO!
ANYONE HERE?
GUESS NOT.
LOOKS LIKE OUR JUMPER HAD COMPANY BEFORE HE TOOK HIS DIVE.
MY GUESS IS THE VISIT DIDN'T GO AS EXPECTED.
SHOULD I BAG THIS, DETECTIVE HARRISON?
DON'T BOTHER.
BUT CHECK AROUND TO SEE IF THE GUY LEFT A NOTE.

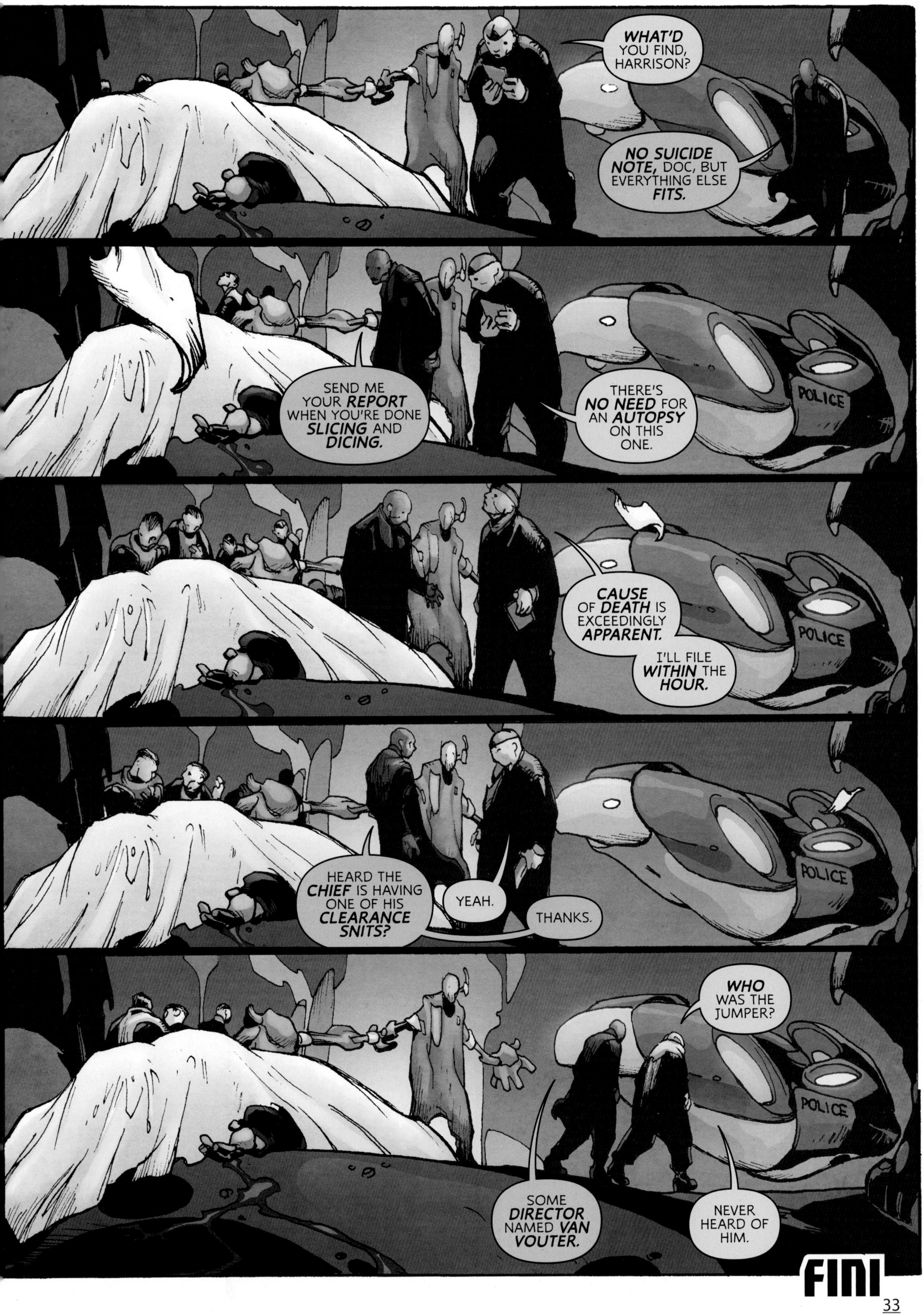
WHAT'D YOU FIND, HARRISON?
NO SUICIDE NOTE, DOC, BUT EVERYTHING ELSE FITS.
SEND ME YOUR REPORT WHEN YOU'RE DONE SLICING AND DICING.
THERE'S NO NEED FOR AN AUTOPSY ON THIS ONE.
POLICE
CAUSE OF DEATH IS EXCEEDINGLY APPARENT.
I'LL FILE WITHIN THE HOUR.
POLICE
HEARD THE CHIEF IS HAVING ONE OF HIS CLEARANCE SNITS?
YEAH.
THANKS.
POLICE
WHO WAS THE JUMPER?
SOME DIRECTOR NAMED VAN VOUTER.
NEVER HEARD OF HIM.
POLICE
FINI

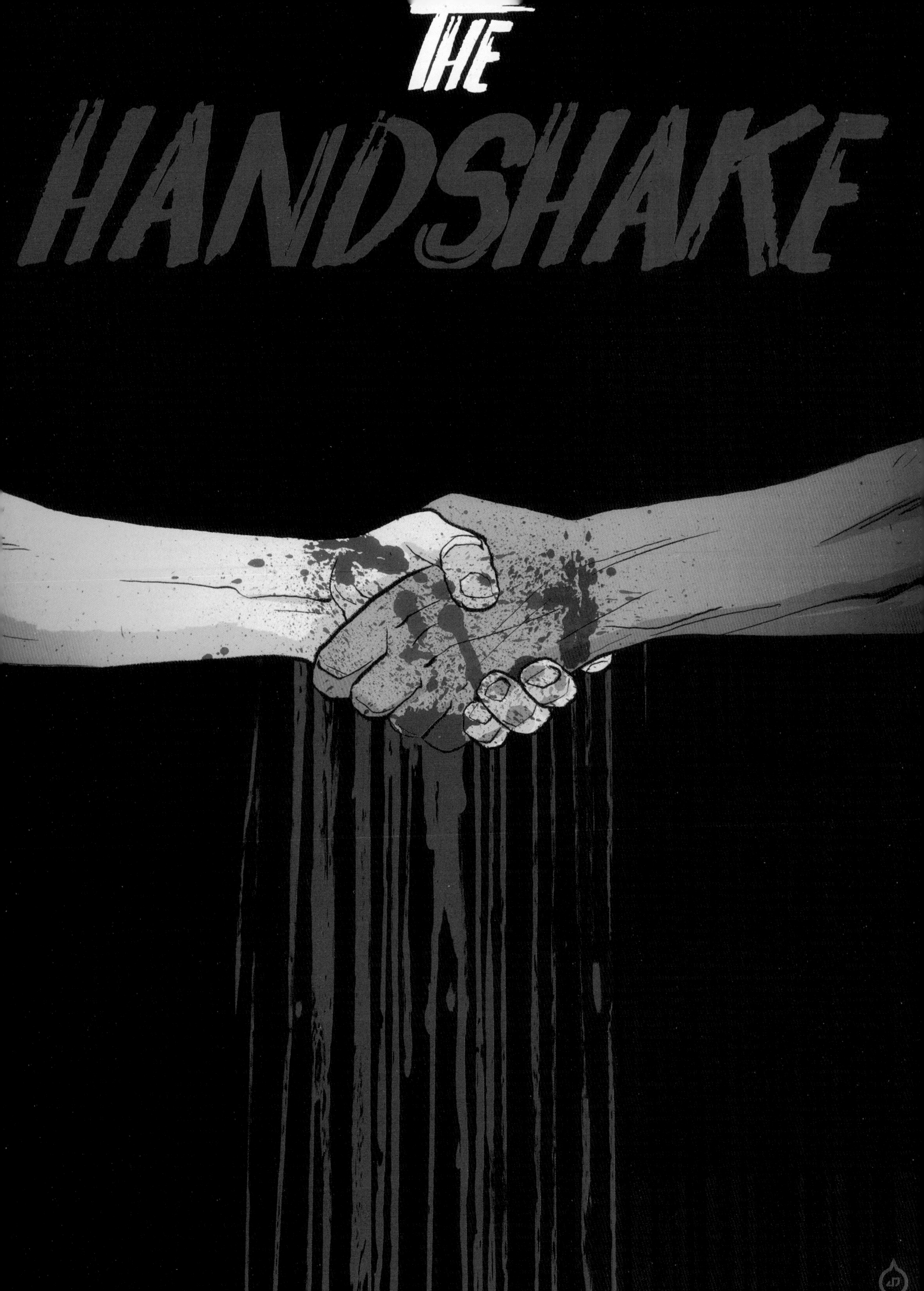
THE
HANDSHAKE

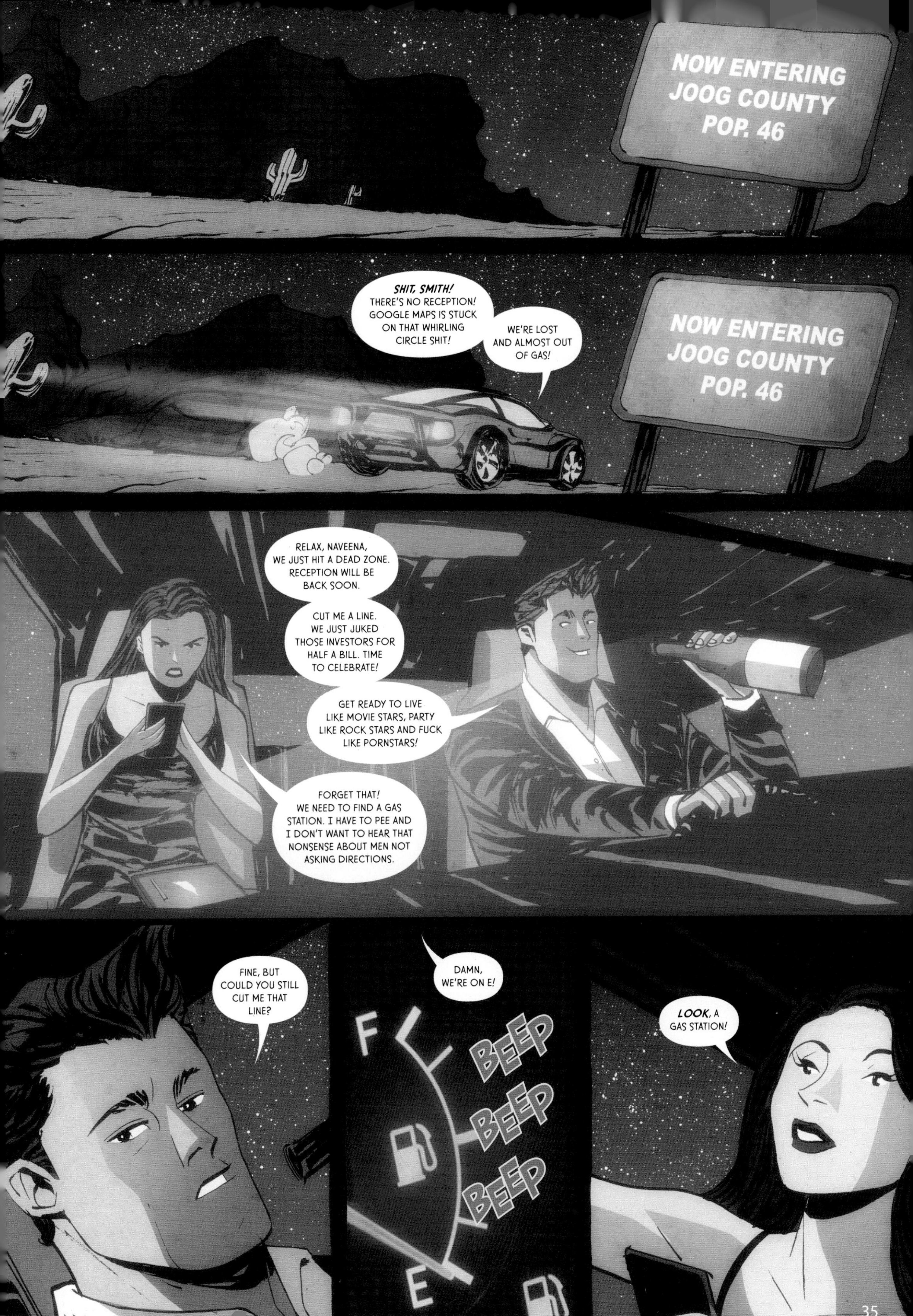
NOW ENTERING JOOG COUNTY POP. 46
SHIT, SMITH! THERE'S NO RECEPTION! GOOGLE MAPS IS STUCK ON THAT WHIRLING CIRCLE SHIT!
WE'RE LOST AND ALMOST OUT OF GAS!
NOW ENTERING JOOG COUNTY POP. 46
RELAX, NAVEENA, WE JUST HIT A DEAD ZONE. RECEPTION WILL BE BACK SOON.
CUT ME A LINE. WE JUST JUKED THOSE INVESTORS FOR HALF A BILL. TIME TO CELEBRATE!
GET READY TO LIVE LIKE MOVIE STARS, PARTY LIKE ROCK STARS AND FUCK LIKE PORNSTARS!
FORGET THAT! WE NEED TO FIND A GAS STATION. I HAVE TO PEE AND I DON'T WANT TO HEAR THAT NONSENSE ABOUT MEN NOT ASKING DIRECTIONS.
FINE, BUT COULD YOU STILL CUT ME THAT LINE?
DAMN, WE'RE ON E!
F
E
BEEP
BEEP
BEEP
LOOK, A GAS STATION!

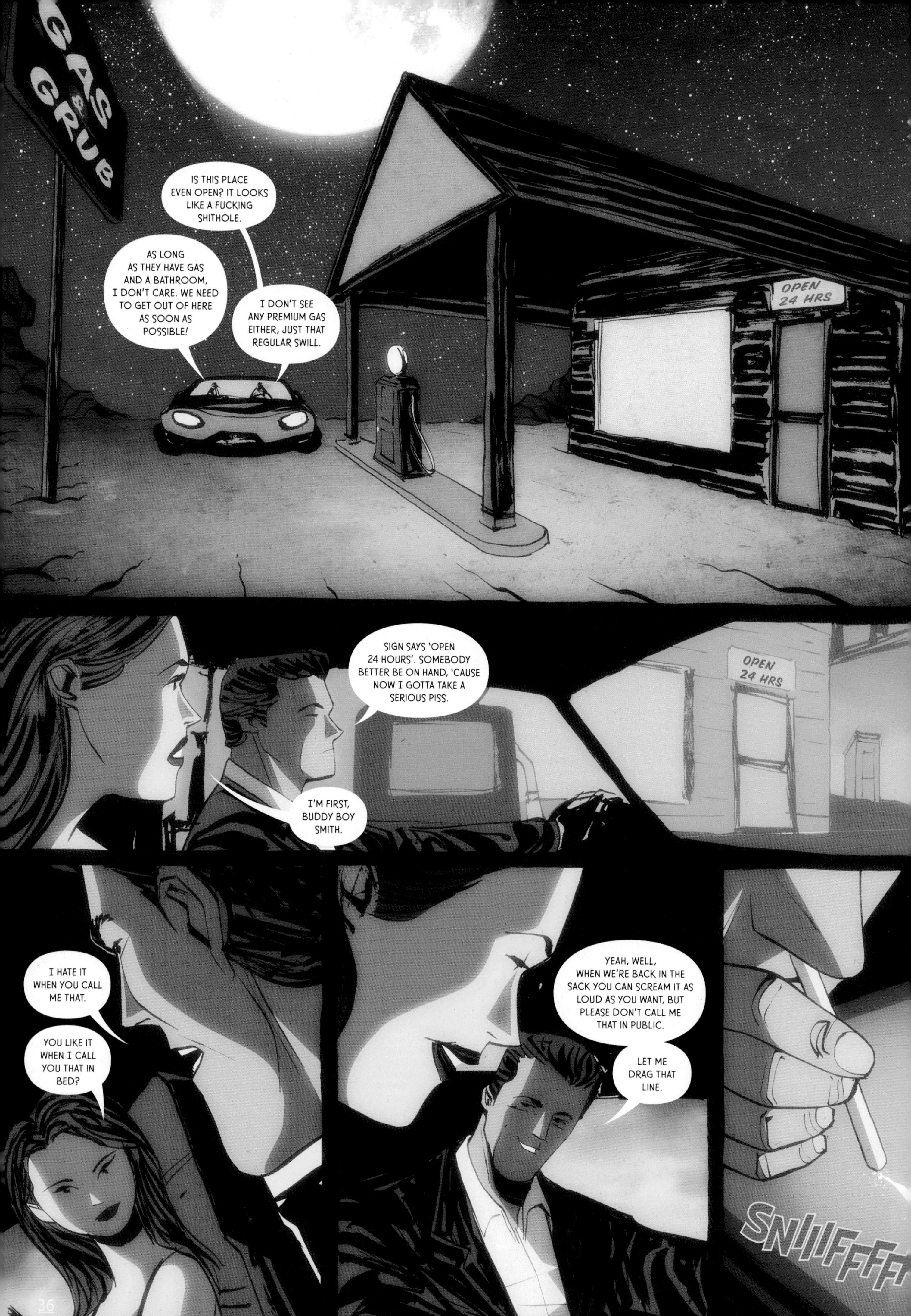
GAS & GRUB
IS THIS PLACE EVEN OPEN? IT LOOKS LIKE A FUCKING SHITHOLE.
AS LONG AS THEY HAVE GAS AND A BATHROOM, I DON'T CARE. WE NEED TO GET OUT OF HERE AS SOON AS POSSIBLE!
I DON'T SEE ANY PREMIUM GAS EITHER, JUST THAT REGULAR SWILL.
OPEN 24 HRS
SIGN SAYS 'OPEN 24 HOURS'. SOMEBODY BETTER BE ON HAND, 'CAUSE NOW I GOTTA TAKE A SERIOUS PISS.
OPEN 24 HRS
I'M FIRST, BUDDY BOY SMITH.
I HATE IT WHEN YOU CALL ME THAT.
YOU LIKE IT WHEN I CALL YOU THAT IN BED?
YEAH, WELL, WHEN WE'RE BACK IN THE SACK YOU CAN SCREAM IT AS LOUD AS YOU WANT, BUT PLEASE DON'T CALL ME THAT IN PUBLIC.
LET ME DRAG THAT LINE.
SNIIIFFFF

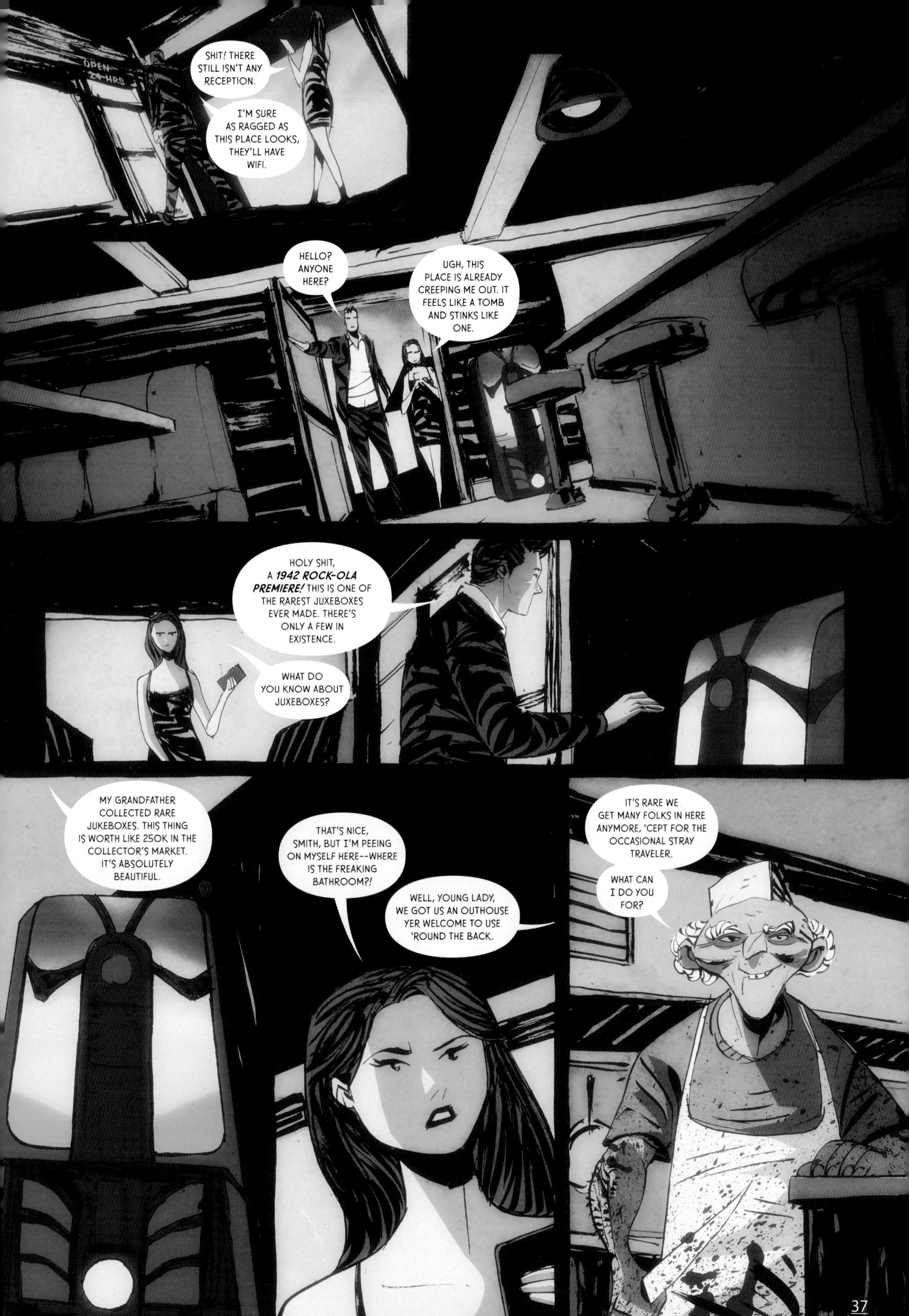
OPEN 24 HRS
SHIT! THERE STILL ISN'T ANY RECEPTION.
I'M SURE AS RAGGED AS THIS PLACE LOOKS, THEY'LL HAVE WIFI.
HELLO? ANYONE HERE?
UGH, THIS PLACE IS ALREADY CREEPING ME OUT. IT FEELS LIKE A TOMB AND STINKS LIKE ONE.
HOLY SHIT, A **1942 ROCK-OLA PREMIERE!** THIS IS ONE OF THE RAREST JUXEBOXES EVER MADE. THERE'S ONLY A FEW IN EXISTENCE.
WHAT DO YOU KNOW ABOUT JUXEBOXES?
MY GRANDFATHER COLLECTED RARE JUKEBOXES. THIS THING IS WORTH LIKE 250K IN THE COLLECTOR'S MARKET. IT'S ABSOLUTELY BEAUTIFUL.
THAT'S NICE, SMITH, BUT I'M PEEING ON MYSELF HERE--WHERE IS THE FREAKING BATHROOM?!
WELL, YOUNG LADY, WE GOT US AN OUTHOUSE YER WELCOME TO USE 'ROUND THE BACK.
IT'S RARE WE GET MANY FOLKS IN HERE ANYMORE, 'CEPT FOR THE OCCASIONAL STRAY TRAVELER.
WHAT CAN I DO YOU FOR?

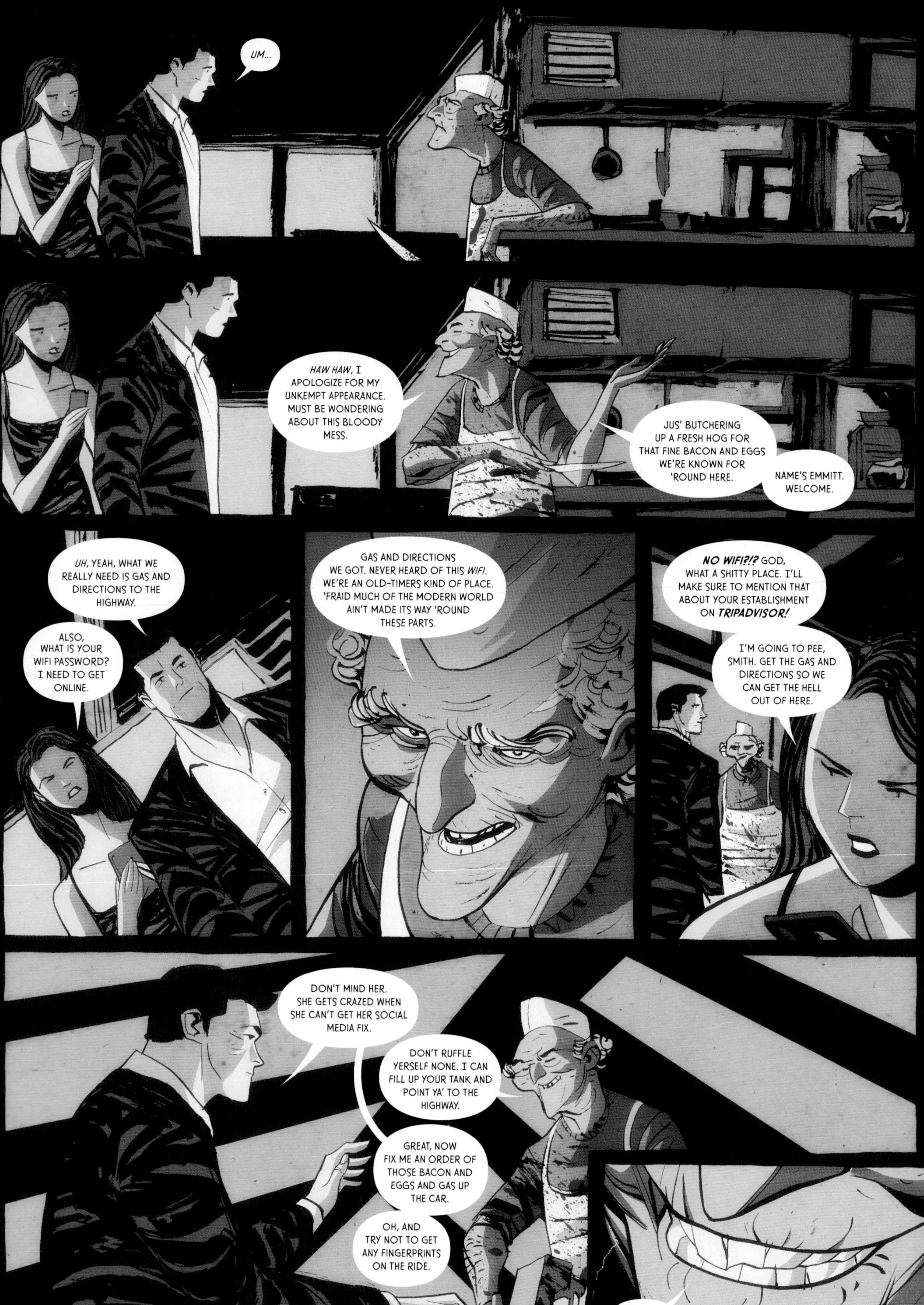
UM...
HAW HAW, I APOLOGIZE FOR MY UNKEMPT APPEARANCE. MUST BE WONDERING ABOUT THIS BLOODY MESS.
JUS' BUTCHERING UP A FRESH HOG FOR THAT FINE BACON AND EGGS WE'RE KNOWN FOR 'ROUND HERE.
NAME'S EMMITT. WELCOME.
UH, YEAH, WHAT WE REALLY NEED IS GAS AND DIRECTIONS TO THE HIGHWAY.
ALSO, WHAT IS YOUR WIFI PASSWORD? I NEED TO GET ONLINE.
GAS AND DIRECTIONS WE GOT. NEVER HEARD OF THIS WIFI. WE'RE AN OLD-TIMERS KIND OF PLACE. 'FRAID MUCH OF THE MODERN WORLD AIN'T MADE ITS WAY 'ROUND THESE PARTS.
NO WIFI?!? GOD, WHAT A SHITTY PLACE. I'LL MAKE SURE TO MENTION THAT ABOUT YOUR ESTABLISHMENT ON TRIPADVISOR!
I'M GOING TO PEE, SMITH. GET THE GAS AND DIRECTIONS SO WE CAN GET THE HELL OUT OF HERE.
DON'T MIND HER. SHE GETS CRAZED WHEN SHE CAN'T GET HER SOCIAL MEDIA FIX.
DON'T RUFFLE YERSELF NONE. I CAN FILL UP YOUR TANK AND POINT YA' TO THE HIGHWAY.
GREAT, NOW FIX ME AN ORDER OF THOSE BACON AND EGGS AND GAS UP THE CAR.
OH, AND TRY NOT TO GET ANY FINGERPRINTS ON THE RIDE.
RIGHT AWAY, SIR.

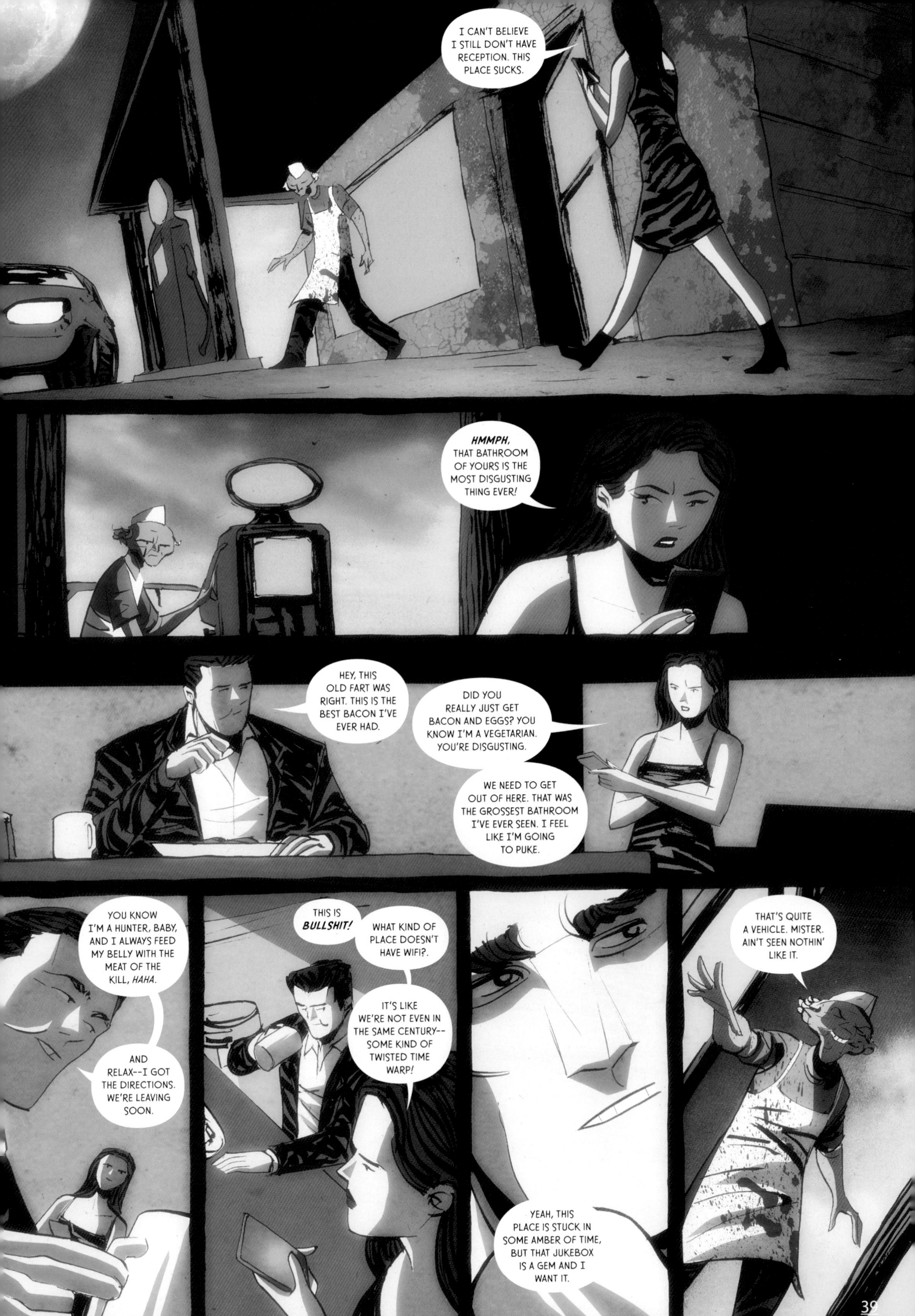
I CAN'T BELIEVE I STILL DON'T HAVE RECEPTION. THIS PLACE SUCKS.
HMMPH, THAT BATHROOM OF YOURS IS THE MOST DISGUSTING THING EVER!
HEY, THIS OLD FART WAS RIGHT. THIS IS THE BEST BACON I'VE EVER HAD.
DID YOU REALLY JUST GET BACON AND EGGS? YOU KNOW I'M A VEGETARIAN. YOU'RE DISGUSTING.
WE NEED TO GET OUT OF HERE. THAT WAS THE GROSSEST BATHROOM I'VE EVER SEEN. I FEEL LIKE I'M GOING TO PUKE.
YOU KNOW I'M A HUNTER, BABY, AND I ALWAYS FEED MY BELLY WITH THE MEAT OF THE KILL, *HAHA*.
AND RELAX--I GOT THE DIRECTIONS. WE'RE LEAVING SOON.
THIS IS ***BULLSHIT!***
WHAT KIND OF PLACE DOESN'T HAVE WIFI?.
IT'S LIKE WE'RE NOT EVEN IN THE SAME CENTURY--SOME KIND OF TWISTED TIME WARP!
YEAH, THIS PLACE IS STUCK IN SOME AMBER OF TIME, BUT THAT JUKEBOX IS A GEM AND I WANT IT.
THAT'S QUITE A VEHICLE. MISTER. AIN'T SEEN NOTHIN' LIKE IT.

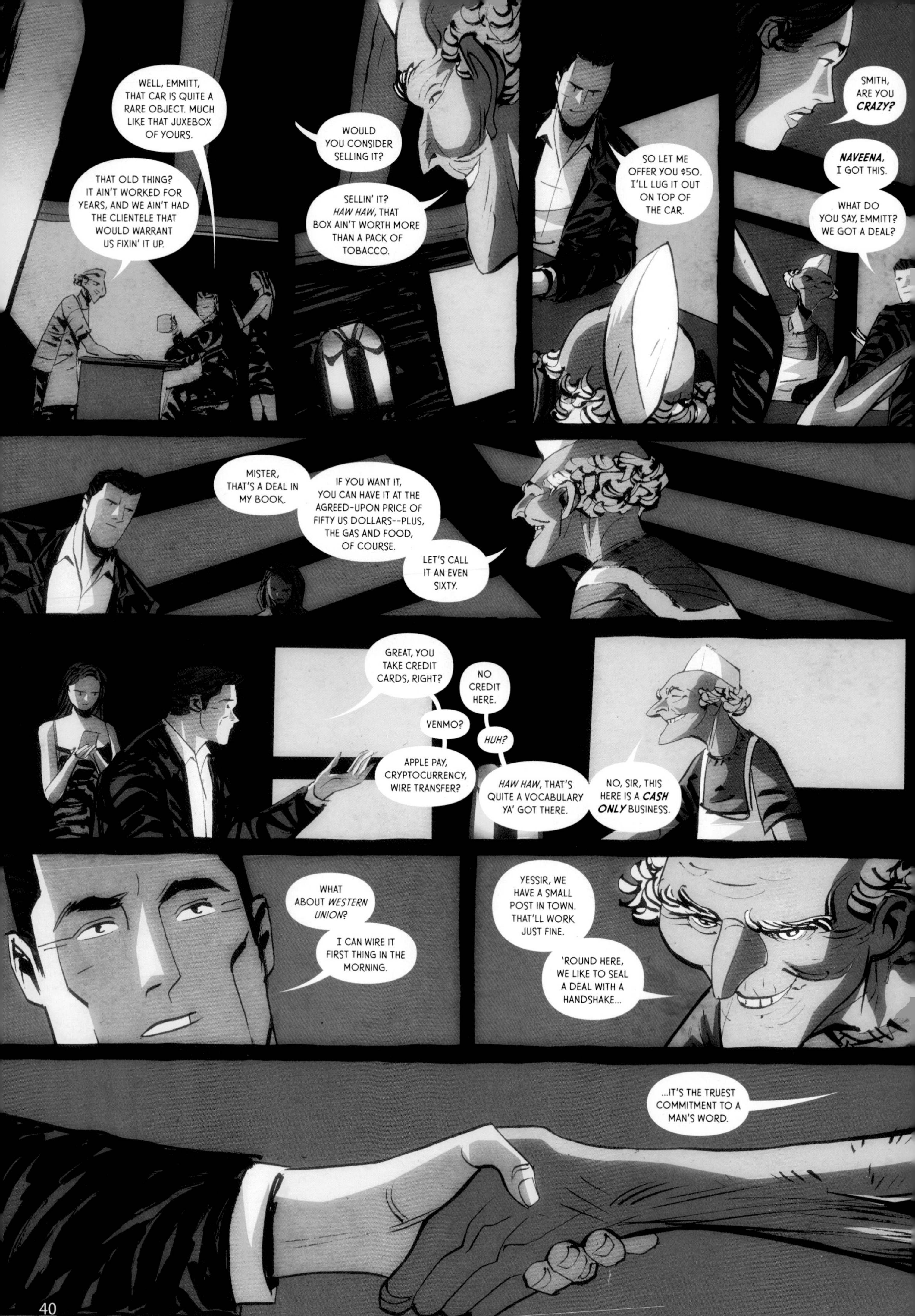

WELL, EMMITT, THAT CAR IS QUITE A RARE OBJECT. MUCH LIKE THAT JUXEBOX OF YOURS.
THAT OLD THING? IT AIN'T WORKED FOR YEARS, AND WE AIN'T HAD THE CLIENTELE THAT WOULD WARRANT US FIXIN' IT UP.
WOULD YOU CONSIDER SELLING IT?
SELLIN' IT? *HAW HAW*, THAT BOX AIN'T WORTH MORE THAN A PACK OF TOBACCO.
SO LET ME OFFER YOU $50. I'LL LUG IT OUT ON TOP OF THE CAR.
SMITH, ARE YOU ***CRAZY?***
NAVEENA, I GOT THIS.
WHAT DO YOU SAY, EMMITT? WE GOT A DEAL?
MISTER, THAT'S A DEAL IN MY BOOK.
IF YOU WANT IT, YOU CAN HAVE IT AT THE AGREED-UPON PRICE OF FIFTY US DOLLARS--PLUS, THE GAS AND FOOD, OF COURSE.
LET'S CALL IT AN EVEN SIXTY.
GREAT, YOU TAKE CREDIT CARDS, RIGHT?
NO CREDIT HERE.
VENMO?
HUH?
APPLE PAY, CRYPTOCURRENCY, WIRE TRANSFER?
HAW HAW, THAT'S QUITE A VOCABULARY YA' GOT THERE.
NO, SIR, THIS HERE IS A ***CASH ONLY*** BUSINESS.
WHAT ABOUT *WESTERN UNION*?
I CAN WIRE IT FIRST THING IN THE MORNING.
YESSIR, WE HAVE A SMALL POST IN TOWN. THAT'LL WORK JUST FINE.
'ROUND HERE, WE LIKE TO SEAL A DEAL WITH A HANDSHAKE...
...IT'S THE TRUEST COMMITMENT TO A MAN'S WORD.

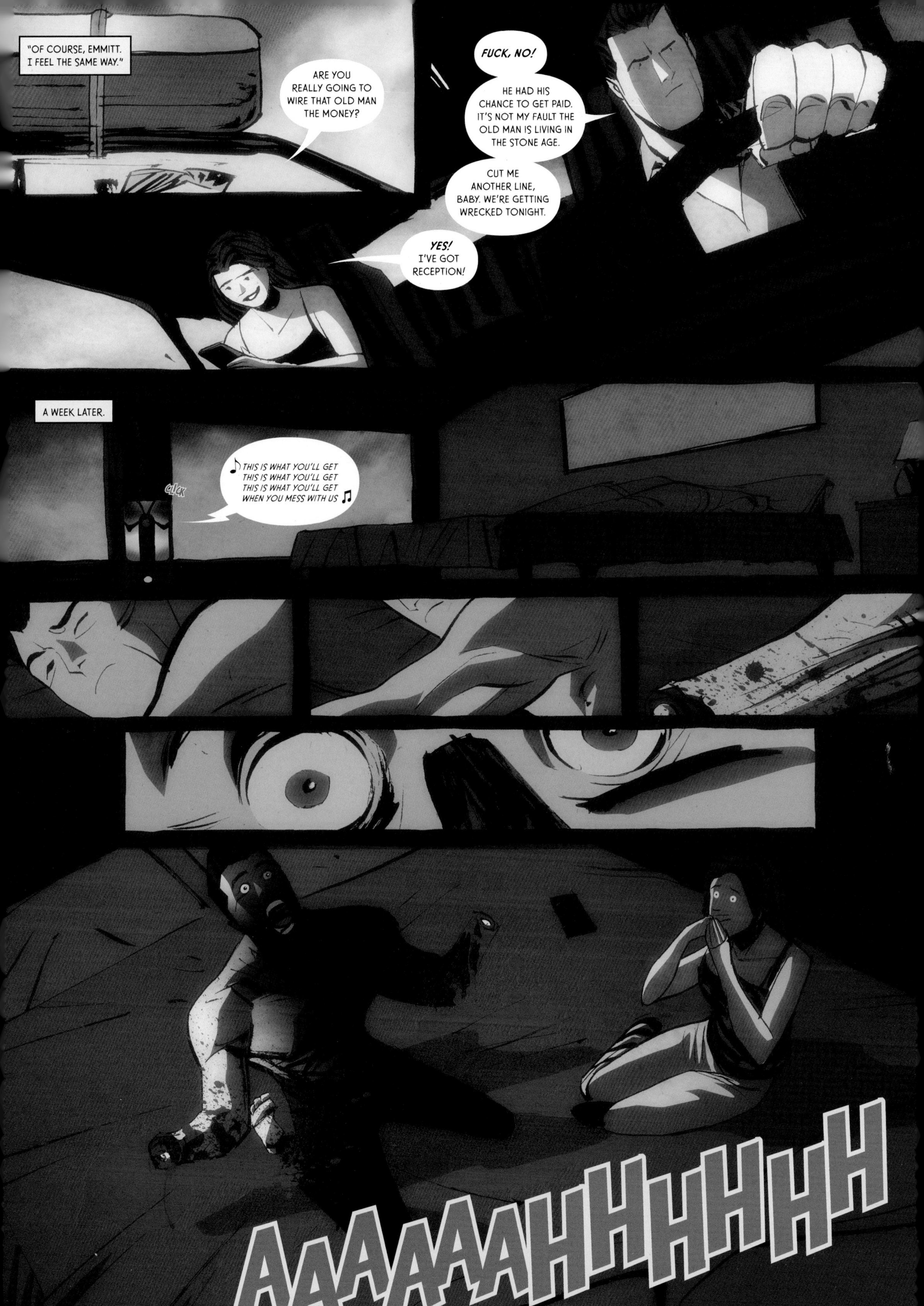

"OF COURSE, EMMITT. I FEEL THE SAME WAY."
ARE YOU REALLY GOING TO WIRE THAT OLD MAN THE MONEY?
FUCK, NO!
HE HAD HIS CHANCE TO GET PAID. IT'S NOT MY FAULT THE OLD MAN IS LIVING IN THE STONE AGE.
CUT ME ANOTHER LINE, BABY. WE'RE GETTING WRECKED TONIGHT.
YES! I'VE GOT RECEPTION!
A WEEK LATER.
♪ THIS IS WHAT YOU'LL GET THIS IS WHAT YOU'LL GET THIS IS WHAT YOU'LL GET WHEN YOU MESS WITH US ♫
AAAAAHHHHHHH

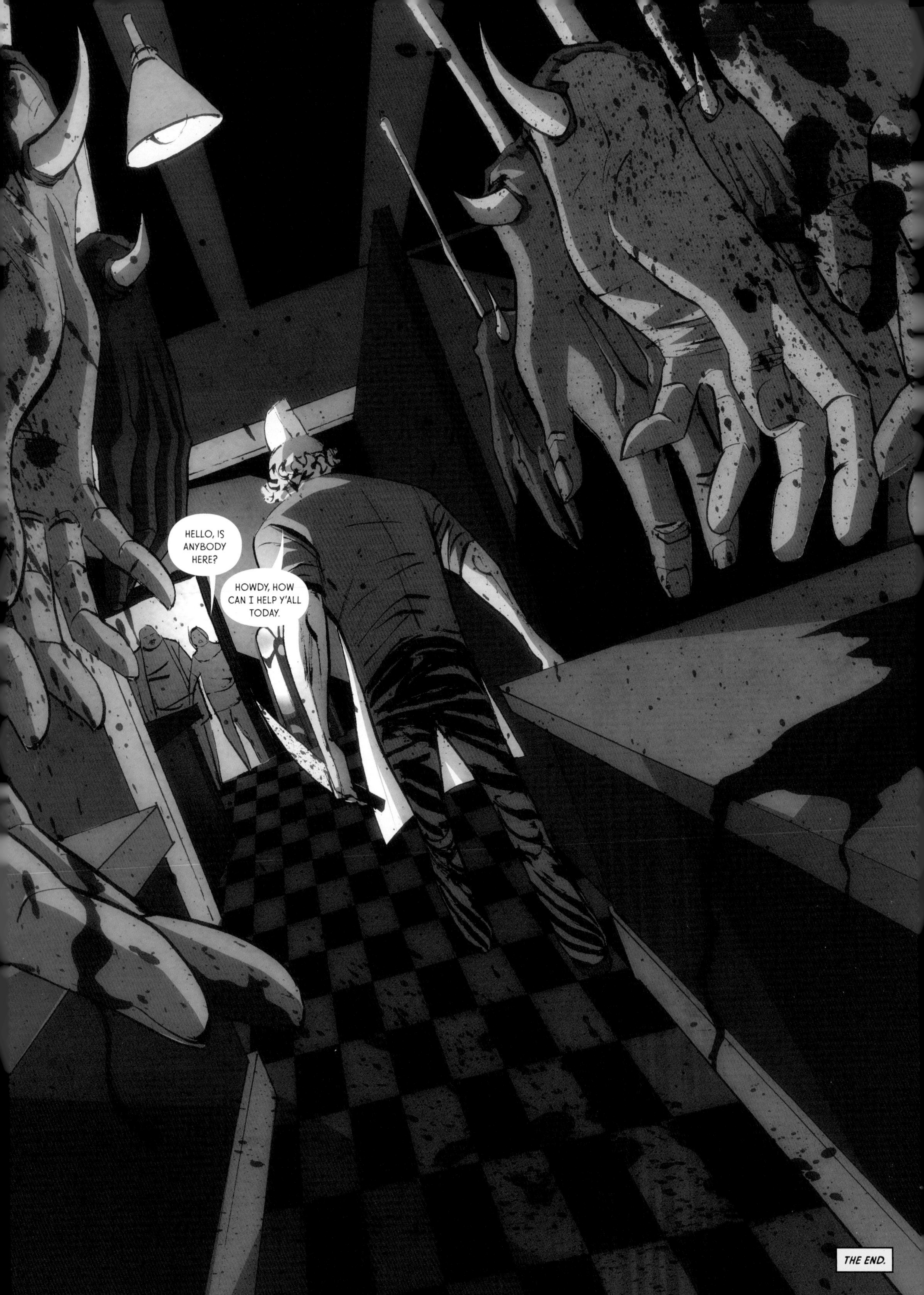
HELLO, IS ANYBODY HERE?
HOWDY, HOW CAN I HELP Y'ALL TODAY.
THE END.

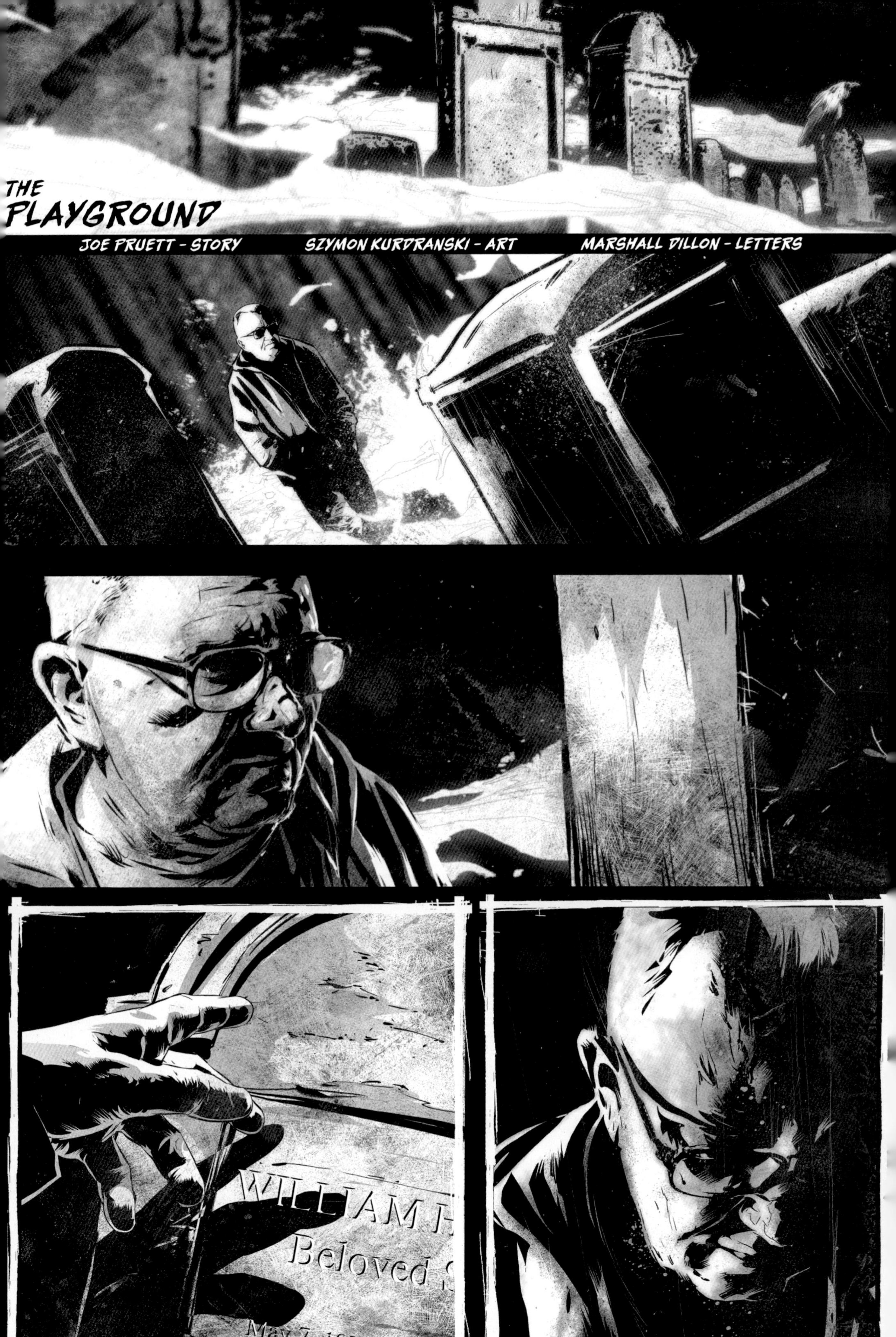
THE PLAYGROUND
JOE PRUETT - STORY
SZYMON KURDRANSKI - ART
MARSHALL DILLON - LETTERS
WILLIAM
Beloved
May 7, 1977-July 2,

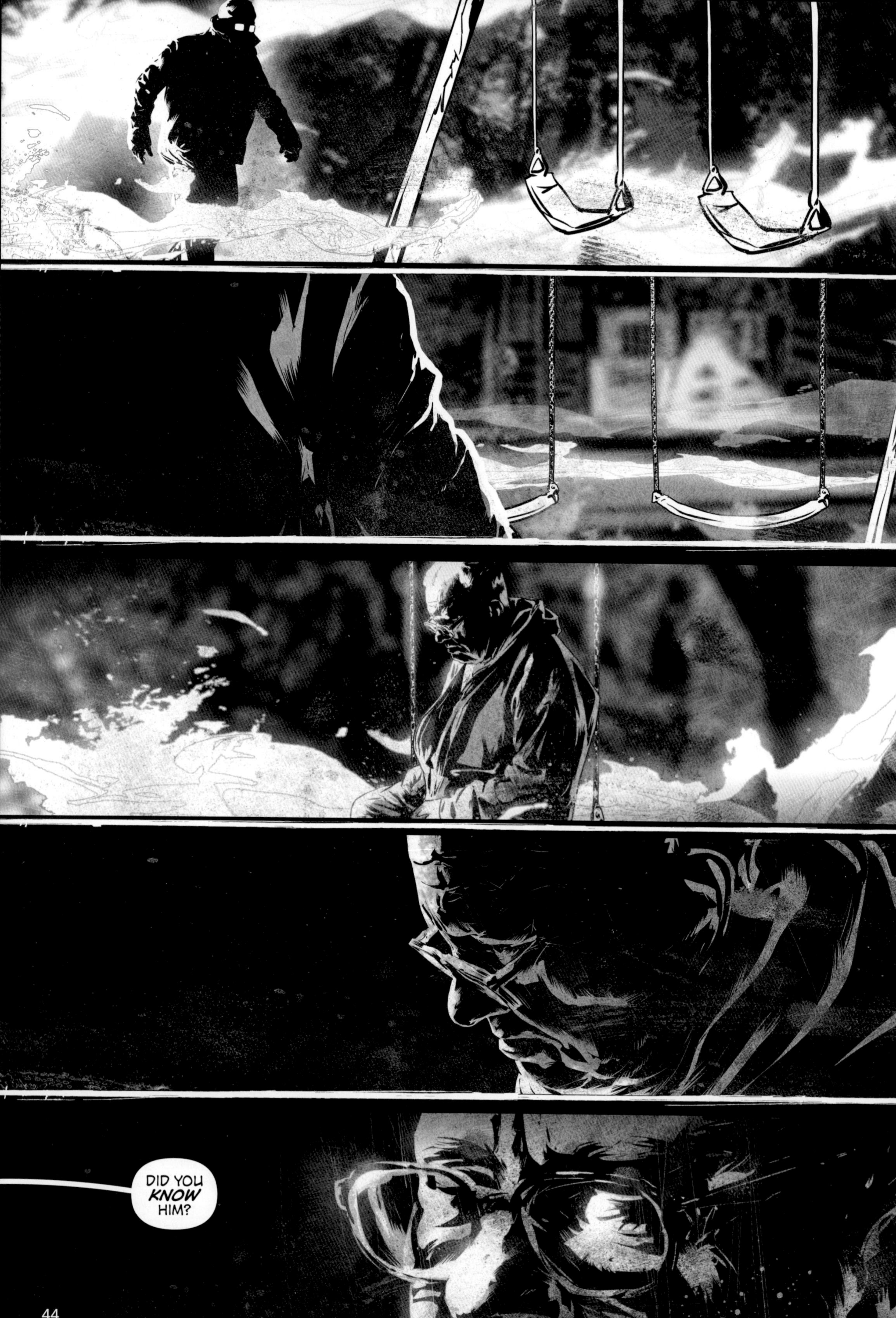
DID YOU *KNOW* HIM?

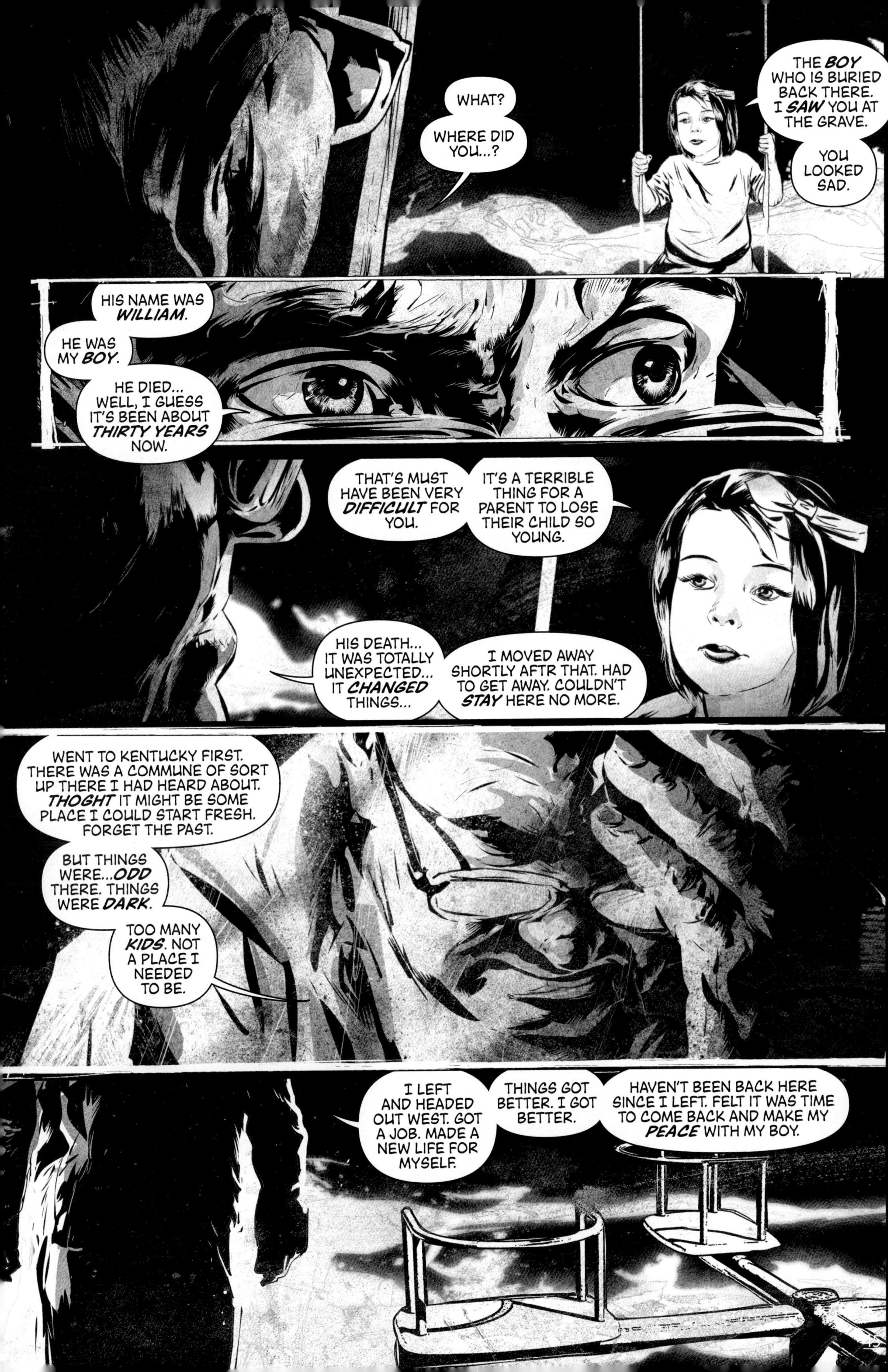
WHAT?
WHERE DID YOU...?
THE BOY WHO IS BURIED BACK THERE. I SAW YOU AT THE GRAVE.
YOU LOOKED SAD.
HIS NAME WAS WILLIAM.
HE WAS MY BOY.
HE DIED... WELL, I GUESS IT'S BEEN ABOUT THIRTY YEARS NOW.
THAT'S MUST HAVE BEEN VERY DIFFICULT FOR YOU.
IT'S A TERRIBLE THING FOR A PARENT TO LOSE THEIR CHILD SO YOUNG.
HIS DEATH... IT WAS TOTALLY UNEXPECTED... IT CHANGED THINGS...
I MOVED AWAY SHORTLY AFTR THAT. HAD TO GET AWAY. COULDN'T STAY HERE NO MORE.
WENT TO KENTUCKY FIRST. THERE WAS A COMMUNE OF SORT UP THERE I HAD HEARD ABOUT. THOGHT IT MIGHT BE SOME PLACE I COULD START FRESH. FORGET THE PAST.
BUT THINGS WERE...ODD THERE. THINGS WERE DARK.
TOO MANY KIDS. NOT A PLACE I NEEDED TO BE.
I LEFT AND HEADED OUT WEST. GOT A JOB. MADE A NEW LIFE FOR MYSELF.
THINGS GOT BETTER. I GOT BETTER.
HAVEN'T BEEN BACK HERE SINCE I LEFT. FELT IT WAS TIME TO COME BACK AND MAKE MY PEACE WITH MY BOY.

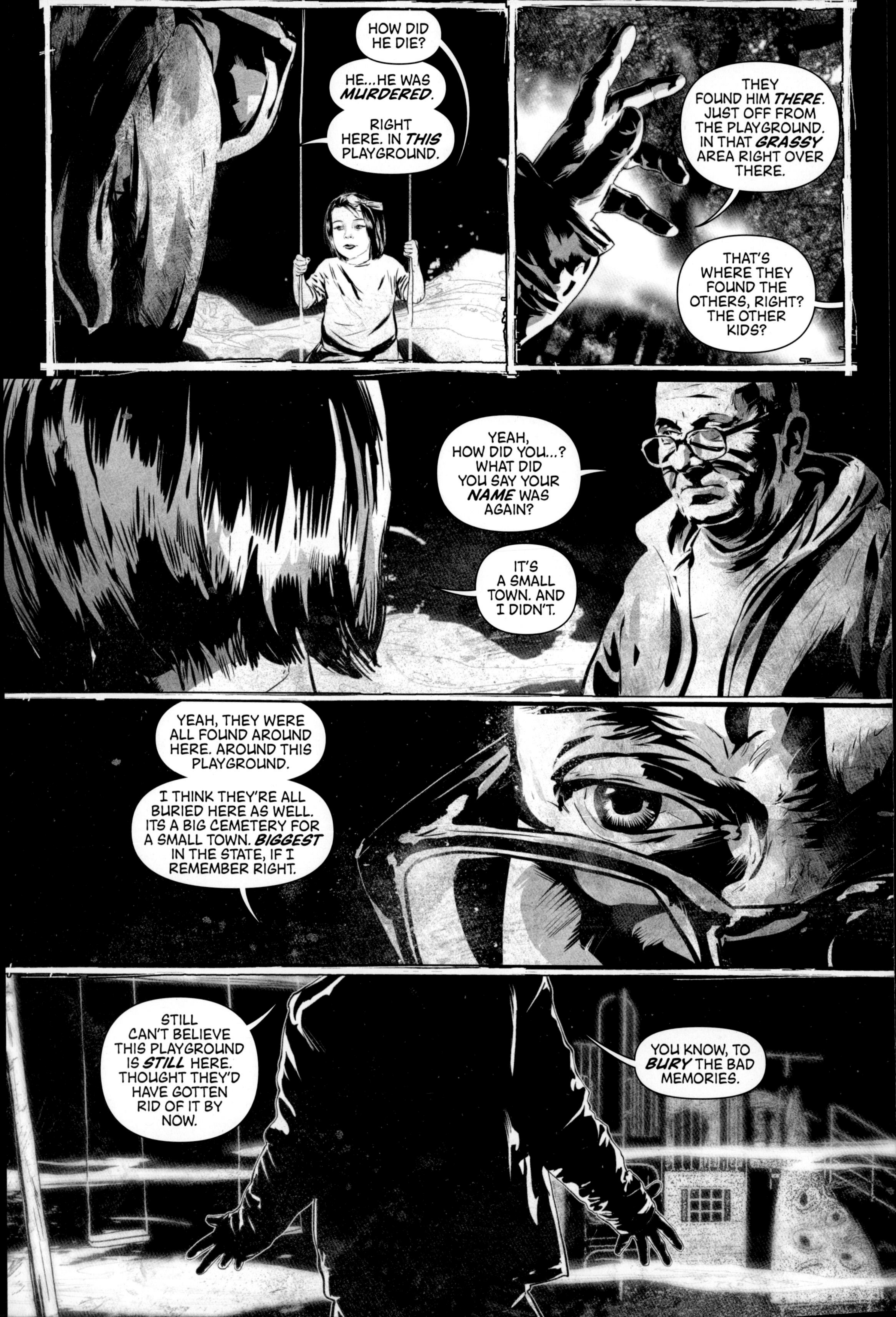
HOW DID HE DIE?
HE...HE WAS MURDERED.
RIGHT HERE. IN THIS PLAYGROUND.
THEY FOUND HIM THERE. JUST OFF FROM THE PLAYGROUND. IN THAT GRASSY AREA RIGHT OVER THERE.
THAT'S WHERE THEY FOUND THE OTHERS, RIGHT? THE OTHER KIDS?
YEAH, HOW DID YOU...? WHAT DID YOU SAY YOUR NAME WAS AGAIN?
IT'S A SMALL TOWN. AND I DIDN'T.
YEAH, THEY WERE ALL FOUND AROUND HERE. AROUND THIS PLAYGROUND.
I THINK THEY'RE ALL BURIED HERE AS WELL. ITS A BIG CEMETERY FOR A SMALL TOWN. BIGGEST IN THE STATE, IF I REMEMBER RIGHT.
STILL CAN'T BELIEVE THIS PLAYGROUND IS STILL HERE. THOUGHT THEY'D HAVE GOTTEN RID OF IT BY NOW.
YOU KNOW, TO BURY THE BAD MEMORIES.

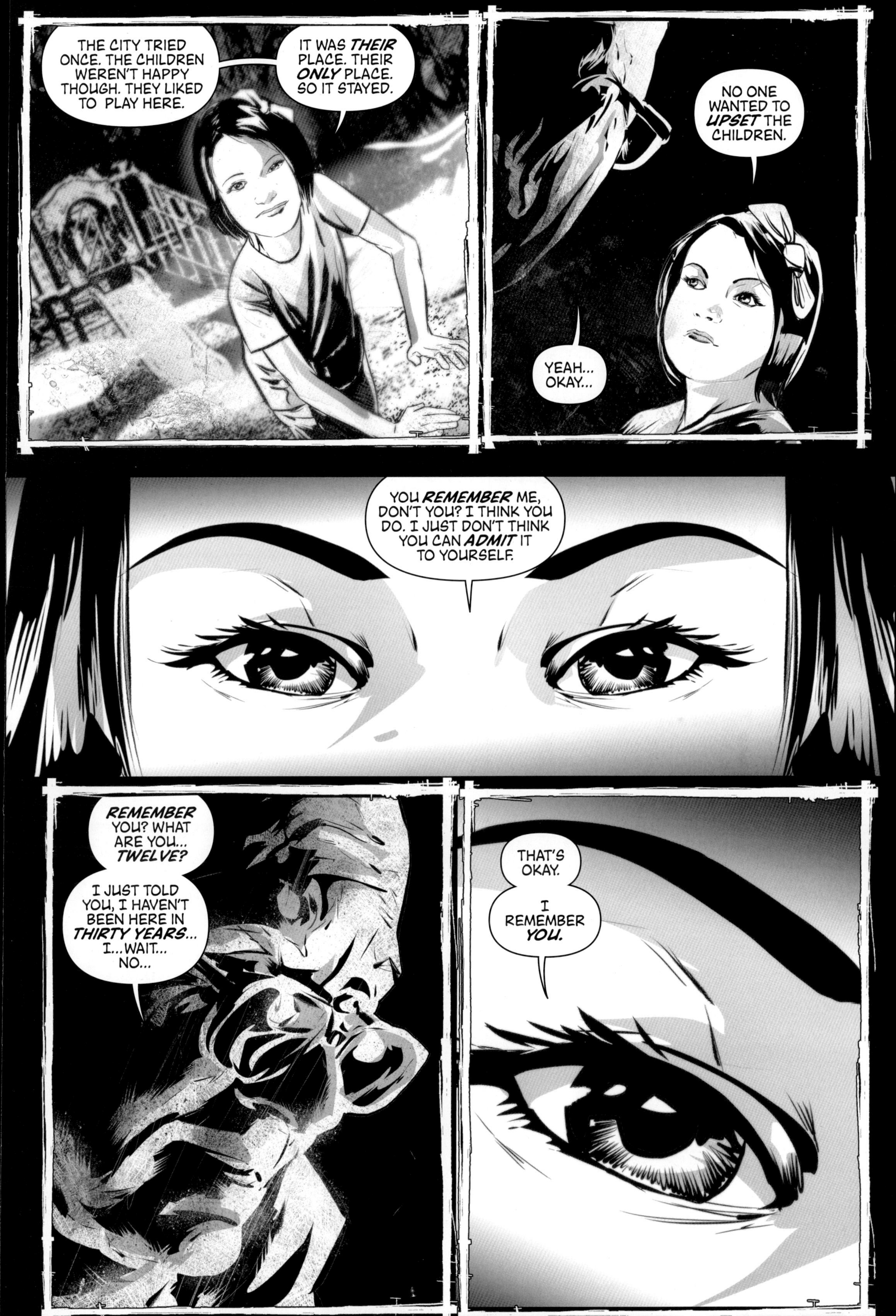
THE CITY TRIED ONCE. THE CHILDREN WEREN'T HAPPY THOUGH. THEY LIKED TO PLAY HERE.
IT WAS *THEIR* PLACE. THEIR *ONLY* PLACE. SO IT STAYED.
NO ONE WANTED TO *UPSET* THE CHILDREN.
YEAH... OKAY...
YOU *REMEMBER* ME, DON'T YOU? I THINK YOU DO. I JUST DON'T THINK YOU CAN *ADMIT* IT TO YOURSELF.
REMEMBER YOU? WHAT ARE YOU... *TWELVE?*
I JUST TOLD YOU, I HAVEN'T BEEN HERE IN *THIRTY YEARS*... I...WAIT... NO...
THAT'S OKAY.
I REMEMBER *YOU.*

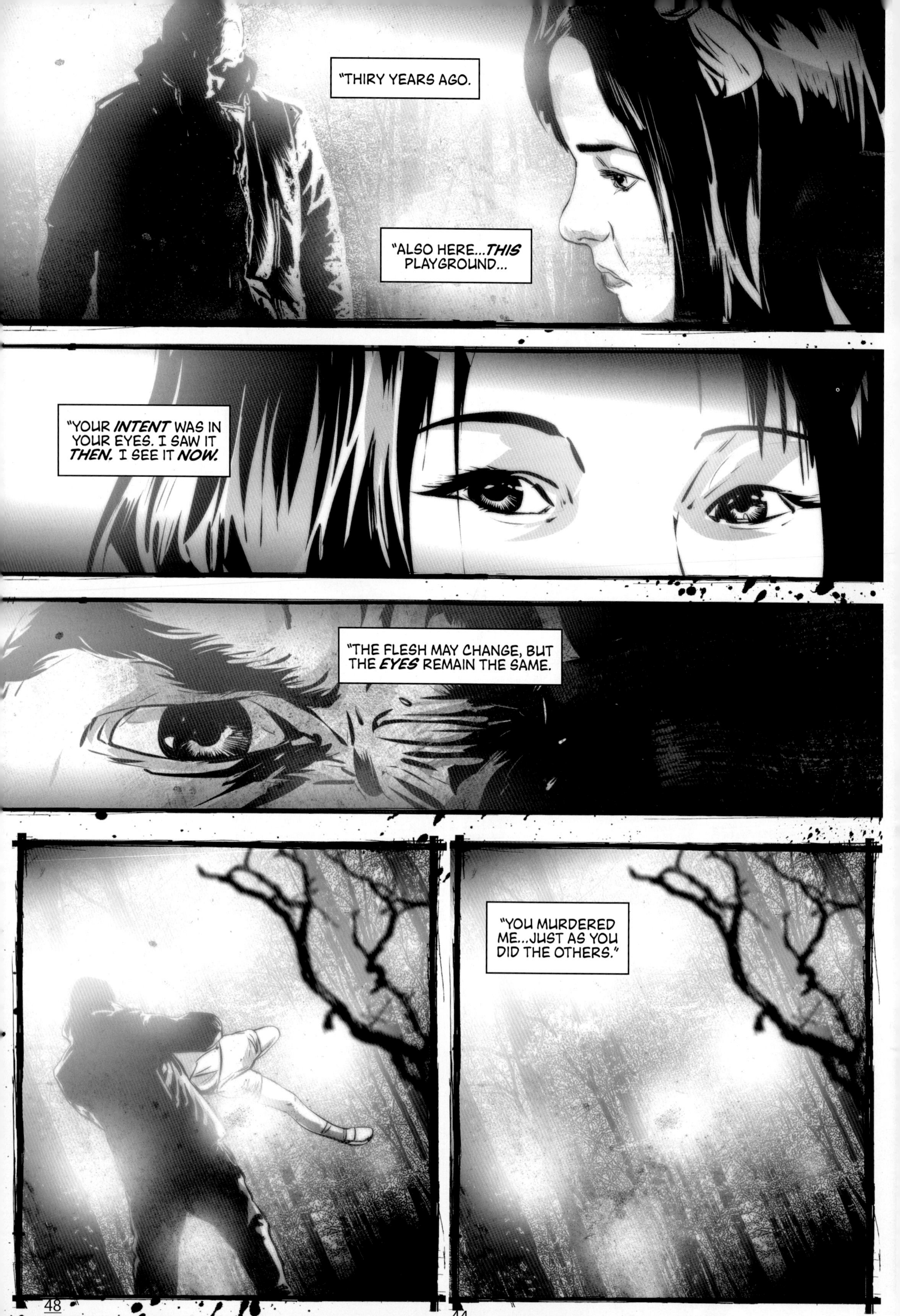
"THIRY YEARS AGO.
"ALSO HERE...THIS PLAYGROUND...
"YOUR INTENT WAS IN YOUR EYES. I SAW IT THEN. I SEE IT NOW.
"THE FLESH MAY CHANGE, BUT THE EYES REMAIN THE SAME.
"YOU MURDERED ME...JUST AS YOU DID THE OTHERS."

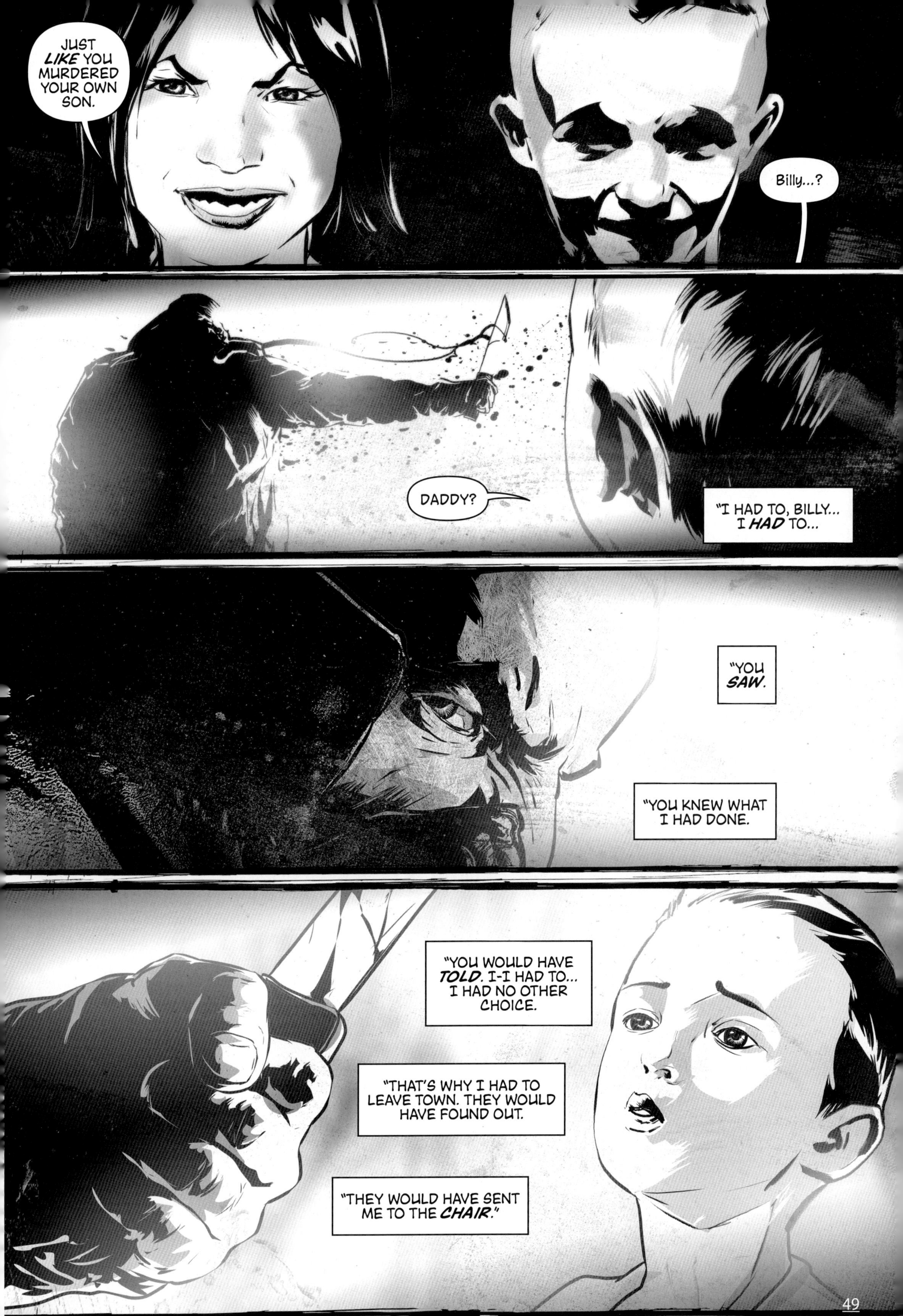
JUST *LIKE* YOU MURDERED YOUR OWN SON.
Billy...?
DADDY?
"I HAD TO, BILLY... I *HAD* TO...
"YOU *SAW*.
"YOU KNEW WHAT I HAD DONE.
"YOU WOULD HAVE *TOLD*. I-I HAD TO... I HAD NO OTHER CHOICE.
"THAT'S WHY I HAD TO LEAVE TOWN. THEY WOULD HAVE FOUND OUT.
"THEY WOULD HAVE SENT ME TO THE *CHAIR*."

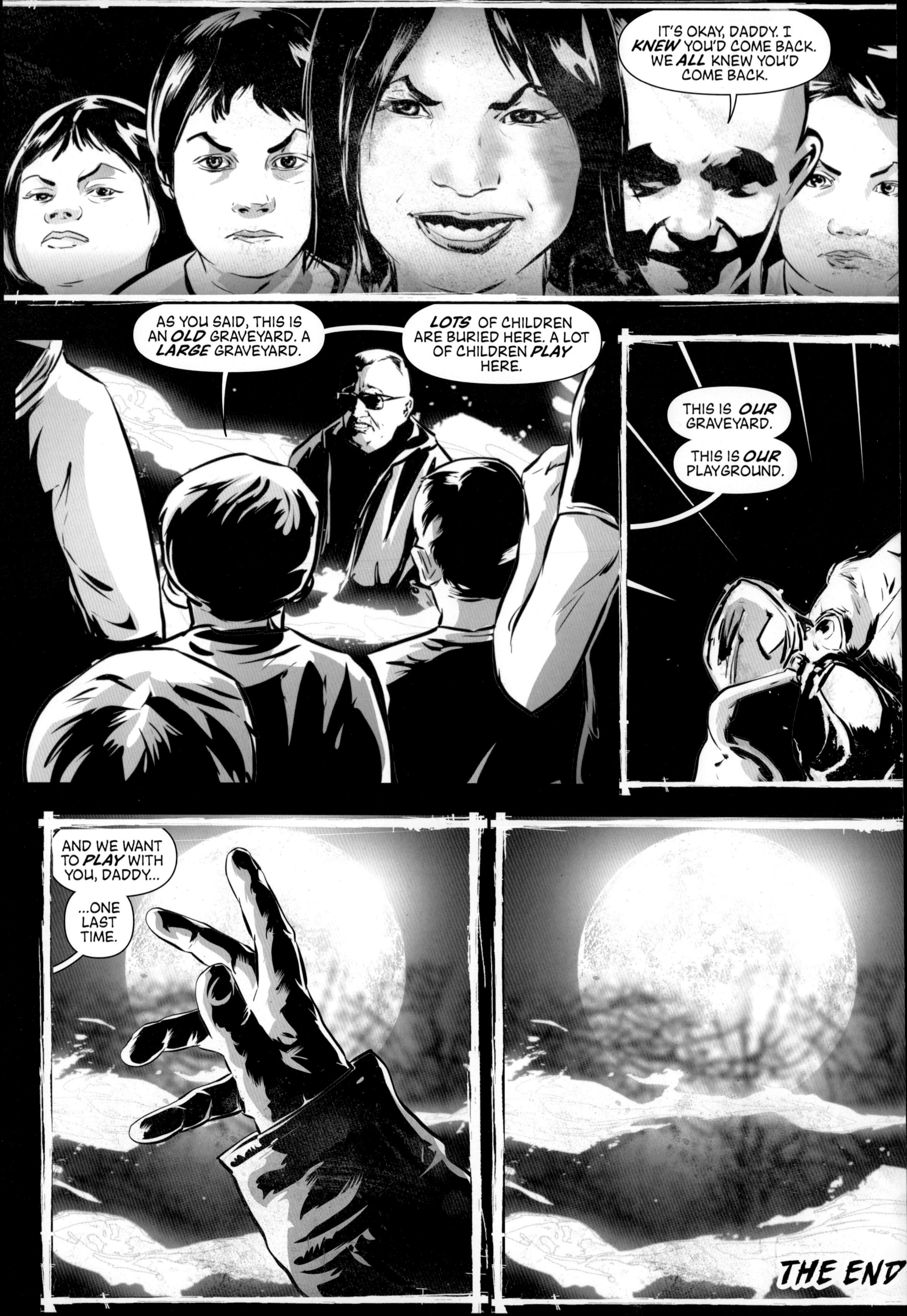
IT'S OKAY, DADDY. I KNEW YOU'D COME BACK. WE ALL KNEW YOU'D COME BACK.
AS YOU SAID, THIS IS AN OLD GRAVEYARD. A LARGE GRAVEYARD.
LOTS OF CHILDREN ARE BURIED HERE. A LOT OF CHILDREN PLAY HERE.
THIS IS OUR GRAVEYARD.
THIS IS OUR PLAYGROUND.
AND WE WANT TO PLAY WITH YOU, DADDY...
...ONE LAST TIME.
THE END

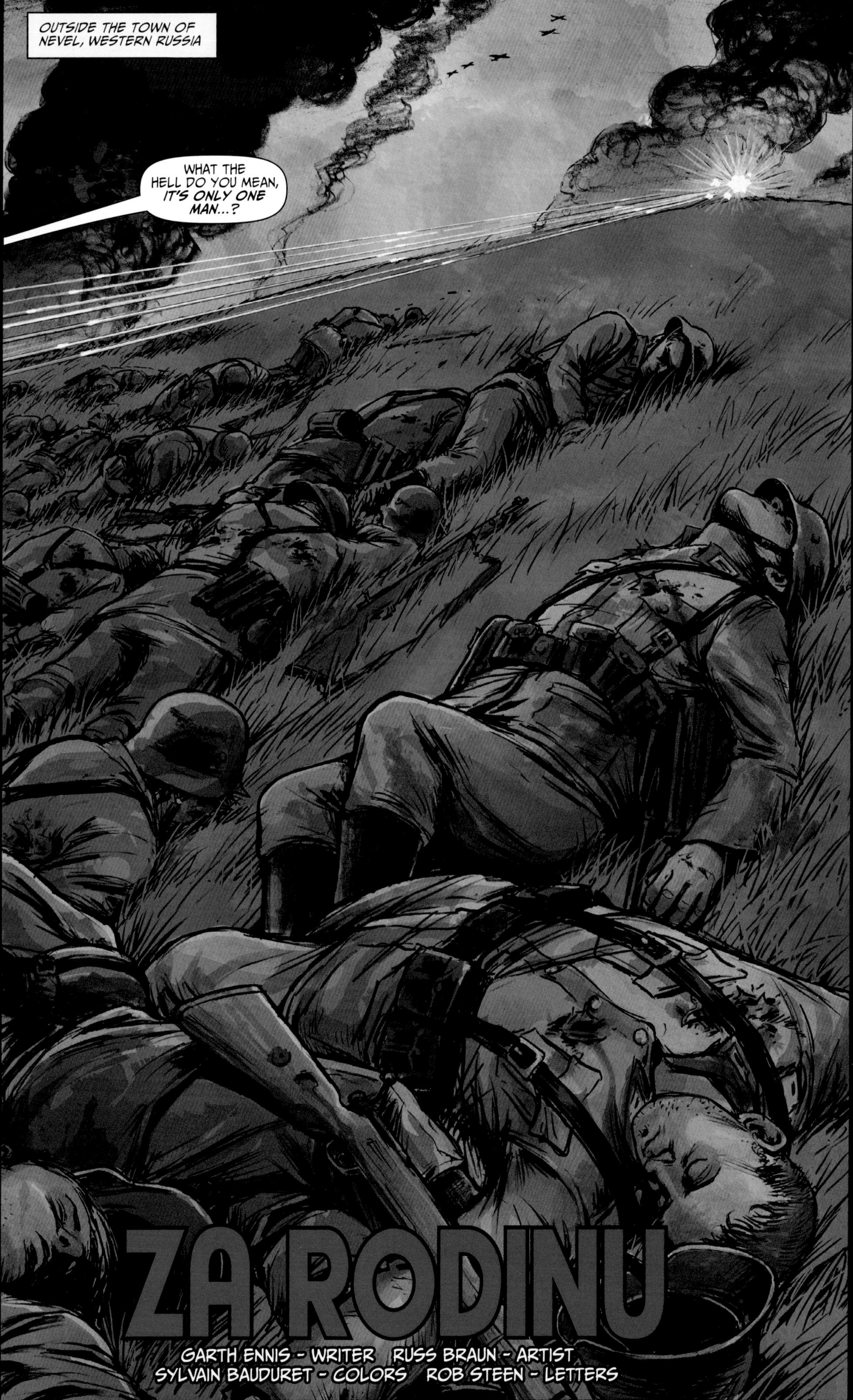
OUTSIDE THE TOWN OF NEVEL, WESTERN RUSSIA
WHAT THE HELL DO YOU MEAN, *IT'S ONLY ONE MAN...?*
ZA RODINU
GARTH ENNIS - WRITER RUSS BRAUN - ARTIST
SYLVAIN BAUDURET - COLORS ROB STEEN - LETTERS

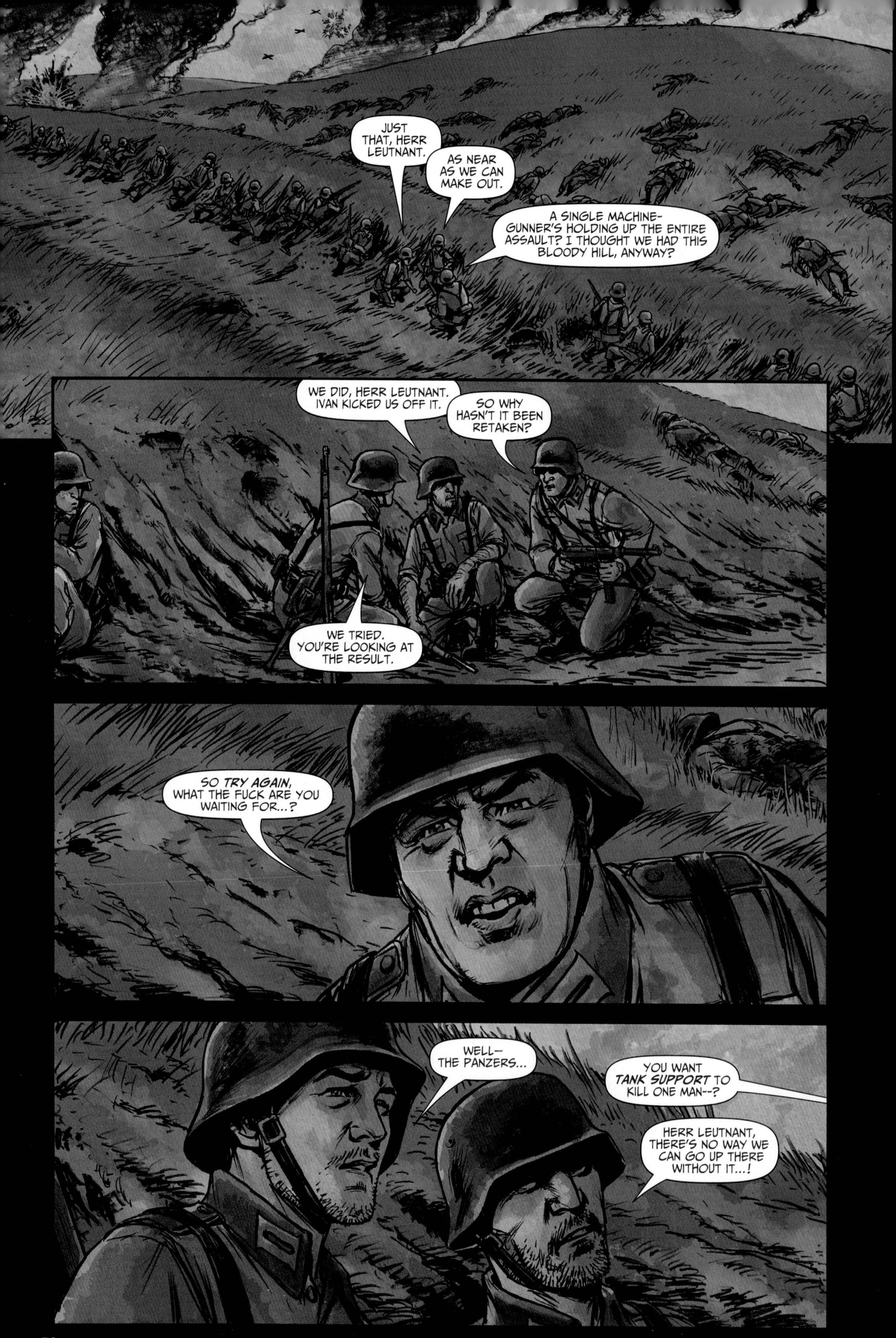
JUST THAT, HERR LEUTNANT.
AS NEAR AS WE CAN MAKE OUT.
A SINGLE MACHINE-GUNNER'S HOLDING UP THE ENTIRE ASSAULT? I THOUGHT WE HAD THIS BLOODY HILL, ANYWAY?
WE DID, HERR LEUTNANT. IVAN KICKED US OFF IT.
SO WHY HASN'T IT BEEN RETAKEN?
WE TRIED. YOU'RE LOOKING AT THE RESULT.
SO ***TRY AGAIN***, WHAT THE FUCK ARE YOU WAITING FOR...?
WELL— THE PANZERS...
YOU WANT ***TANK SUPPORT*** TO KILL ONE MAN--?
HERR LEUTNANT, THERE'S NO WAY WE CAN GO UP THERE WITHOUT IT...!

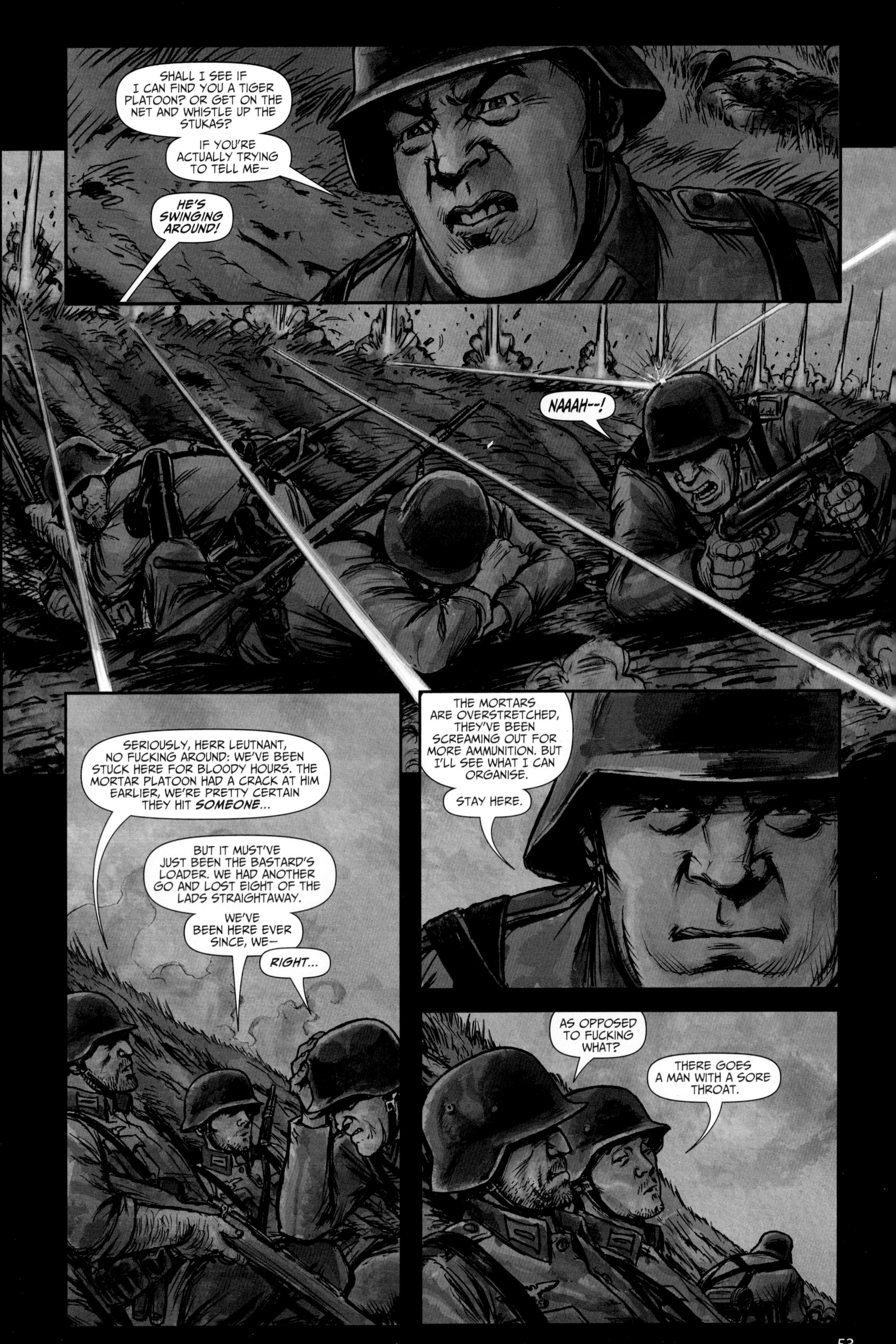

SHALL I SEE IF I CAN FIND YOU A TIGER PLATOON? OR GET ON THE NET AND WHISTLE UP THE STUKAS?
IF YOU'RE ACTUALLY TRYING TO TELL ME–
HE'S SWINGING AROUND!
NAAAH--!
SERIOUSLY, HERR LEUTNANT, NO FUCKING AROUND: WE'VE BEEN STUCK HERE FOR BLOODY HOURS. THE MORTAR PLATOON HAD A CRACK AT HIM EARLIER, WE'RE PRETTY CERTAIN THEY HIT SOMEONE...
BUT IT MUST'VE JUST BEEN THE BASTARD'S LOADER. WE HAD ANOTHER GO AND LOST EIGHT OF THE LADS STRAIGHTAWAY.
WE'VE BEEN HERE EVER SINCE, WE–
RIGHT...
THE MORTARS ARE OVERSTRETCHED, THEY'VE BEEN SCREAMING OUT FOR MORE AMMUNITION. BUT I'LL SEE WHAT I CAN ORGANISE.
STAY HERE.
AS OPPOSED TO FUCKING WHAT?
THERE GOES A MAN WITH A SORE THROAT.

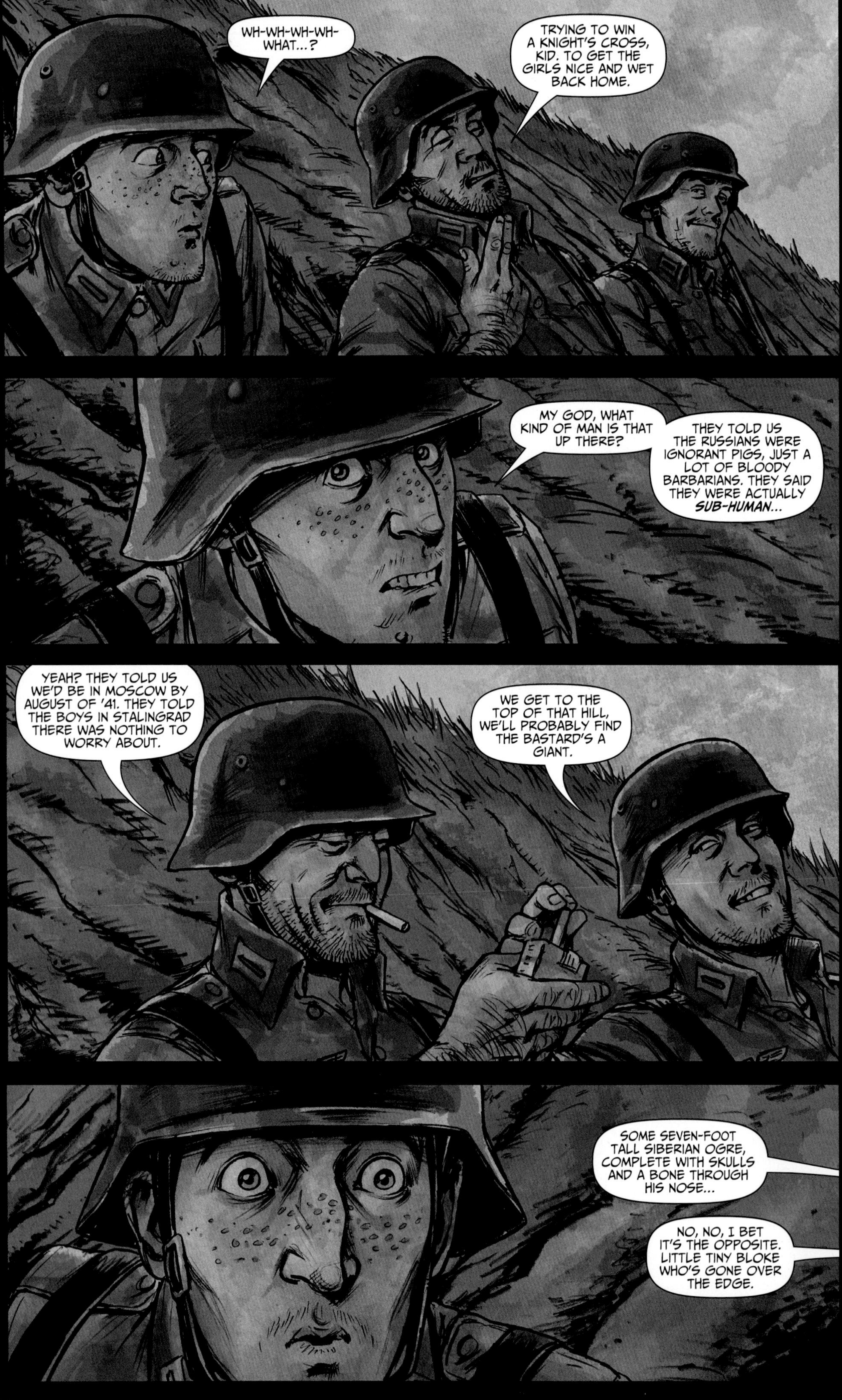
WH-WH-WH-WH-WHAT...?
TRYING TO WIN A KNIGHT'S CROSS, KID. TO GET THE GIRLS NICE AND WET BACK HOME.
MY GOD, WHAT KIND OF MAN IS THAT UP THERE?
THEY TOLD US THE RUSSIANS WERE IGNORANT PIGS, JUST A LOT OF BLOODY BARBARIANS. THEY SAID THEY WERE ACTUALLY SUB-HUMAN...
YEAH? THEY TOLD US WE'D BE IN MOSCOW BY AUGUST OF '41. THEY TOLD THE BOYS IN STALINGRAD THERE WAS NOTHING TO WORRY ABOUT.
WE GET TO THE TOP OF THAT HILL, WE'LL PROBABLY FIND THE BASTARD'S A GIANT.
SOME SEVEN-FOOT TALL SIBERIAN OGRE, COMPLETE WITH SKULLS AND A BONE THROUGH HIS NOSE...
NO, NO, I BET IT'S THE OPPOSITE. LITTLE TINY BLOKE WHO'S GONE OVER THE EDGE.

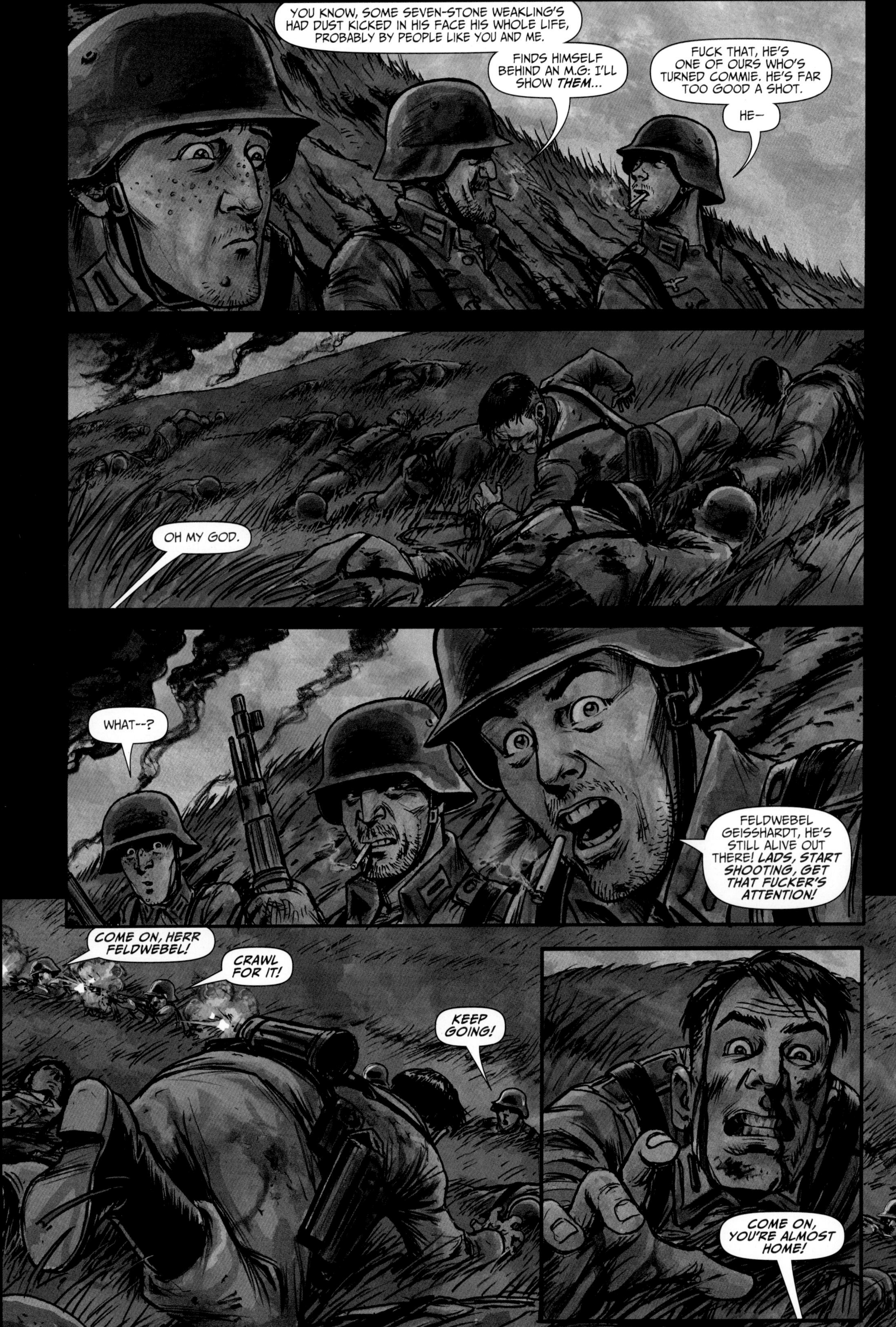

YOU KNOW, SOME SEVEN-STONE WEAKLING'S HAD DUST KICKED IN HIS FACE HIS WHOLE LIFE, PROBABLY BY PEOPLE LIKE YOU AND ME.
FINDS HIMSELF BEHIND AN M.G: I'LL SHOW *THEM*...
FUCK THAT, HE'S ONE OF OURS WHO'S TURNED COMMIE. HE'S FAR TOO GOOD A SHOT.
HE–
OH MY GOD.
WHAT--?
FELDWEBEL GEISSHARDT, HE'S STILL ALIVE OUT THERE! *LADS, START SHOOTING, GET THAT FUCKER'S ATTENTION!*
COME ON, HERR FELDWEBEL!
CRAWL FOR IT!
KEEP GOING!
COME ON, YOU'RE ALMOST HOME!

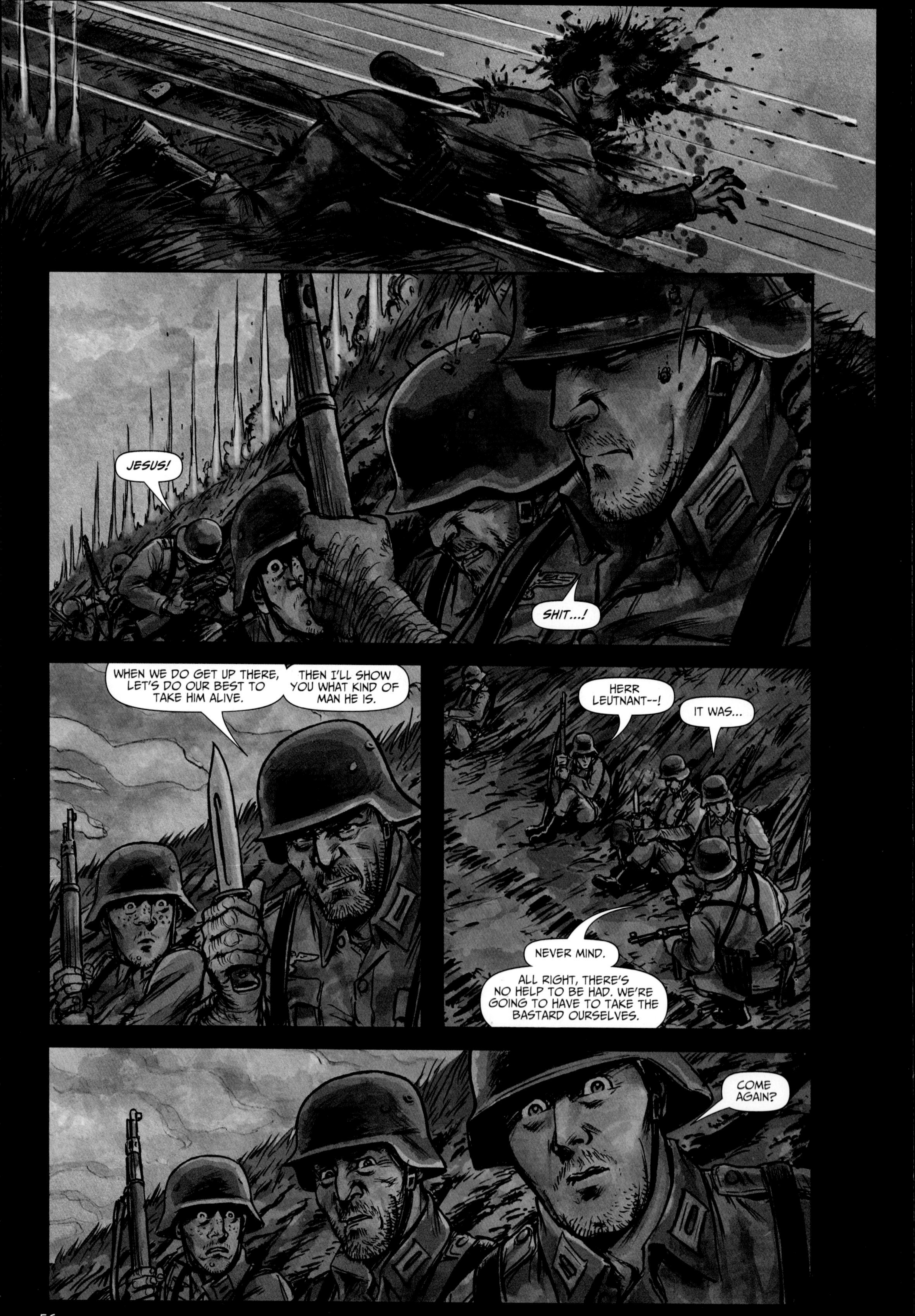
JESUS!
SHIT...!
WHEN WE DO GET UP THERE, LET'S DO OUR BEST TO TAKE HIM ALIVE.
THEN I'LL SHOW YOU WHAT KIND OF MAN HE IS.
HERR LEUTNANT--!
IT WAS...
NEVER MIND.
ALL RIGHT, THERE'S NO HELP TO BE HAD. WE'RE GOING TO HAVE TO TAKE THE BASTARD OURSELVES.
COME AGAIN?

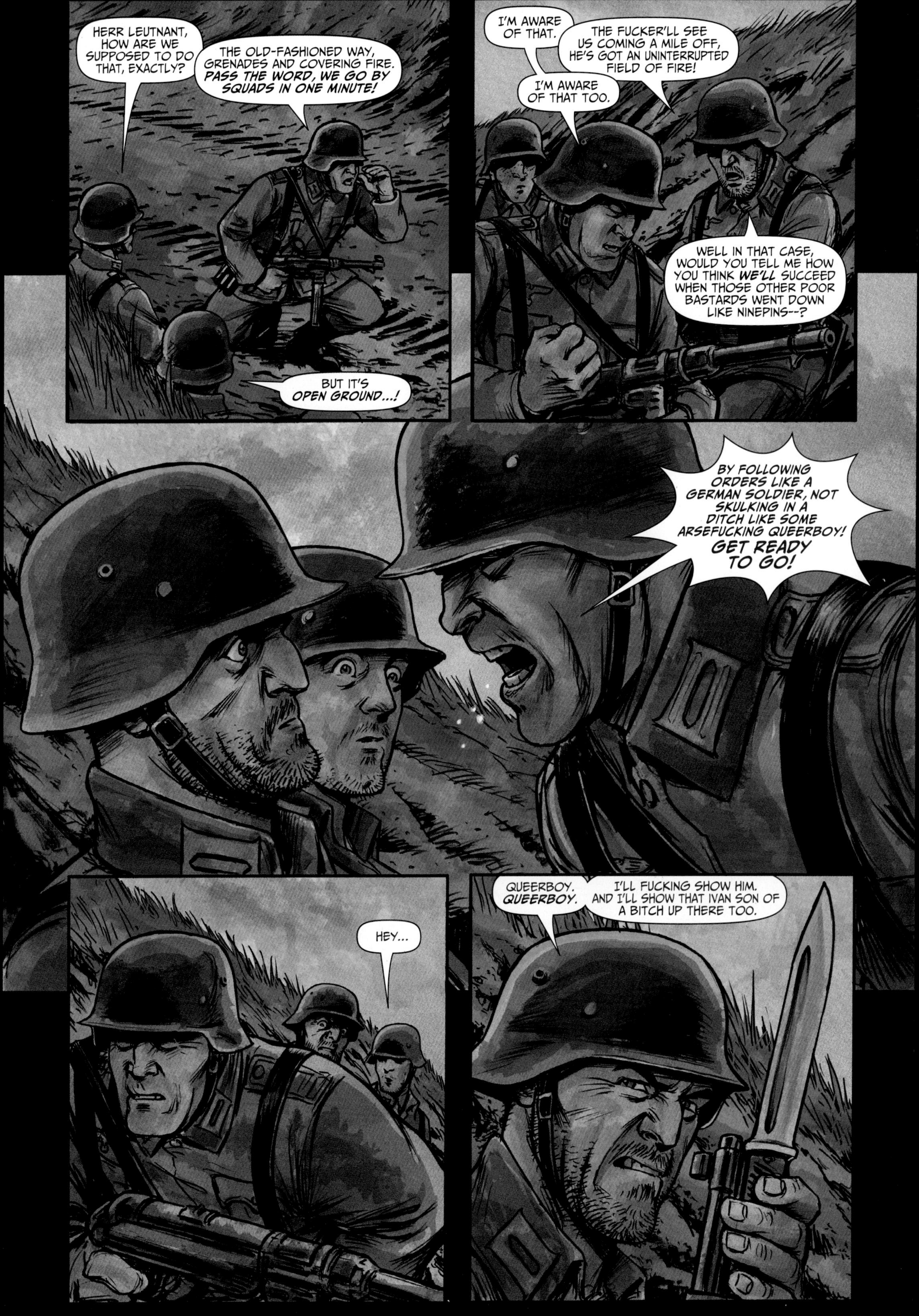
HERR LEUTNANT, HOW ARE WE SUPPOSED TO DO THAT, EXACTLY?
THE OLD-FASHIONED WAY, GRENADES AND COVERING FIRE. PASS THE WORD, WE GO BY SQUADS IN ONE MINUTE!
BUT IT'S OPEN GROUND...!
I'M AWARE OF THAT.
THE FUCKER'LL SEE US COMING A MILE OFF, HE'S GOT AN UNINTERRUPTED FIELD OF FIRE!
I'M AWARE OF THAT TOO.
WELL IN THAT CASE, WOULD YOU TELL ME HOW YOU THINK WE'LL SUCCEED WHEN THOSE OTHER POOR BASTARDS WENT DOWN LIKE NINEPINS--?
BY FOLLOWING ORDERS LIKE A GERMAN SOLDIER, NOT SKULKING IN A DITCH LIKE SOME ARSEFUCKING QUEERBOY! GET READY TO GO!
HEY...
QUEERBOY. QUEERBOY.
I'LL FUCKING SHOW HIM. AND I'LL SHOW THAT IVAN SON OF A BITCH UP THERE TOO.

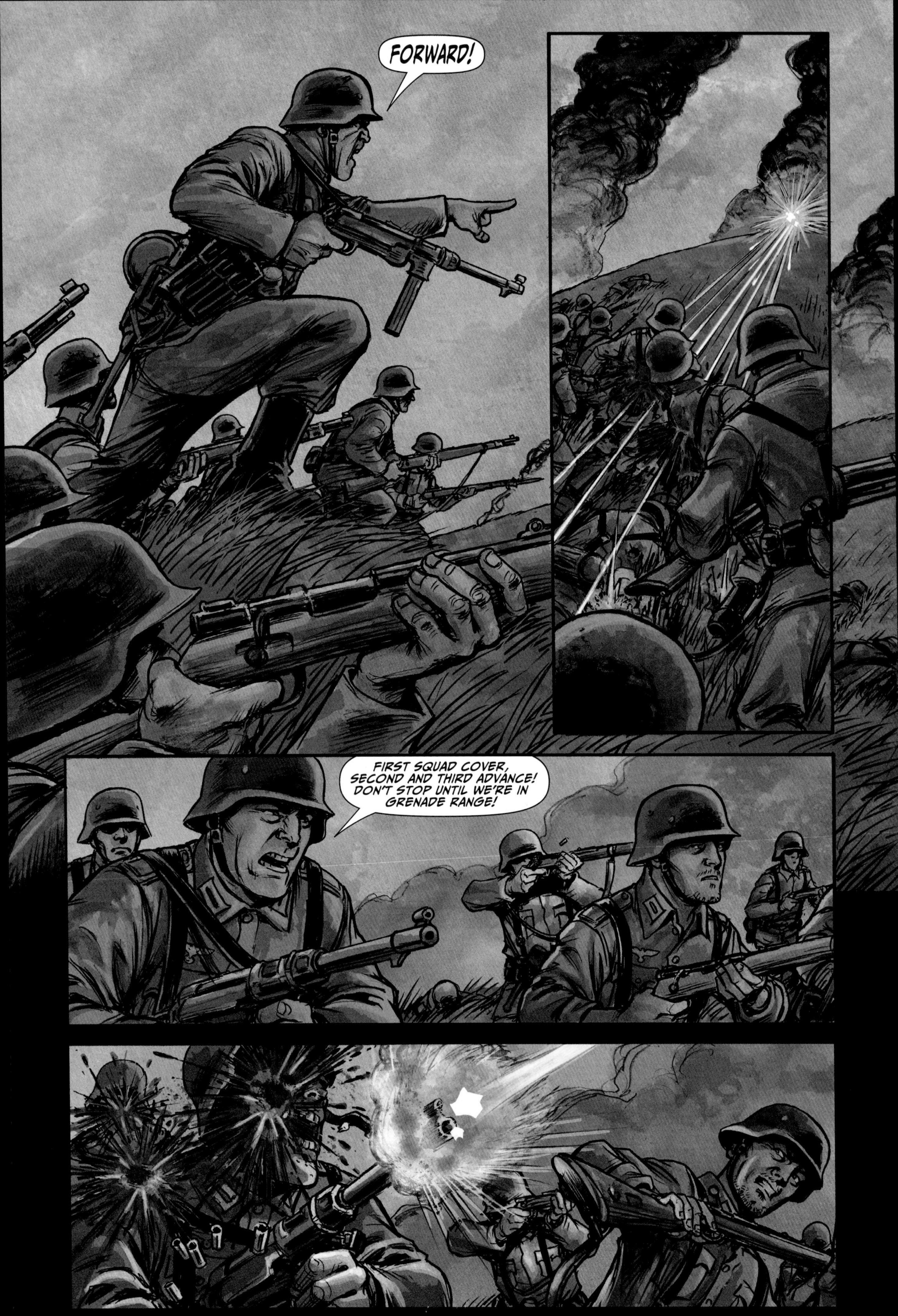
FORWARD!
FIRST SQUAD COVER, SECOND AND THIRD ADVANCE! DON'T STOP UNTIL WE'RE IN GRENADE RANGE!

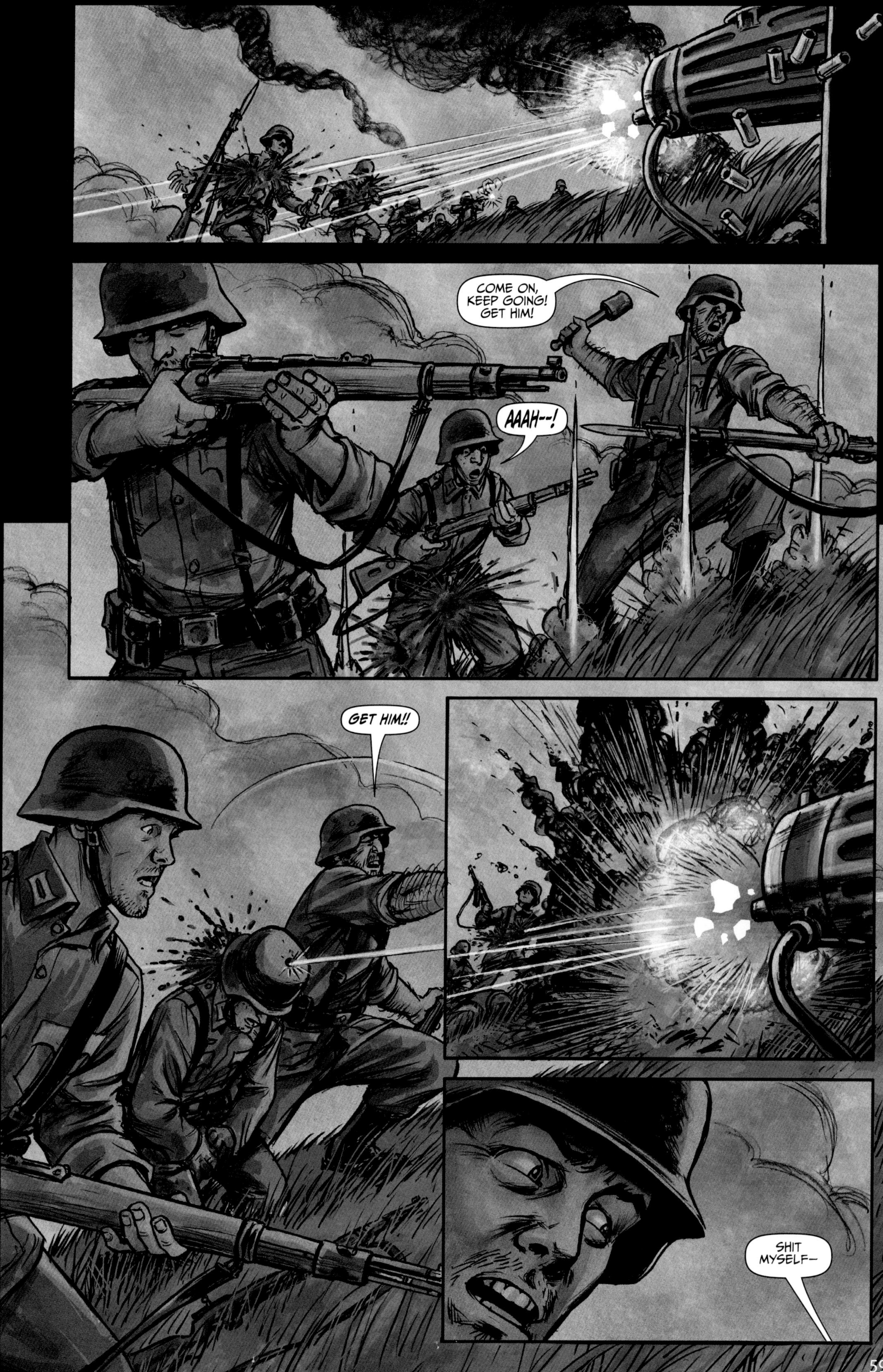
COME ON, KEEP GOING! GET HIM!
AAAH--!
GET HIM!!
SHIT MYSELF—

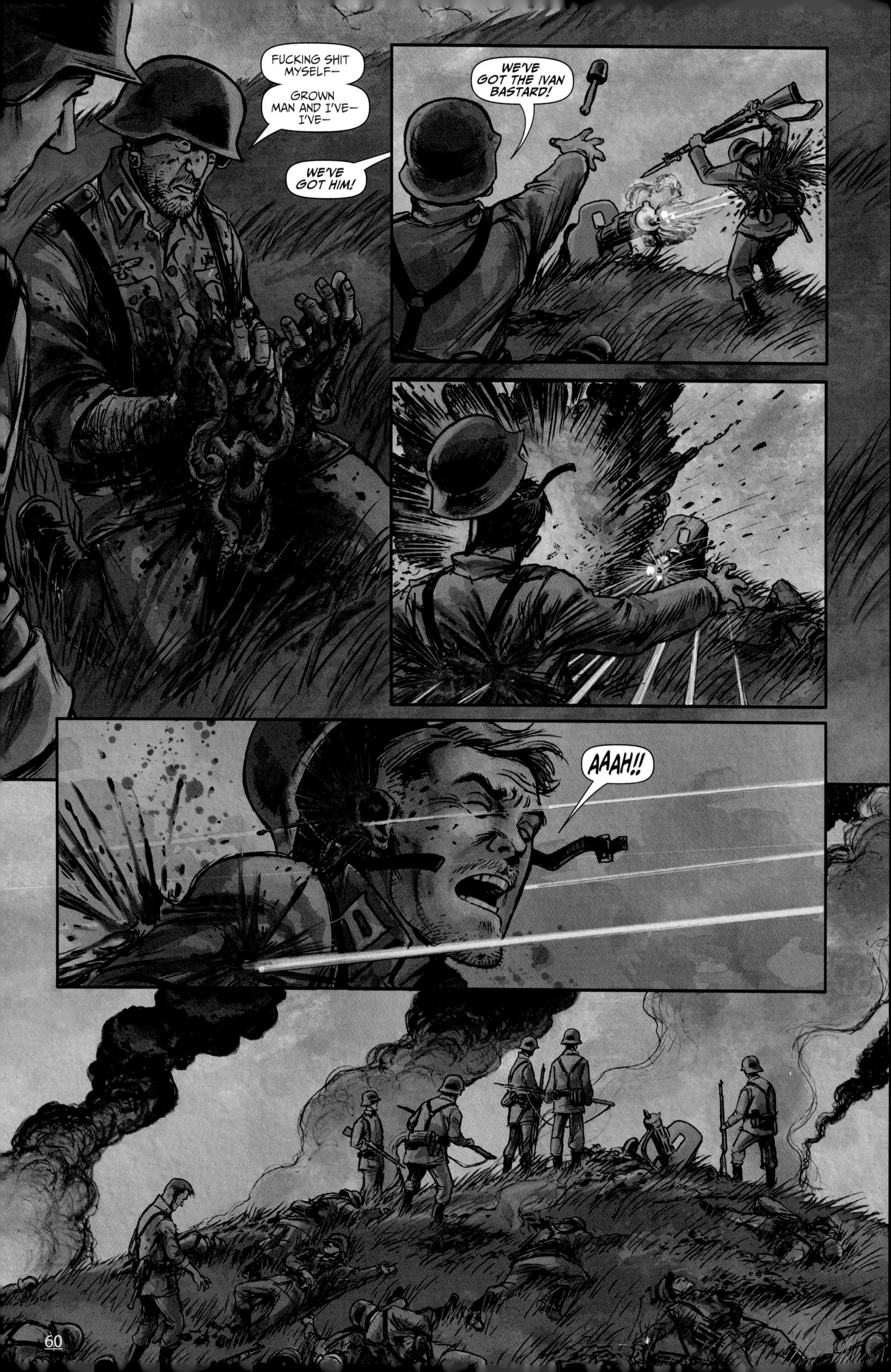
FUCKING SHIT MYSELF—
GROWN MAN AND I'VE— I'VE—
WE'VE GOT HIM!
WE'VE GOT THE IVAN BASTARD!
AAAH!!

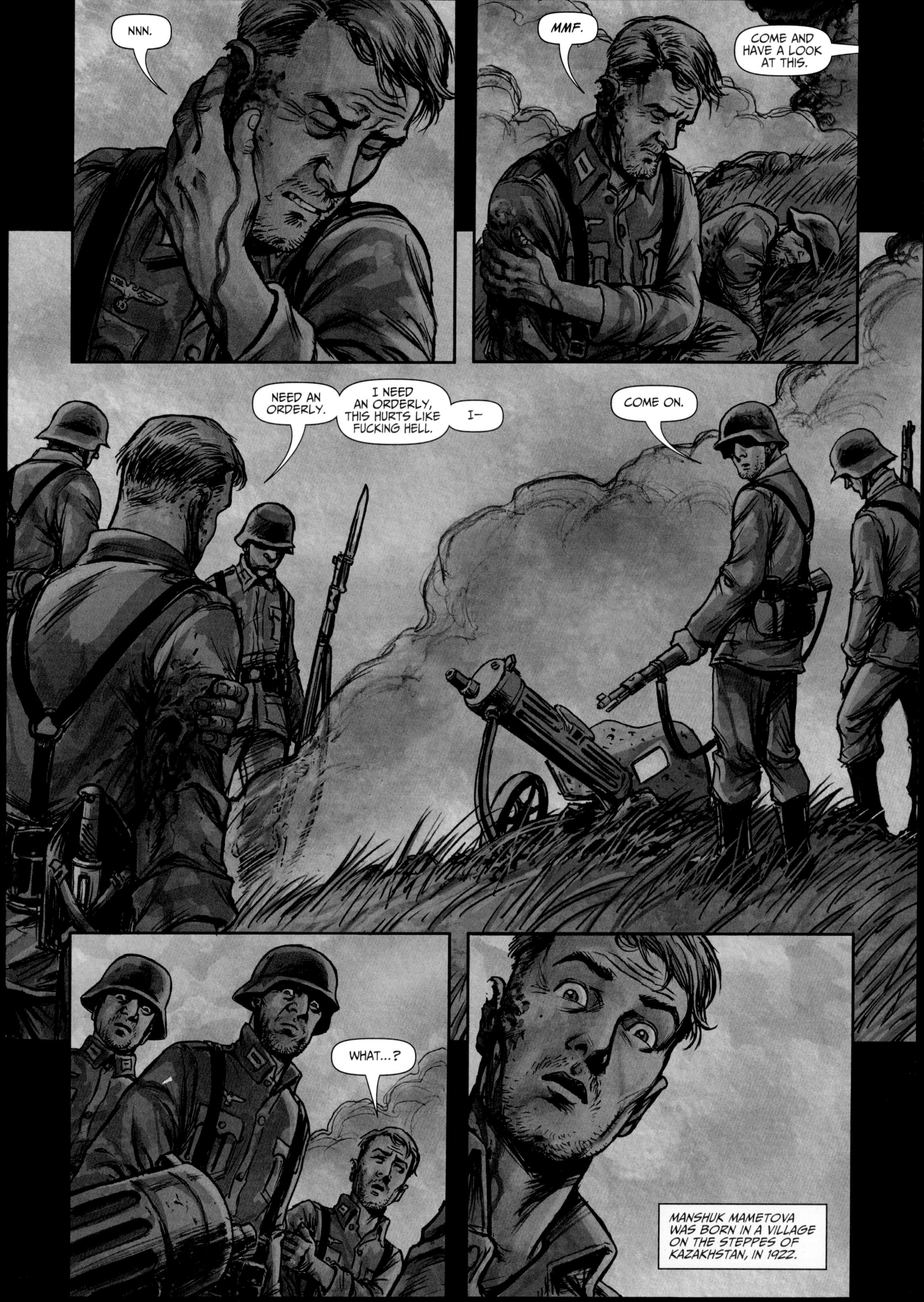
NNN.
MMF.
COME AND HAVE A LOOK AT THIS.
NEED AN ORDERLY.
I NEED AN ORDERLY, THIS HURTS LIKE FUCKING HELL.
I—
COME ON.
WHAT...?
MANSHUK MAMETOVA WAS BORN IN A VILLAGE ON THE STEPPES OF KAZAKHSTAN, IN 1922.

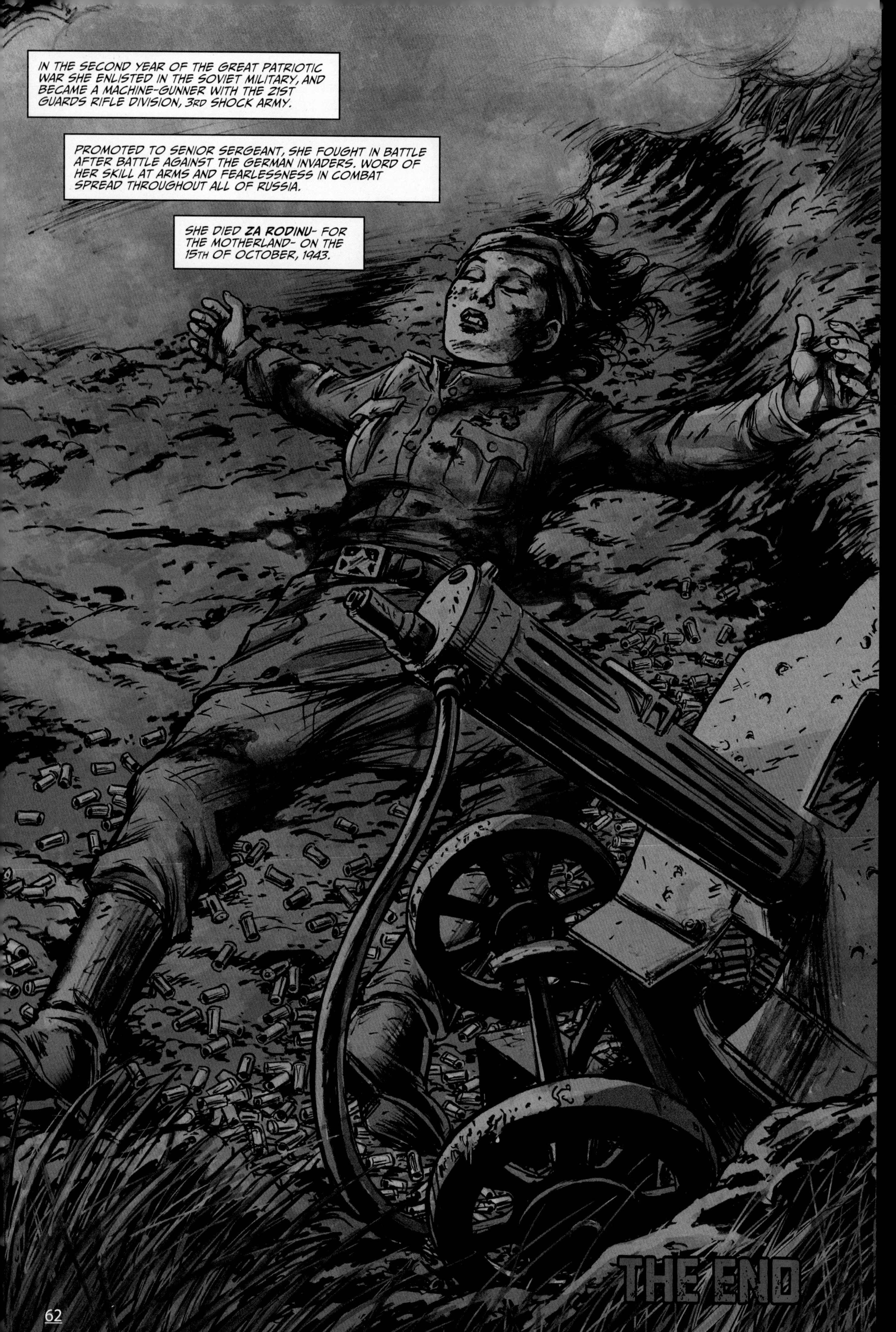
IN THE SECOND YEAR OF THE GREAT PATRIOTIC WAR SHE ENLISTED IN THE SOVIET MILITARY, AND BECAME A MACHINE-GUNNER WITH THE 21ST GUARDS RIFLE DIVISION, 3RD SHOCK ARMY.
PROMOTED TO SENIOR SERGEANT, SHE FOUGHT IN BATTLE AFTER BATTLE AGAINST THE GERMAN INVADERS. WORD OF HER SKILL AT ARMS AND FEARLESSNESS IN COMBAT SPREAD THROUGHOUT ALL OF RUSSIA.
SHE DIED **ZA RODINU**- FOR THE MOTHERLAND- ON THE 15TH OF OCTOBER, 1943.
THE END

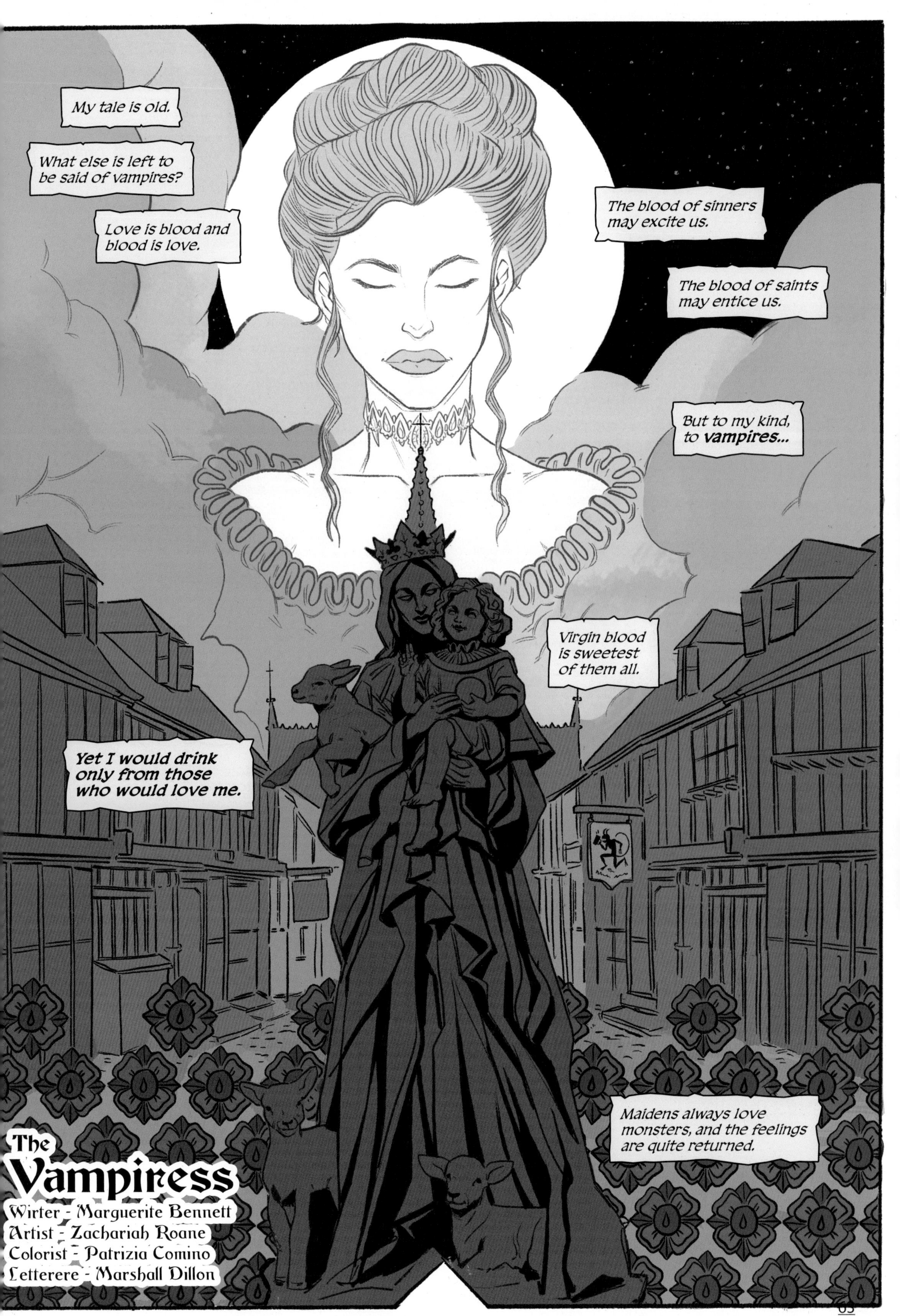
My tale is old.
What else is left to be said of vampires?
Love is blood and blood is love.
The blood of sinners may excite us.
The blood of saints may entice us.
But to my kind, to **vampires...**
Virgin blood is sweetest of them all.
Yet I would drink only from those who would love me.
Maidens always love monsters, and the feelings are quite returned.
The Vampiress
Wirter - Marguerite Bennett
Artist - Zachariah Roane
Colorist - Patrizia Comino
Letterere - Marshall Dillon

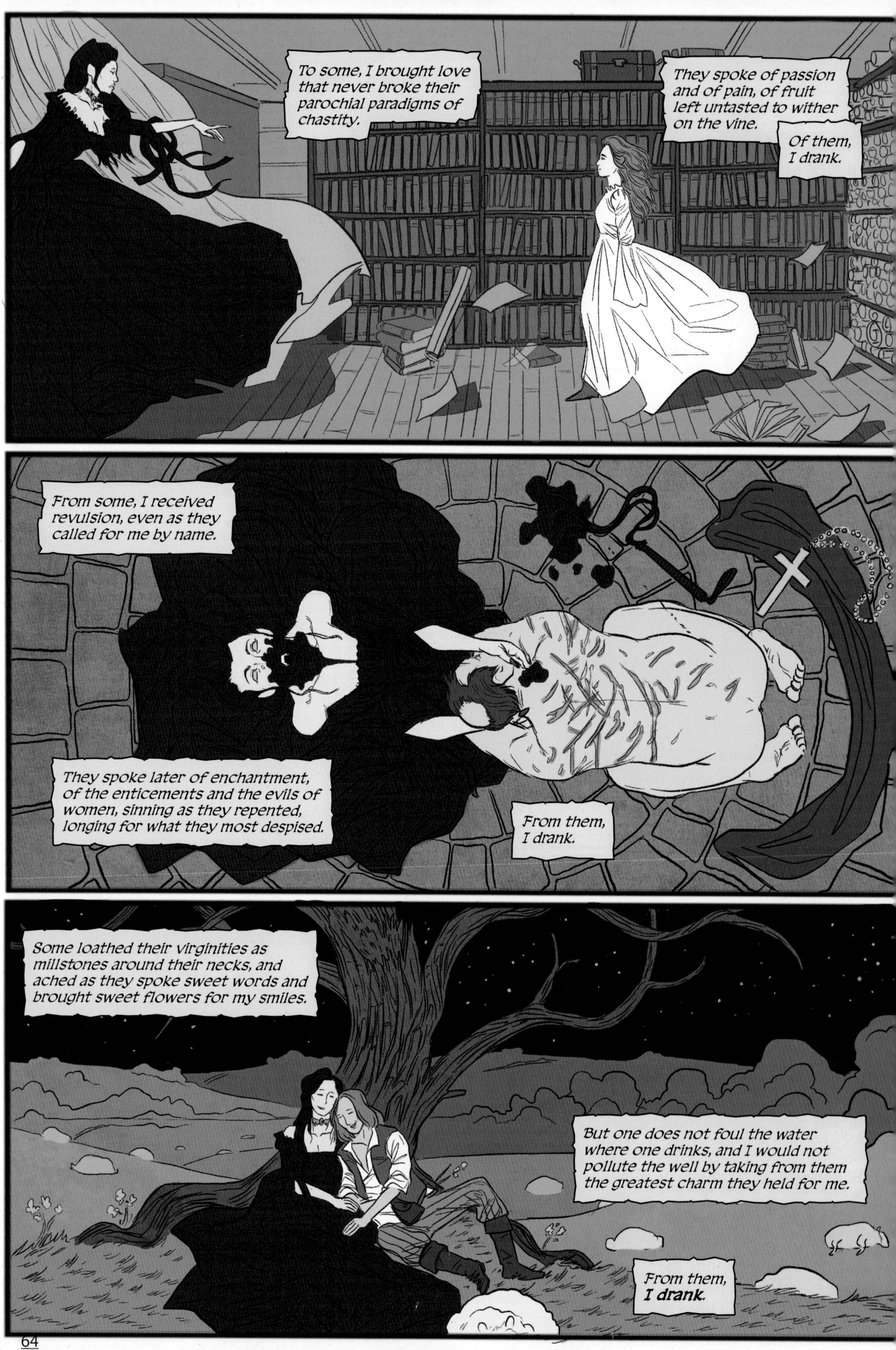
To some, I brought love that never broke their parochial paradigms of chastity.
They spoke of passion and of pain, of fruit left untasted to wither on the vine.
Of them, I drank.
From some, I received revulsion, even as they called for me by name.
They spoke later of enchantment, of the enticements and the evils of women, sinning as they repented, longing for what they most despised.
From them, I drank.
Some loathed their virginities as millstones around their necks, and ached as they spoke sweet words and brought sweet flowers for my smiles.
But one does not foul the water where one drinks, and I would not pollute the well by taking from them the greatest charm they held for me.
From them, **I drank.**

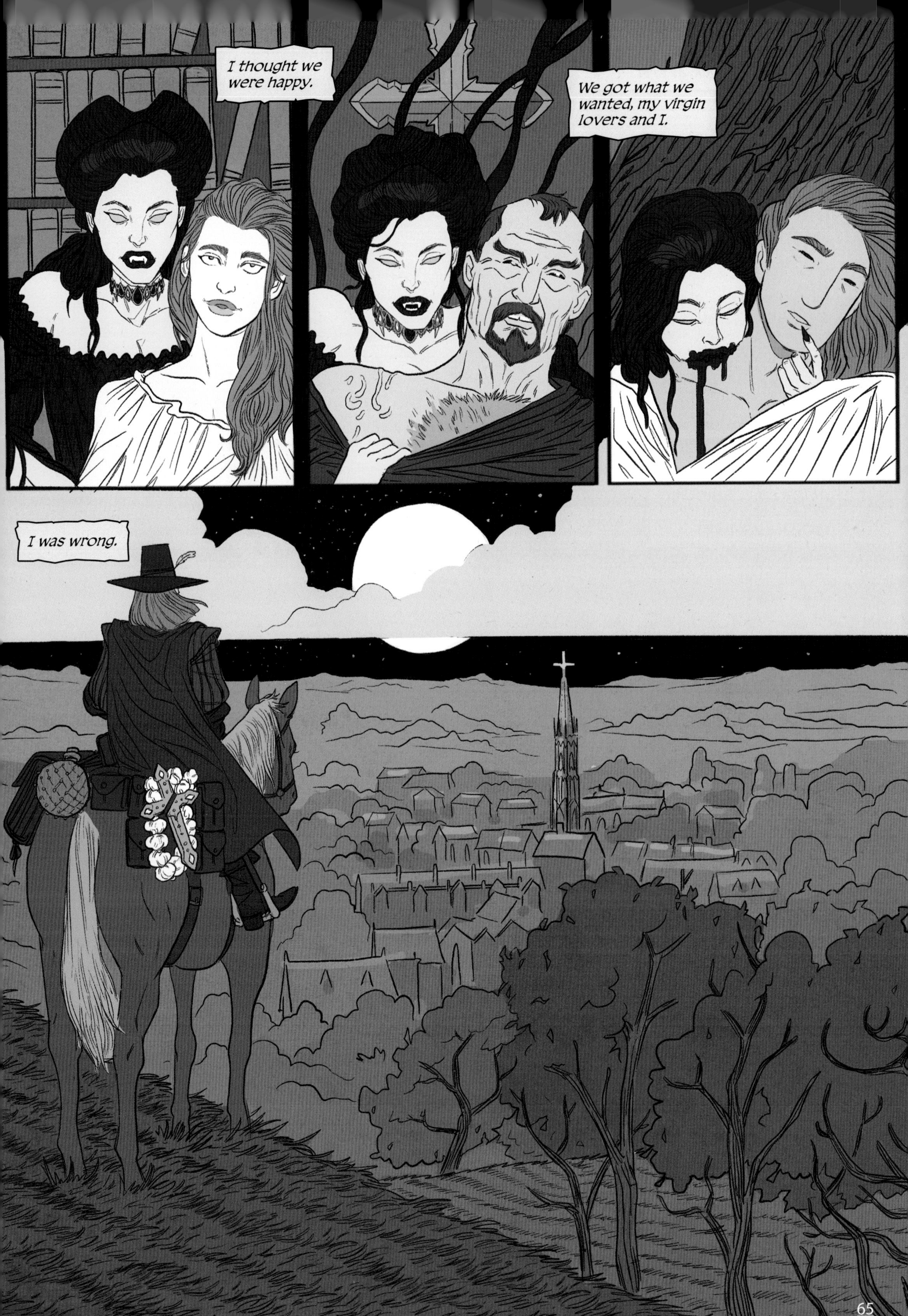
I thought we were happy.
We got what we wanted, my virgin lovers and I.
I was wrong.

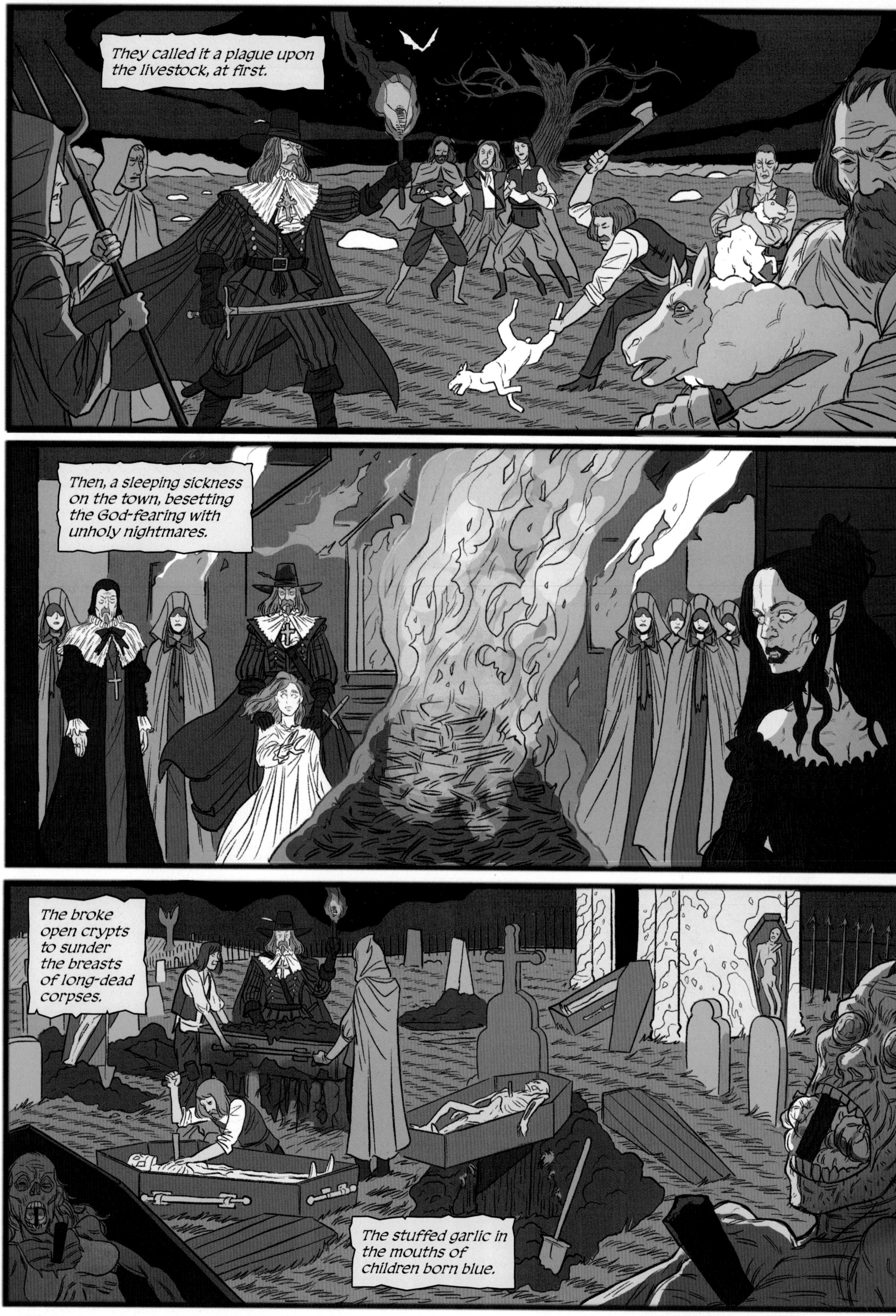
They called it a plague upon the livestock, at first.
Then, a sleeping sickness on the town, besetting the God-fearing with unholy nightmares.
The broke open crypts to sunder the breasts of long-dead corpses.
The stuffed garlic in the mouths of children born blue.

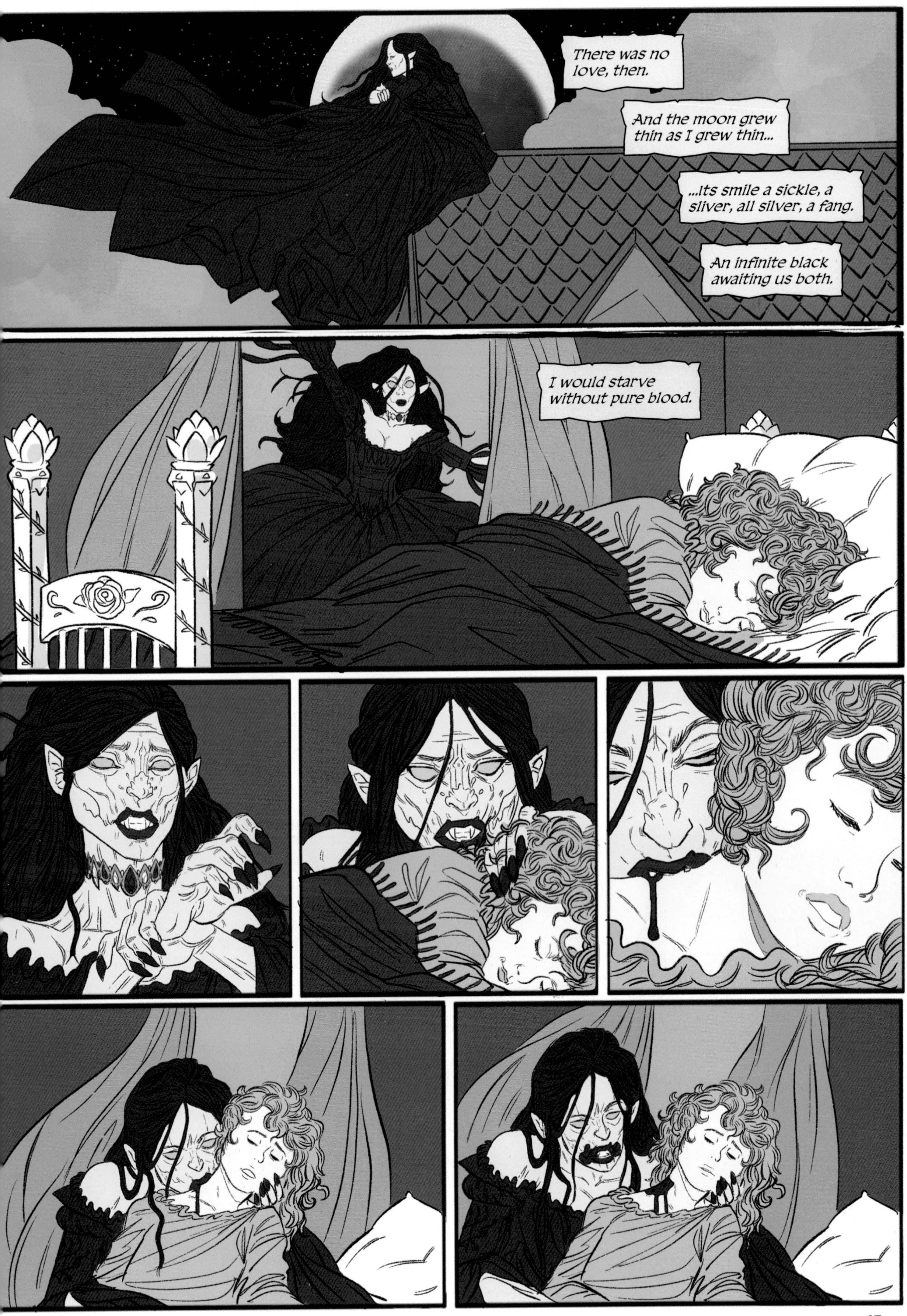
There was no love, then.
And the moon grew thin as I grew thin...
...its smile a sickle, a sliver, all silver, a fang.
An infinite black awaiting us both.
I would starve without pure blood.

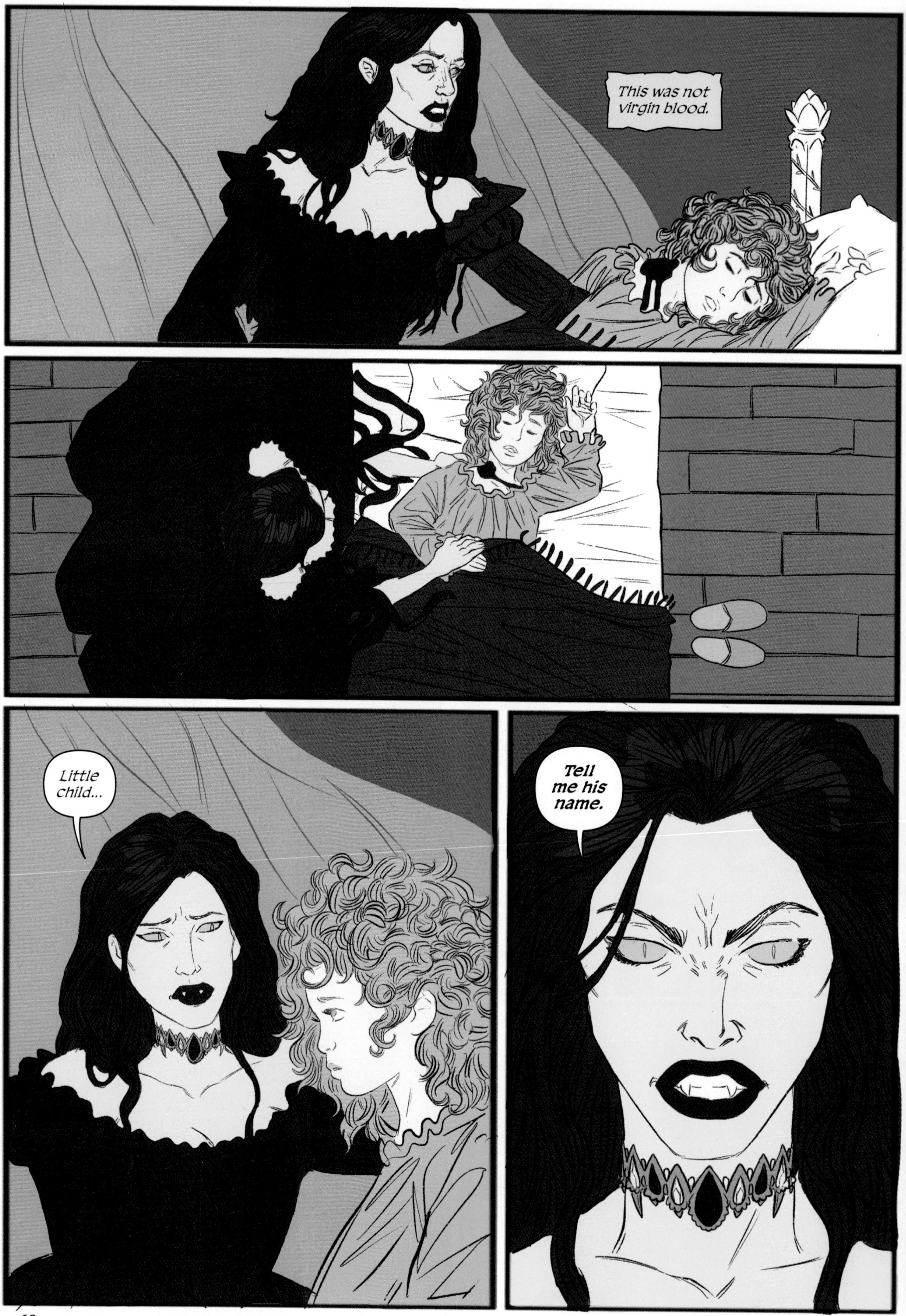
This was not virgin blood.
Little child...
Tell me his name.

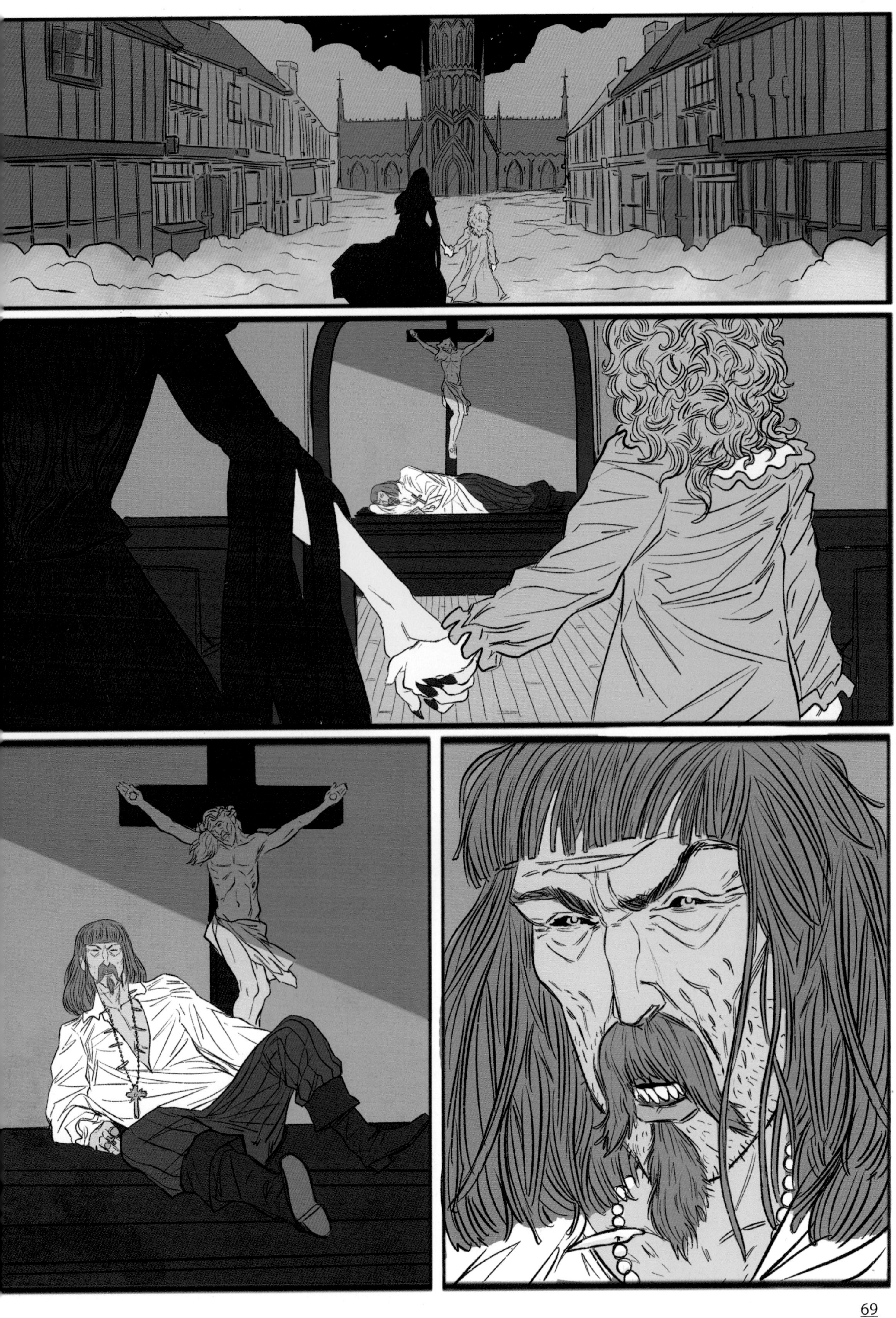

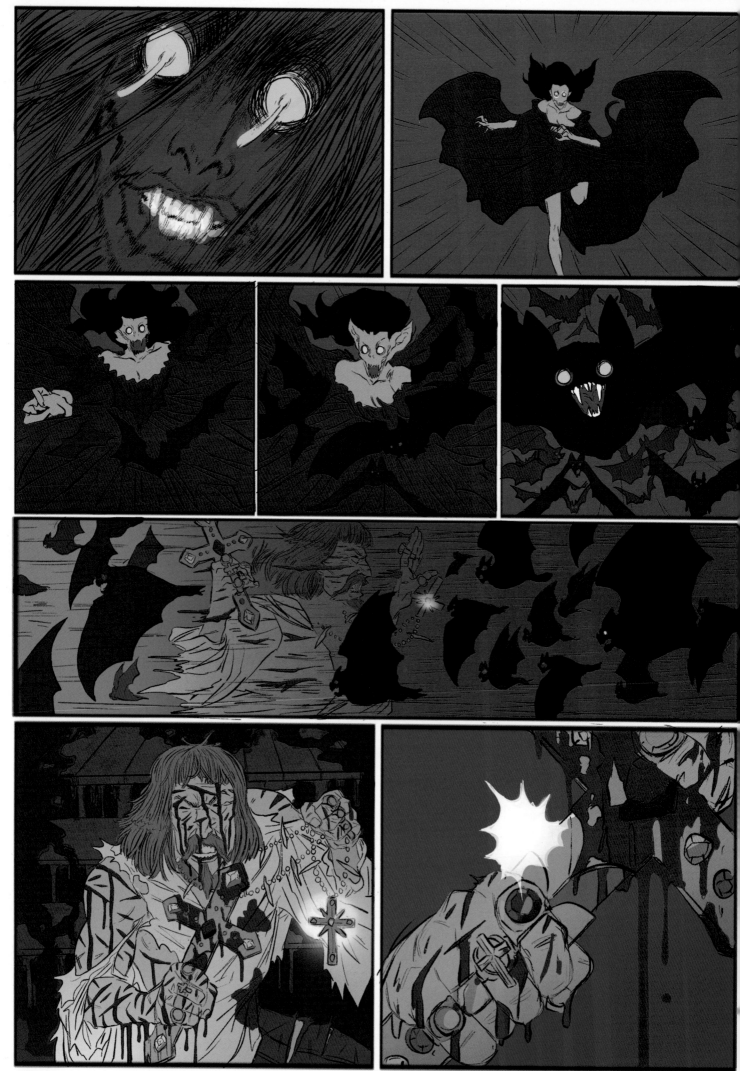

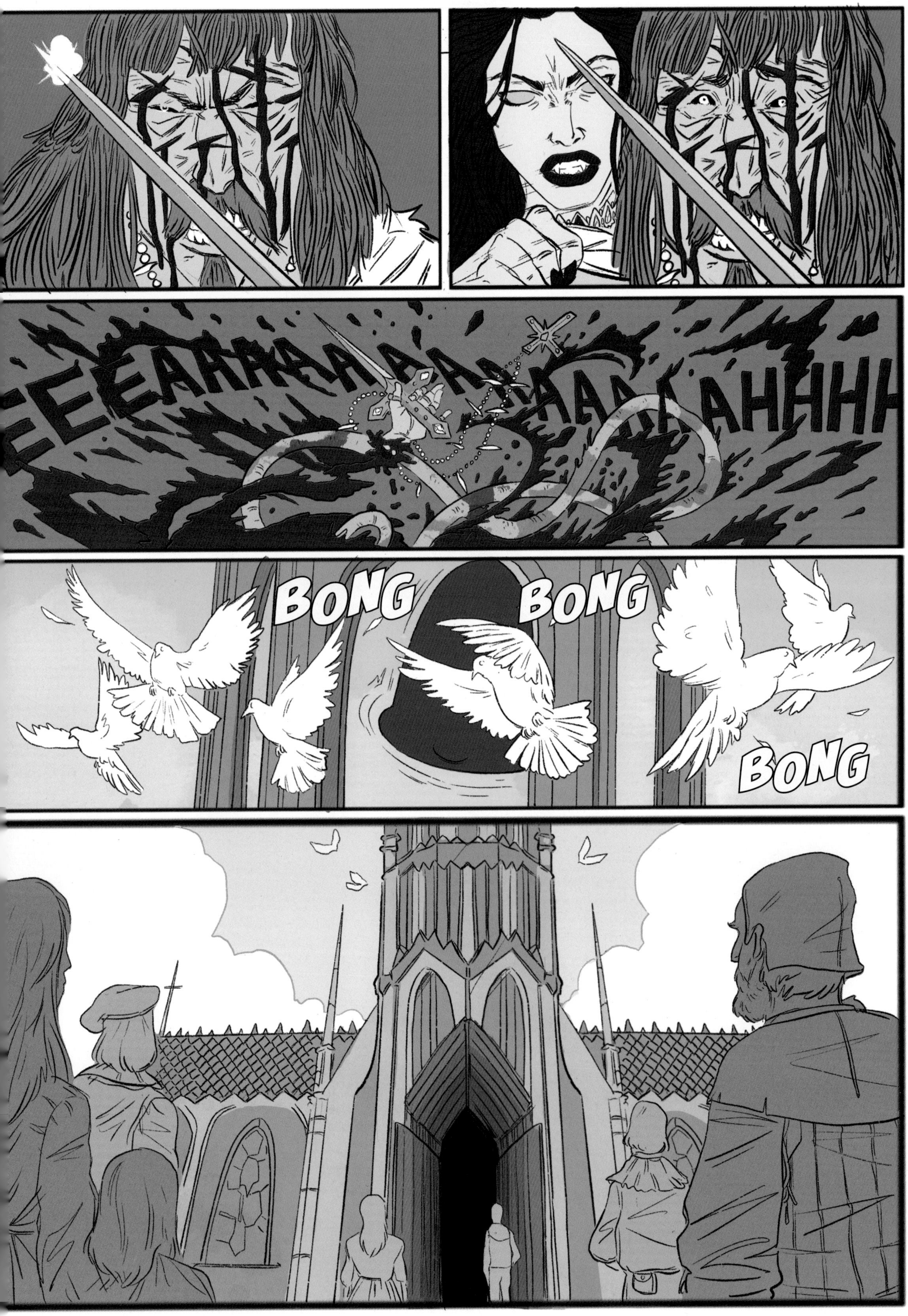
EEEARRRAAAAAAAAAAHHHHH
BONG
BONG
BONG

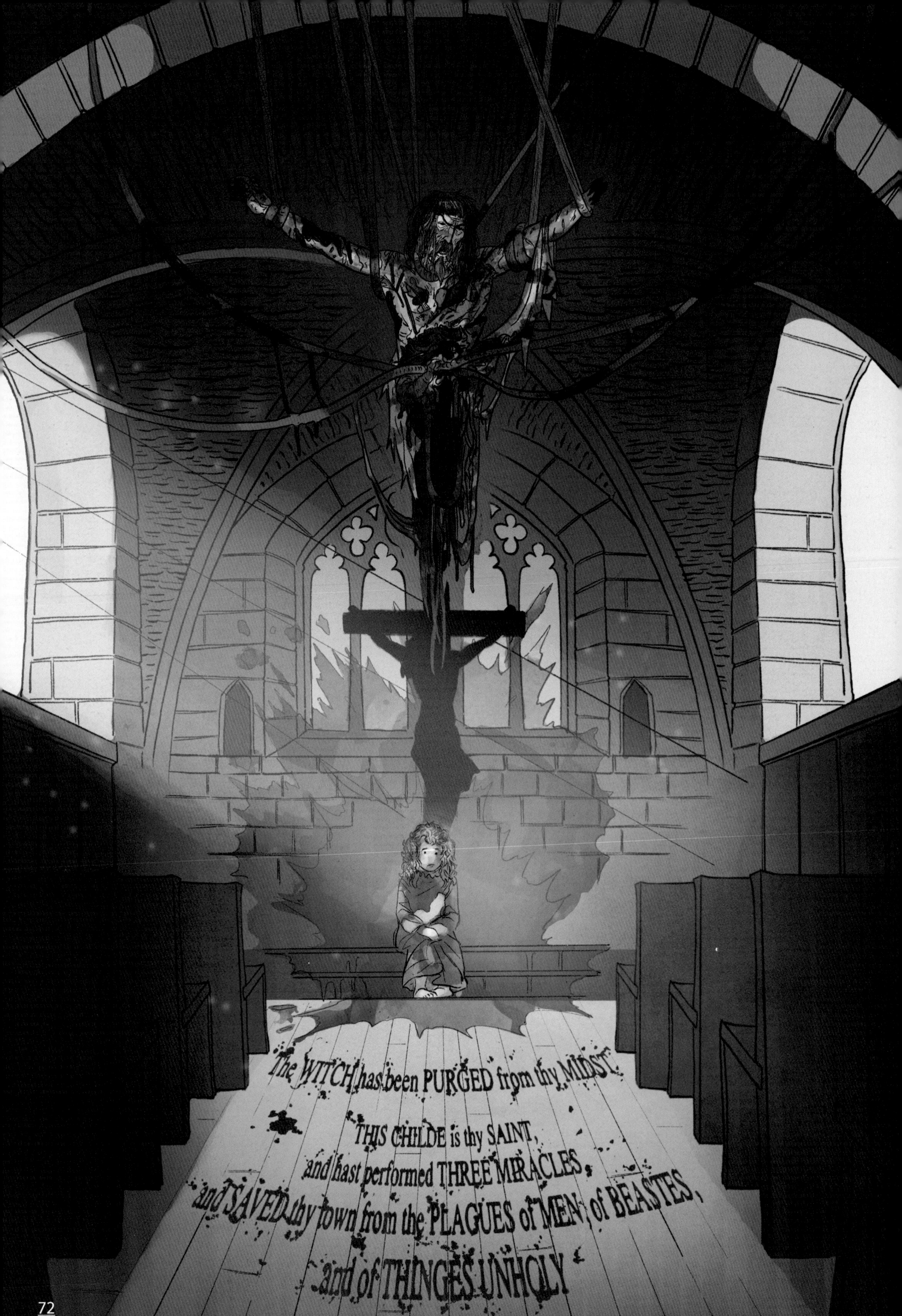
The WITCH has been PURGED from thy MIDST.
THIS CHILDE is thy SAINT,
and hast performed THREE MIRACLES,
and SAVED thy town from the PLAGUES of MEN, of BEASTES,
and of THINGES UNHOLY

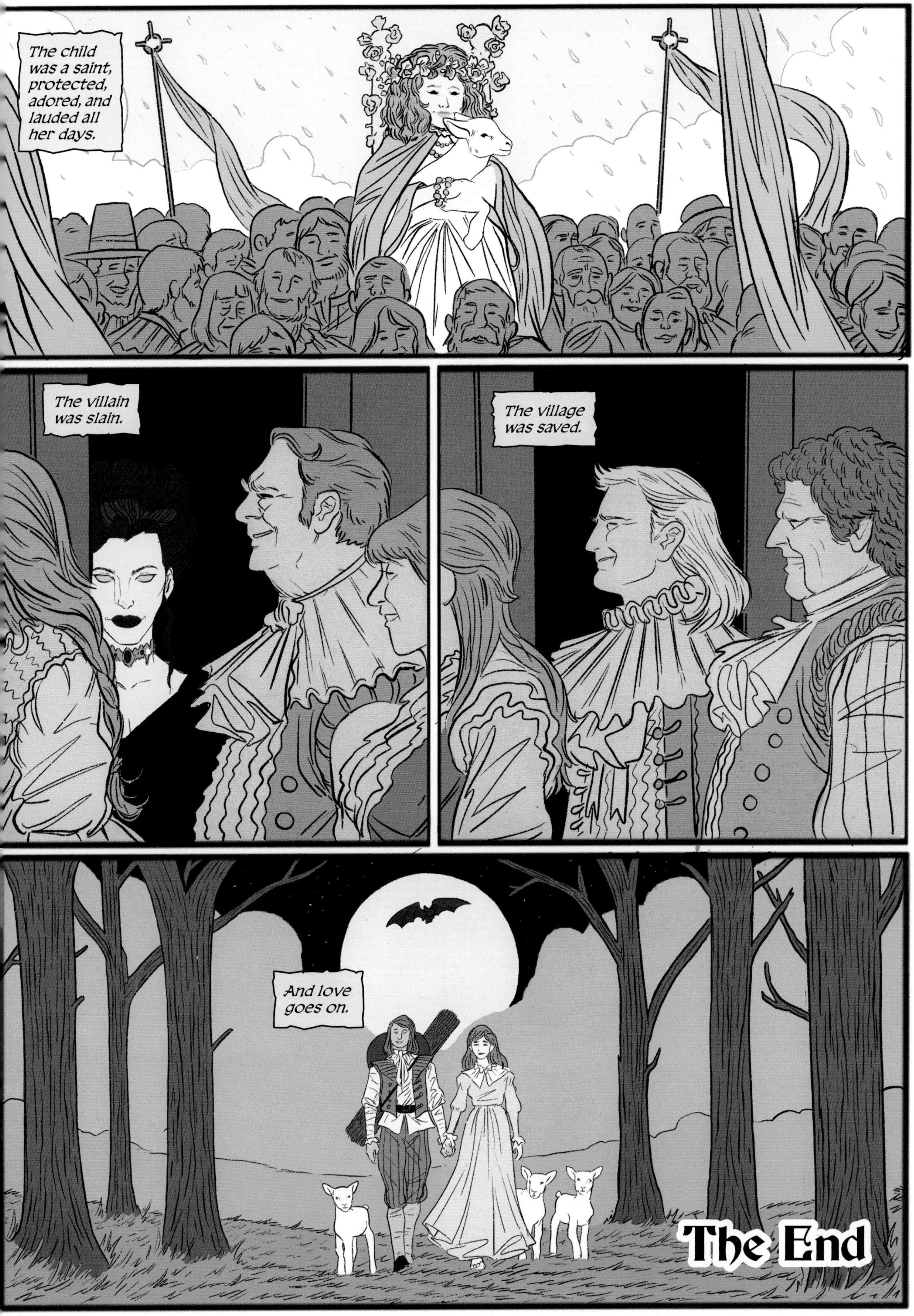
The child was a saint, protected, adored, and lauded all her days.
The villain was slain.
The village was saved.
And love goes on.
The End

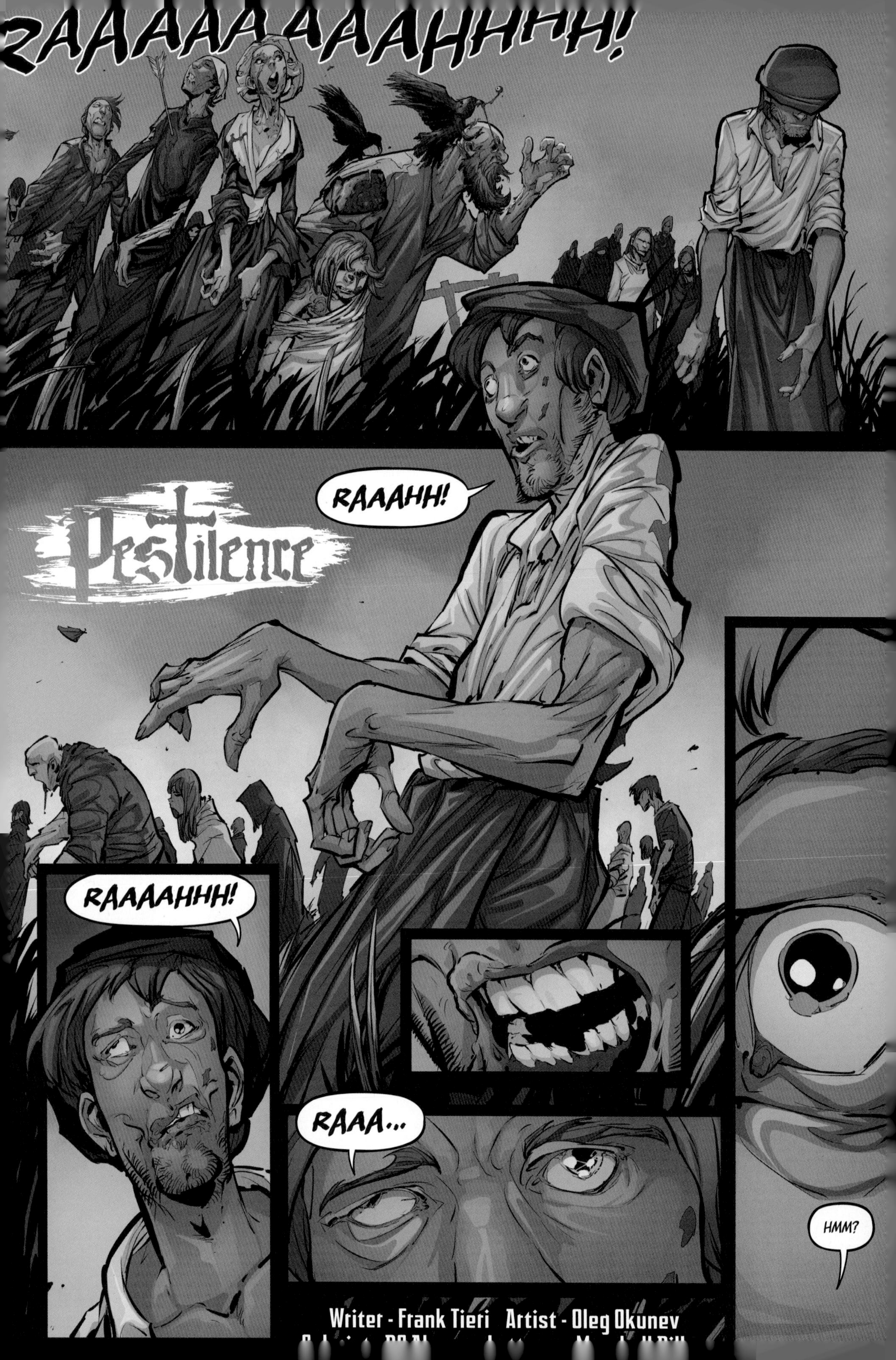
RAAAAAA AAAAHHHH!
Pestilence
RAAAHH!
RAAAAHHH!
RAAA...
HMM?
Writer - Frank Tieri Artist - Oleg Okunev

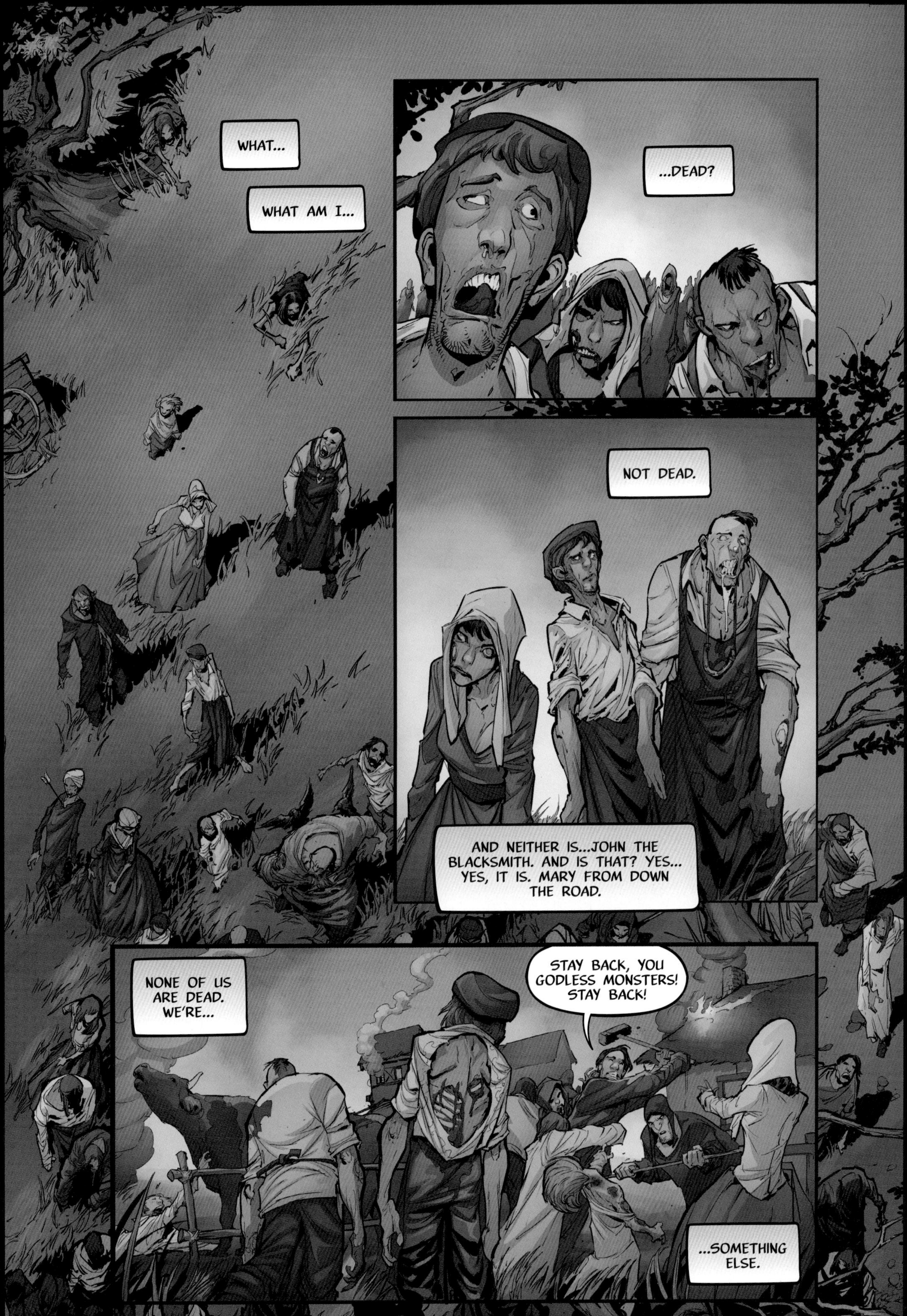
WHAT...
WHAT AM I...
...DEAD?
NOT DEAD.
AND NEITHER IS...JOHN THE BLACKSMITH. AND IS THAT? YES... YES, IT IS. MARY FROM DOWN THE ROAD.
NONE OF US ARE DEAD. WE'RE...
STAY BACK, YOU GODLESS MONSTERS! STAY BACK!
...SOMETHING ELSE.

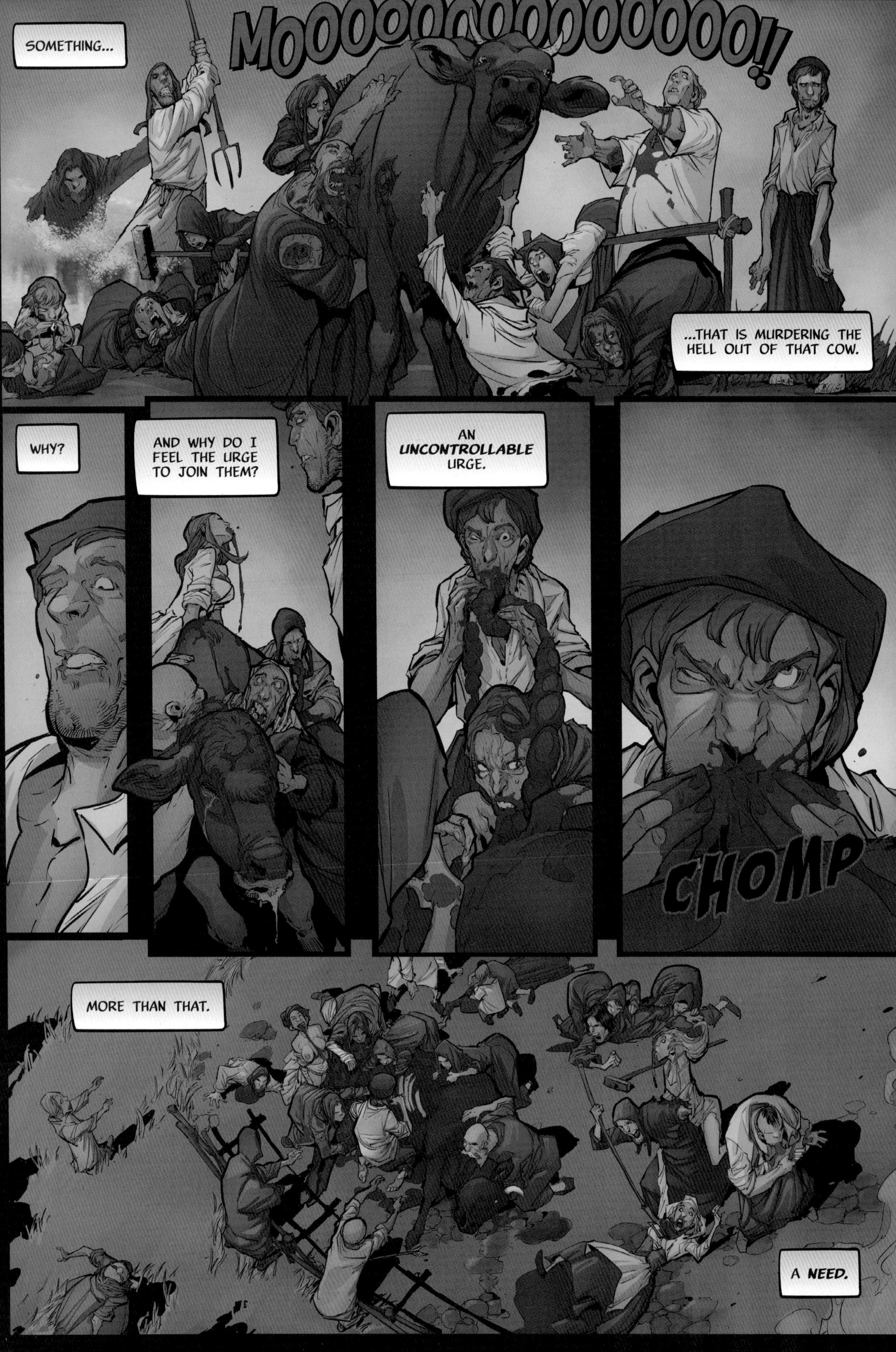
SOMETHING...
MOOOOOOOOOOOOOOOO!!
...THAT IS MURDERING THE HELL OUT OF THAT COW.
WHY?
AND WHY DO I FEEL THE URGE TO JOIN THEM?
AN UNCONTROLLABLE URGE.
CHOMP
MORE THAN THAT.
A NEED.

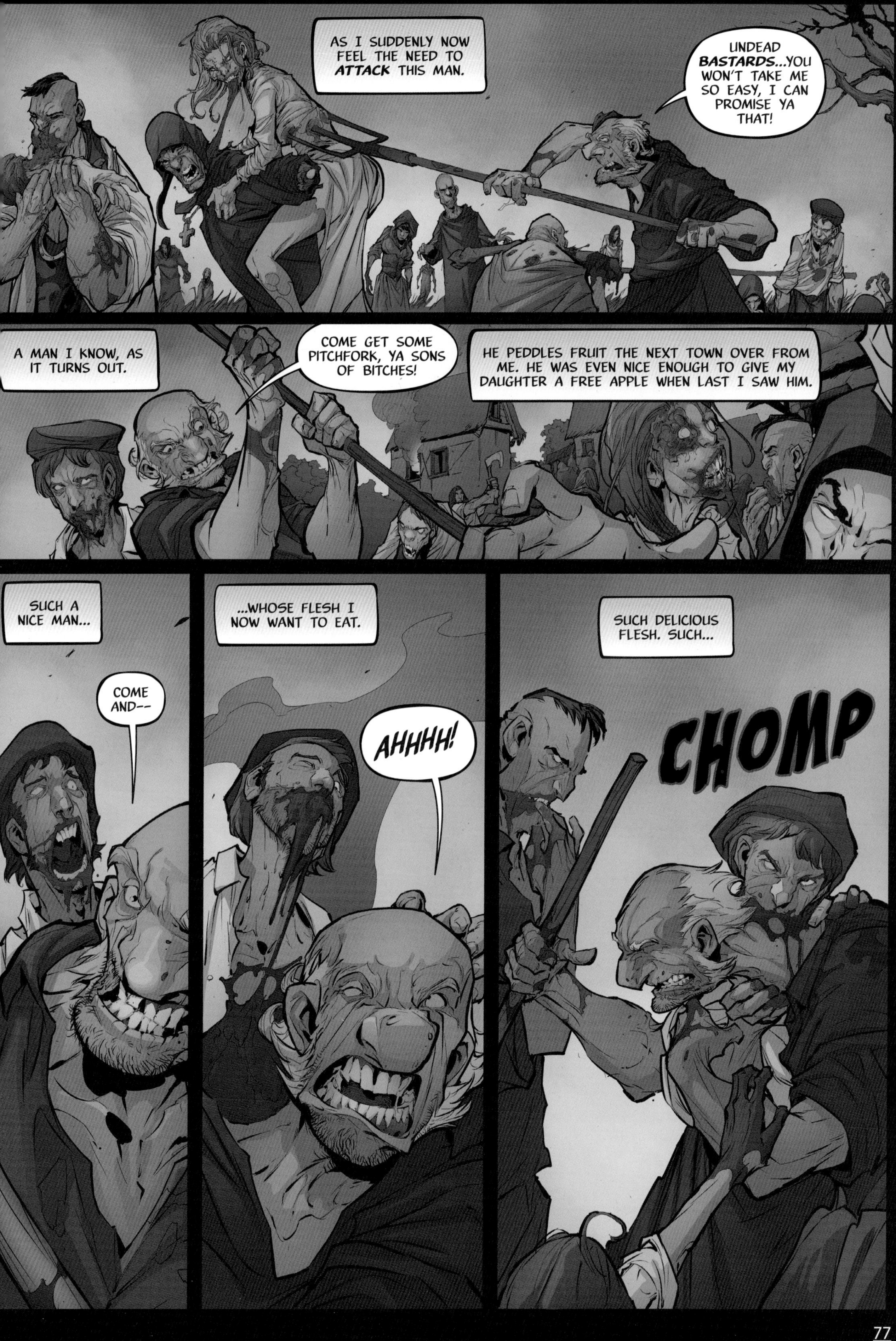

AS I SUDDENLY NOW FEEL THE NEED TO ATTACK THIS MAN.
UNDEAD BASTARDS...YOU WON'T TAKE ME SO EASY, I CAN PROMISE YA THAT!
A MAN I KNOW, AS IT TURNS OUT.
COME GET SOME PITCHFORK, YA SONS OF BITCHES!
HE PEDDLES FRUIT THE NEXT TOWN OVER FROM ME. HE WAS EVEN NICE ENOUGH TO GIVE MY DAUGHTER A FREE APPLE WHEN LAST I SAW HIM.
SUCH A NICE MAN...
COME AND--
...WHOSE FLESH I NOW WANT TO EAT.
AHHHH!
SUCH DELICIOUS FLESH. SUCH...
CHOMP

MY LORD...
...WHAT THE HELL AM I DOING?
THIS IS... WRONG.
I KNOW THIS. OF COURSE, I KNOW THIS.
AND ALL THESE...UNDEAD, THEY HAVE TO SOMEHOW KNOW IT, TOO. THEY WERE GOOD PEOPLE ONCE.
AND THEY CAN BE AGAIN, DAMNIT. SURELY THERE ARE MORE LIKE ME. MORE...AWAKENED.
THERE ARE AND I WILL FIND THEM. I WILL PUT AN **END** TO THIS.
I WILL WORK WITHIN THE ***INFECTED*** COMMUNITY AND START A REBELLION IF I HAVE TO!
AND THEN SLOWLY BUT SURELY, FINALLY...
FINALLY THERE WILL BE PEACE BETWEEN THE UNDEAD AND THE LIVING.
FINALLY, THERE WILL--

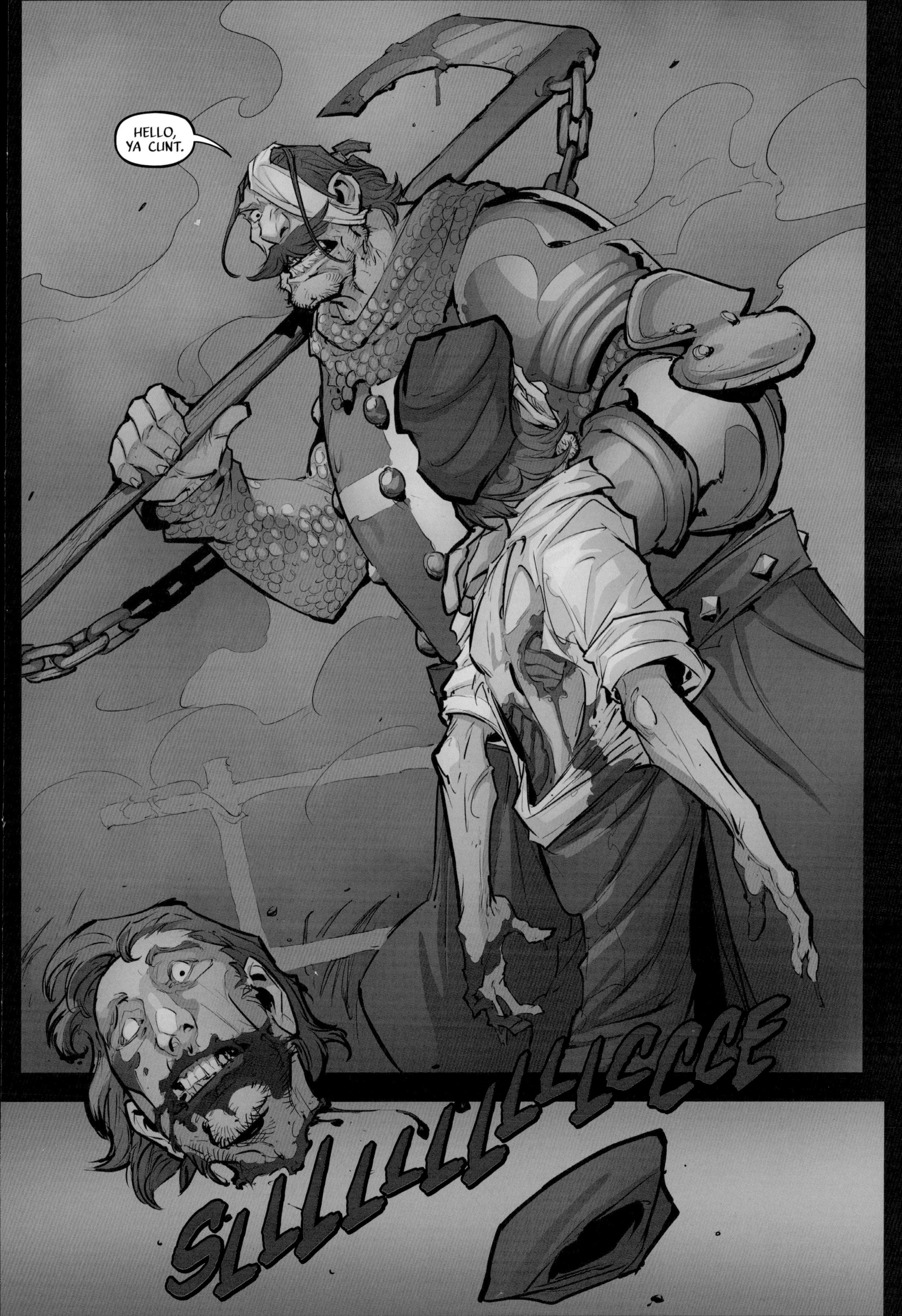
HELLO,
YA CUNT.
SLLLLLLLLLICCCCE

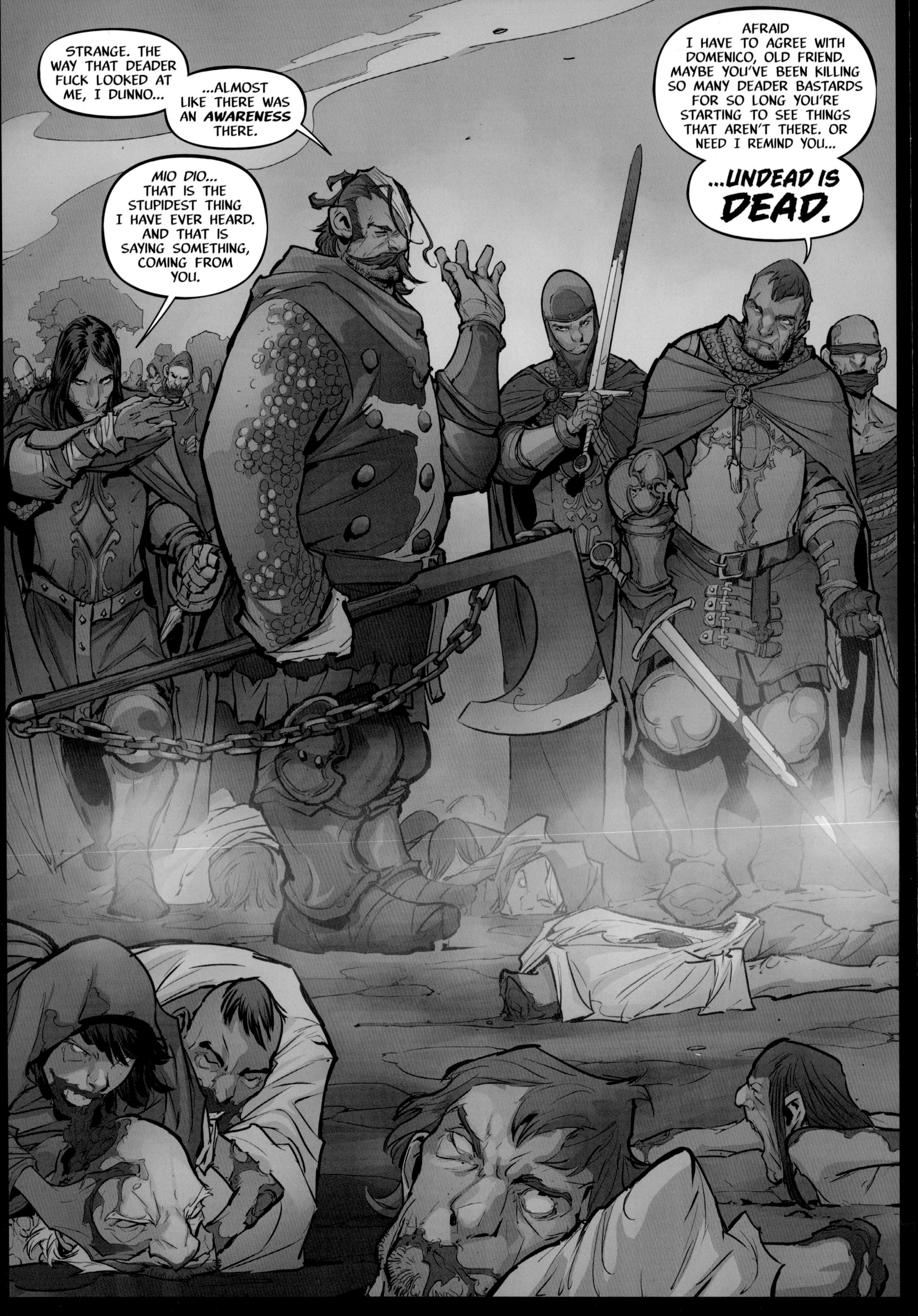
STRANGE. THE WAY THAT DEADER FUCK LOOKED AT ME, I DUNNO...
...ALMOST LIKE THERE WAS AN **AWARENESS** THERE.
MIO DIO... THAT IS THE STUPIDEST THING I HAVE EVER HEARD. AND THAT IS SAYING SOMETHING, COMING FROM YOU.
AFRAID I HAVE TO AGREE WITH DOMENICO, OLD FRIEND. MAYBE YOU'VE BEEN KILLING SO MANY DEADER BASTARDS FOR SO LONG YOU'RE STARTING TO SEE THINGS THAT AREN'T THERE. OR NEED I REMIND YOU...
...UNDEAD IS DEAD.

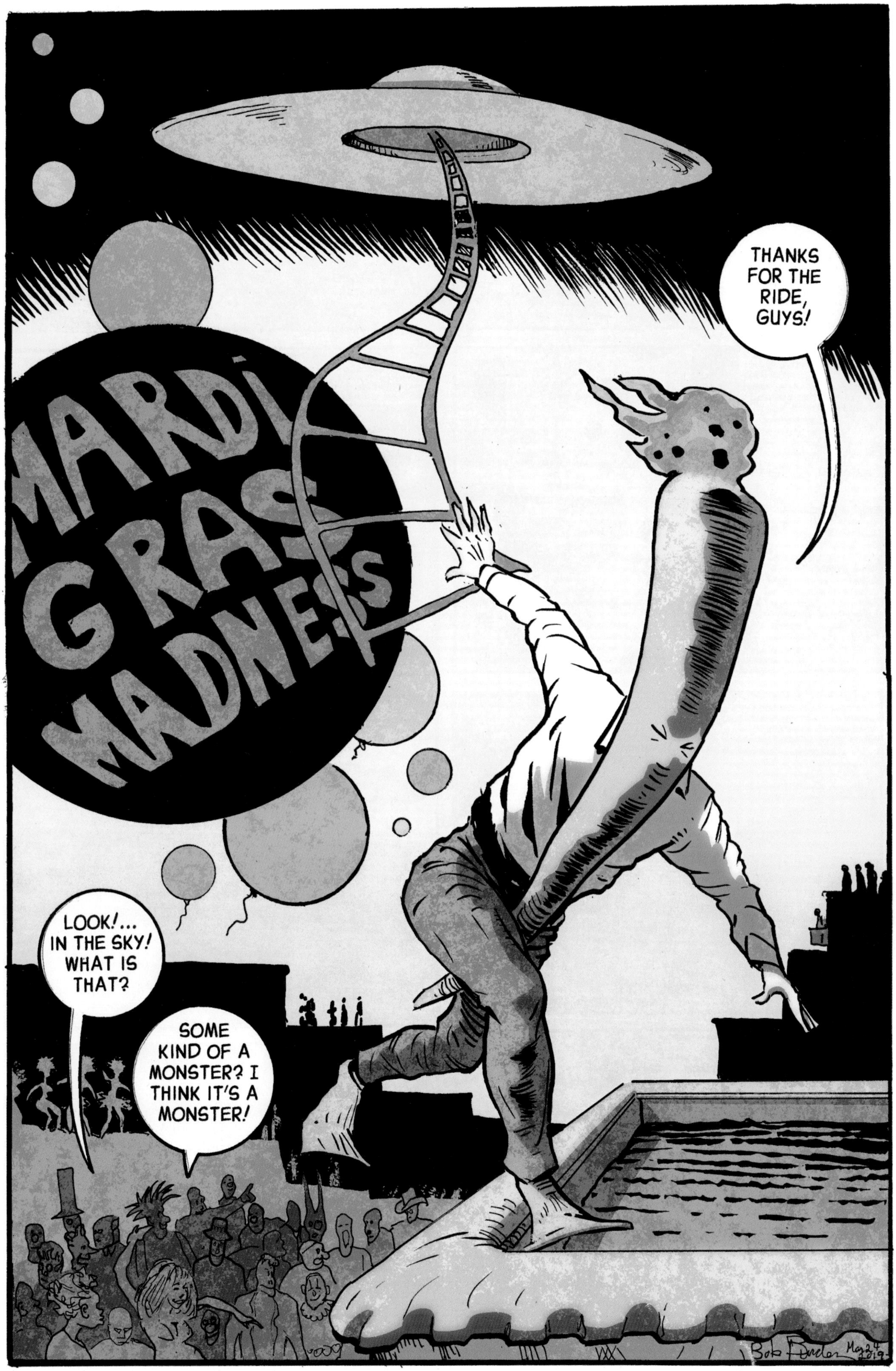
MARDI GRAS MADNESS
THANKS FOR THE RIDE, GUYS!
LOOK!... IN THE SKY! WHAT IS THAT?
SOME KIND OF A MONSTER? I THINK IT'S A MONSTER!

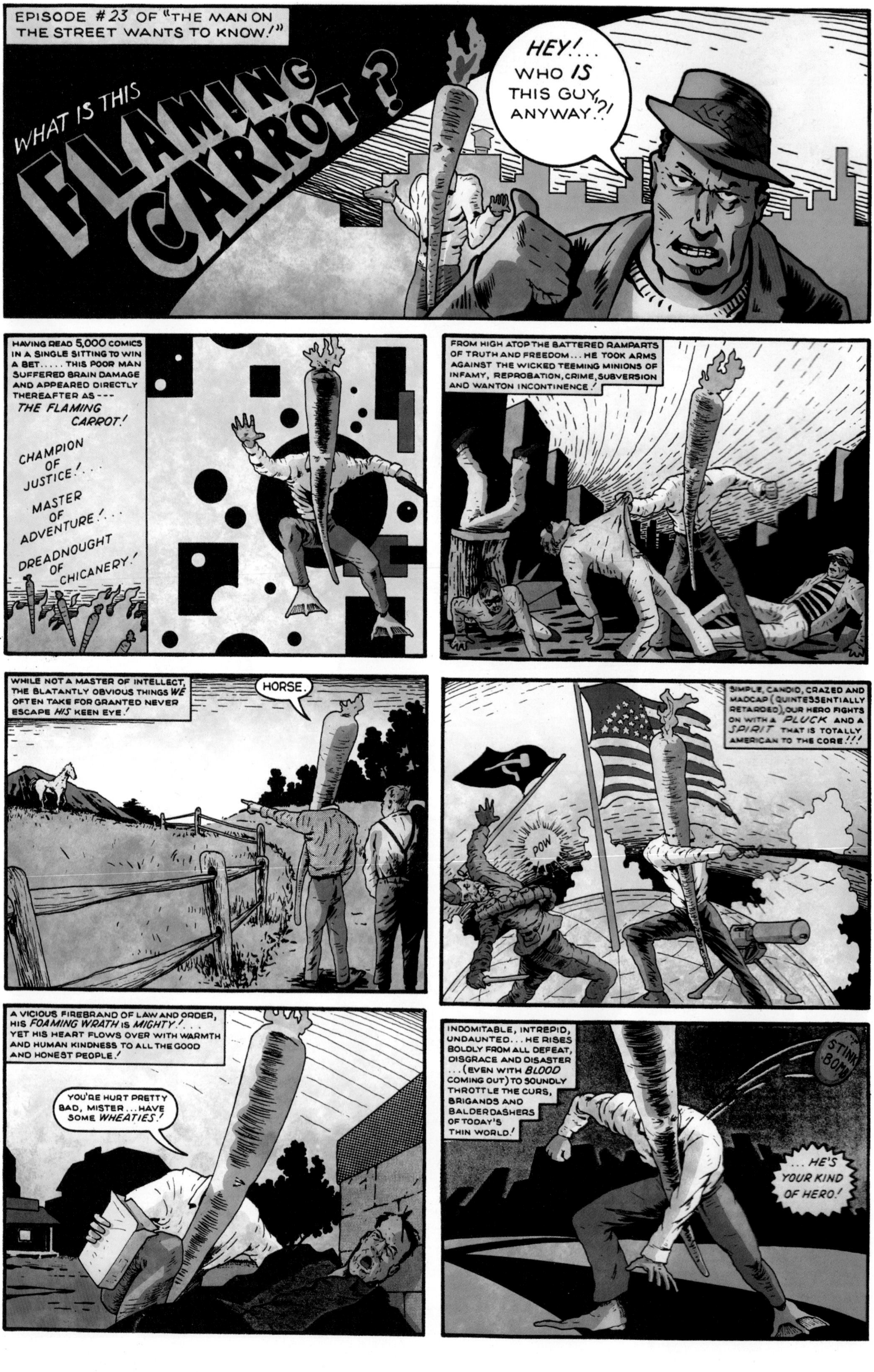
EPISODE #23 OF "THE MAN ON THE STREET WANTS TO KNOW!"
WHAT IS THIS FLAMING CARROT?
HEY!... WHO IS THIS GUY,?! ANYWAY..?!
HAVING READ 5,000 COMICS IN A SINGLE SITTING TO WIN A BET..... THIS POOR MAN SUFFERED BRAIN DAMAGE AND APPEARED DIRECTLY THEREAFTER AS --- THE FLAMING CARROT!
CHAMPION OF JUSTICE!...
MASTER OF ADVENTURE!...
DREADNOUGHT OF CHICANERY!
FROM HIGH ATOP THE BATTERED RAMPARTS OF TRUTH AND FREEDOM... HE TOOK ARMS AGAINST THE WICKED TEEMING MINIONS OF INFAMY, REPROBATION, CRIME, SUBVERSION AND WANTON INCONTINENCE!
WHILE NOT A MASTER OF INTELLECT, THE BLATANTLY OBVIOUS THINGS WE OFTEN TAKE FOR GRANTED NEVER ESCAPE HIS KEEN EYE!
HORSE.
SIMPLE, CANDID, CRAZED AND MADCAP (QUINTESSENTIALLY RETARDED), OUR HERO FIGHTS ON WITH A PLUCK AND A SPIRIT THAT IS TOTALLY AMERICAN TO THE CORE!!!
POW
A VICIOUS FIREBRAND OF LAW AND ORDER, HIS FOAMING WRATH IS MIGHTY!... YET HIS HEART FLOWS OVER WITH WARMTH AND HUMAN KINDNESS TO ALL THE GOOD AND HONEST PEOPLE!
YOU'RE HURT PRETTY BAD, MISTER... HAVE SOME WHEATIES!
INDOMITABLE, INTREPID, UNDAUNTED... HE RISES BOLDLY FROM ALL DEFEAT, DISGRACE AND DISASTER ...(EVEN WITH BLOOD COMING OUT) TO SOUNDLY THROTTLE THE CURS, BRIGANDS AND BALDERDASHERS OF TODAY'S THIN WORLD!
STINK BOMB
...HE'S YOUR KIND OF HERO!

WHERE ARE YOU BOLD WEEVIL AND LUMMOX?
WHAT THE?
WRIST LOCATOR SAYS THEY'RE RIGHT HERE! GOTTA GET A BIRD'S EYE VIEW NOW.
LOOK HE'S FLYING!
AHH... SOME SPECIAL EFFECT!
MEET BOLD WEEVIL AND THE LUMMOX!
HERE THEY ARE!
HEY GUYS! WHY ARE YOU UP HERE ON THE ROOF?
FLAMING CARROT! YOU'RE FLYING NOW?
HOW WAS BOHEMIAN GROVE? DID YOU SET THEM STRAIGHT OUT THERE?
ALL SET STRAIGHT!
BUT HOW? HOW DO YOU FLY NOW?
FLYING PILLS!
MADE FROM MAGIC MOJO, SOME SPARKLING DROPS OF RETSIN AND *A SECRET INGREDIENT ORIGINALLY FOUND IN JELLYFISH!*

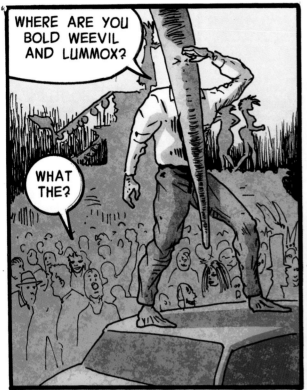

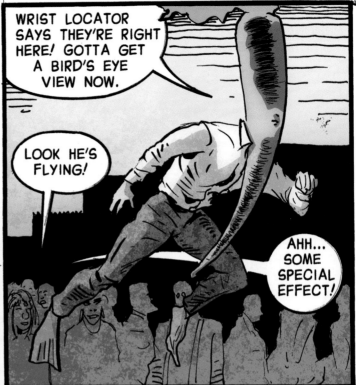

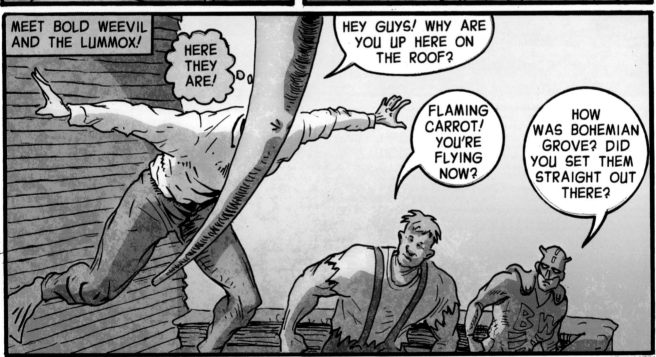

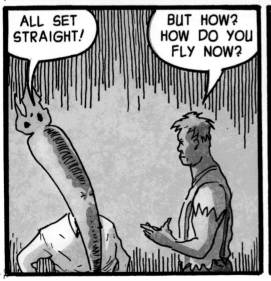

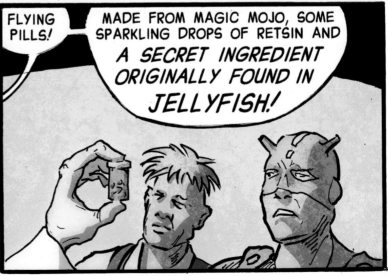

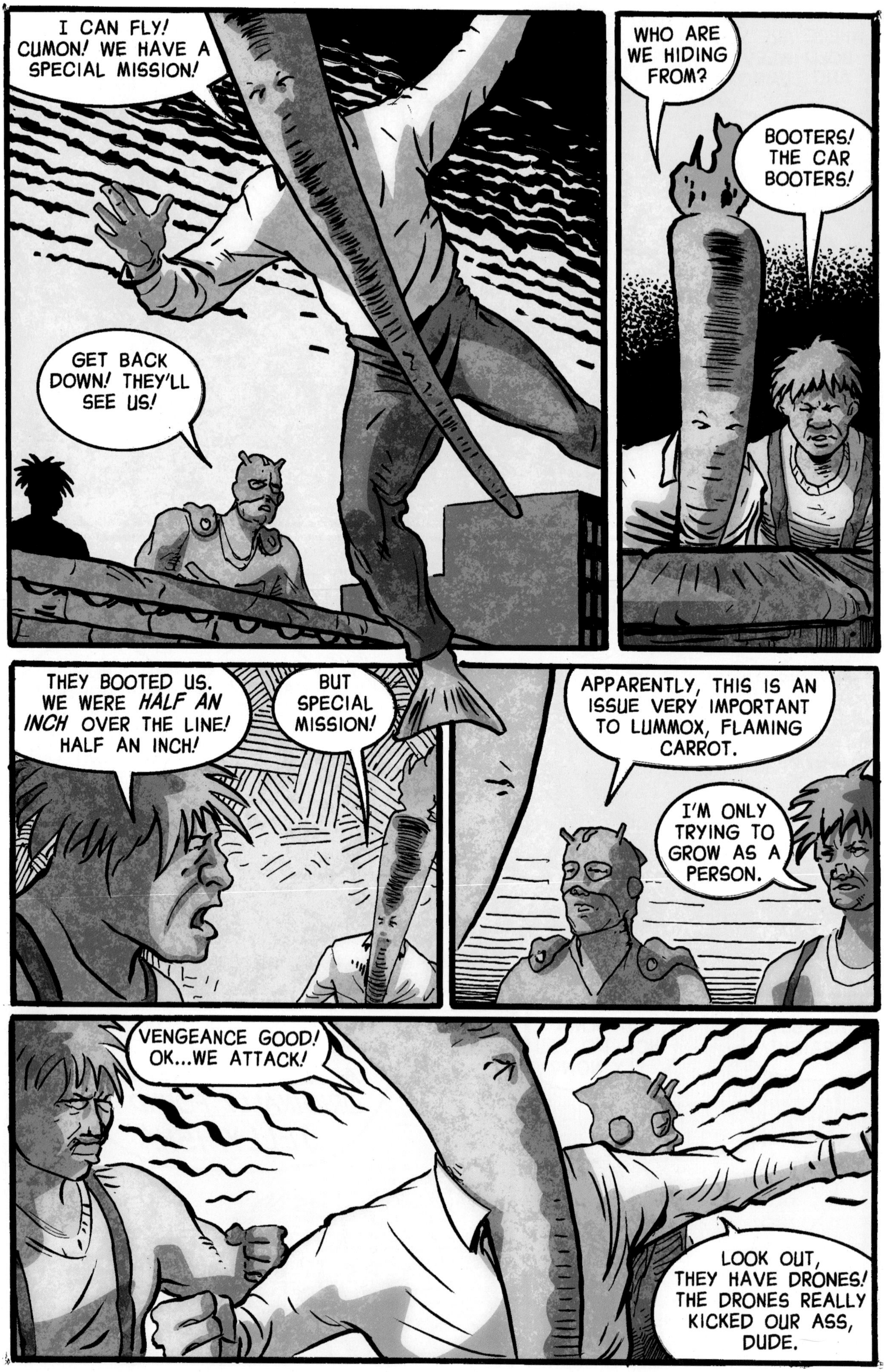

I CAN FLY! CUMON! WE HAVE A SPECIAL MISSION!
GET BACK DOWN! THEY'LL SEE US!
WHO ARE WE HIDING FROM?
BOOTERS! THE CAR BOOTERS!
THEY BOOTED US. WE WERE *HALF AN INCH* OVER THE LINE! HALF AN INCH!
BUT SPECIAL MISSION!
APPARENTLY, THIS IS AN ISSUE VERY IMPORTANT TO LUMMOX, FLAMING CARROT.
I'M ONLY TRYING TO GROW AS A PERSON.
VENGEANCE GOOD! OK...WE ATTACK!
LOOK OUT, THEY HAVE DRONES! THE DRONES REALLY KICKED OUR ASS, DUDE.

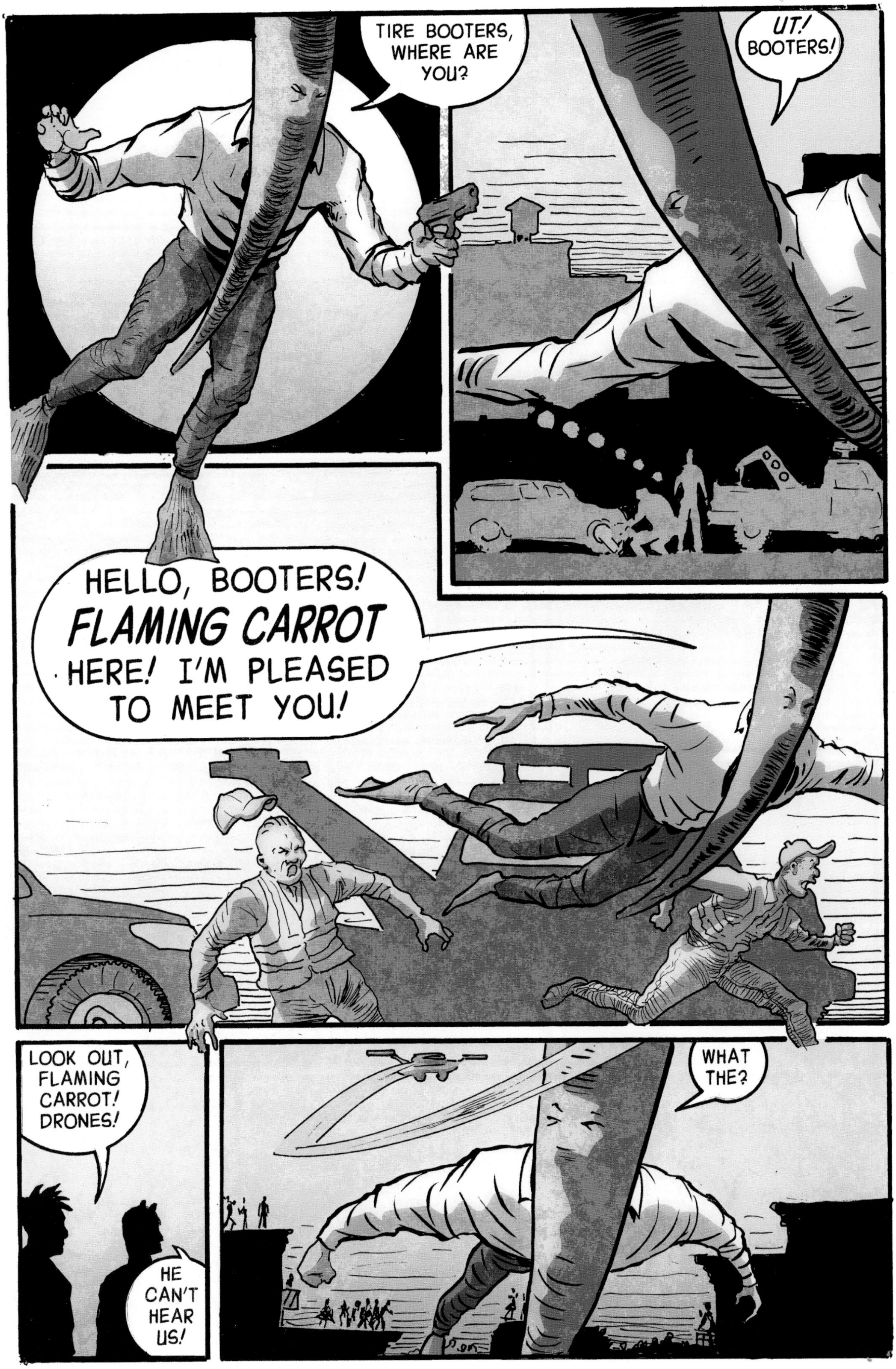
TIRE BOOTERS, WHERE ARE YOU?
UT! BOOTERS!
HELLO, BOOTERS! FLAMING CARROT HERE! I'M PLEASED TO MEET YOU!
LOOK OUT, FLAMING CARROT! DRONES!
HE CAN'T HEAR US!
WHAT THE?

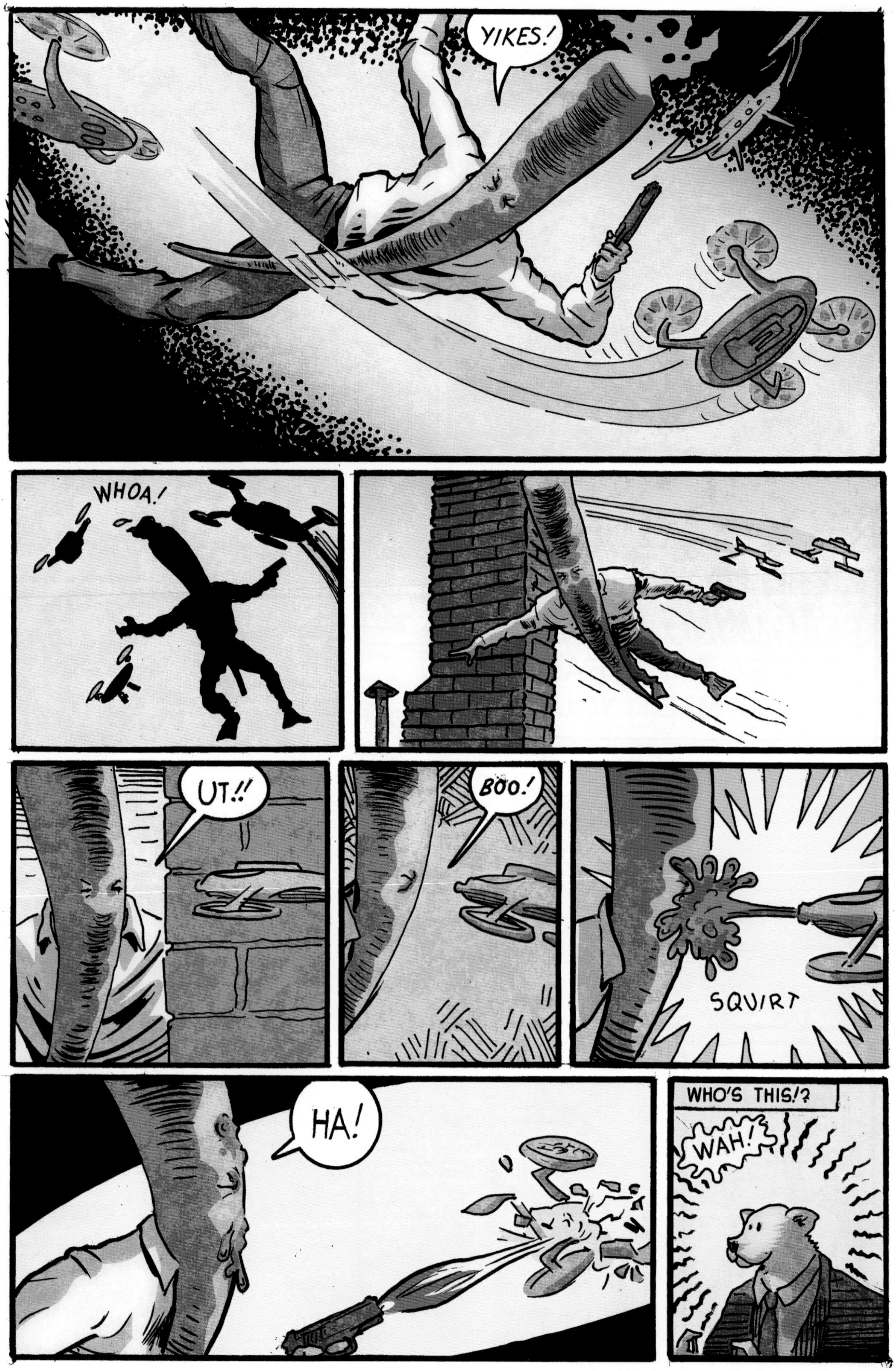
YIKES!
WHOA!
UT!!
BOO!
SQUIRT
HA!
WHO'S THIS!?
WAH!

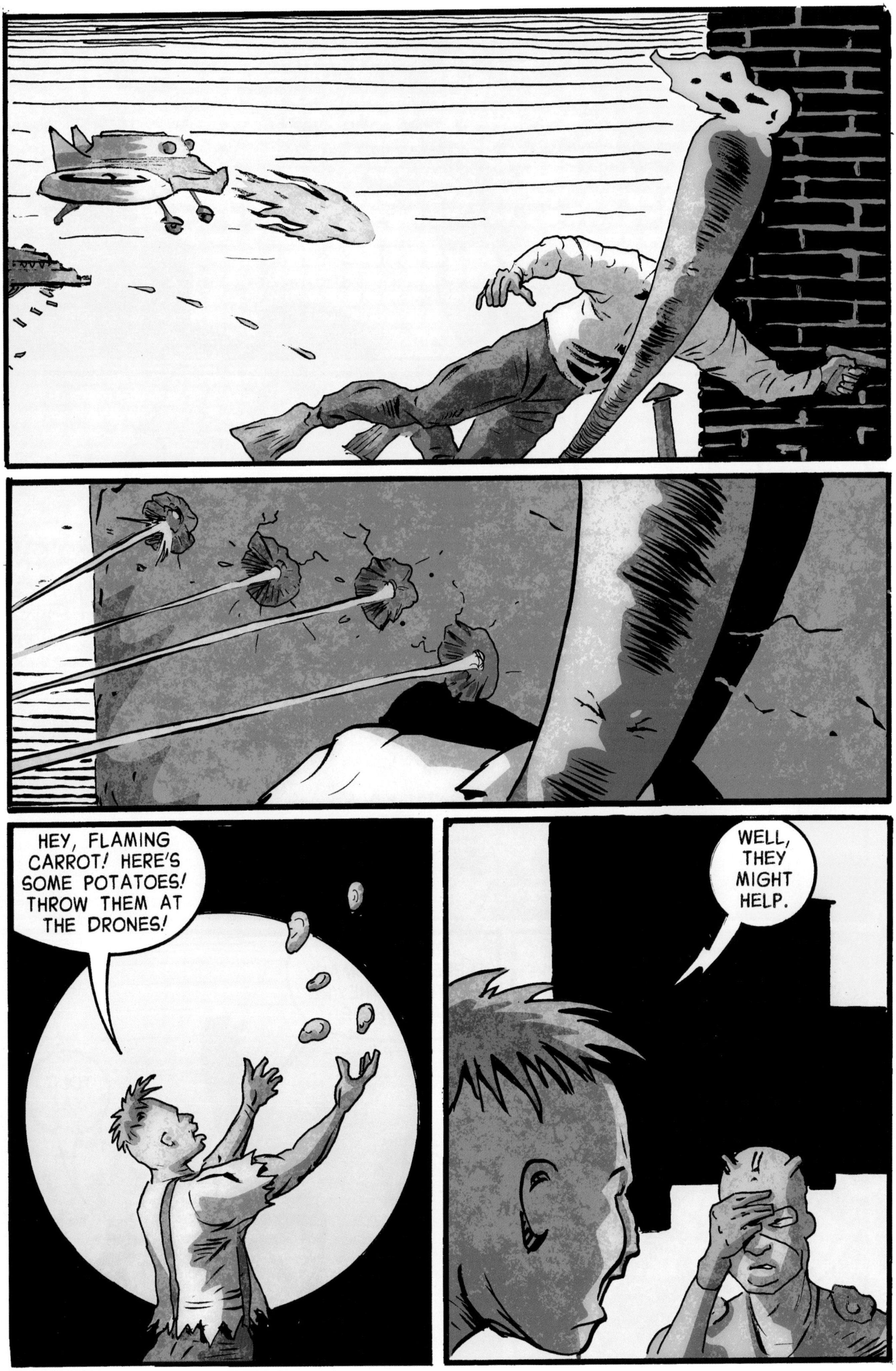
HEY, FLAMING CARROT! HERE'S SOME POTATOES! THROW THEM AT THE DRONES!
WELL, THEY MIGHT HELP.

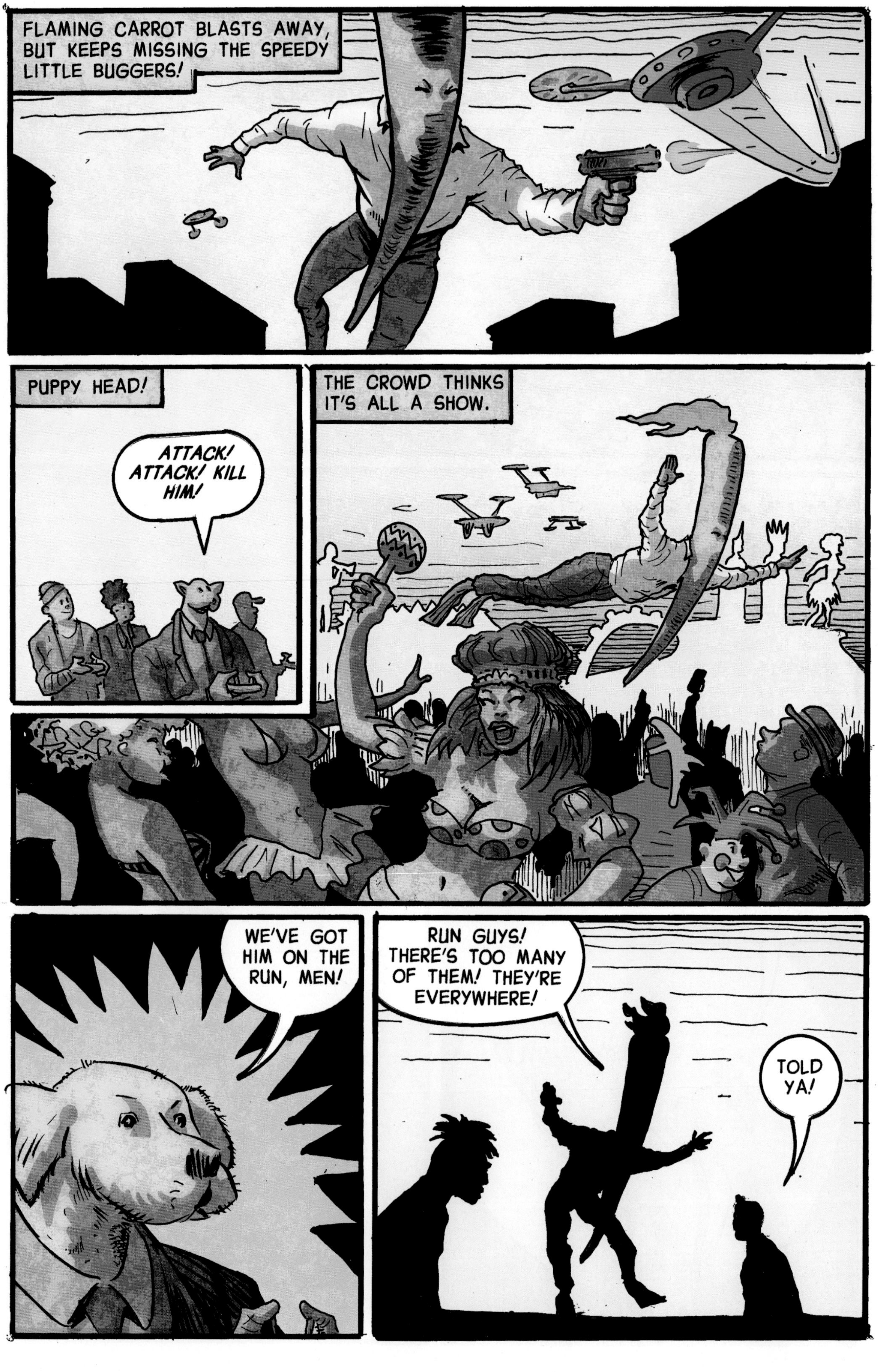
FLAMING CARROT BLASTS AWAY, BUT KEEPS MISSING THE SPEEDY LITTLE BUGGERS!
PUPPY HEAD!
ATTACK! ATTACK! KILL HIM!
THE CROWD THINKS IT'S ALL A SHOW.
WE'VE GOT HIM ON THE RUN, MEN!
RUN GUYS! THERE'S TOO MANY OF THEM! THEY'RE EVERYWHERE!
TOLD YA!

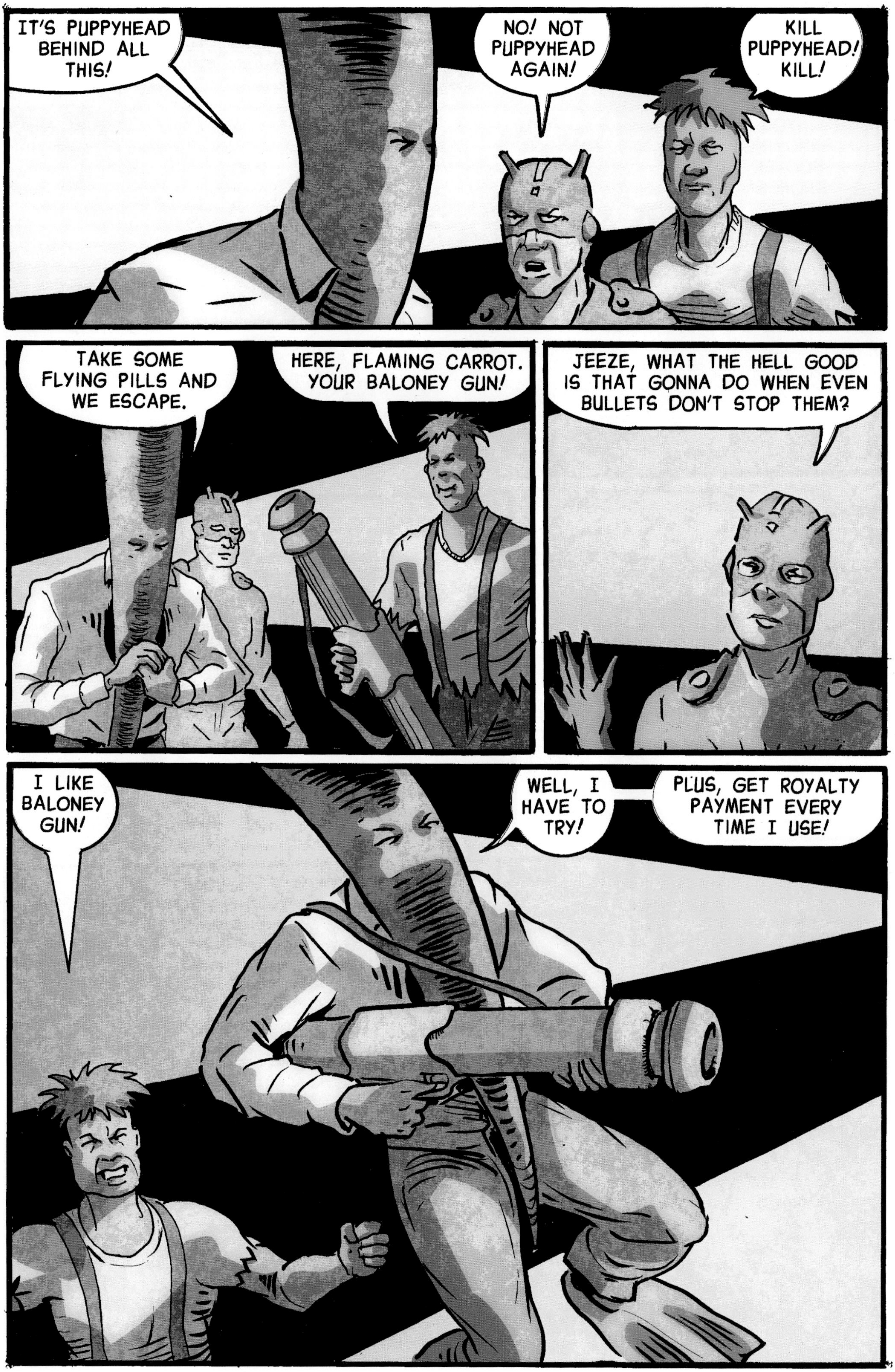
IT'S PUPPYHEAD BEHIND ALL THIS!
NO! NOT PUPPYHEAD AGAIN!
KILL PUPPYHEAD! KILL!
TAKE SOME FLYING PILLS AND WE ESCAPE.
HERE, FLAMING CARROT. YOUR BALONEY GUN!
JEEZE, WHAT THE HELL GOOD IS THAT GONNA DO WHEN EVEN BULLETS DON'T STOP THEM?
I LIKE BALONEY GUN!
WELL, I HAVE TO TRY!
PLUS, GET ROYALTY PAYMENT EVERY TIME I USE!

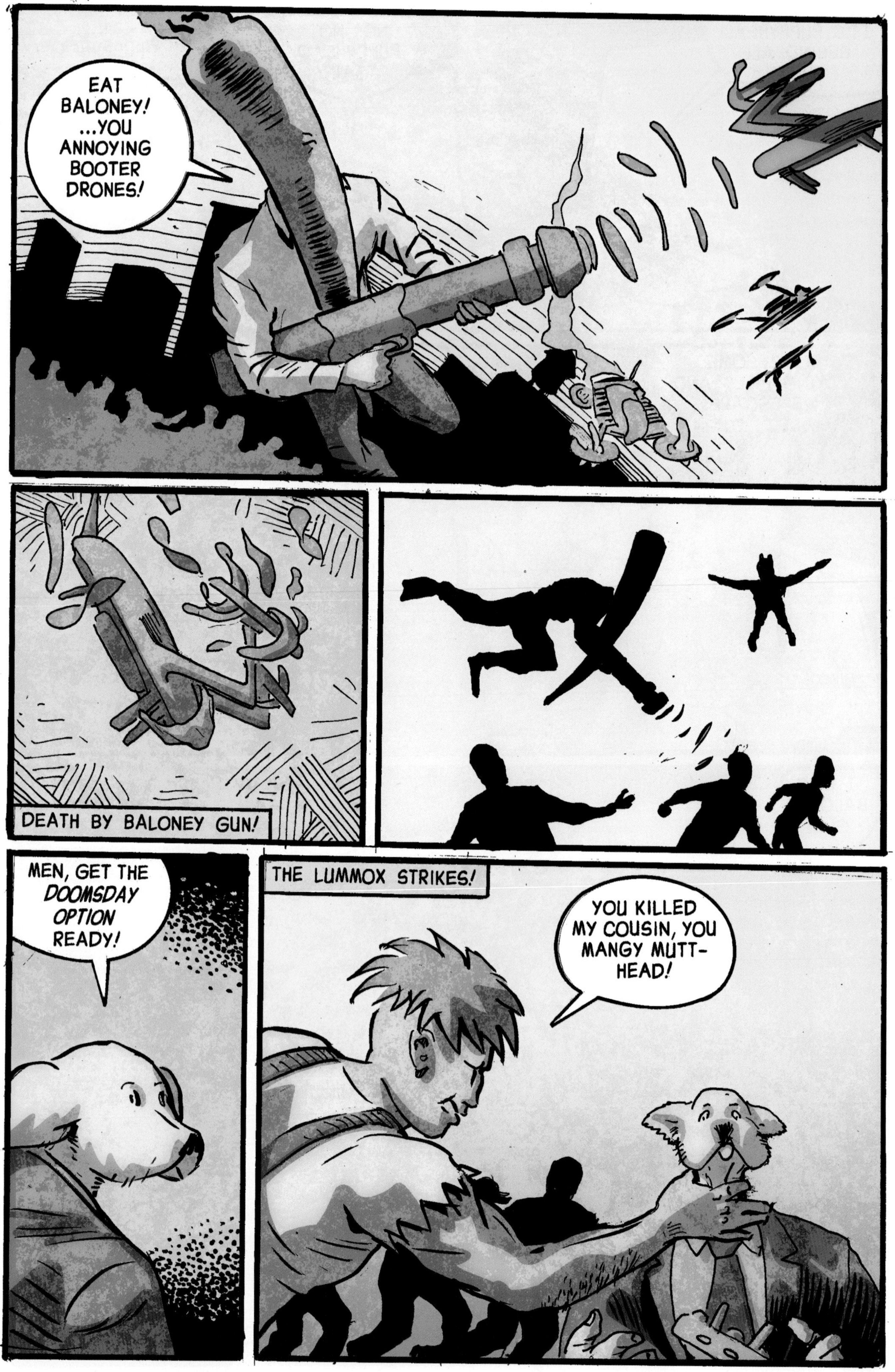
EAT BALONEY! ...YOU ANNOYING BOOTER DRONES!
DEATH BY BALONEY GUN!
MEN, GET THE DOOMSDAY OPTION READY!
THE LUMMOX STRIKES!
YOU KILLED MY COUSIN, YOU MANGY MUTT-HEAD!

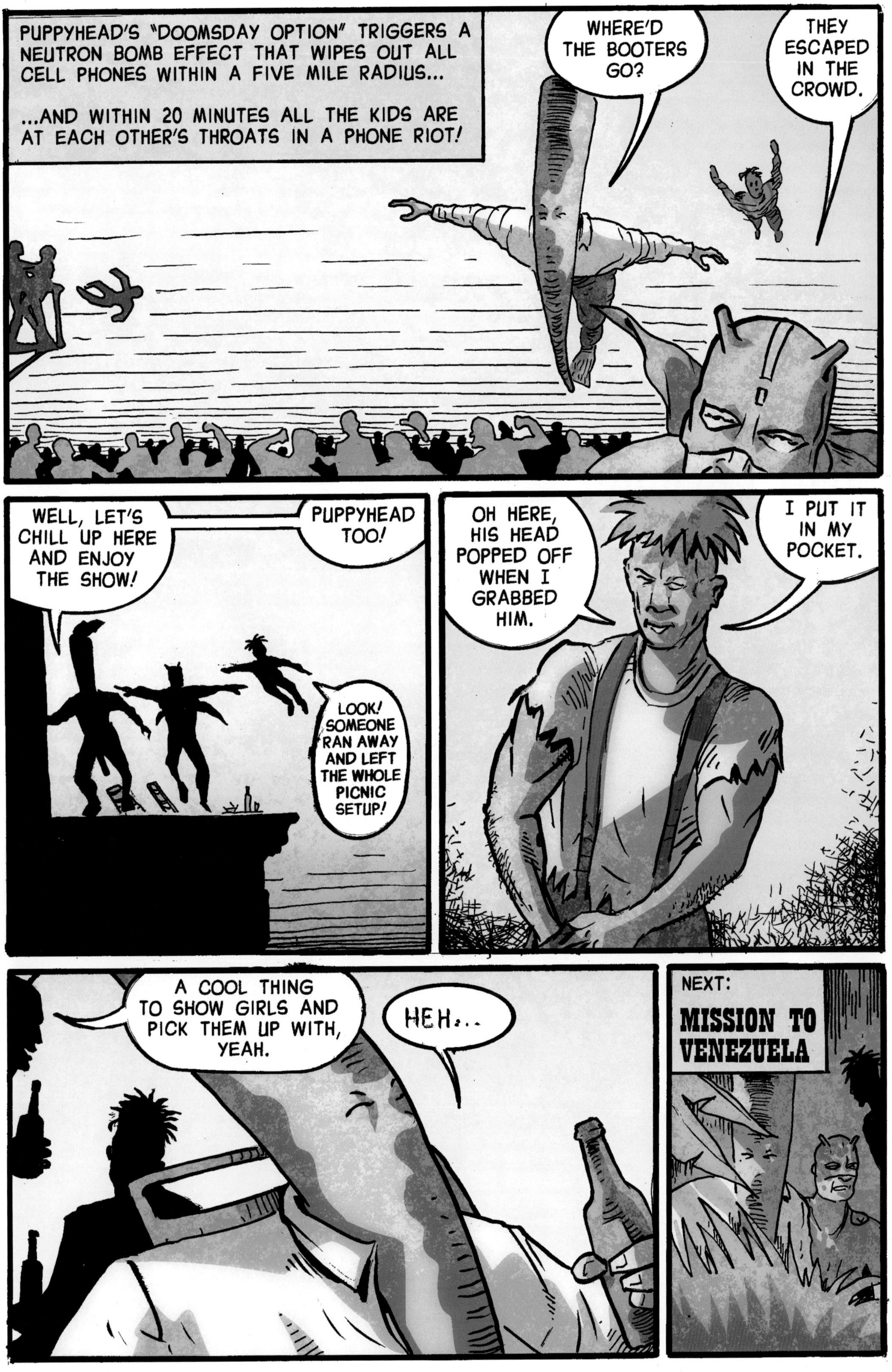

PUPPYHEAD'S "DOOMSDAY OPTION" TRIGGERS A NEUTRON BOMB EFFECT THAT WIPES OUT ALL CELL PHONES WITHIN A FIVE MILE RADIUS...
...AND WITHIN 20 MINUTES ALL THE KIDS ARE AT EACH OTHER'S THROATS IN A PHONE RIOT!
WHERE'D THE BOOTERS GO?
THEY ESCAPED IN THE CROWD.
WELL, LET'S CHILL UP HERE AND ENJOY THE SHOW!
PUPPYHEAD TOO!
LOOK! SOMEONE RAN AWAY AND LEFT THE WHOLE PICNIC SETUP!
OH HERE, HIS HEAD POPPED OFF WHEN I GRABBED HIM.
I PUT IT IN MY POCKET.
A COOL THING TO SHOW GIRLS AND PICK THEM UP WITH, YEAH.
HEH...
NEXT:
MISSION TO VENEZUELA

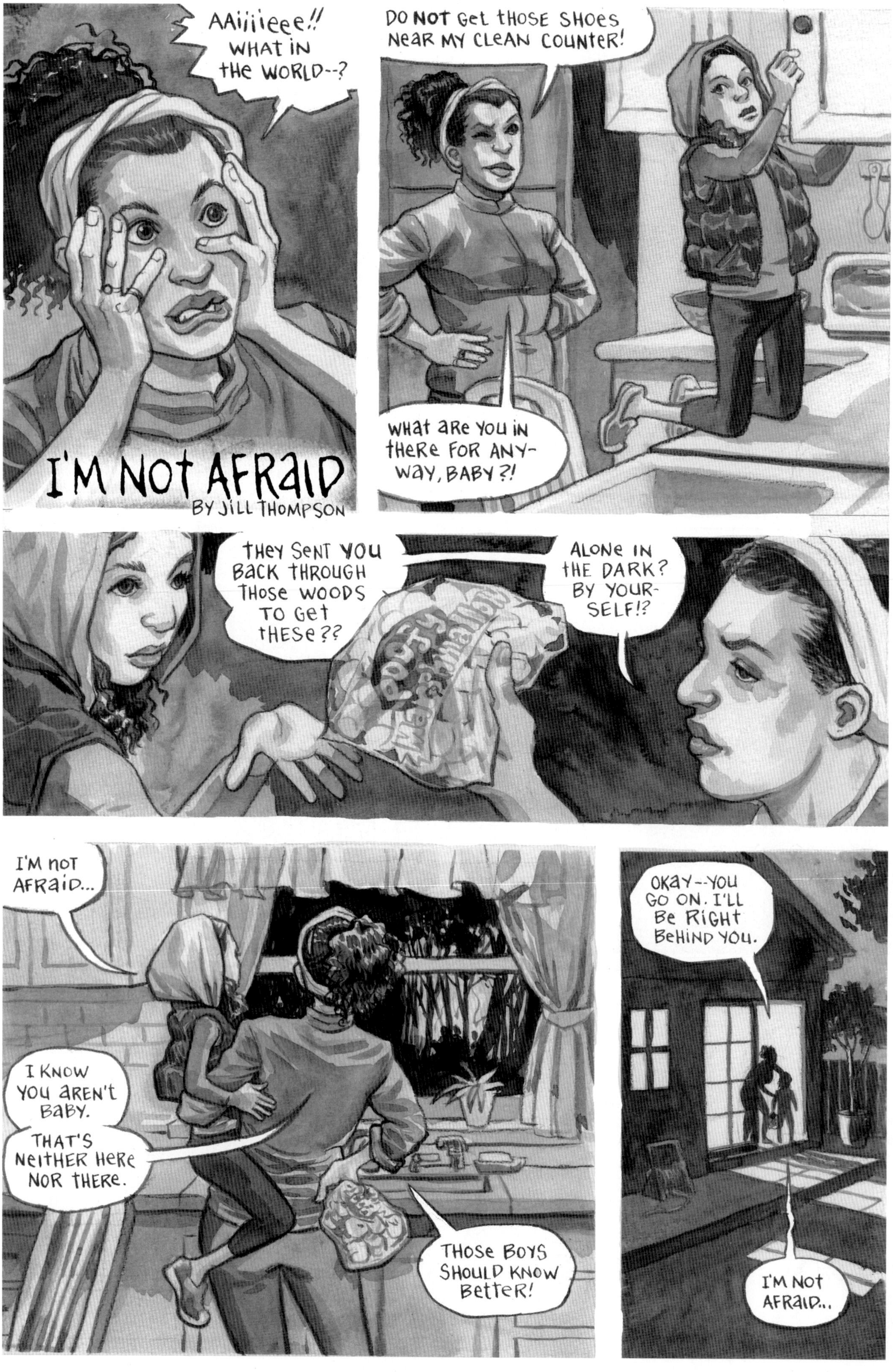
AAiiiieee!! WHAT IN THE WORLD--?
I'M NOT AFRAID
BY JILL THOMPSON
DO NOT GET THOSE SHOES NEAR MY CLEAN COUNTER!
WHAT ARE YOU IN THERE FOR ANY-WAY, BABY?!
THEY SENT YOU BACK THROUGH THOSE WOODS TO GET THESE??
ALONE IN THE DARK? BY YOUR-SELF!?
I'M NOT AFRAID...
I KNOW YOU AREN'T BABY.
THAT'S NEITHER HERE NOR THERE.
THOSE BOYS SHOULD KNOW BETTER!
OKAY--YOU GO ON. I'LL BE RIGHT BEHIND YOU.
I'M NOT AFRAID...

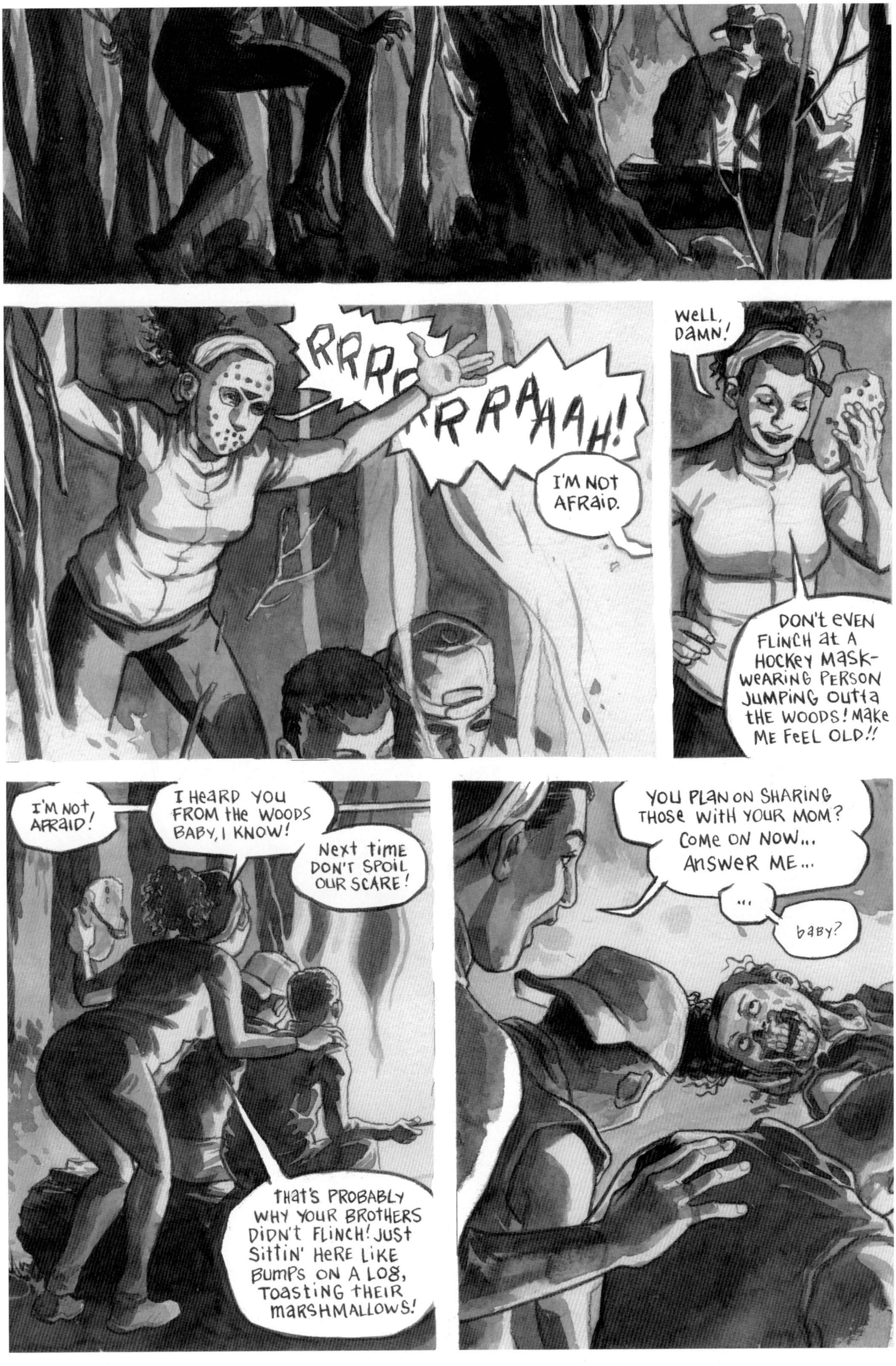
RRRRRRRAAAH!
I'M NOT AFRAID.
WeLL, DAMN!
DON'T EVEN FLINCH AT A HOCKEY MASK-WEARING PERSON JUMPING OUTTA THE WOODS! MAKE ME FEEL OLD!!
I'M NOT AFRAID!
I HEARD YOU FROM THE WOODS BABY, I KNOW!
Next time DON'T SPOIL OUR SCARE!
THAT'S PROBABLY WHY YOUR BROTHERS DIDN'T FLINCH! JUST SITTIN' HERE LIKE BUMPS ON A LOG, TOASTING THEIR MARSHMALLOWS!
YOU PLAN ON SHARING THOSE WITH YOUR MOM? COME ON NOW... ANSWER ME...
...
baby?

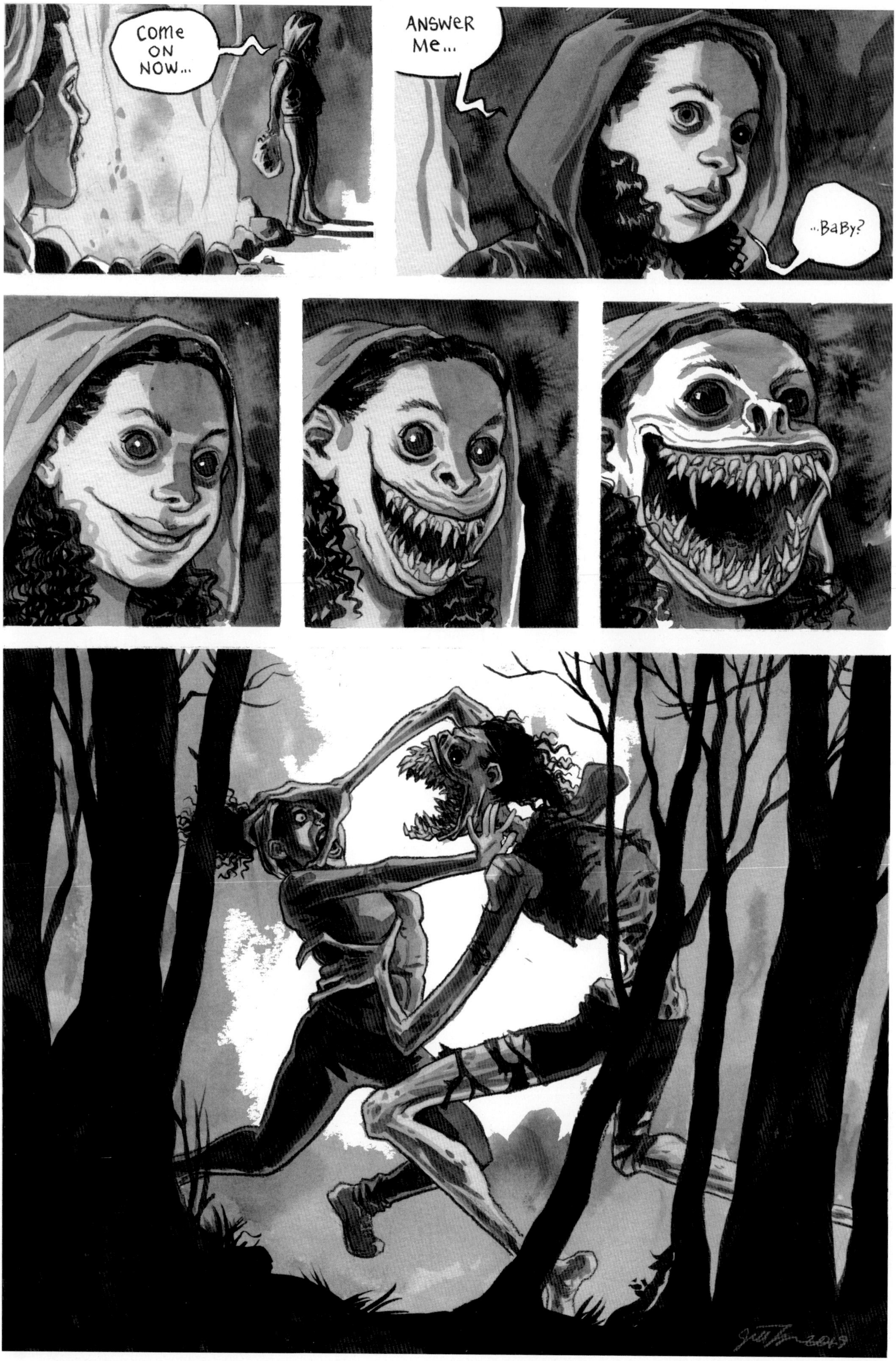
Come ON NOW...
ANSWER Me...
...BaBy?

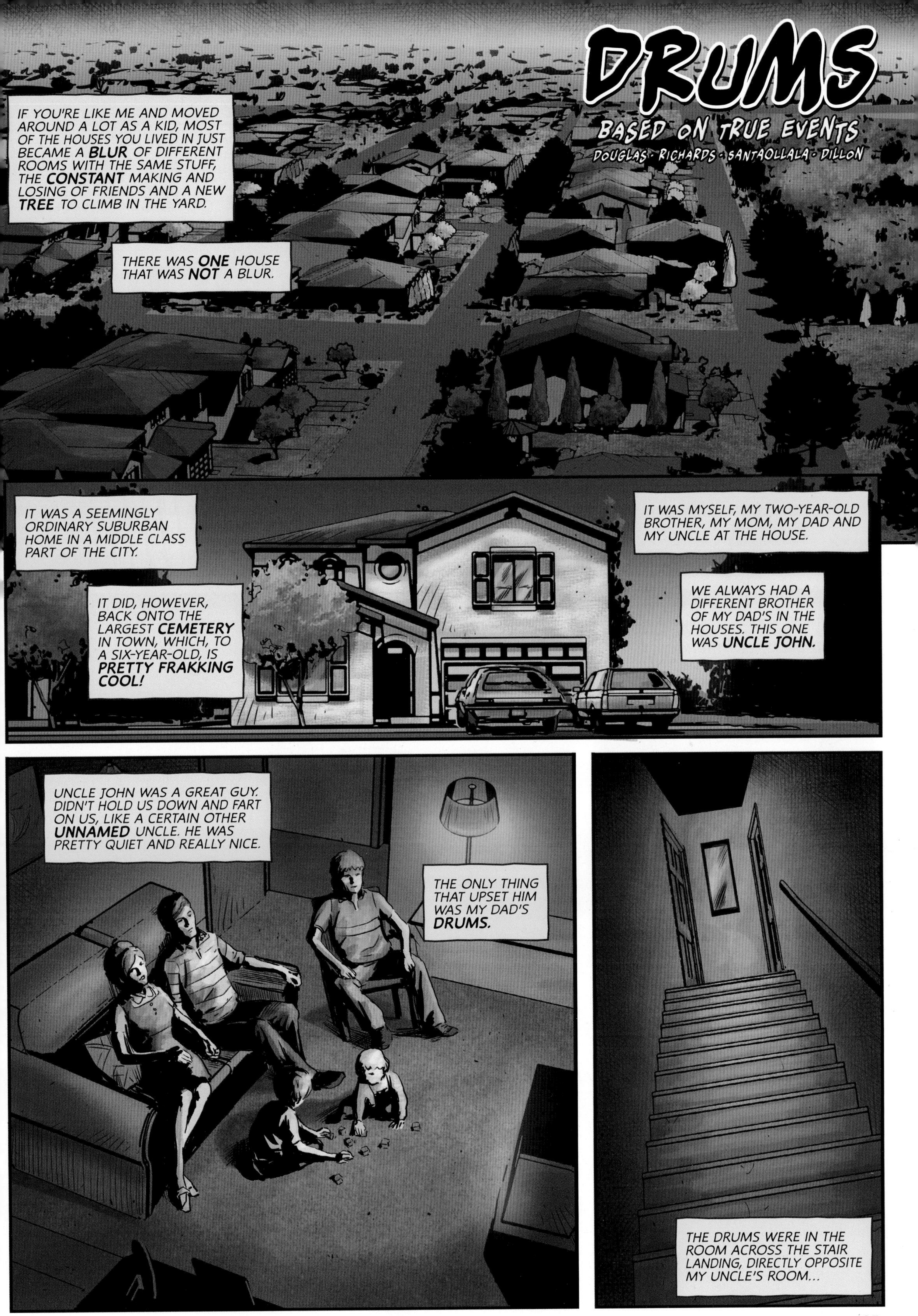
DRUMS
BASED ON TRUE EVENTS
DOUGLAS · RICHARDS · SANTAOLLALA · DILLON
IF YOU'RE LIKE ME AND MOVED AROUND A LOT AS A KID, MOST OF THE HOUSES YOU LIVED IN JUST BECAME A BLUR OF DIFFERENT ROOMS WITH THE SAME STUFF, THE CONSTANT MAKING AND LOSING OF FRIENDS AND A NEW TREE TO CLIMB IN THE YARD.
THERE WAS ONE HOUSE THAT WAS NOT A BLUR.
IT WAS A SEEMINGLY ORDINARY SUBURBAN HOME IN A MIDDLE CLASS PART OF THE CITY.
IT DID, HOWEVER, BACK ONTO THE LARGEST CEMETERY IN TOWN, WHICH, TO A SIX-YEAR-OLD, IS PRETTY FRAKKING COOL!
IT WAS MYSELF, MY TWO-YEAR-OLD BROTHER, MY MOM, MY DAD AND MY UNCLE AT THE HOUSE.
WE ALWAYS HAD A DIFFERENT BROTHER OF MY DAD'S IN THE HOUSES. THIS ONE WAS UNCLE JOHN.
UNCLE JOHN WAS A GREAT GUY. DIDN'T HOLD US DOWN AND FART ON US, LIKE A CERTAIN OTHER UNNAMED UNCLE. HE WAS PRETTY QUIET AND REALLY NICE.
THE ONLY THING THAT UPSET HIM WAS MY DAD'S DRUMS.
THE DRUMS WERE IN THE ROOM ACROSS THE STAIR LANDING, DIRECTLY OPPOSITE MY UNCLE'S ROOM...

...WHICH ALSO HAPPENED TO BE RIGHT UPSTAIRS FROM MY OWN ROOM.

I'D LAY IN BED AT NIGHT AND LISTEN TO THE **SOUND** OF THE DRUMS THROUGH THE FLOOR ABOVE.

NO MATTER HOW MUCH I WOULD **WISH** IT, MY PARENTS NEVER CAME OUT TO TELL JOHN TO **'KNOCK IT OFF!'**

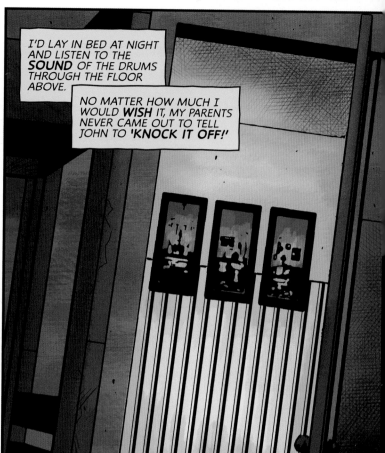

I WAS TOO YOUNG TO HAVE A ROOM AT THE TOP OF THE STAIRS, SO THE DRUMS GOT THE ROOM THAT SHOULD HAVE BEEN MINE.

THEY'D SIT THERE, ALL ALONE, IN THIS COOL BEDROOM.

BUT EVEN **ALONE**...

...SOME NIGHTS...

...THE DRUMS WOULD **PLAY.**

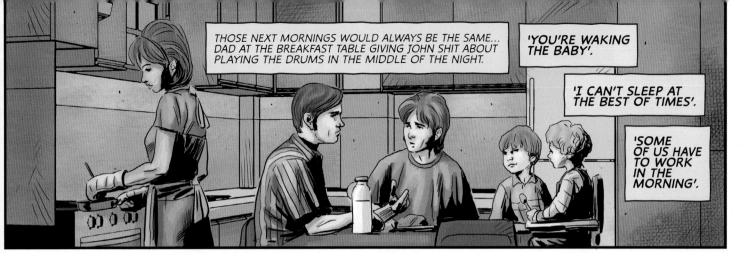

THOSE NEXT MORNINGS WOULD ALWAYS BE THE SAME... DAD AT THE BREAKFAST TABLE GIVING JOHN SHIT ABOUT PLAYING THE DRUMS IN THE MIDDLE OF THE NIGHT.

'YOU'RE WAKING THE BABY'.

'I CAN'T SLEEP AT THE BEST OF TIMES'.

'SOME OF US HAVE TO WORK IN THE MORNING'.

UNCLE WOULD SWEAR HE NEVER **TOUCHED** THE DRUMS.

SWEAR IT!

MY BROTHER AND I WOULD JUST SIT AND SMILE BECAUSE NO ONE WAS CRUSHING **US** FOR DOING SOMETHING STUPID THAT MORNING.

JOHN ALWAYS THOUGHT IT WAS ME OR MY DAD PLAYING A GAME ON HIM.

WHEN HE'D HEAR THE DRUMS PLAY, HE'D SLIP FROM HIS ROOM, CREEP TO THE DOOR...AND...

BA-DRUM DUM DUM-DA-DA-DUM BRUM-PUM-PUM

...**WHAM!** HE'D FLIP THAT DOOR OPEN READY TO **CATCH** ONE OF US IN THE ACT!

BUT...

CLATT

...THE STICKS WOULD JUST CLATTER TO THE FLOOR...

...IN AN **EMPTY** ROOM.

CLAT-ADAT-A-DAT

MY DAD **NEVER** BELIEVED HIM.

MY MOM WOULD LISTEN, BUT SHE'D KEEP HER THOUGHTS TO HERSELF.

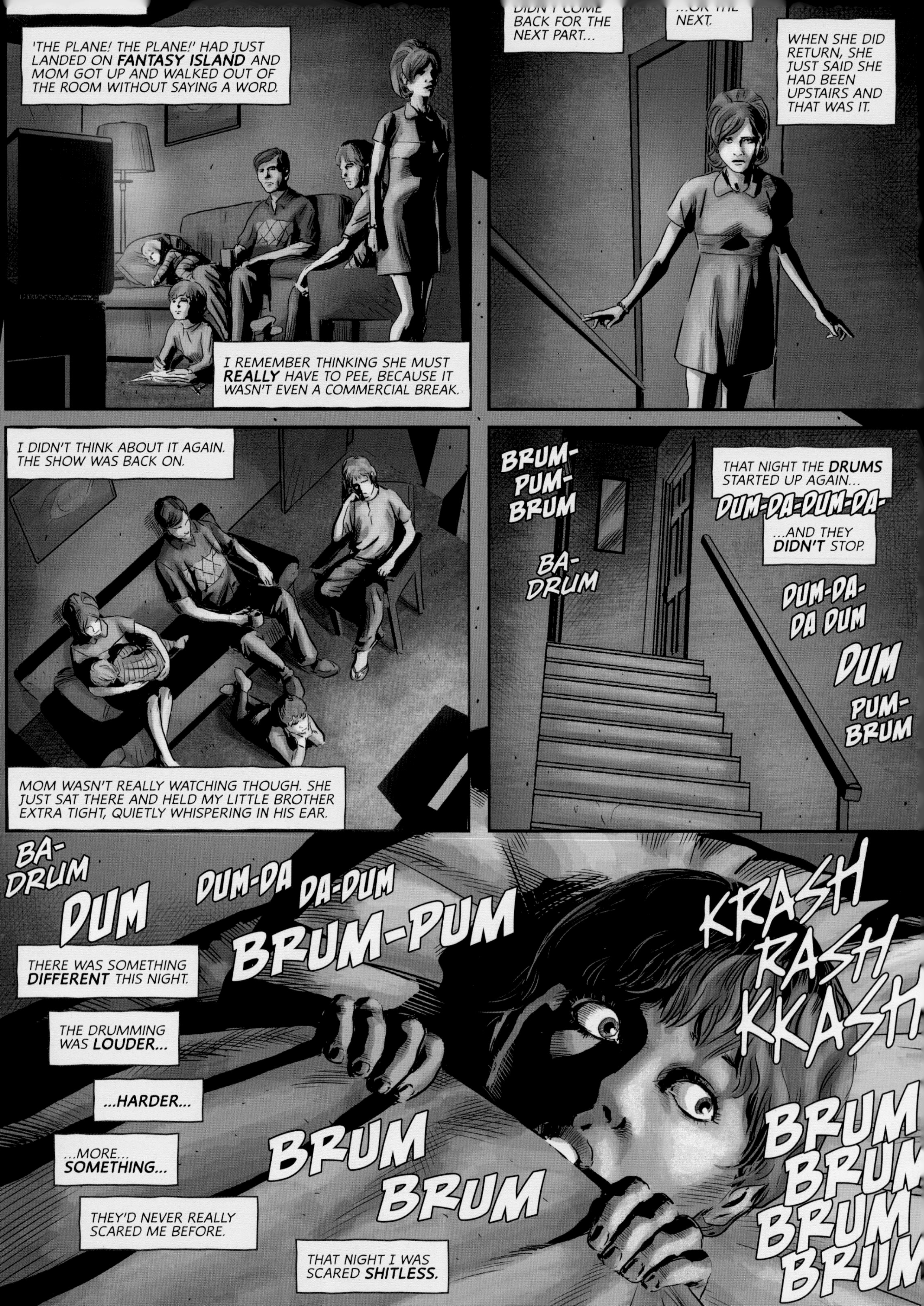
'THE PLANE! THE PLANE!' HAD JUST LANDED ON **FANTASY ISLAND** AND MOM GOT UP AND WALKED OUT OF THE ROOM WITHOUT SAYING A WORD.
I REMEMBER THINKING SHE MUST **REALLY** HAVE TO PEE, BECAUSE IT WASN'T EVEN A COMMERCIAL BREAK.
BACK FOR THE NEXT PART...
NEXT.
WHEN SHE DID RETURN, SHE JUST SAID SHE HAD BEEN UPSTAIRS AND THAT WAS IT.
I DIDN'T THINK ABOUT IT AGAIN. THE SHOW WAS BACK ON.
MOM WASN'T REALLY WATCHING THOUGH. SHE JUST SAT THERE AND HELD MY LITTLE BROTHER EXTRA TIGHT, QUIETLY WHISPERING IN HIS EAR.
BRUM-PUM-BRUM
BA-DRUM
THAT NIGHT THE **DRUMS** STARTED UP AGAIN...
DUM-DA-DUM-DA-
...AND THEY **DIDN'T** STOP.
DUM-DA-DA DUM
DUM
PUM-BRUM
BA-DRUM
DUM
DUM-DA
DA-DUM
BRUM-PUM
THERE WAS SOMETHING **DIFFERENT** THIS NIGHT.
THE DRUMMING WAS **LOUDER...**
...HARDER...
...MORE... **SOMETHING...**
THEY'D NEVER REALLY SCARED ME BEFORE.
BRUM
BRUM
THAT NIGHT I WAS SCARED **SHITLESS.**
KRASH
RASH
KKASH
BRUM
BRUM
BRUM
BRUM

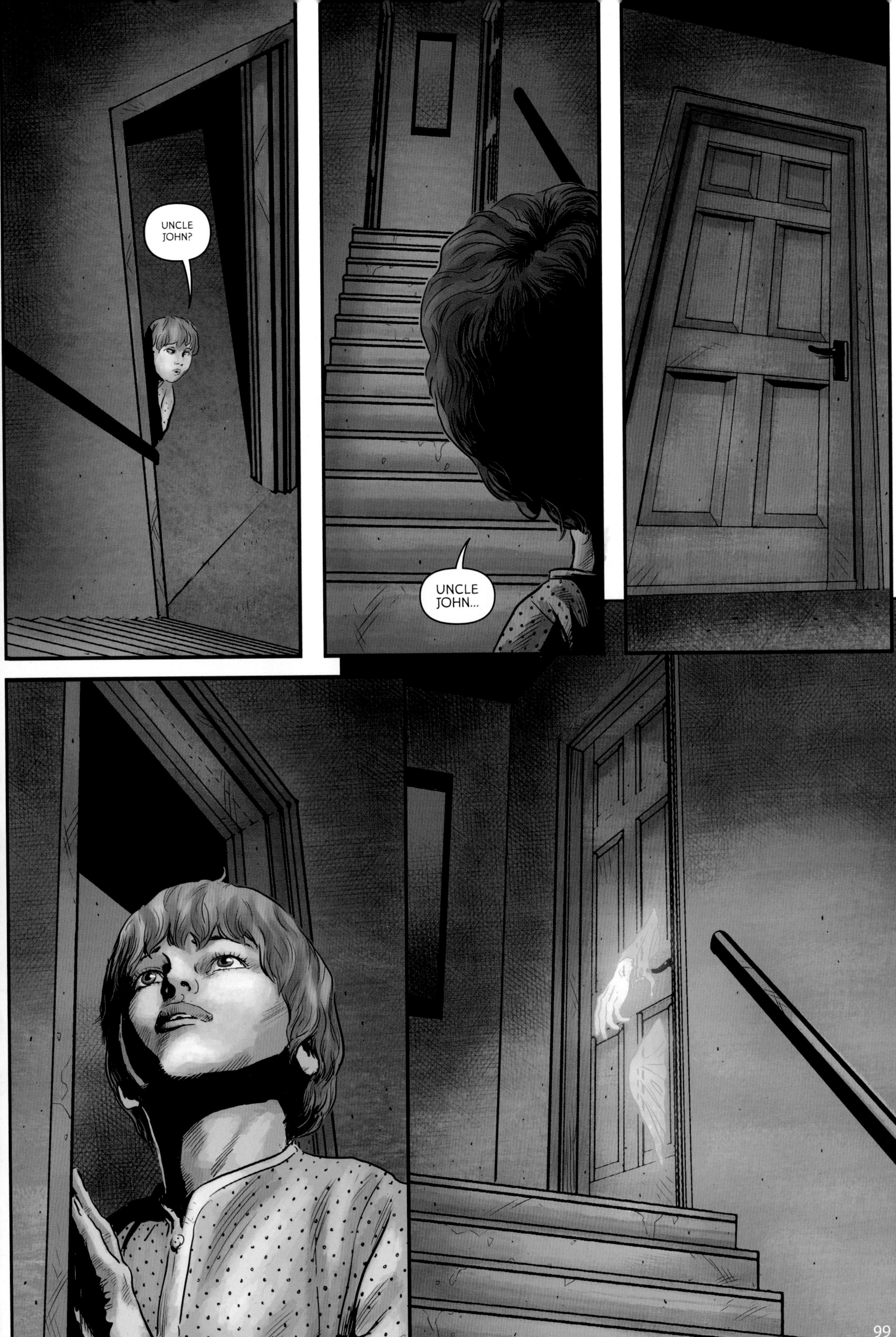
UNCLE JOHN?
UNCLE JOHN...

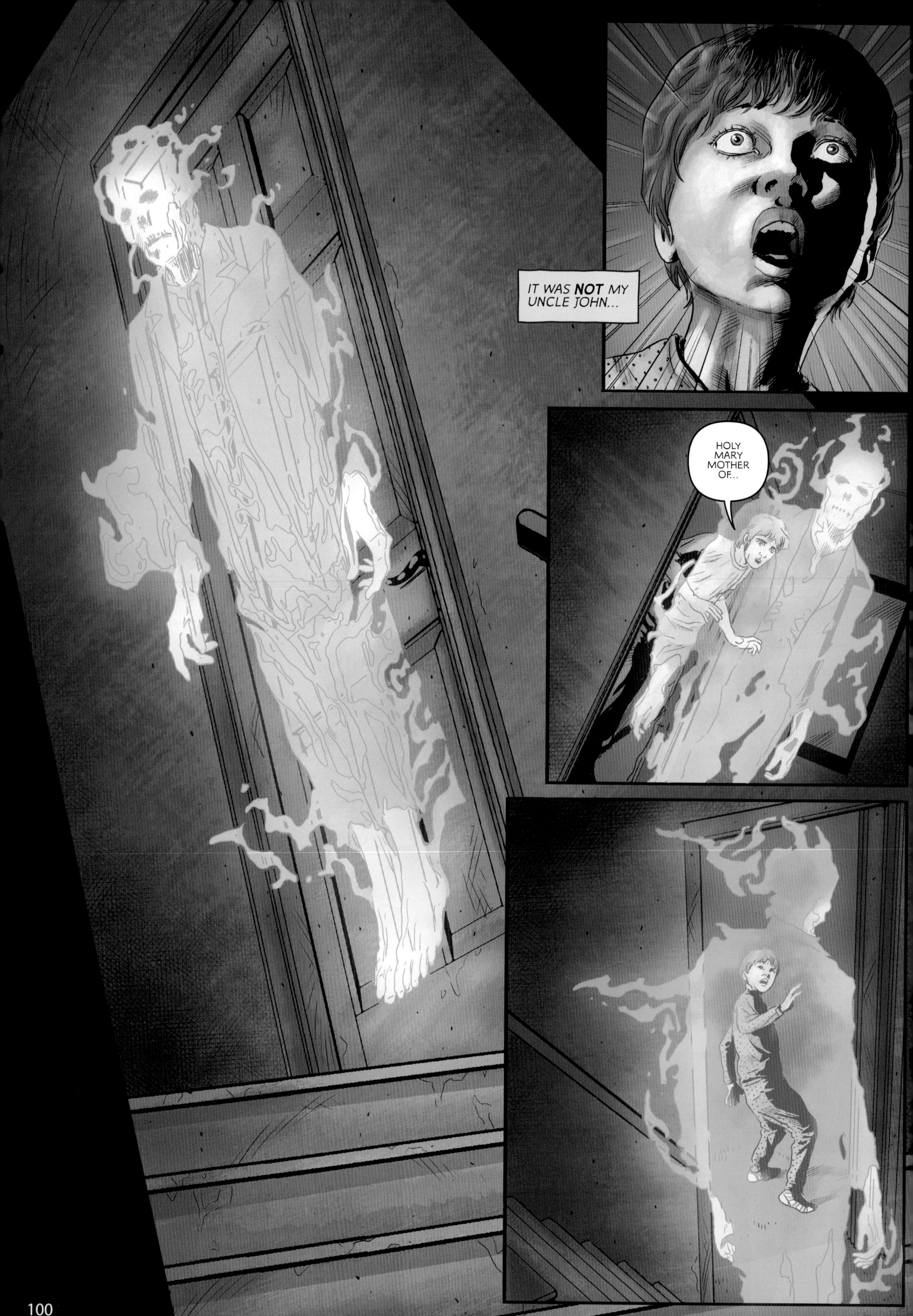
IT WAS **NOT** MY UNCLE JOHN...
HOLY MARY MOTHER OF...

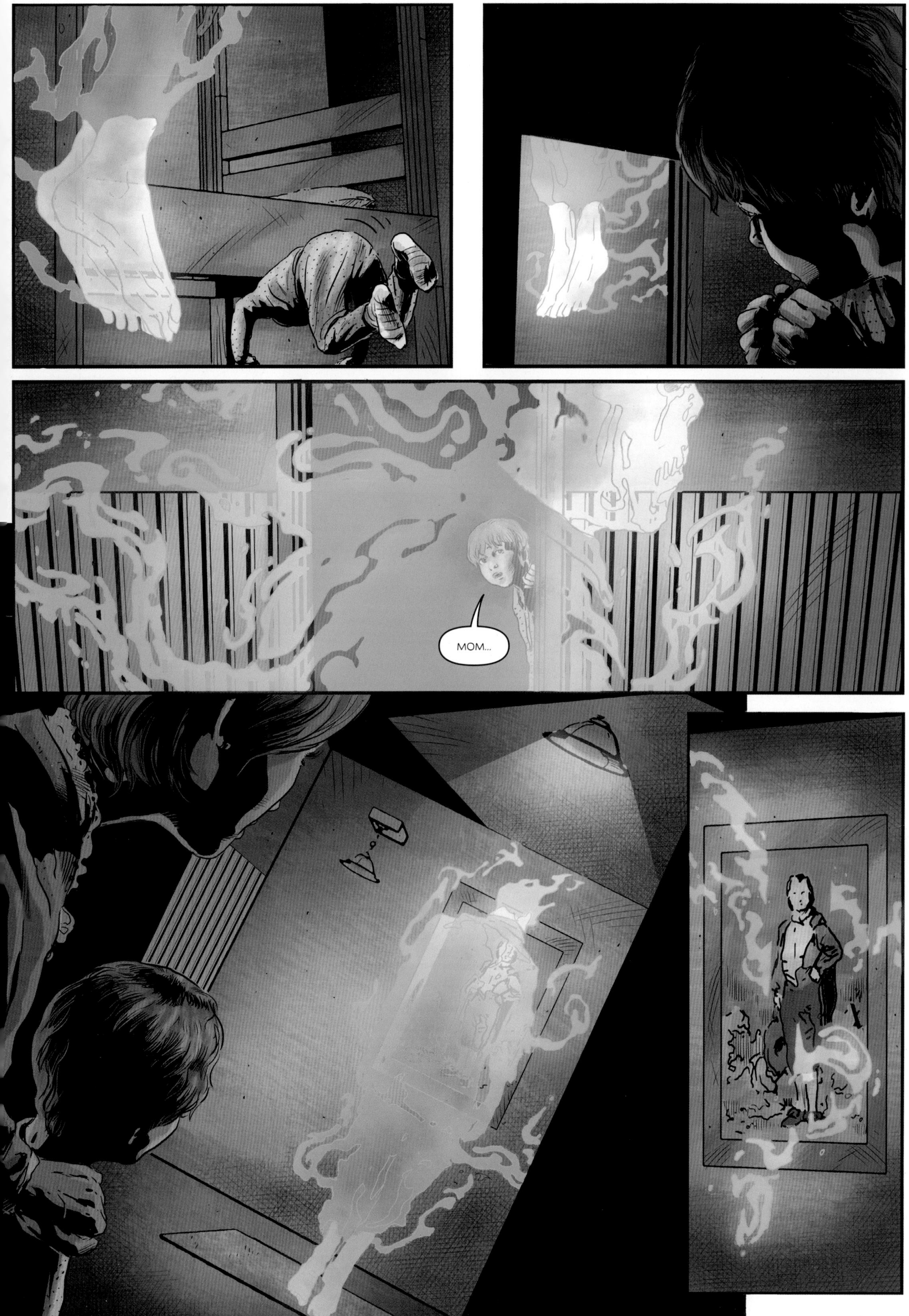
MOM...

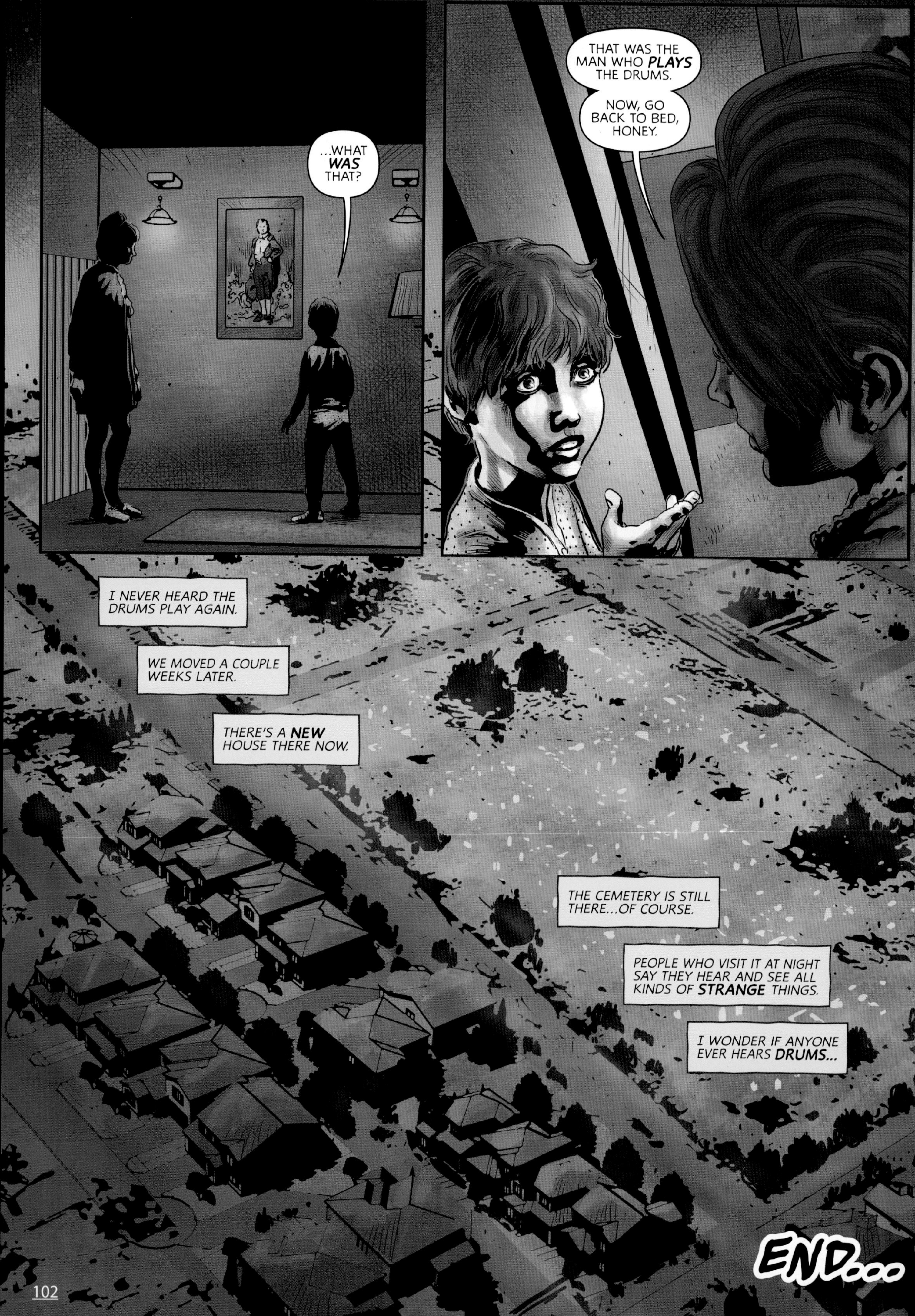

...WHAT WAS THAT?
THAT WAS THE MAN WHO PLAYS THE DRUMS.
NOW, GO BACK TO BED, HONEY.
I NEVER HEARD THE DRUMS PLAY AGAIN.
WE MOVED A COUPLE WEEKS LATER.
THERE'S A NEW HOUSE THERE NOW.
THE CEMETERY IS STILL THERE...OF COURSE.
PEOPLE WHO VISIT IT AT NIGHT SAY THEY HEAR AND SEE ALL KINDS OF STRANGE THINGS.
I WONDER IF ANYONE EVER HEARS DRUMS...
END...

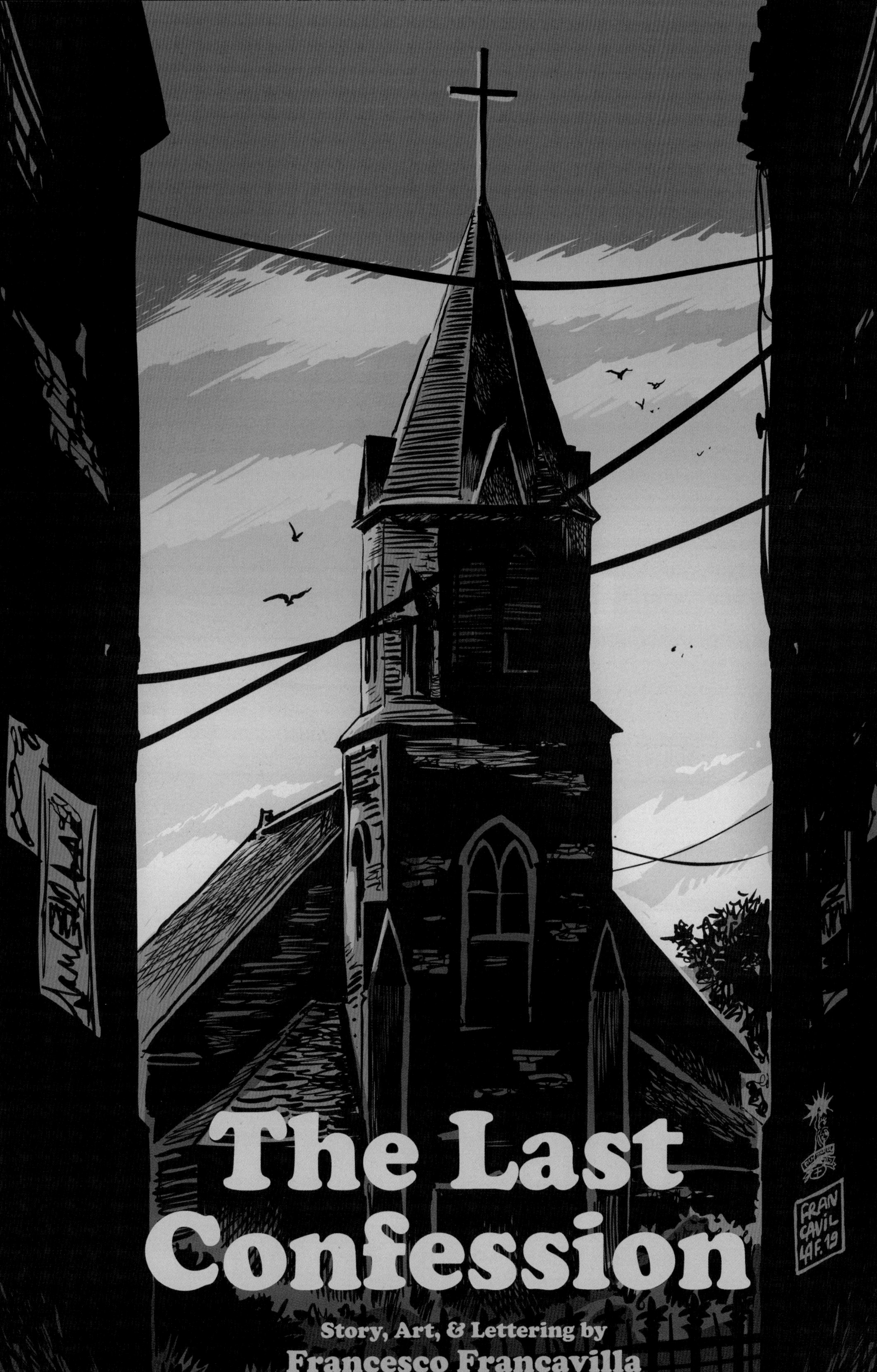
The Last Confession
Story, Art, & Lettering by
Francesco Francavilla

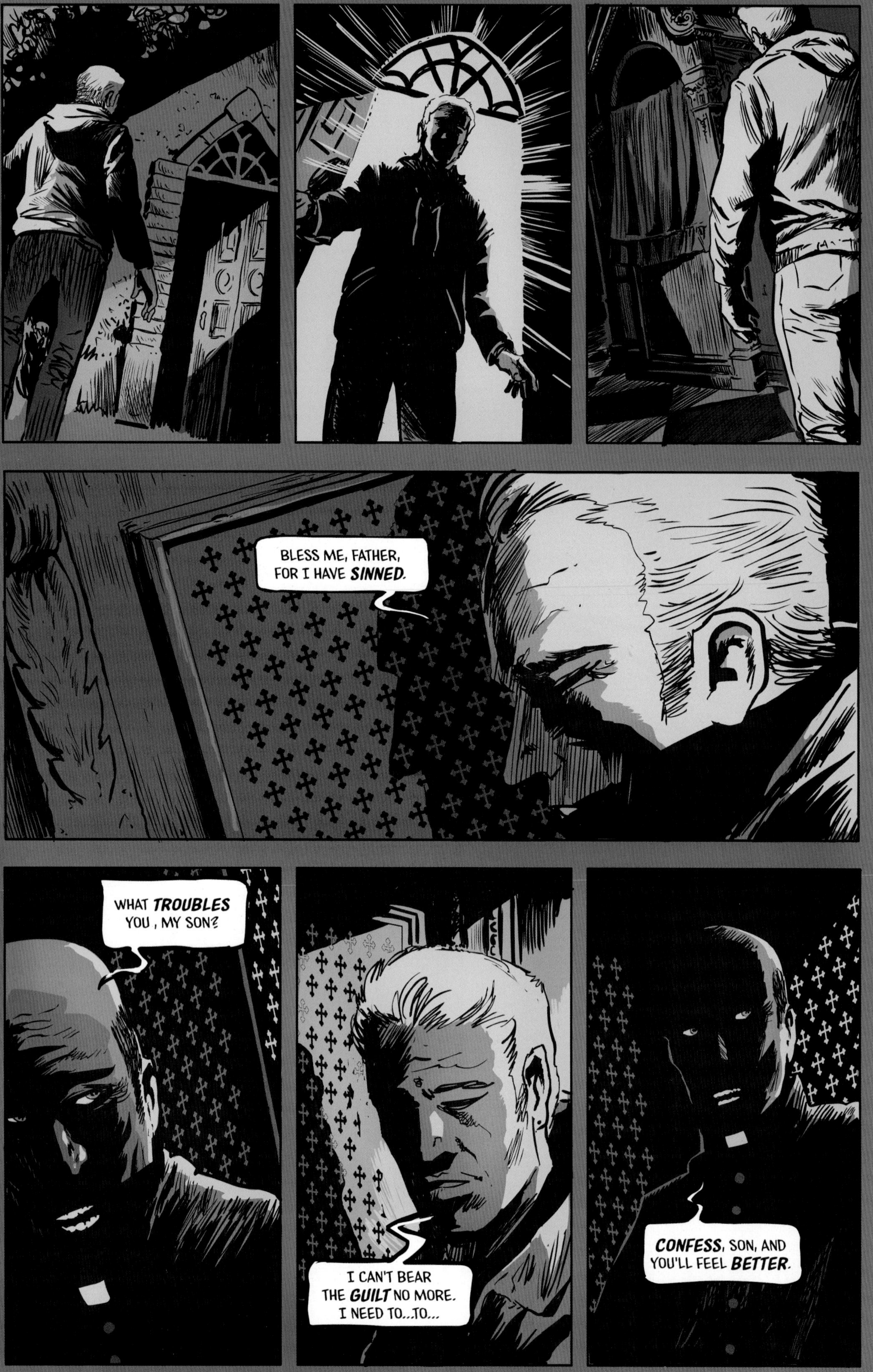
BLESS ME, FATHER, FOR I HAVE SINNED.
WHAT TROUBLES YOU , MY SON?
I CAN'T BEAR THE GUILT NO MORE. I NEED TO...TO...
CONFESS, SON, AND YOU'LL FEEL BETTER.

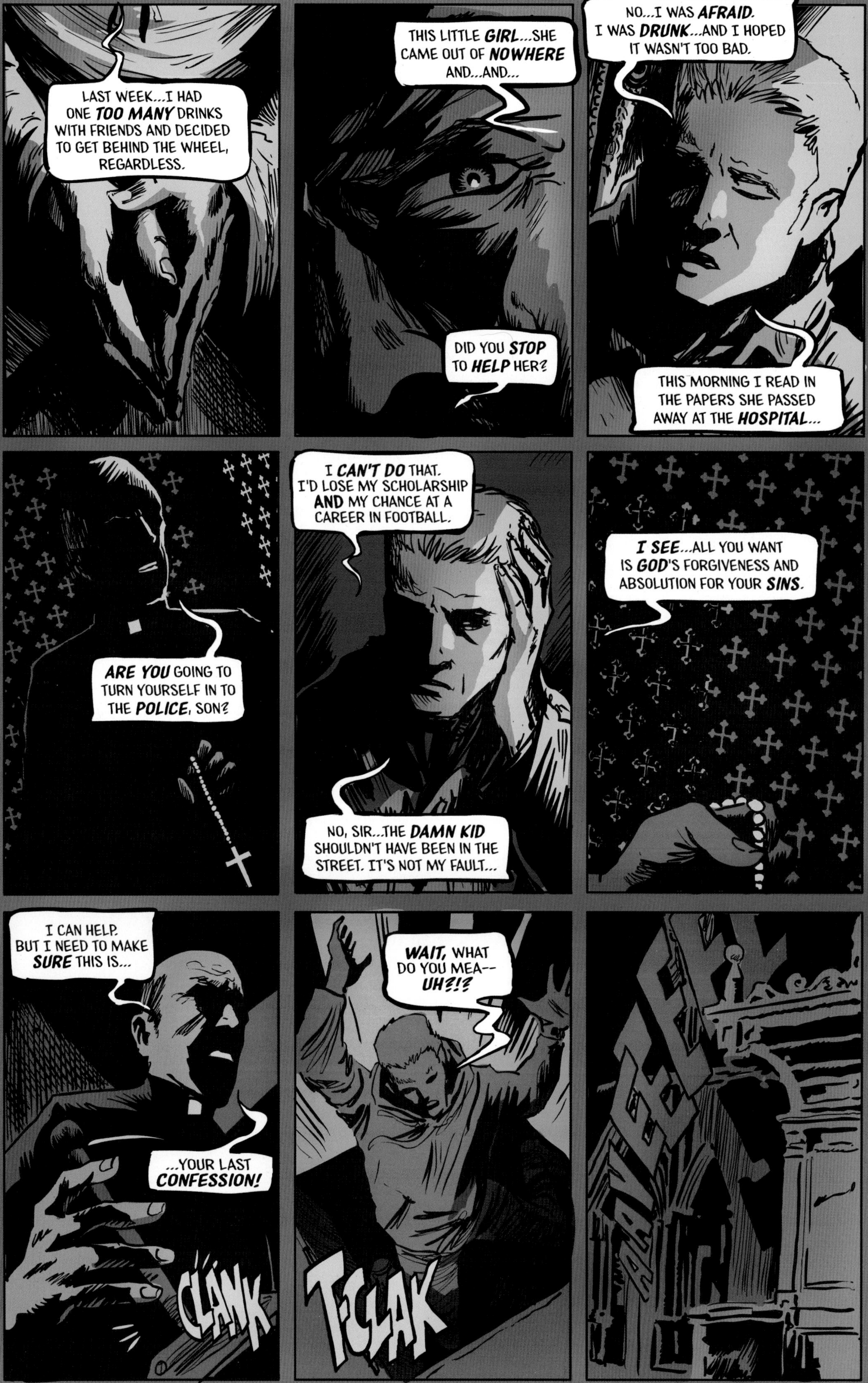
LAST WEEK...I HAD ONE TOO MANY DRINKS WITH FRIENDS AND DECIDED TO GET BEHIND THE WHEEL, REGARDLESS.
THIS LITTLE GIRL...SHE CAME OUT OF NOWHERE AND...AND...
DID YOU STOP TO HELP HER?
NO...I WAS AFRAID. I WAS DRUNK...AND I HOPED IT WASN'T TOO BAD.
THIS MORNING I READ IN THE PAPERS SHE PASSED AWAY AT THE HOSPITAL...
ARE YOU GOING TO TURN YOURSELF IN TO THE POLICE, SON?
I CAN'T DO THAT. I'D LOSE MY SCHOLARSHIP AND MY CHANCE AT A CAREER IN FOOTBALL.
NO, SIR...THE DAMN KID SHOULDN'T HAVE BEEN IN THE STREET. IT'S NOT MY FAULT...
I SEE...ALL YOU WANT IS GOD'S FORGIVENESS AND ABSOLUTION FOR YOUR SINS.
I CAN HELP. BUT I NEED TO MAKE SURE THIS IS...
...YOUR LAST CONFESSION!
CLANK
WAIT, WHAT DO YOU MEA-- UH?!?
T-CLAK

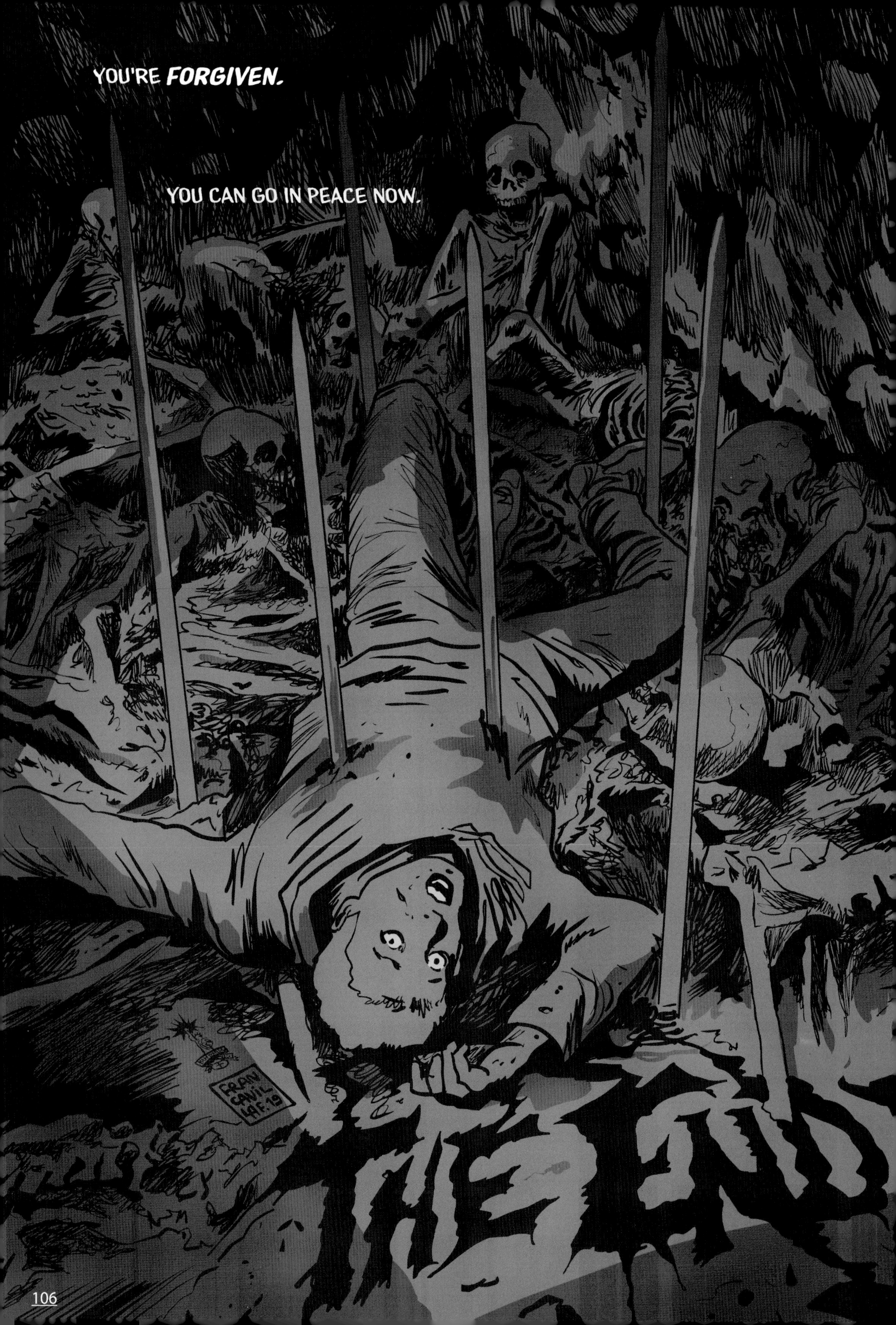
YOU'RE FORGIVEN.
YOU CAN GO IN PEACE NOW.
FRAN GAVIL 19F.19
THE END

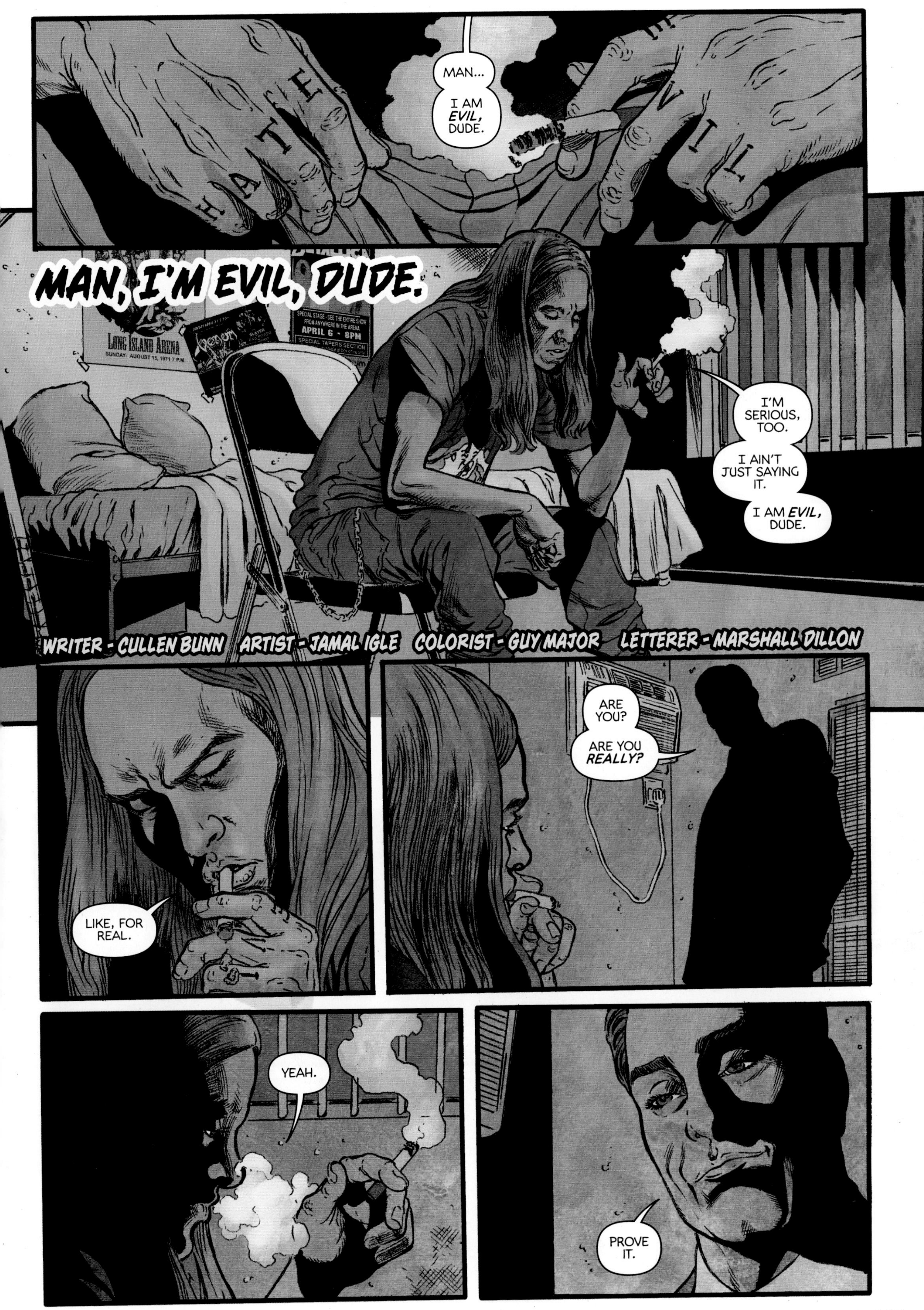
MAN...
I AM EVIL, DUDE.
HATE
EVIL
MAN, I'M EVIL, DUDE.
LONG ISLAND ARENA
SUNDAY · AUGUST 15, 1971 7 P.M.
SPECIAL STAGE - SEE THE ENTIRE SHOW FROM ANYWHERE IN THE ARENA
APRIL 6 - 8PM
SPECIAL TAPERS SECTION
I'M SERIOUS, TOO.
I AIN'T JUST SAYING IT.
I AM EVIL, DUDE.
WRITER - CULLEN BUNN ARTIST - JAMAL IGLE COLORIST - GUY MAJOR LETTERER - MARSHALL DILLON
LIKE, FOR REAL.
ARE YOU?
ARE YOU REALLY?
YEAH.
PROVE IT.

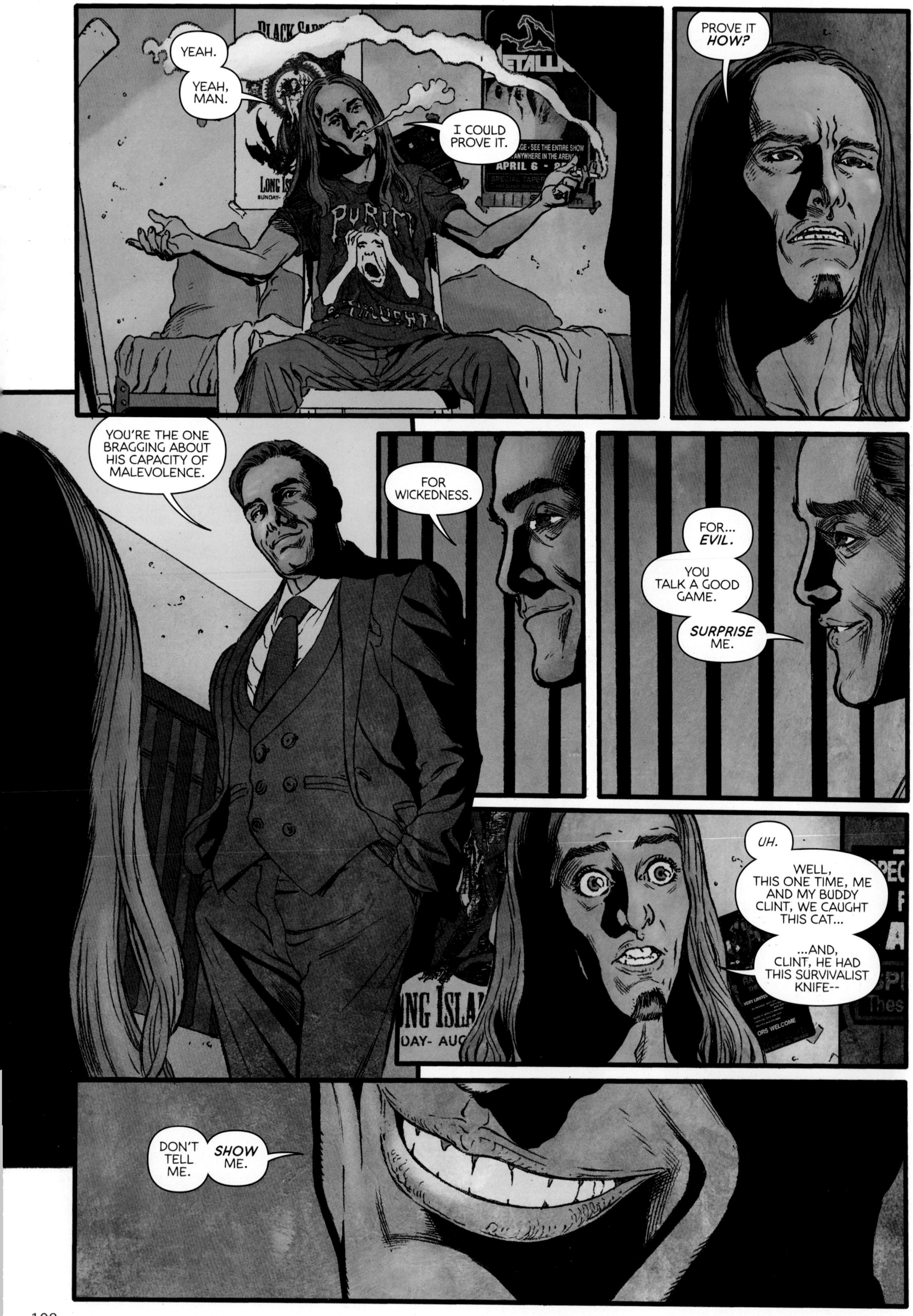
YEAH.
YEAH, MAN.
I COULD PROVE IT.
PROVE IT HOW?
YOU'RE THE ONE BRAGGING ABOUT HIS CAPACITY OF MALEVOLENCE.
FOR WICKEDNESS.
FOR... EVIL.
YOU TALK A GOOD GAME.
SURPRISE ME.
UH.
WELL, THIS ONE TIME, ME AND MY BUDDY CLINT, WE CAUGHT THIS CAT...
...AND, CLINT, HE HAD THIS SURVIVALIST KNIFE--
DON'T TELL ME.
SHOW ME.

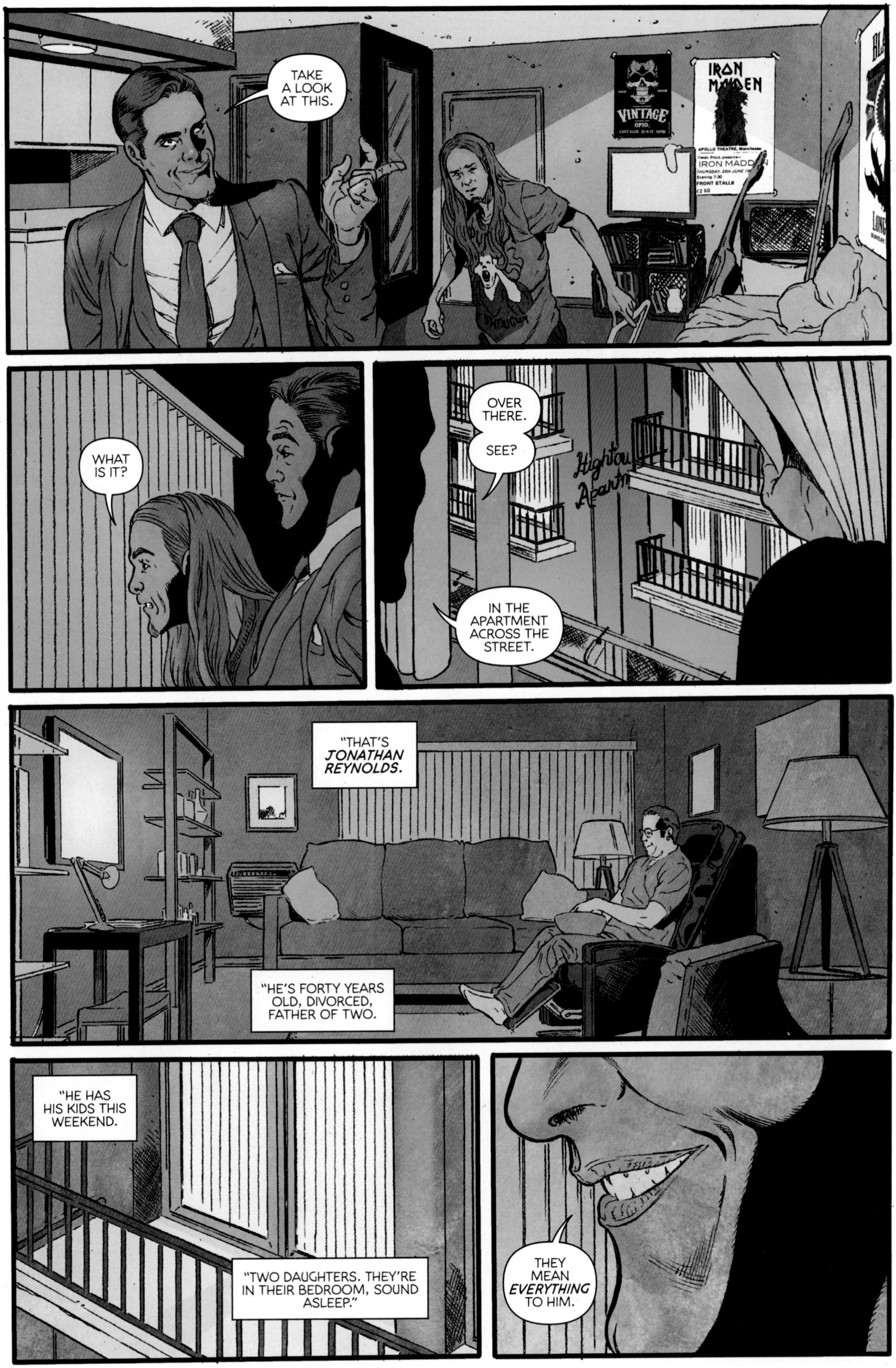

TAKE A LOOK AT THIS.
VINTAGE
IRON MAIDEN
WHAT IS IT?
OVER THERE.
SEE?
IN THE APARTMENT ACROSS THE STREET.
"THAT'S *JONATHAN REYNOLDS.*
"HE'S FORTY YEARS OLD, DIVORCED, FATHER OF TWO.
"HE HAS HIS KIDS THIS WEEKEND.
"TWO DAUGHTERS. THEY'RE IN THEIR BEDROOM, SOUND ASLEEP."
THEY MEAN *EVERYTHING* TO HIM.

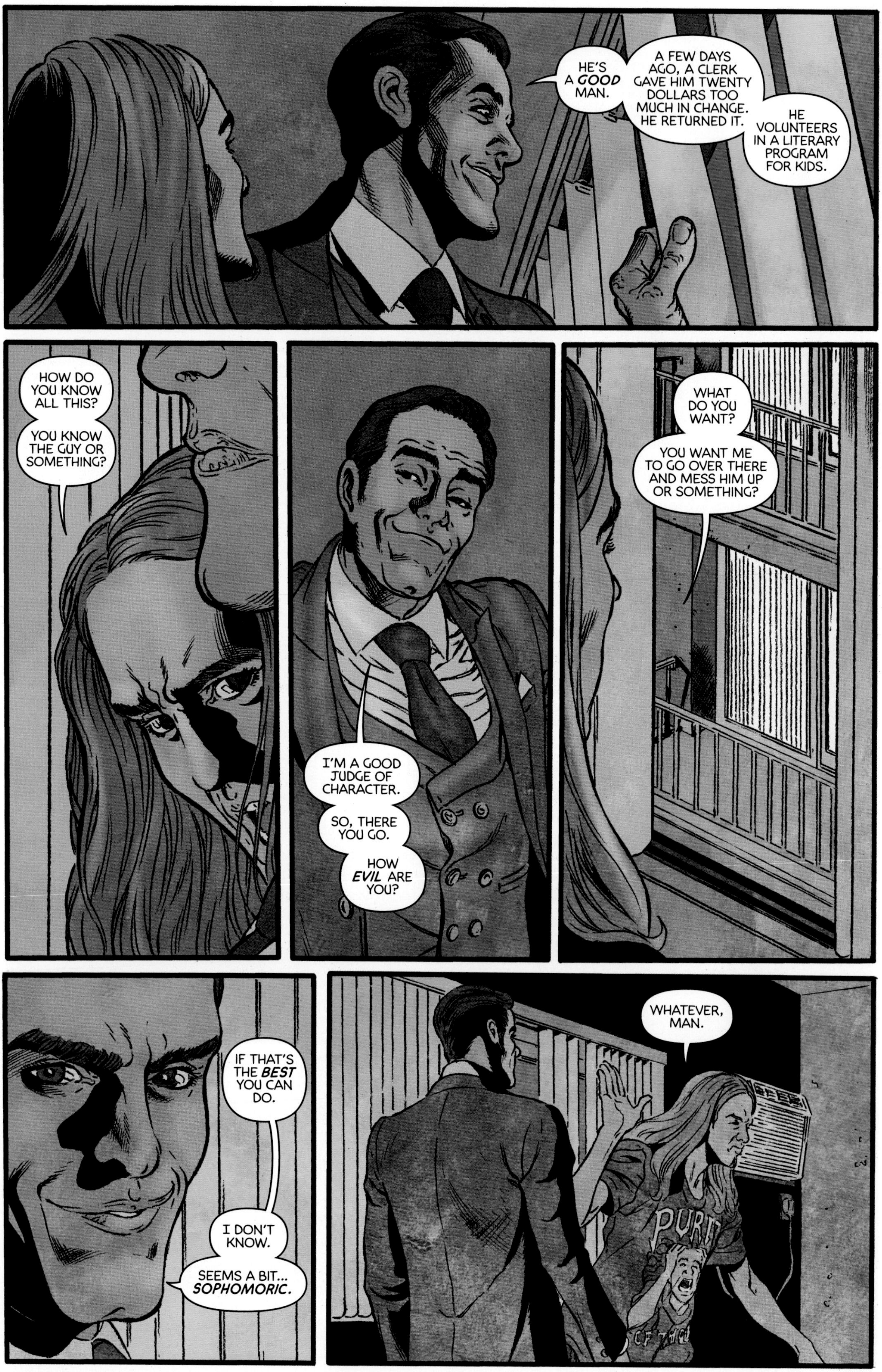
HE'S A GOOD MAN.
A FEW DAYS AGO, A CLERK GAVE HIM TWENTY DOLLARS TOO MUCH IN CHANGE. HE RETURNED IT.
HE VOLUNTEERS IN A LITERARY PROGRAM FOR KIDS.
HOW DO YOU KNOW ALL THIS?
YOU KNOW THE GUY OR SOMETHING?
I'M A GOOD JUDGE OF CHARACTER.
SO, THERE YOU GO.
HOW EVIL ARE YOU?
WHAT DO YOU WANT?
YOU WANT ME TO GO OVER THERE AND MESS HIM UP OR SOMETHING?
IF THAT'S THE BEST YOU CAN DO.
I DON'T KNOW.
SEEMS A BIT... SOPHOMORIC.
WHATEVER, MAN.

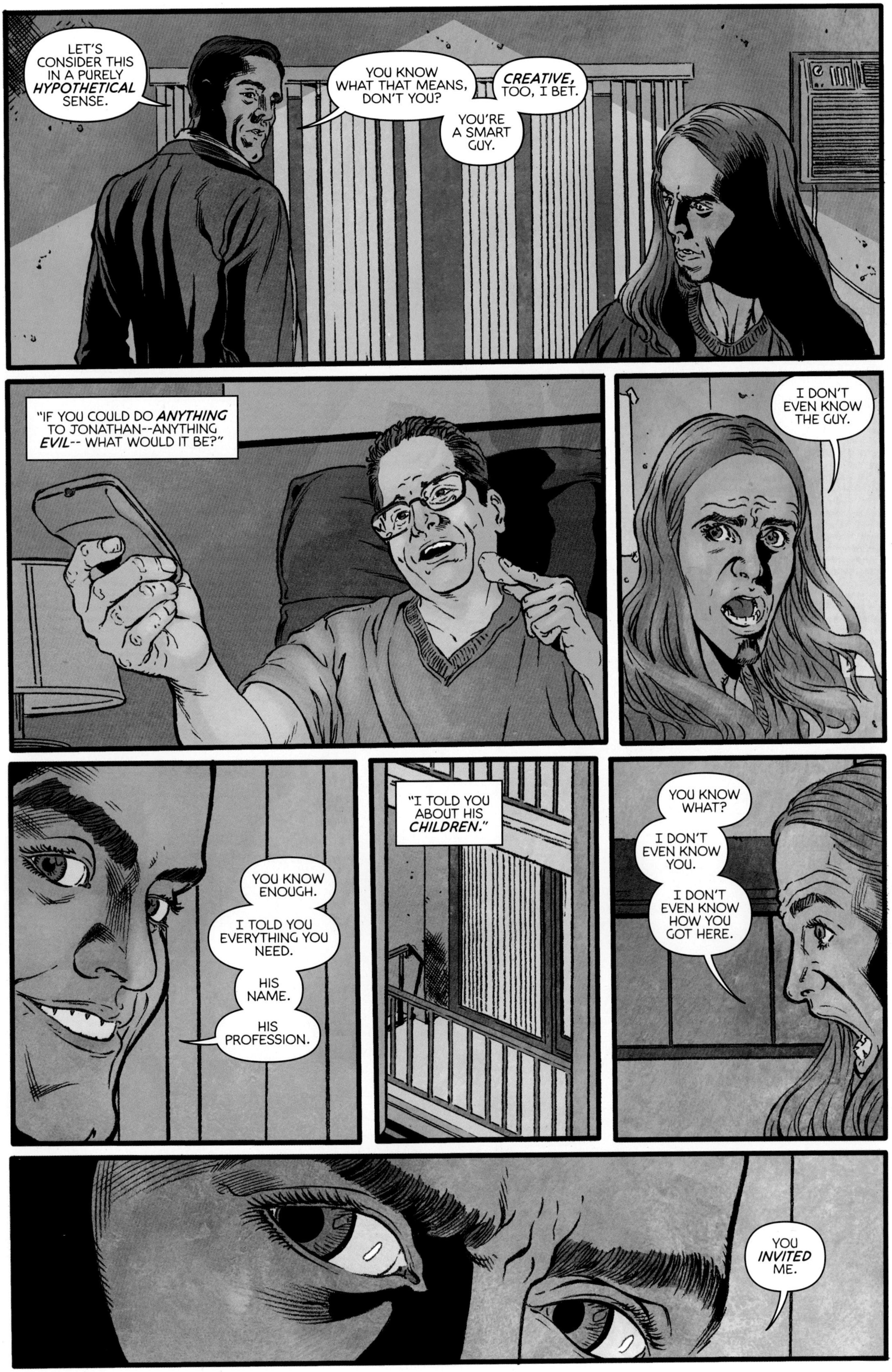
LET'S CONSIDER THIS IN A PURELY HYPOTHETICAL SENSE.
YOU KNOW WHAT THAT MEANS, DON'T YOU?
YOU'RE A SMART GUY.
CREATIVE, TOO, I BET.
"IF YOU COULD DO ANYTHING TO JONATHAN--ANYTHING EVIL-- WHAT WOULD IT BE?"
I DON'T EVEN KNOW THE GUY.
YOU KNOW ENOUGH.
I TOLD YOU EVERYTHING YOU NEED.
HIS NAME.
HIS PROFESSION.
"I TOLD YOU ABOUT HIS CHILDREN."
YOU KNOW WHAT?
I DON'T EVEN KNOW YOU.
I DON'T EVEN KNOW HOW YOU GOT HERE.
YOU INVITED ME.

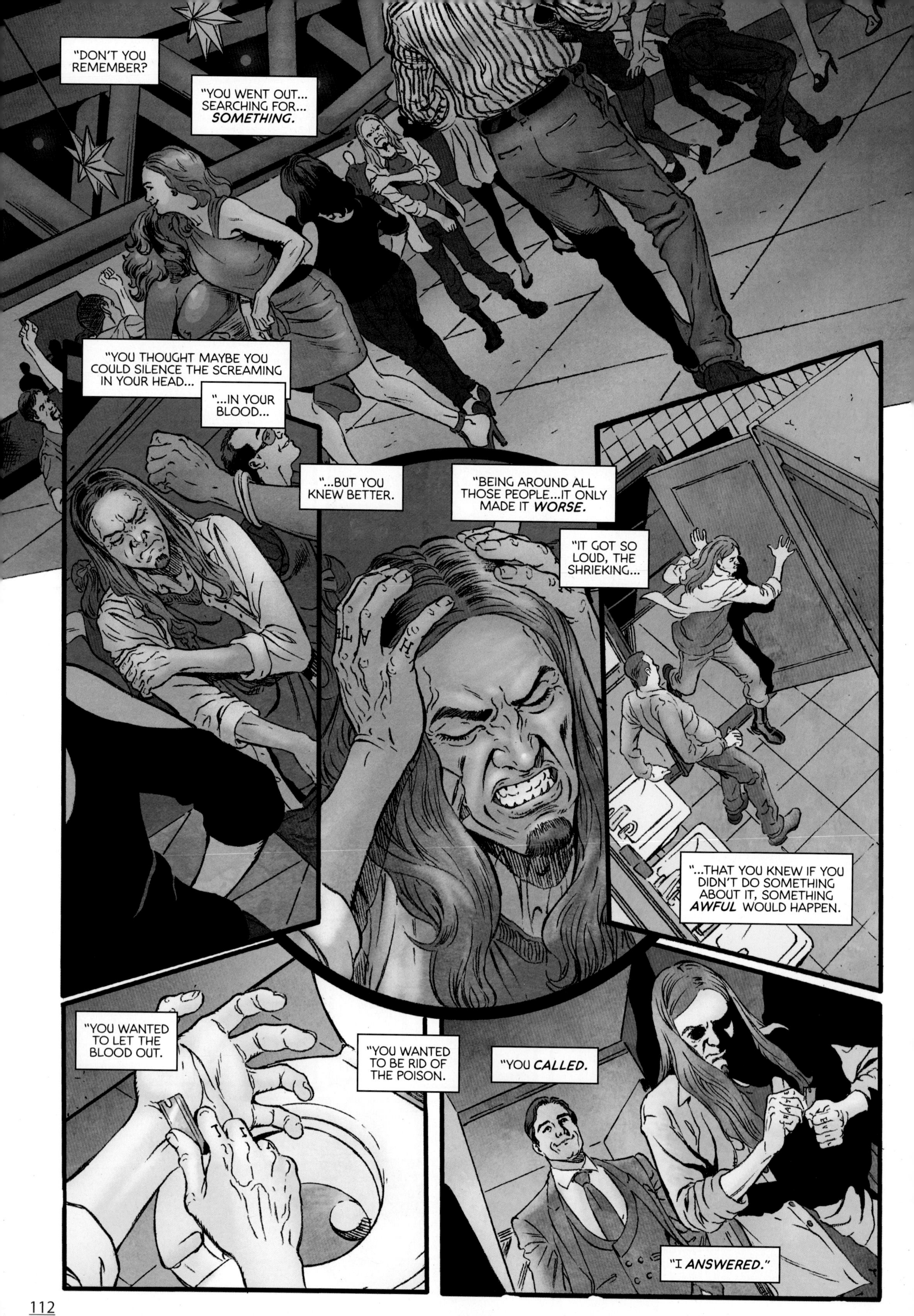
"DON'T YOU REMEMBER?
"YOU WENT OUT... SEARCHING FOR... SOMETHING.
"YOU THOUGHT MAYBE YOU COULD SILENCE THE SCREAMING IN YOUR HEAD...
"...IN YOUR BLOOD...
"...BUT YOU KNEW BETTER.
"BEING AROUND ALL THOSE PEOPLE...IT ONLY MADE IT WORSE.
"IT GOT SO LOUD, THE SHRIEKING...
"...THAT YOU KNEW IF YOU DIDN'T DO SOMETHING ABOUT IT, SOMETHING AWFUL WOULD HAPPEN.
"YOU WANTED TO LET THE BLOOD OUT.
"YOU WANTED TO BE RID OF THE POISON.
"YOU CALLED.
"I ANSWERED."

I DIDN'T--

SEE FOR YOURSELF.

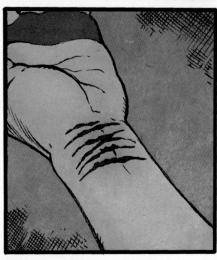

SO. SHOW ME.

SHOW ME HOW *EVIL* YOU ARE.

I'M NOT--

OH! THAT'S *GOOD.*

WHAT A *WONDERFUL* SUGGESTION.

I DIDN'T SAY ANYTHING.

YOU DIDN'T NEED TO.

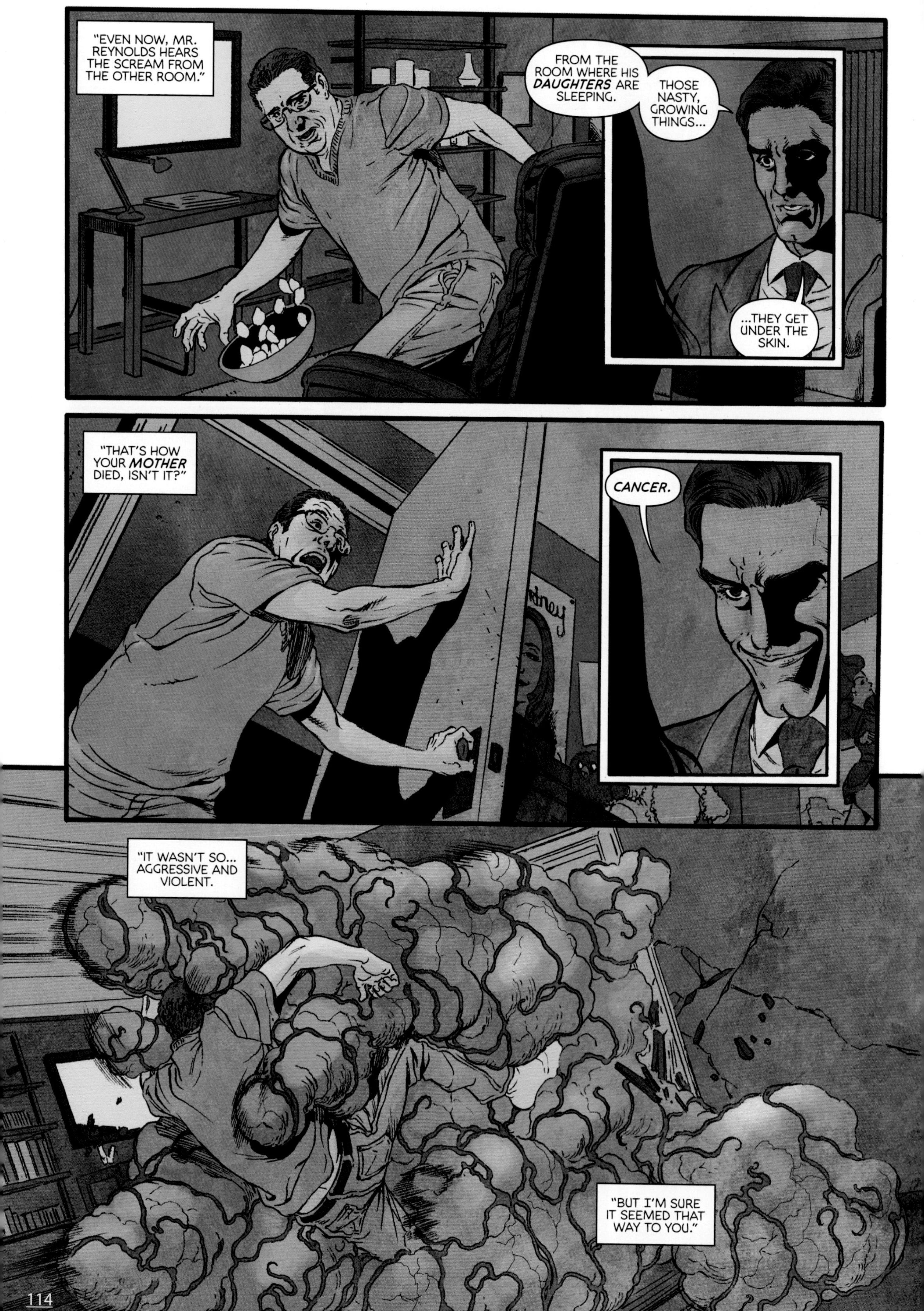
"EVEN NOW, MR. REYNOLDS HEARS THE SCREAM FROM THE OTHER ROOM."
FROM THE ROOM WHERE HIS DAUGHTERS ARE SLEEPING.
THOSE NASTY, GROWING THINGS...
...THEY GET UNDER THE SKIN.
"THAT'S HOW YOUR MOTHER DIED, ISN'T IT?"
CANCER.
"IT WASN'T SO... AGGRESSIVE AND VIOLENT.
"BUT I'M SURE IT SEEMED THAT WAY TO YOU."

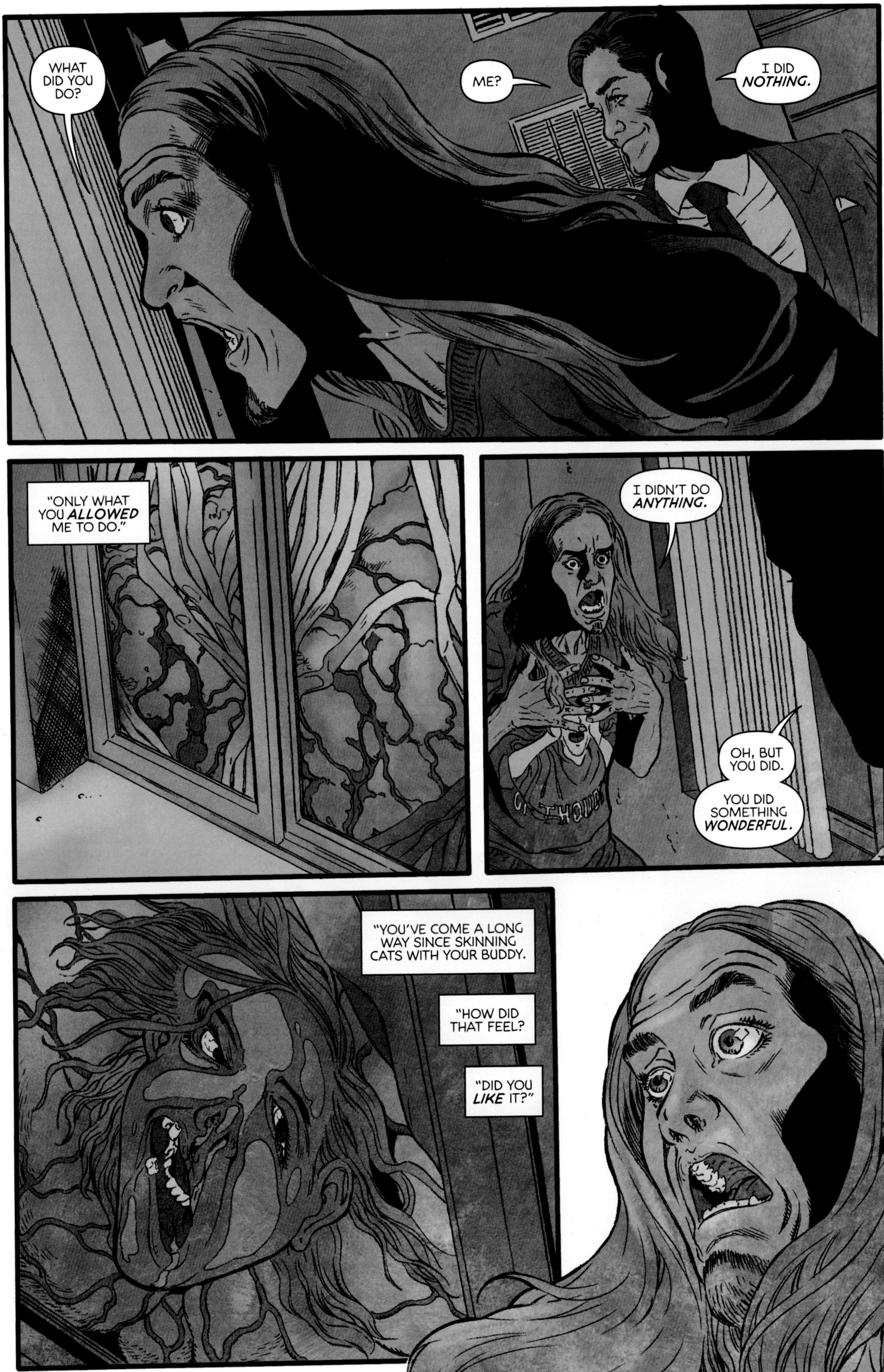
WHAT DID YOU DO?
ME?
I DID *NOTHING.*
"ONLY WHAT YOU *ALLOWED* ME TO DO."
I DIDN'T DO *ANYTHING.*
OH, BUT YOU DID.
YOU DID SOMETHING *WONDERFUL.*
"YOU'VE COME A LONG WAY SINCE SKINNING CATS WITH YOUR BUDDY.
"HOW DID THAT FEEL?
"DID YOU *LIKE* IT?"

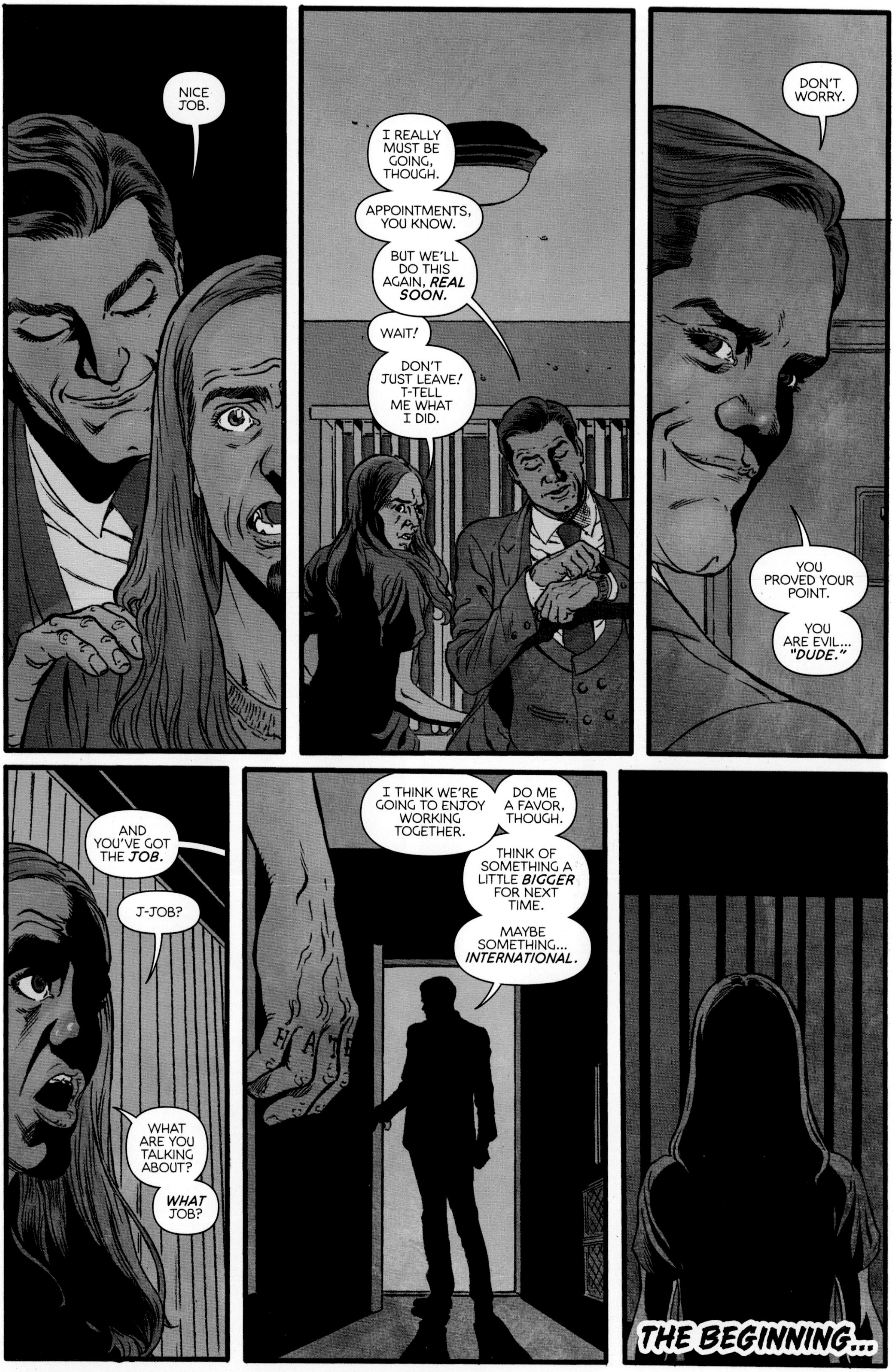
NICE JOB.
I REALLY MUST BE GOING, THOUGH.
APPOINTMENTS, YOU KNOW.
BUT WE'LL DO THIS AGAIN, *REAL SOON.*
WAIT!
DON'T JUST LEAVE! T-TELL ME WHAT I DID.
DON'T WORRY.
YOU PROVED YOUR POINT.
YOU ARE EVIL... *"DUDE."*
AND YOU'VE GOT THE *JOB.*
J-JOB?
WHAT ARE YOU TALKING ABOUT?
WHAT JOB?
I THINK WE'RE GOING TO ENJOY WORKING TOGETHER.
DO ME A FAVOR, THOUGH.
THINK OF SOMETHING A LITTLE *BIGGER* FOR NEXT TIME.
MAYBE SOMETHING... *INTERNATIONAL.*
THE BEGINNING...

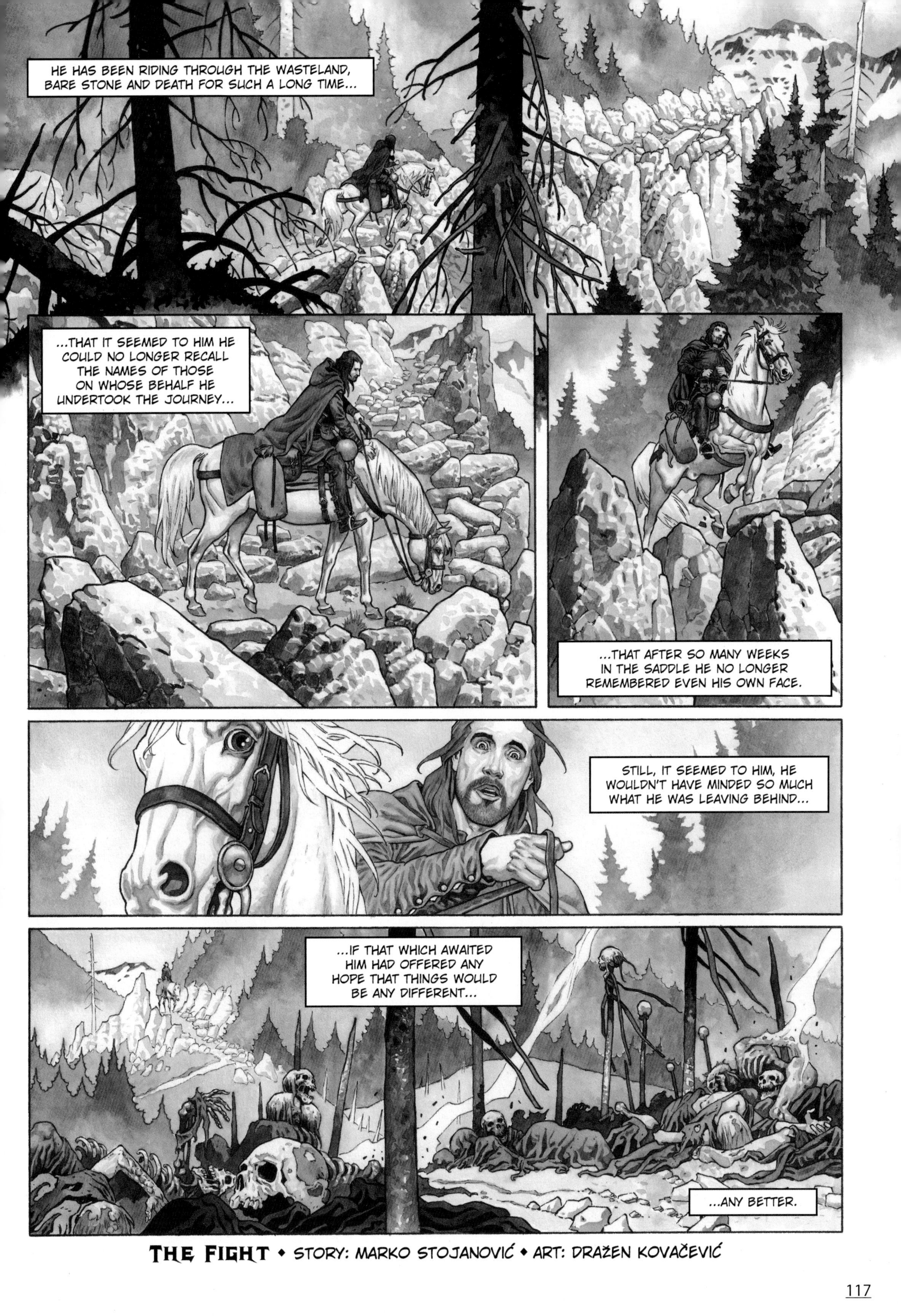
HE HAS BEEN RIDING THROUGH THE WASTELAND, BARE STONE AND DEATH FOR SUCH A LONG TIME...
...THAT IT SEEMED TO HIM HE COULD NO LONGER RECALL THE NAMES OF THOSE ON WHOSE BEHALF HE UNDERTOOK THE JOURNEY...
...THAT AFTER SO MANY WEEKS IN THE SADDLE HE NO LONGER REMEMBERED EVEN HIS OWN FACE.
STILL, IT SEEMED TO HIM, HE WOULDN'T HAVE MINDED SO MUCH WHAT HE WAS LEAVING BEHIND...
...IF THAT WHICH AWAITED HIM HAD OFFERED ANY HOPE THAT THINGS WOULD BE ANY DIFFERENT...
...ANY BETTER.

THE FIGHT • STORY: MARKO STOJANOVIĆ • ART: DRAŽEN KOVAČEVIĆ

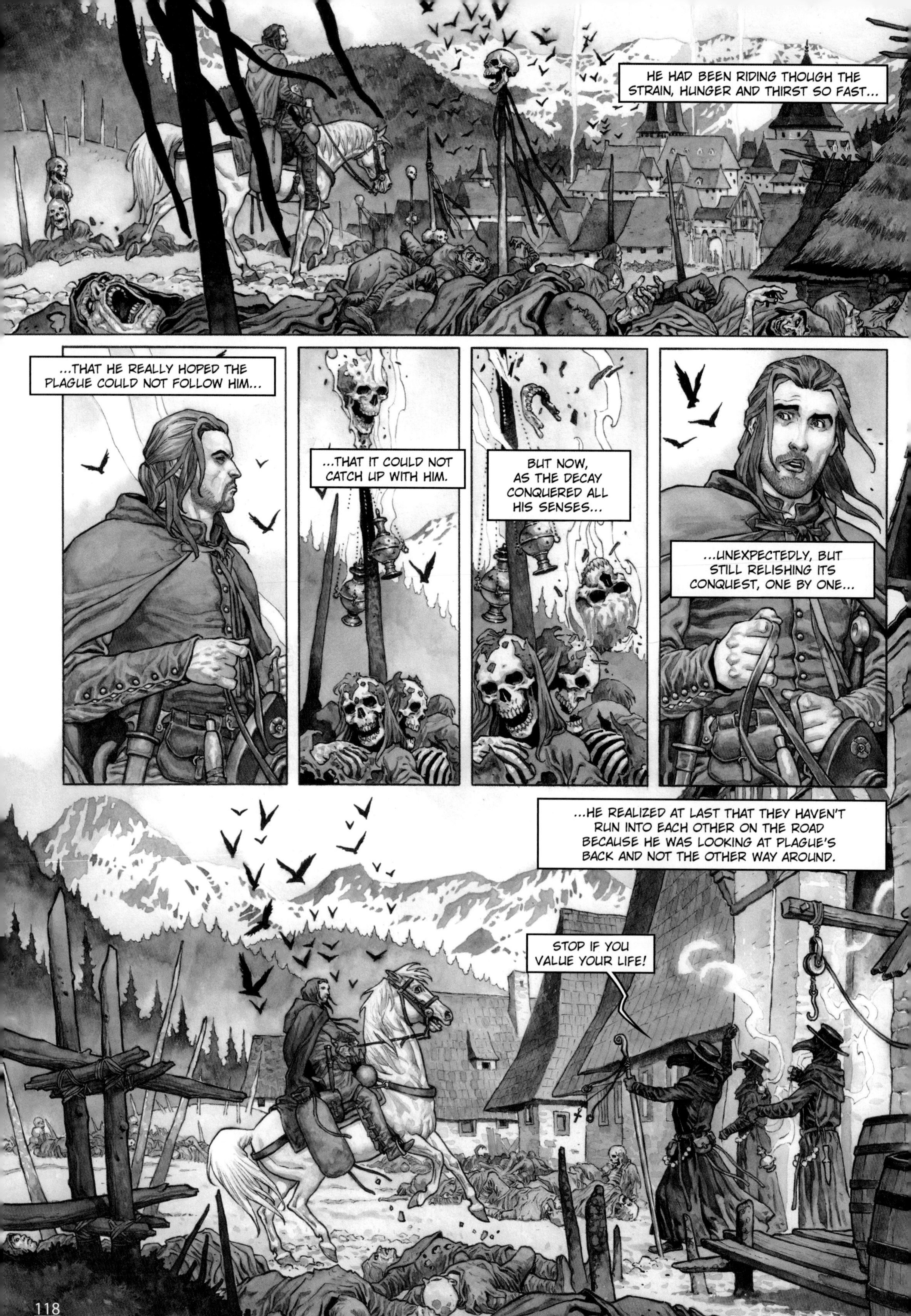

HE HAD BEEN RIDING THOUGH THE STRAIN, HUNGER AND THIRST SO FAST...
...THAT HE REALLY HOPED THE PLAGUE COULD NOT FOLLOW HIM...
...THAT IT COULD NOT CATCH UP WITH HIM.
BUT NOW, AS THE DECAY CONQUERED ALL HIS SENSES...
...UNEXPECTEDLY, BUT STILL RELISHING ITS CONQUEST, ONE BY ONE...
...HE REALIZED AT LAST THAT THEY HAVEN'T RUN INTO EACH OTHER ON THE ROAD BECAUSE HE WAS LOOKING AT PLAGUE'S BACK AND NOT THE OTHER WAY AROUND.
STOP IF YOU VALUE YOUR LIFE!

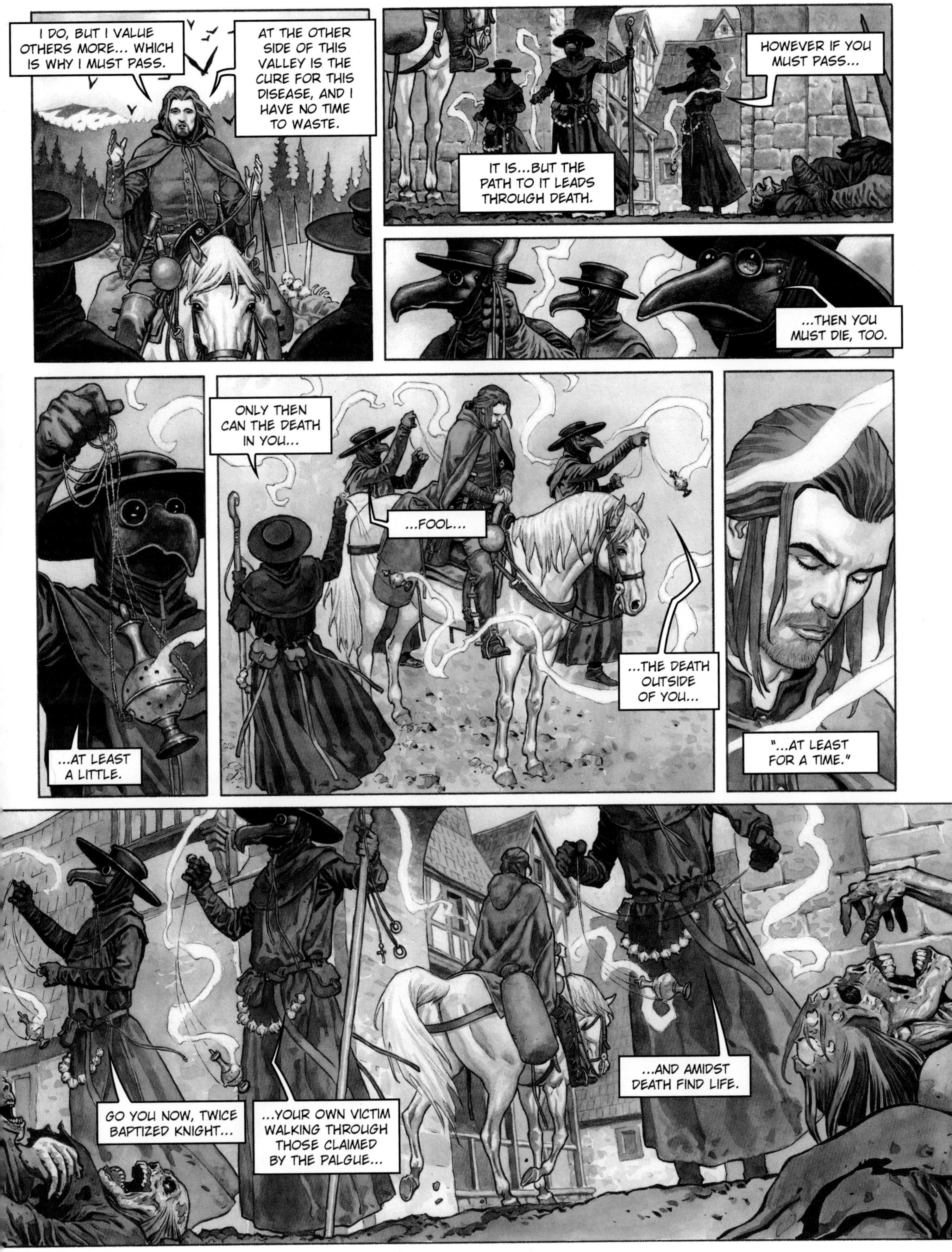

I DO, BUT I VALUE OTHERS MORE... WHICH IS WHY I MUST PASS.
AT THE OTHER SIDE OF THIS VALLEY IS THE CURE FOR THIS DISEASE, AND I HAVE NO TIME TO WASTE.
IT IS...BUT THE PATH TO IT LEADS THROUGH DEATH.
HOWEVER IF YOU MUST PASS...
...THEN YOU MUST DIE, TOO.
...AT LEAST A LITTLE.
ONLY THEN CAN THE DEATH IN YOU...
...FOOL...
...THE DEATH OUTSIDE OF YOU...
"...AT LEAST FOR A TIME."
GO YOU NOW, TWICE BAPTIZED KNIGHT...
...YOUR OWN VICTIM WALKING THROUGH THOSE CLAIMED BY THE PALGUE...
...AND AMIDST DEATH FIND LIFE.

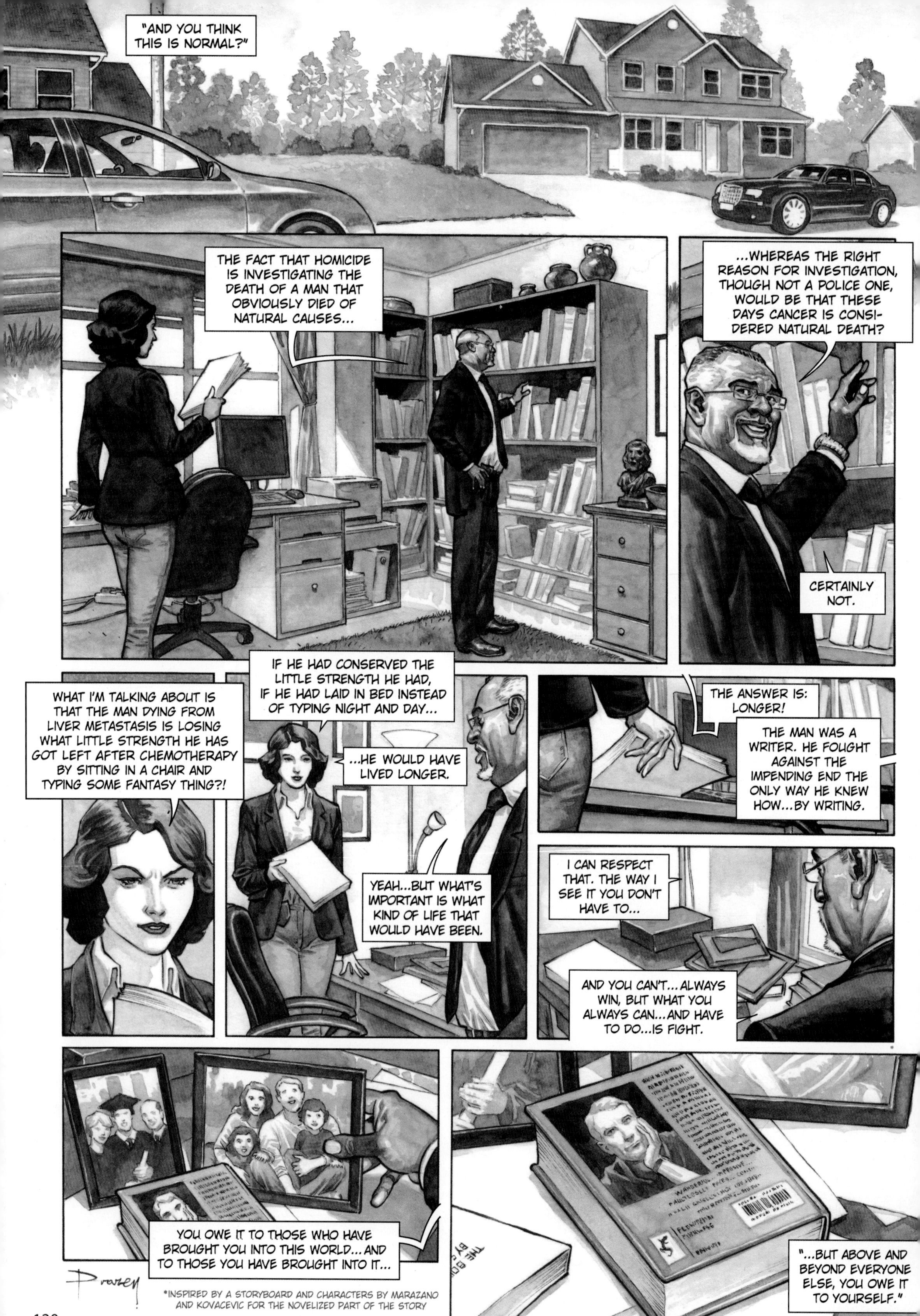
"AND YOU THINK THIS IS NORMAL?"
THE FACT THAT HOMICIDE IS INVESTIGATING THE DEATH OF A MAN THAT OBVIOUSLY DIED OF NATURAL CAUSES...
...WHEREAS THE RIGHT REASON FOR INVESTIGATION, THOUGH NOT A POLICE ONE, WOULD BE THAT THESE DAYS CANCER IS CONSI-DERED NATURAL DEATH?
CERTAINLY NOT.
WHAT I'M TALKING ABOUT IS THAT THE MAN DYING FROM LIVER METASTASIS IS LOSING WHAT LITTLE STRENGTH HE HAS GOT LEFT AFTER CHEMOTHERAPY BY SITTING IN A CHAIR AND TYPING SOME FANTASY THING?!
IF HE HAD CONSERVED THE LITTLE STRENGTH HE HAD, IF HE HAD LAID IN BED INSTEAD OF TYPING NIGHT AND DAY...
...HE WOULD HAVE LIVED LONGER.
YEAH...BUT WHAT'S IMPORTANT IS WHAT KIND OF LIFE THAT WOULD HAVE BEEN.
THE ANSWER IS: LONGER!
THE MAN WAS A WRITER. HE FOUGHT AGAINST THE IMPENDING END THE ONLY WAY HE KNEW HOW...BY WRITING.
I CAN RESPECT THAT. THE WAY I SEE IT YOU DON'T HAVE TO...
AND YOU CAN'T...ALWAYS WIN, BUT WHAT YOU ALWAYS CAN...AND HAVE TO DO...IS FIGHT.
YOU OWE IT TO THOSE WHO HAVE BROUGHT YOU INTO THIS WORLD...AND TO THOSE YOU HAVE BROUGHT INTO IT...
"...BUT ABOVE AND BEYOND EVERYONE ELSE, YOU OWE IT TO YOURSELF."
Drazen

*INSPIRED BY A STORYBOARD AND CHARACTERS BY MARAZANO AND KOVACEVIC FOR THE NOVELIZED PART OF THE STORY

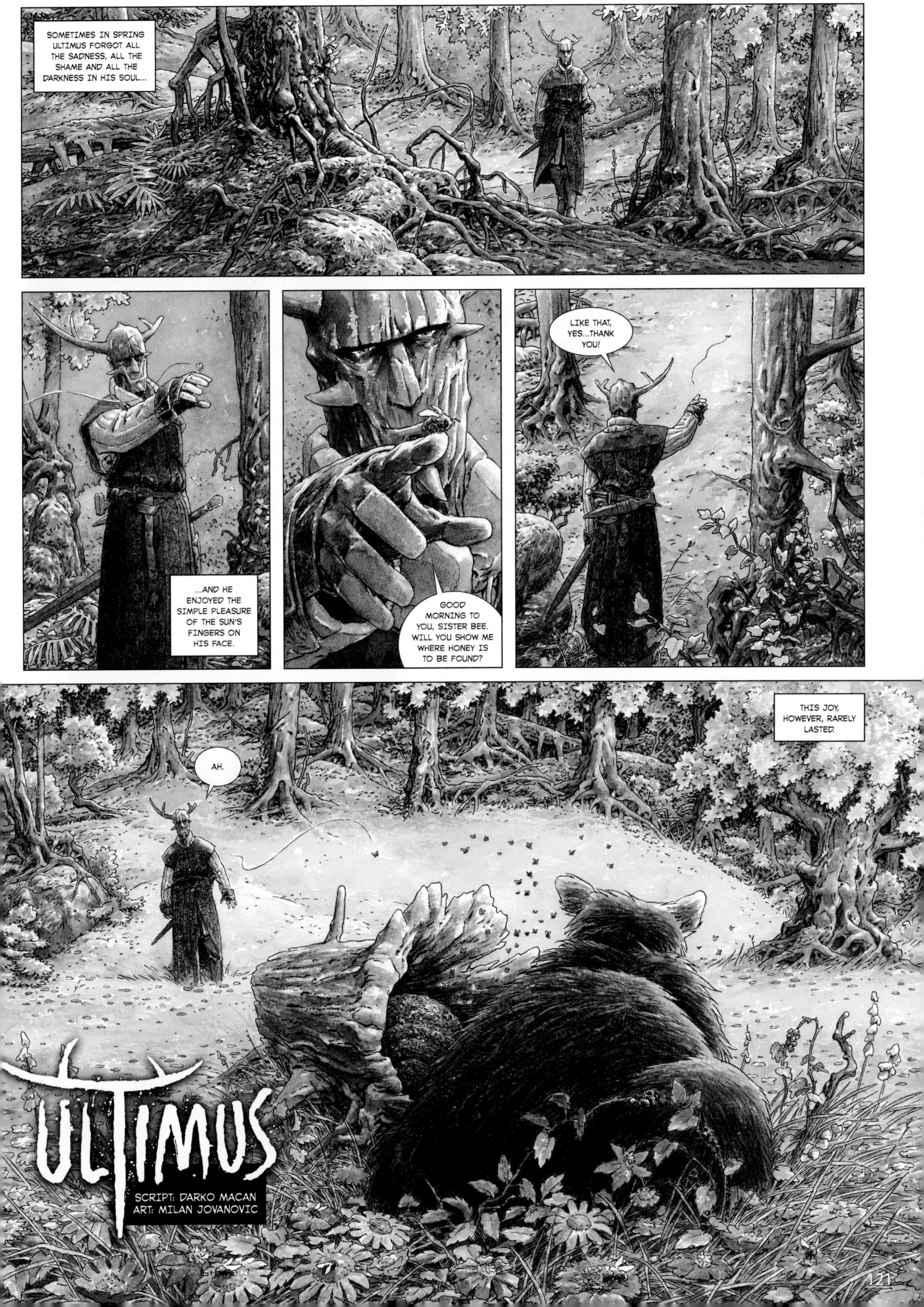

SOMETIMES IN SPRING ULTIMUS FORGOT ALL THE SADNESS, ALL THE SHAME AND ALL THE DARKNESS IN HIS SOUL...
...AND HE ENJOYED THE SIMPLE PLEASURE OF THE SUN'S FINGERS ON HIS FACE.
GOOD MORNING TO YOU, SISTER BEE. WILL YOU SHOW ME WHERE HONEY IS TO BE FOUND?
LIKE THAT, YES...THANK YOU!
THIS JOY, HOWEVER, RARELY LASTED.
AH.
ULTIMUS
SCRIPT: DARKO MACAN
ART: MILAN JOVANOVIC

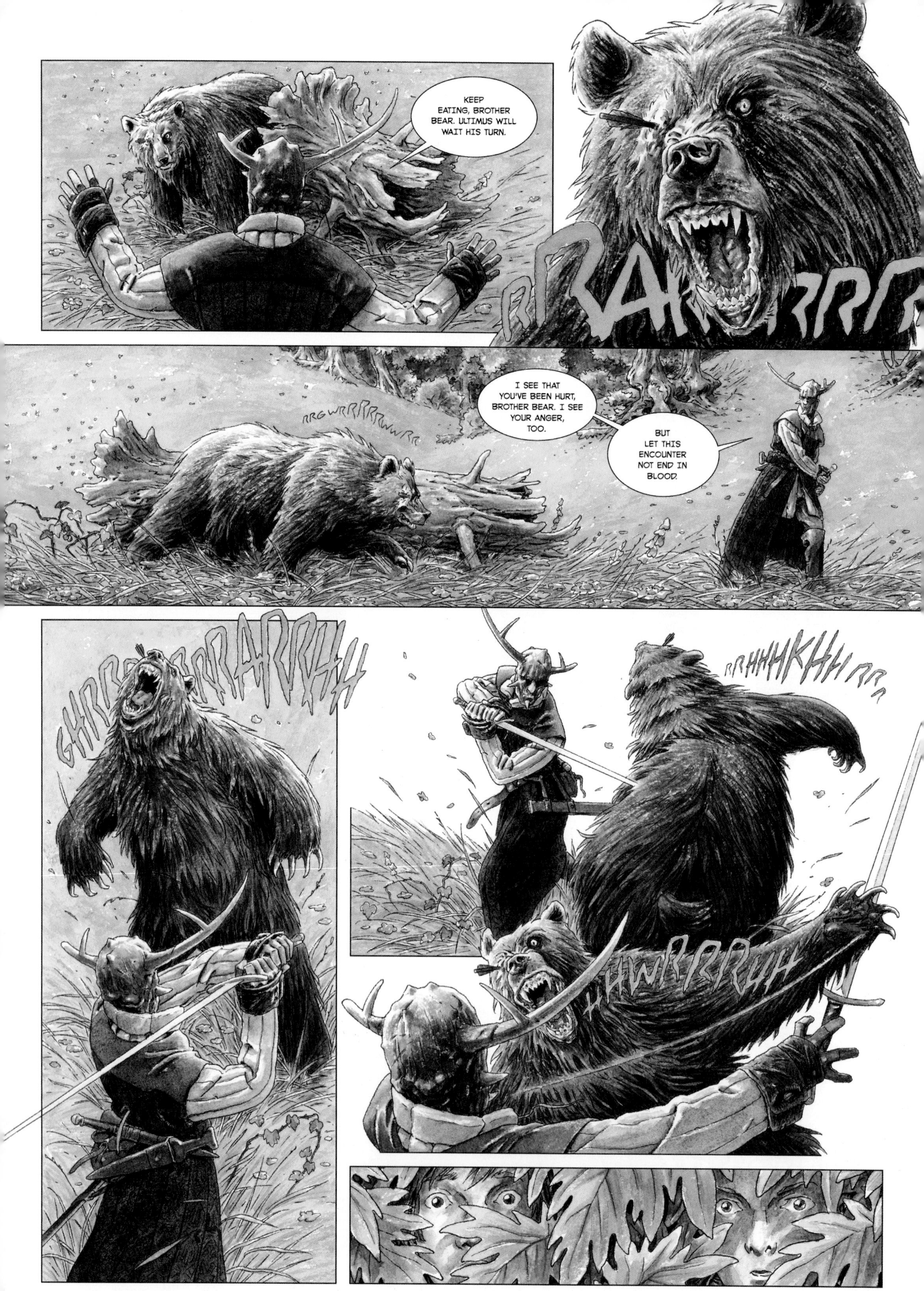
KEEP EATING, BROTHER BEAR. ULTIMUS WILL WAIT HIS TURN.
I SEE THAT YOU'VE BEEN HURT, BROTHER BEAR. I SEE YOUR ANGER, TOO.
BUT LET THIS ENCOUNTER NOT END IN BLOOD.

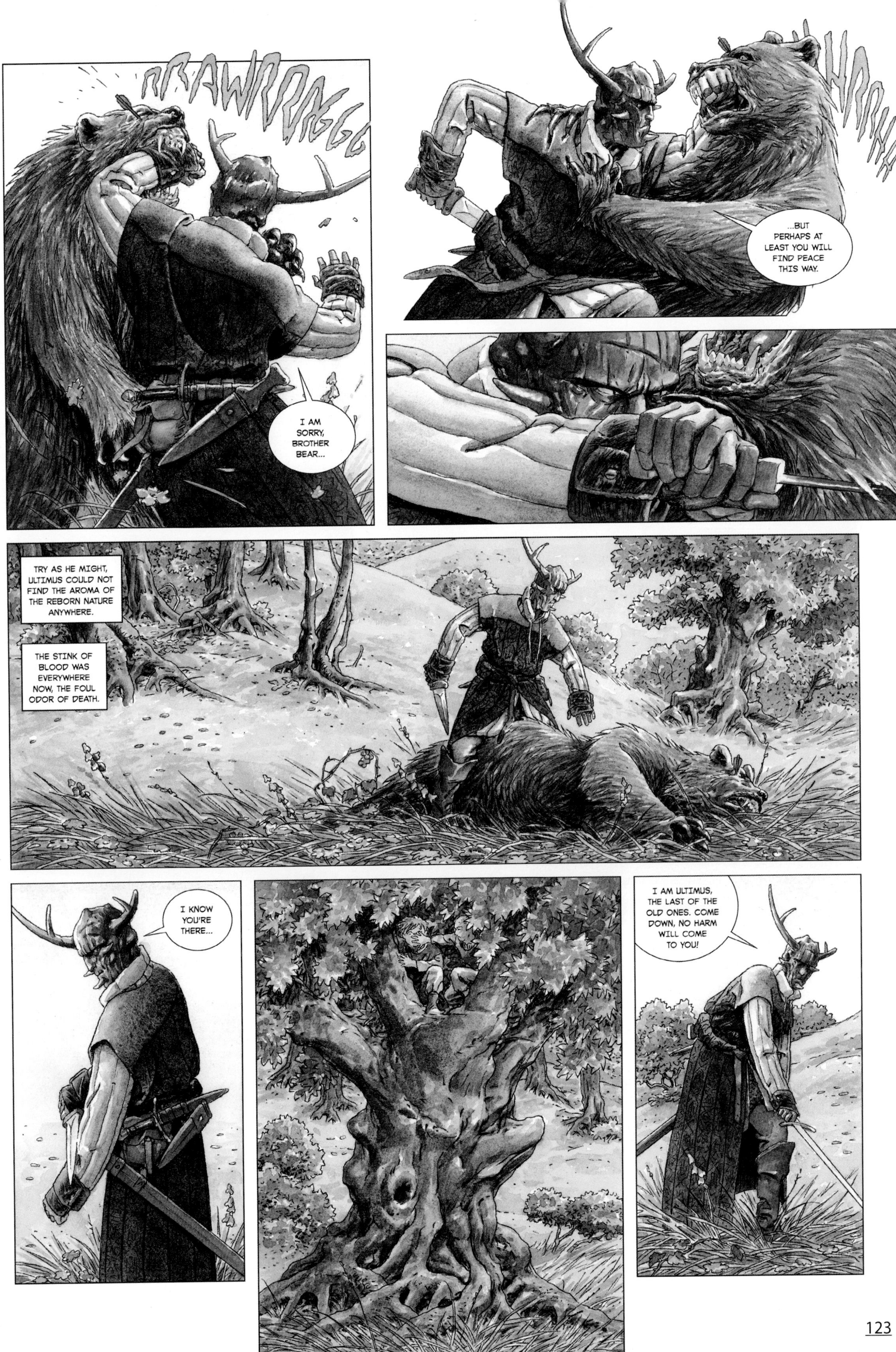
RRAWRRRGG
I AM SORRY, BROTHER BEAR...
...BUT PERHAPS AT LEAST YOU WILL FIND PEACE THIS WAY.
TRY AS HE MIGHT, ULTIMUS COULD NOT FIND THE AROMA OF THE REBORN NATURE ANYWHERE.
THE STINK OF BLOOD WAS EVERYWHERE NOW, THE FOUL ODOR OF DEATH.
I KNOW YOU'RE THERE...
I AM ULTIMUS, THE LAST OF THE OLD ONES. COME DOWN, NO HARM WILL COME TO YOU!

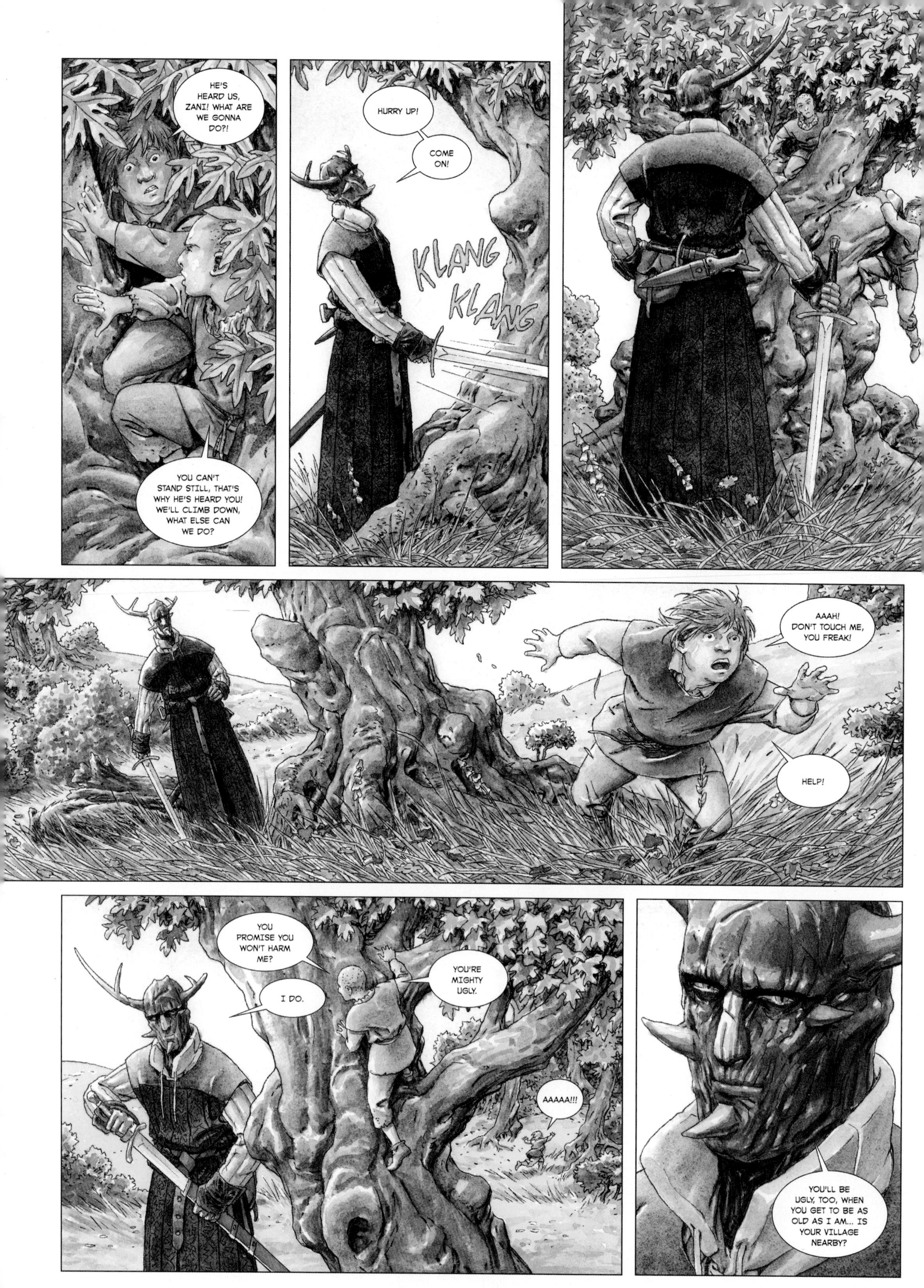
HE'S HEARD US, ZANI! WHAT ARE WE GONNA DO?!
YOU CAN'T STAND STILL, THAT'S WHY HE'S HEARD YOU! WE'LL CLIMB DOWN, WHAT ELSE CAN WE DO?
HURRY UP!
COME ON!
KLANG
KLANG
AAAH! DON'T TOUCH ME, YOU FREAK!
HELP!
YOU PROMISE YOU WON'T HARM ME?
I DO.
YOU'RE MIGHTY UGLY.
AAAAA!!!
YOU'LL BE UGLY, TOO, WHEN YOU GET TO BE AS OLD AS I AM... IS YOUR VILLAGE NEARBY?

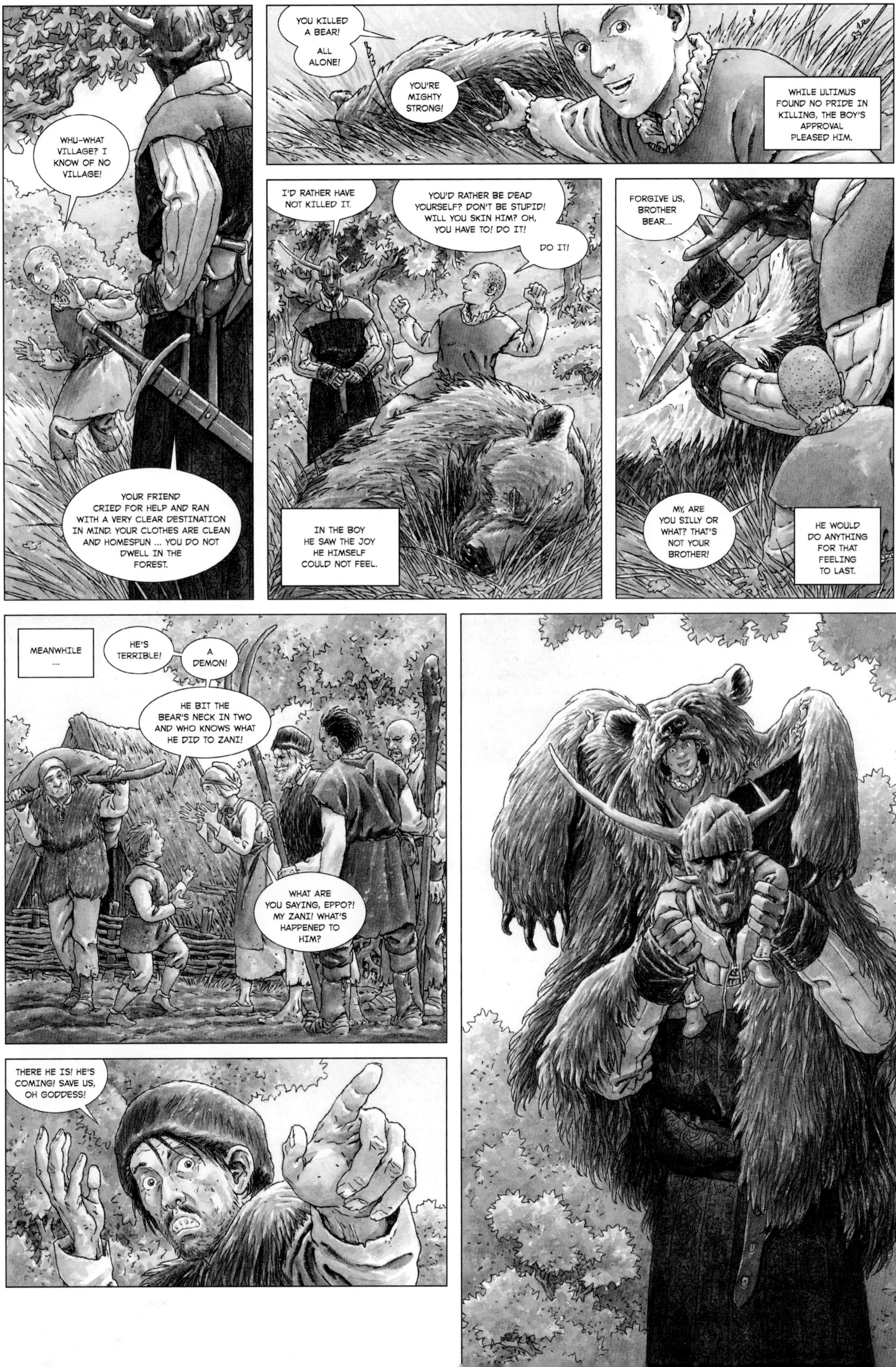
WHU-WHAT VILLAGE? I KNOW OF NO VILLAGE!
YOUR FRIEND CRIED FOR HELP AND RAN WITH A VERY CLEAR DESTINATION IN MIND. YOUR CLOTHES ARE CLEAN AND HOMESPUN ... YOU DO NOT DWELL IN THE FOREST.
YOU KILLED A BEAR!
ALL ALONE!
YOU'RE MIGHTY STRONG!
WHILE ULTIMUS FOUND NO PRIDE IN KILLING, THE BOY'S APPROVAL PLEASED HIM.
I'D RATHER HAVE NOT KILLED IT.
YOU'D RATHER BE DEAD YOURSELF? DON'T BE STUPID! WILL YOU SKIN HIM? OH, YOU HAVE TO! DO IT!
DO IT!
IN THE BOY HE SAW THE JOY HE HIMSELF COULD NOT FEEL.
FORGIVE US, BROTHER BEAR...
MY, ARE YOU SILLY OR WHAT? THAT'S NOT YOUR BROTHER!
HE WOULD DO ANYTHING FOR THAT FEELING TO LAST.
MEANWHILE ...
HE'S TERRIBLE!
A DEMON!
HE BIT THE BEAR'S NECK IN TWO AND WHO KNOWS WHAT HE DID TO ZANI!
WHAT ARE YOU SAYING, EPPO?! MY ZANI! WHAT'S HAPPENED TO HIM?
THERE HE IS! HE'S COMING! SAVE US, OH GODDESS!

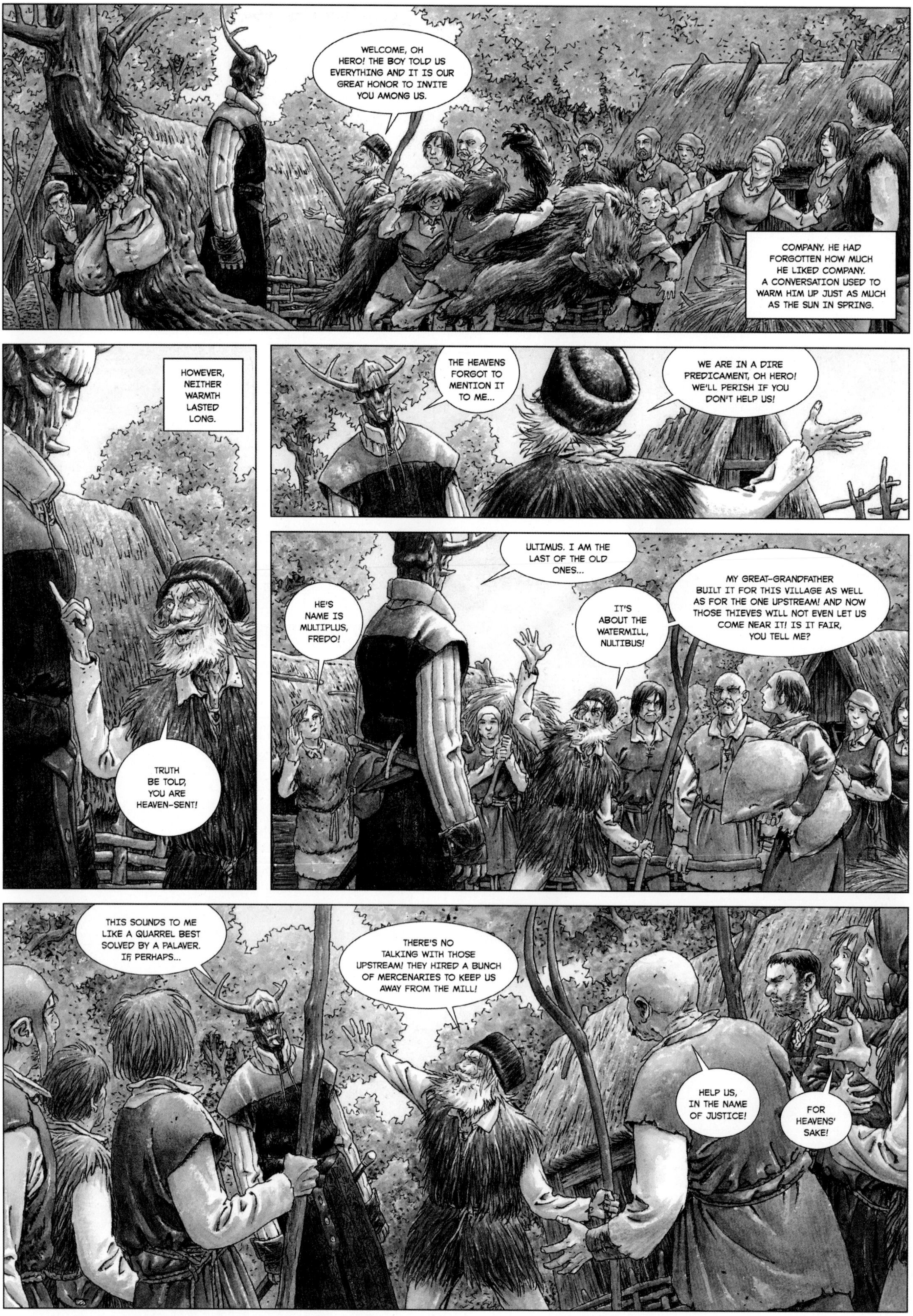
WELCOME, OH HERO! THE BOY TOLD US EVERYTHING AND IT IS OUR GREAT HONOR TO INVITE YOU AMONG US.
COMPANY. HE HAD FORGOTTEN HOW MUCH HE LIKED COMPANY. A CONVERSATION USED TO WARM HIM UP JUST AS MUCH AS THE SUN IN SPRING.
HOWEVER, NEITHER WARMTH LASTED LONG.
TRUTH BE TOLD, YOU ARE HEAVEN-SENT!
THE HEAVENS FORGOT TO MENTION IT TO ME...
WE ARE IN A DIRE PREDICAMENT, OH HERO! WE'LL PERISH IF YOU DON'T HELP US!
ULTIMUS. I AM THE LAST OF THE OLD ONES...
HE'S NAME IS MULTIPLUS, FREDO!
IT'S ABOUT THE WATERMILL, NULTIBUS!
MY GREAT-GRANDFATHER BUILT IT FOR THIS VILLAGE AS WELL AS FOR THE ONE UPSTREAM! AND NOW THOSE THIEVES WILL NOT EVEN LET US COME NEAR IT! IS IT FAIR, YOU TELL ME?
THIS SOUNDS TO ME LIKE A QUARREL BEST SOLVED BY A PALAVER. IF, PERHAPS...
THERE'S NO TALKING WITH THOSE UPSTREAM! THEY HIRED A BUNCH OF MERCENARIES TO KEEP US AWAY FROM THE MILL!
HELP US, IN THE NAME OF JUSTICE!
FOR HEAVENS' SAKE!

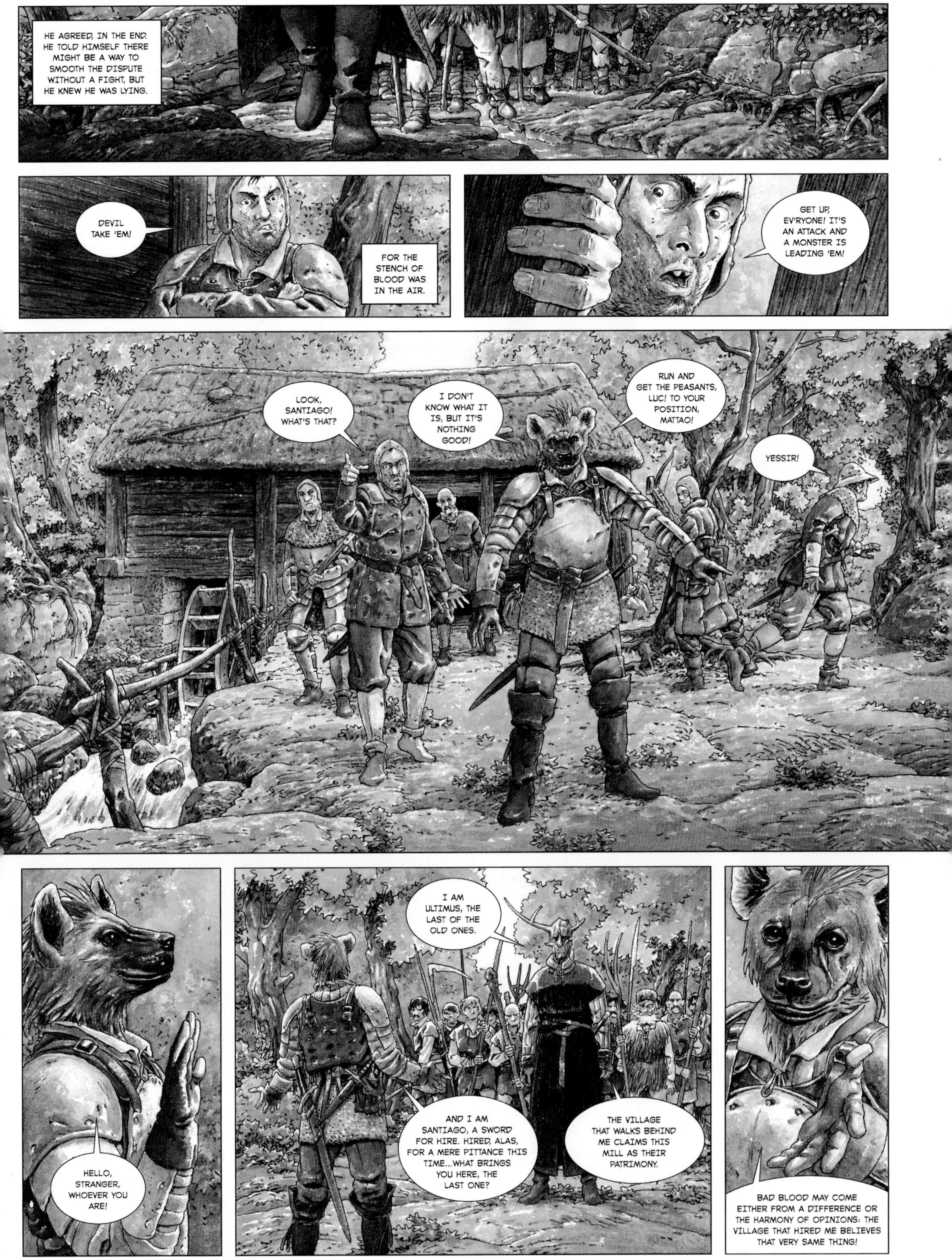
HE AGREED, IN THE END. HE TOLD HIMSELF THERE MIGHT BE A WAY TO SMOOTH THE DISPUTE WITHOUT A FIGHT, BUT HE KNEW HE WAS LYING.
DEVIL TAKE 'EM!
FOR THE STENCH OF BLOOD WAS IN THE AIR.
GET UP, EV'RYONE! IT'S AN ATTACK AND A MONSTER IS LEADING 'EM!
LOOK, SANTIAGO! WHAT'S THAT?
I DON'T KNOW WHAT IT IS, BUT IT'S NOTHING GOOD!
RUN AND GET THE PEASANTS, LUC! TO YOUR POSITION, MATTAO!
YESSIR!
HELLO, STRANGER, WHOEVER YOU ARE!
I AM ULTIMUS, THE LAST OF THE OLD ONES.
AND I AM SANTIAGO, A SWORD FOR HIRE. HIRED, ALAS, FOR A MERE PITTANCE THIS TIME...WHAT BRINGS YOU HERE, THE LAST ONE?
THE VILLAGE THAT WALKS BEHIND ME CLAIMS THIS MILL AS THEIR PATRIMONY.
BAD BLOOD MAY COME EITHER FROM A DIFFERENCE OR THE HARMONY OF OPINIONS: THE VILLAGE THAT HIRED ME BELIEVES THAT VERY SAME THING!

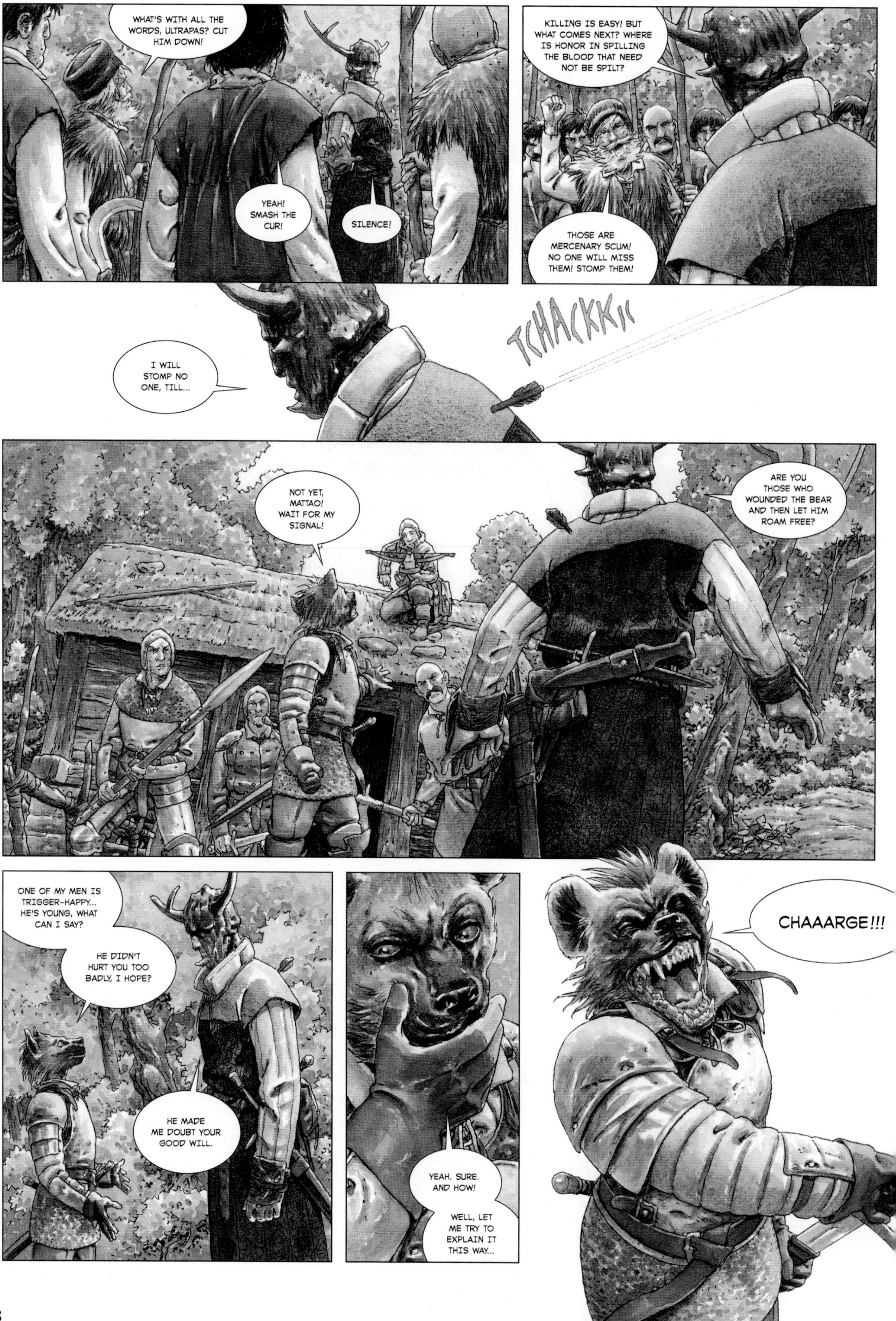

WHAT'S WITH ALL THE WORDS, ULTRAPAS? CUT HIM DOWN!
YEAH! SMASH THE CUR!
SILENCE!
KILLING IS EASY! BUT WHAT COMES NEXT? WHERE IS HONOR IN SPILLING THE BLOOD THAT NEED NOT BE SPILT?
THOSE ARE MERCENARY SCUM! NO ONE WILL MISS THEM! STOMP THEM!
I WILL STOMP NO ONE, TILL...
TCHACKK!!
NOT YET, MATTAO! WAIT FOR MY SIGNAL!
ARE YOU THOSE WHO WOUNDED THE BEAR AND THEN LET HIM ROAM FREE?
ONE OF MY MEN IS TRIGGER-HAPPY... HE'S YOUNG, WHAT CAN I SAY?
HE DIDN'T HURT YOU TOO BADLY, I HOPE?
HE MADE ME DOUBT YOUR GOOD WILL.
YEAH. SURE. AND HOW!
WELL, LET ME TRY TO EXPLAIN IT THIS WAY...
CHAAARGE!!!

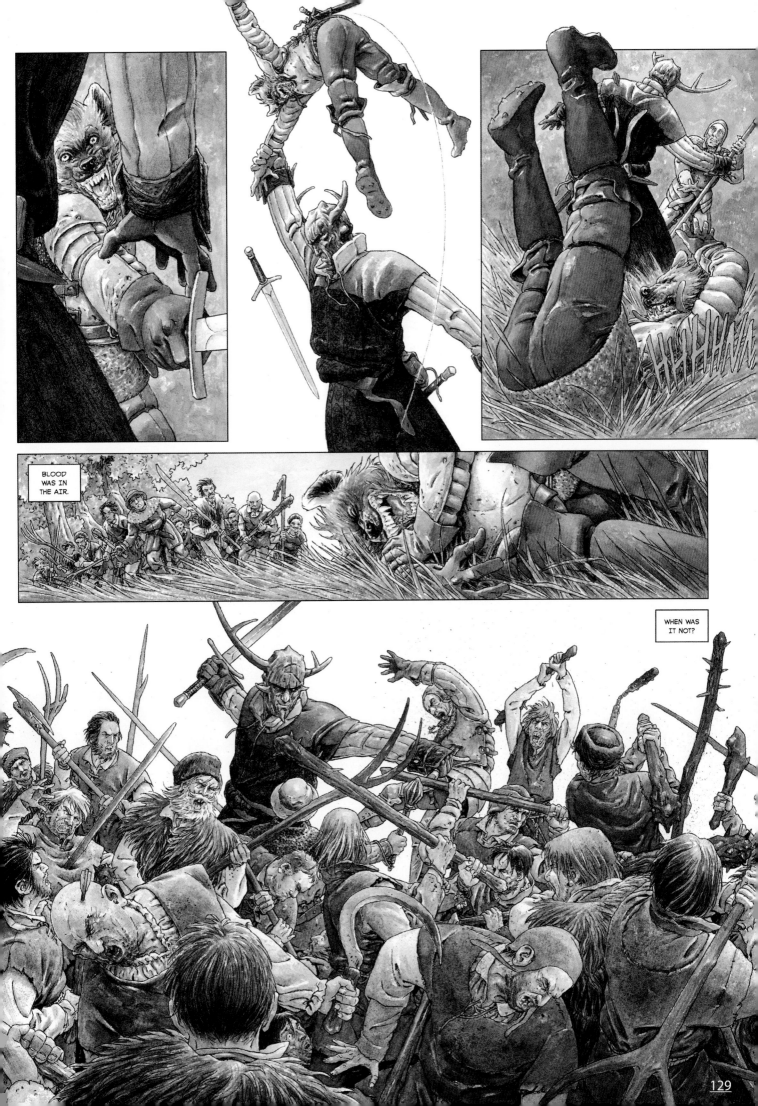

BLOOD WAS IN THE AIR.

WHEN WAS IT NOT?

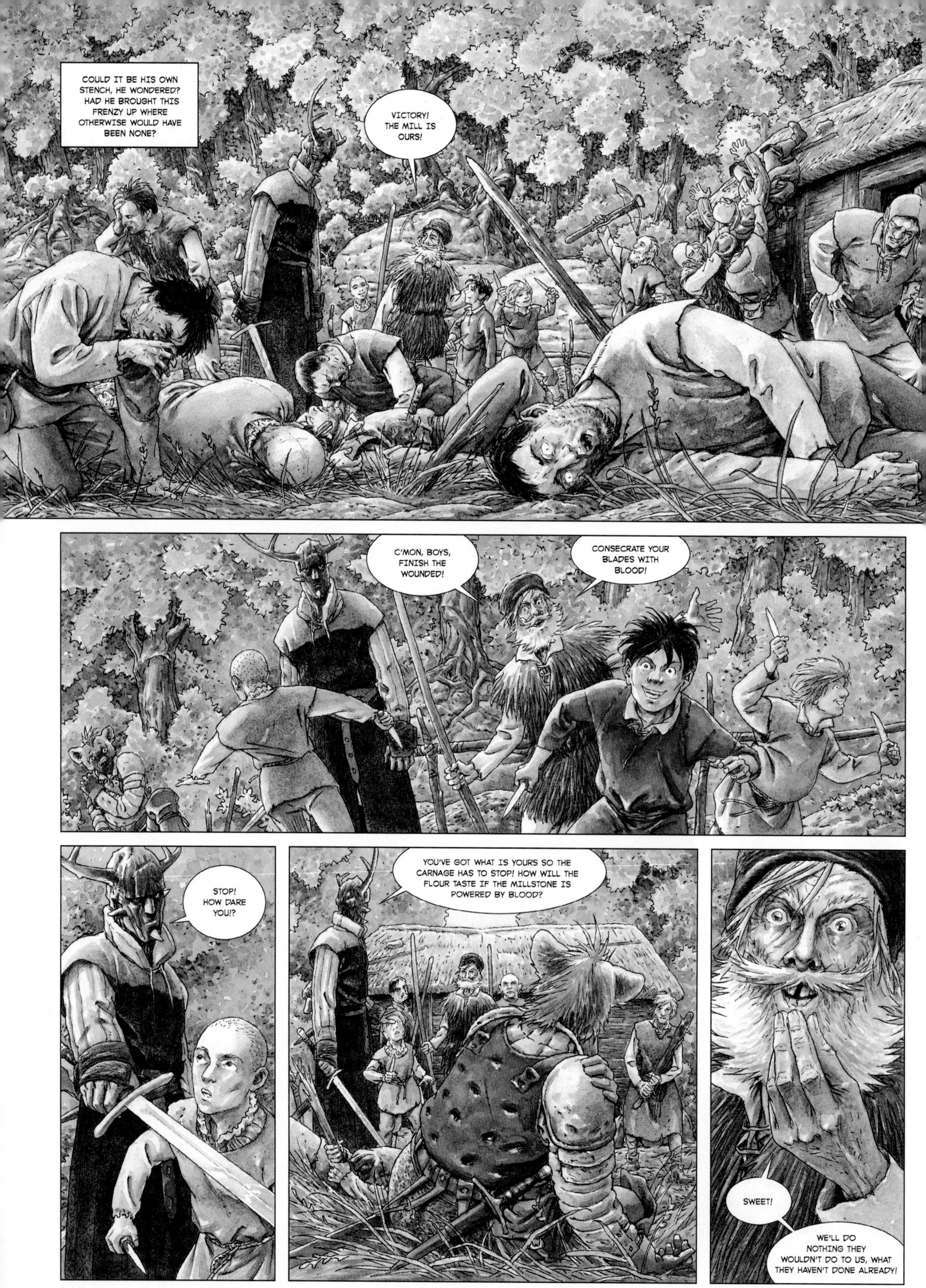
COULD IT BE HIS OWN STENCH, HE WONDERED? HAD HE BROUGHT THIS FRENZY UP WHERE OTHERWISE WOULD HAVE BEEN NONE?
VICTORY! THE MILL IS OURS!
C'MON, BOYS, FINISH THE WOUNDED!
CONSECRATE YOUR BLADES WITH BLOOD!
STOP! HOW DARE YOU!?
YOU'VE GOT WHAT IS YOURS SO THE CARNAGE HAS TO STOP! HOW WILL THE FLOUR TASTE IF THE MILLSTONE IS POWERED BY BLOOD?
SWEET!
WE'LL DO NOTHING THEY WOULDN'T DO TO US, WHAT THEY HAVEN'T DONE ALREADY!

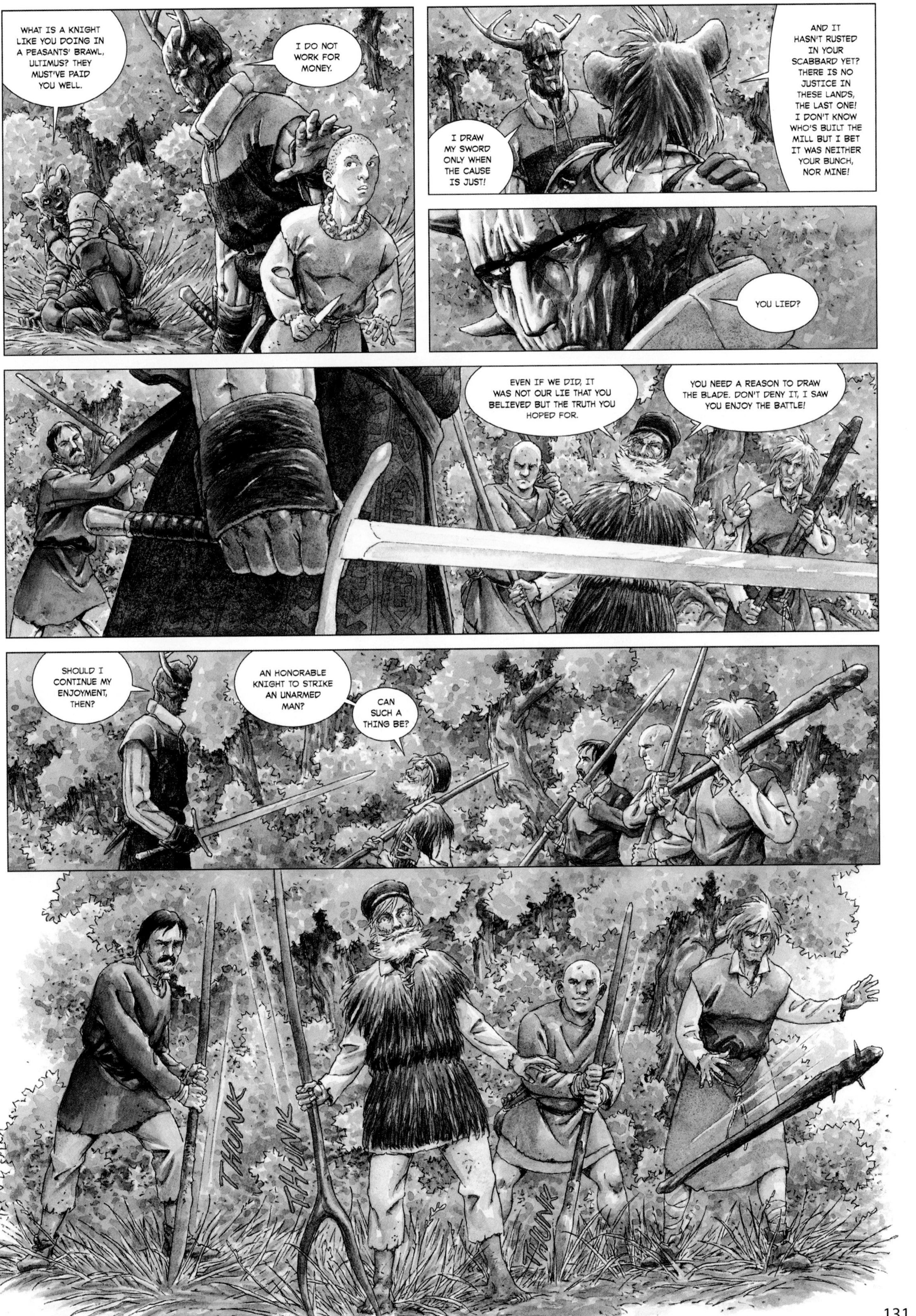
WHAT IS A KNIGHT LIKE YOU DOING IN A PEASANTS' BRAWL, ULTIMUS? THEY MUST'VE PAID YOU WELL.
I DO NOT WORK FOR MONEY.
AND IT HASN'T RUSTED IN YOUR SCABBARD YET? THERE IS NO JUSTICE IN THESE LANDS, THE LAST ONE! I DON'T KNOW WHO'S BUILT THE MILL BUT I BET IT WAS NEITHER YOUR BUNCH, NOR MINE!
I DRAW MY SWORD ONLY WHEN THE CAUSE IS JUST!
YOU LIED?
EVEN IF WE DID, IT WAS NOT OUR LIE THAT YOU BELIEVED BUT THE TRUTH YOU HOPED FOR.
YOU NEED A REASON TO DRAW THE BLADE. DON'T DENY IT, I SAW YOU ENJOY THE BATTLE!
SHOULD I CONTINUE MY ENJOYMENT, THEN?
AN HONORABLE KNIGHT TO STRIKE AN UNARMED MAN?
CAN SUCH A THING BE?
THUNK
THUNK
THUNK

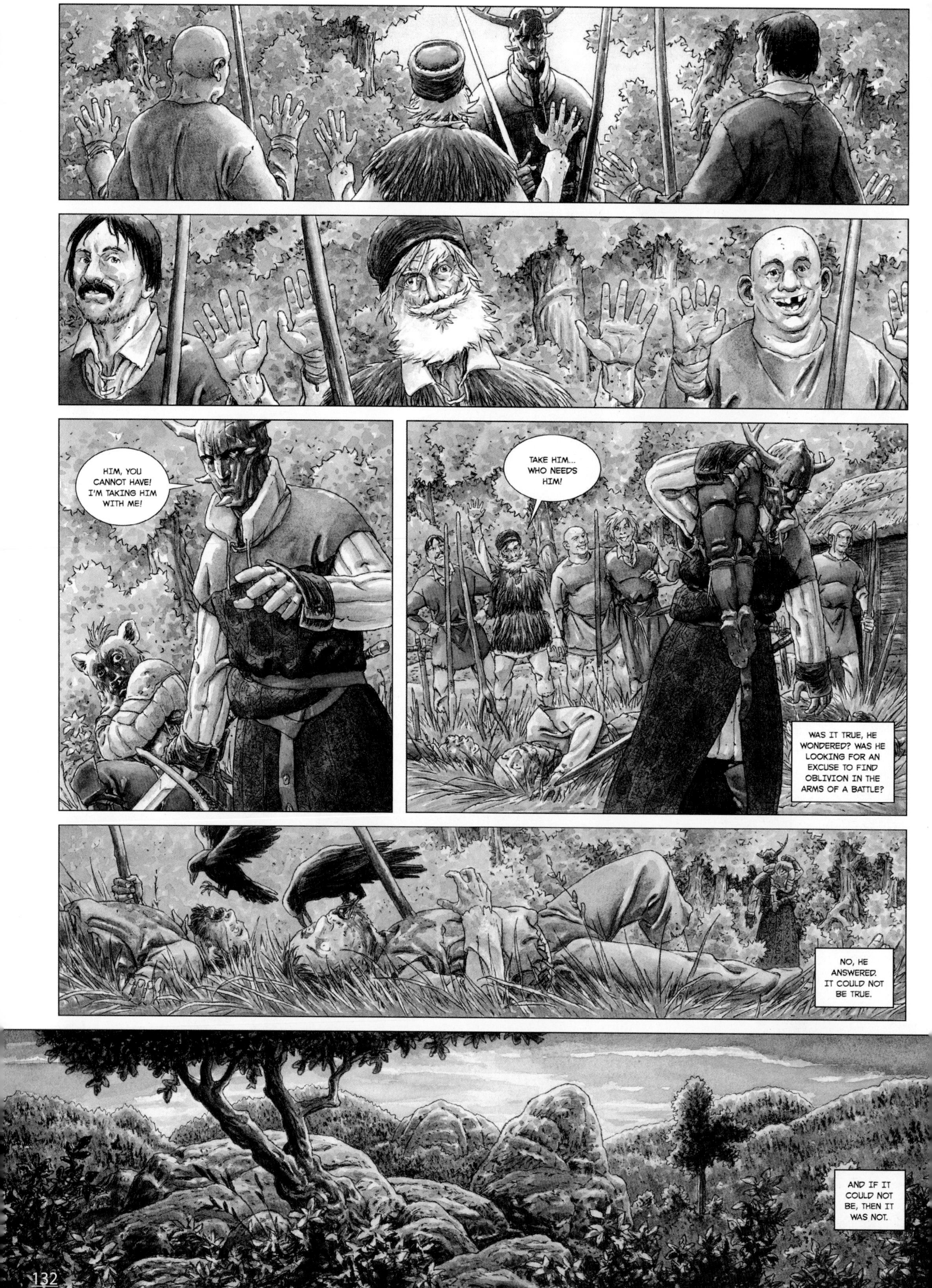
HIM, YOU CANNOT HAVE! I'M TAKING HIM WITH ME!
TAKE HIM... WHO NEEDS HIM!
WAS IT TRUE, HE WONDERED? WAS HE LOOKING FOR AN EXCUSE TO FIND OBLIVION IN THE ARMS OF A BATTLE?
NO, HE ANSWERED. IT COULD NOT BE TRUE.
AND IF IT COULD NOT BE, THEN IT WAS NOT.

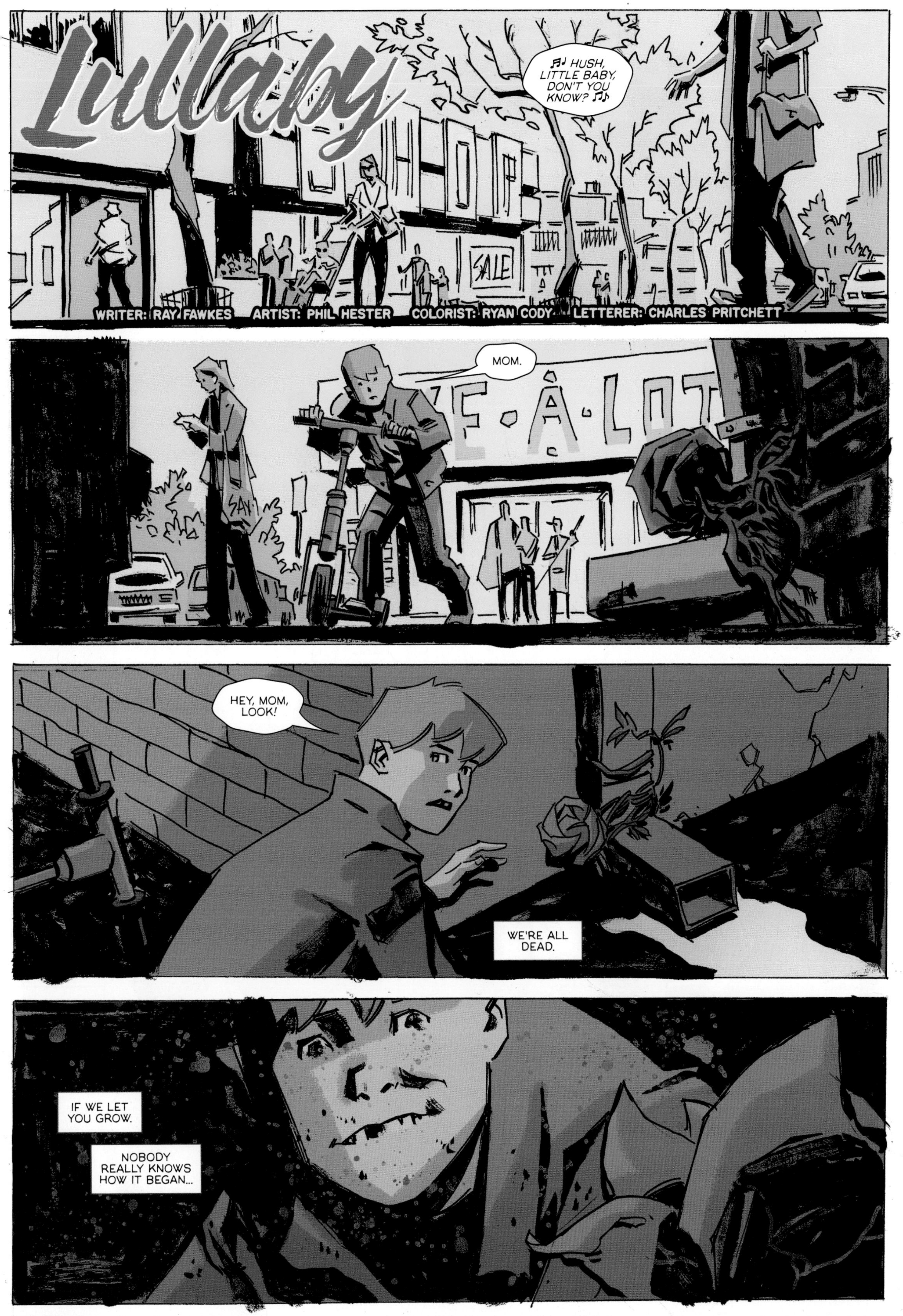

Lullaby
♬♩ HUSH, LITTLE BABY, DON'T YOU KNOW? ♫♪
SALE
WRITER: RAY FAWKES ARTIST: PHIL HESTER COLORIST: RYAN CODY LETTERER: CHARLES PRITCHETT
MOM.
HEY, MOM, LOOK!
WE'RE ALL DEAD.
IF WE LET YOU GROW.
NOBODY REALLY KNOWS HOW IT BEGAN...

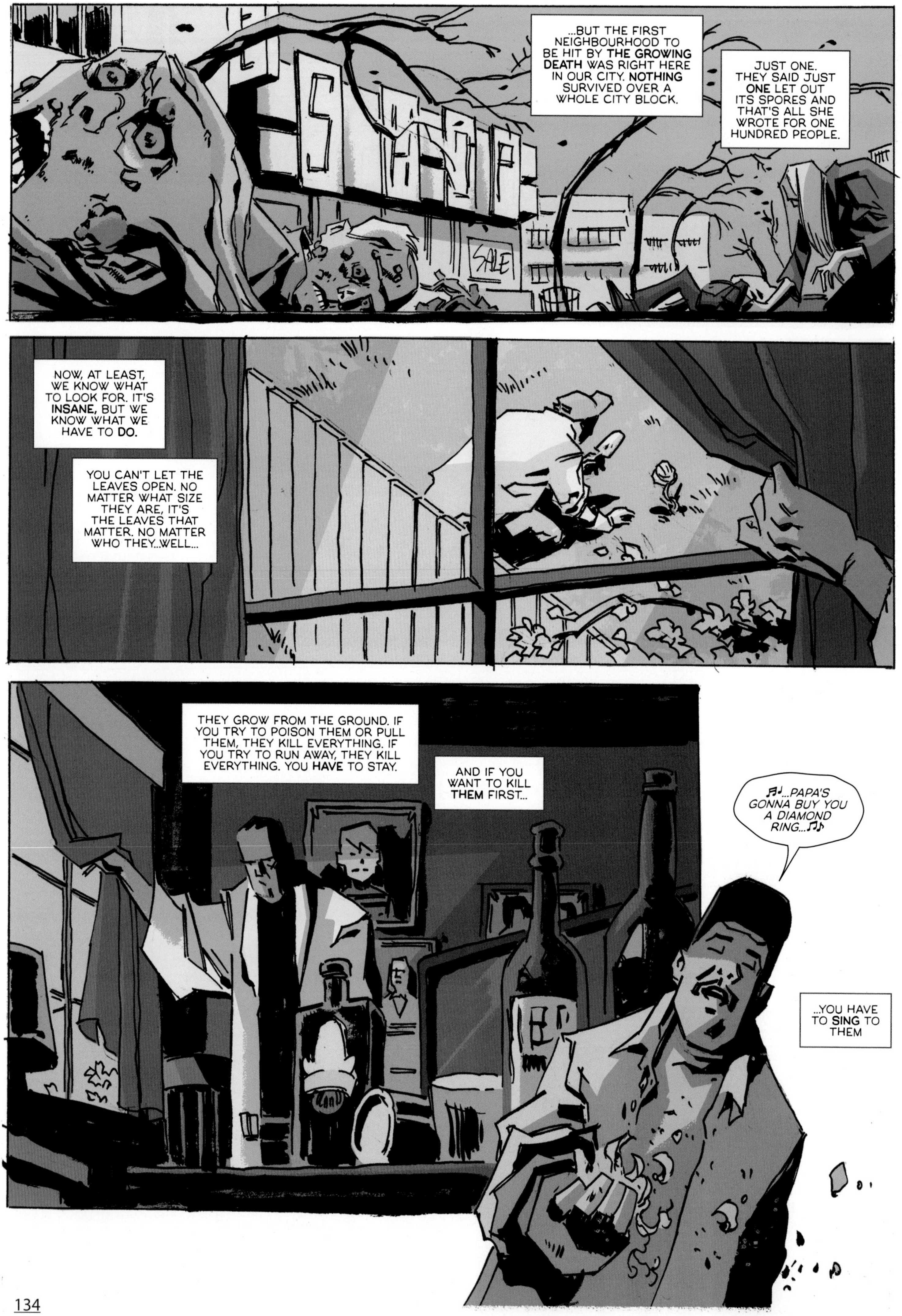

...BUT THE FIRST NEIGHBOURHOOD TO BE HIT BY **THE GROWING DEATH** WAS RIGHT HERE IN OUR CITY. **NOTHING** SURVIVED OVER A WHOLE CITY BLOCK.
JUST ONE. THEY SAID JUST **ONE** LET OUT ITS SPORES AND THAT'S ALL SHE WROTE FOR ONE HUNDRED PEOPLE.
SALE
NOW, AT LEAST, WE KNOW WHAT TO LOOK FOR. IT'S **INSANE,** BUT WE KNOW WHAT WE HAVE TO **DO.**
YOU CAN'T LET THE LEAVES OPEN. NO MATTER WHAT SIZE THEY ARE, IT'S THE LEAVES THAT MATTER. NO MATTER WHO THEY...WELL...
THEY GROW FROM THE GROUND. IF YOU TRY TO POISON THEM OR PULL THEM, THEY KILL EVERYTHING. IF YOU TRY TO RUN AWAY, THEY KILL EVERYTHING. YOU **HAVE** TO STAY.
AND IF YOU WANT TO KILL **THEM** FIRST...
♬♩...PAPA'S GONNA BUY YOU A DIAMOND RING...♫♪
...YOU HAVE TO **SING** TO THEM

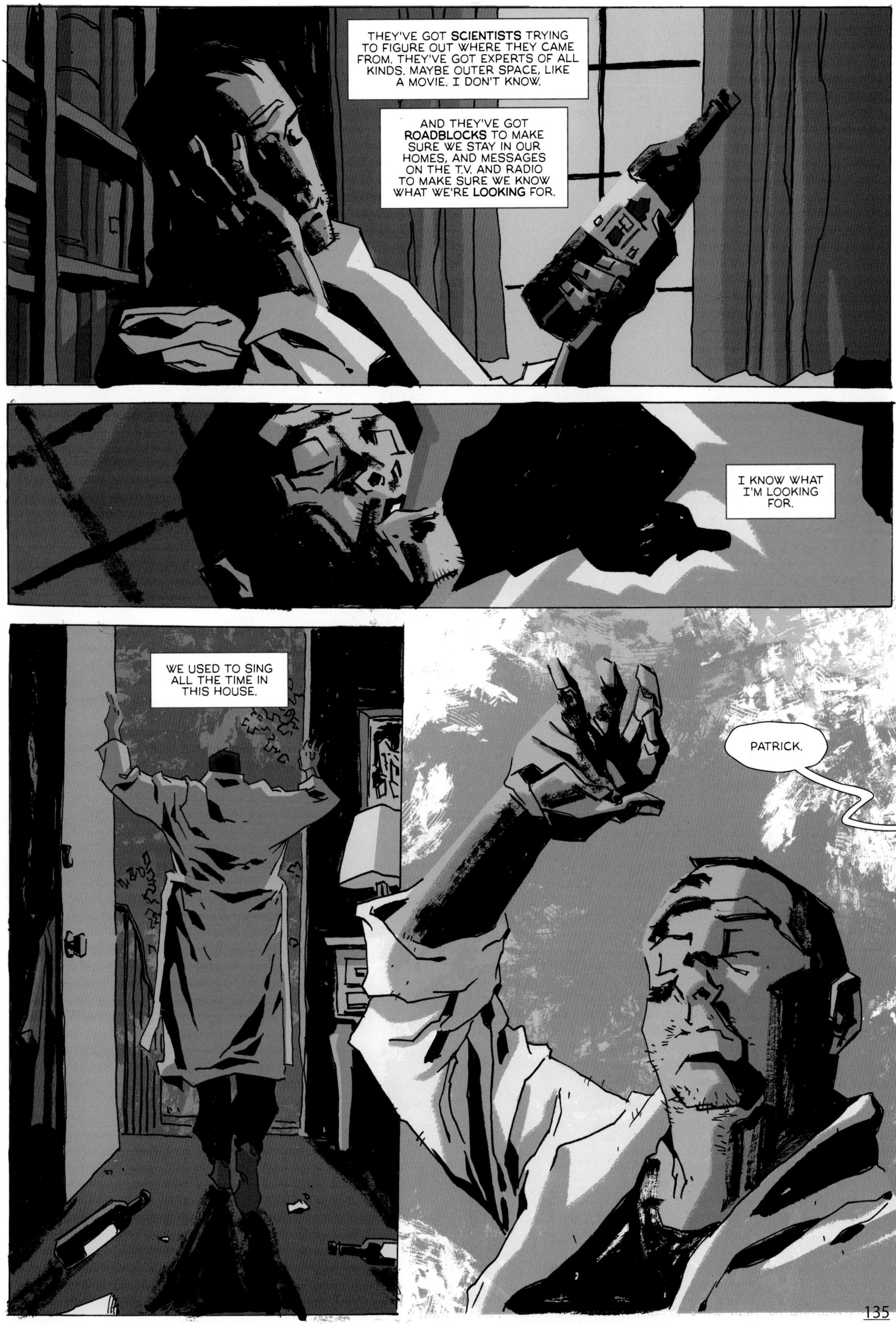
THEY'VE GOT **SCIENTISTS** TRYING TO FIGURE OUT WHERE THEY CAME FROM. THEY'VE GOT EXPERTS OF ALL KINDS. MAYBE OUTER SPACE, LIKE A MOVIE. I DON'T KNOW.
AND THEY'VE GOT **ROADBLOCKS** TO MAKE SURE WE STAY IN OUR HOMES, AND MESSAGES ON THE T.V. AND RADIO TO MAKE SURE WE KNOW WHAT WE'RE **LOOKING** FOR.
I KNOW WHAT I'M LOOKING FOR.
WE USED TO SING ALL THE TIME IN THIS HOUSE.
PATRICK.

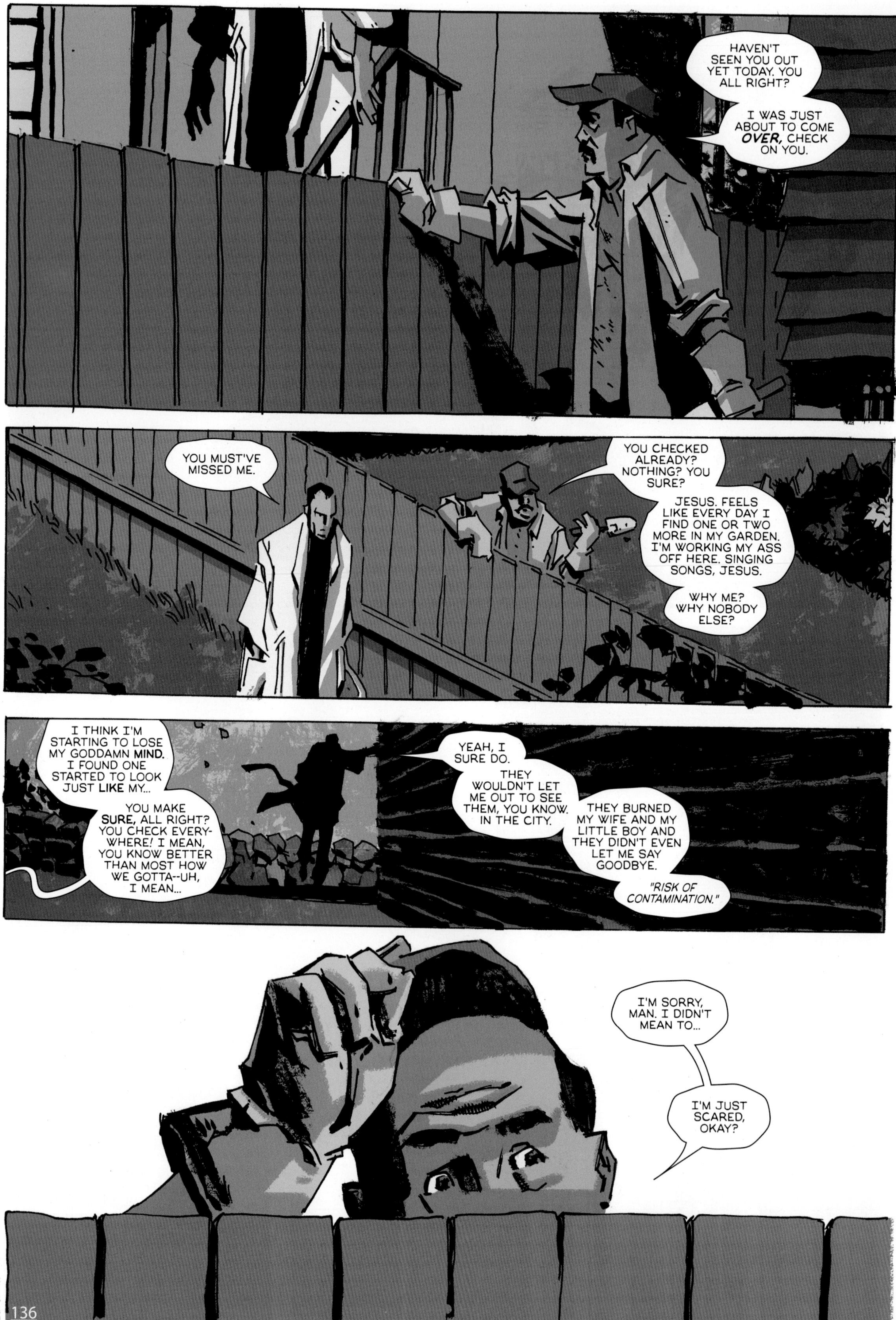
HAVEN'T SEEN YOU OUT YET TODAY. YOU ALL RIGHT?
I WAS JUST ABOUT TO COME **OVER,** CHECK ON YOU.
YOU MUST'VE MISSED ME.
YOU CHECKED ALREADY? NOTHING? YOU SURE?
JESUS. FEELS LIKE EVERY DAY I FIND ONE OR TWO MORE IN MY GARDEN. I'M WORKING MY ASS OFF HERE. SINGING SONGS, JESUS.
WHY ME? WHY NOBODY ELSE?
I THINK I'M STARTING TO LOSE MY GODDAMN **MIND.** I FOUND ONE STARTED TO LOOK JUST **LIKE** MY...
YOU MAKE **SURE,** ALL RIGHT? YOU CHECK EVERY-WHERE! I MEAN, YOU KNOW BETTER THAN MOST HOW WE GOTTA--UH, I MEAN...
YEAH, I SURE DO.
THEY WOULDN'T LET ME OUT TO SEE THEM, YOU KNOW. IN THE CITY.
THEY BURNED MY WIFE AND MY LITTLE BOY AND THEY DIDN'T EVEN LET ME SAY GOODBYE.
"RISK OF CONTAMINATION."
I'M SORRY, MAN. I DIDN'T MEAN TO...
I'M JUST SCARED, OKAY?

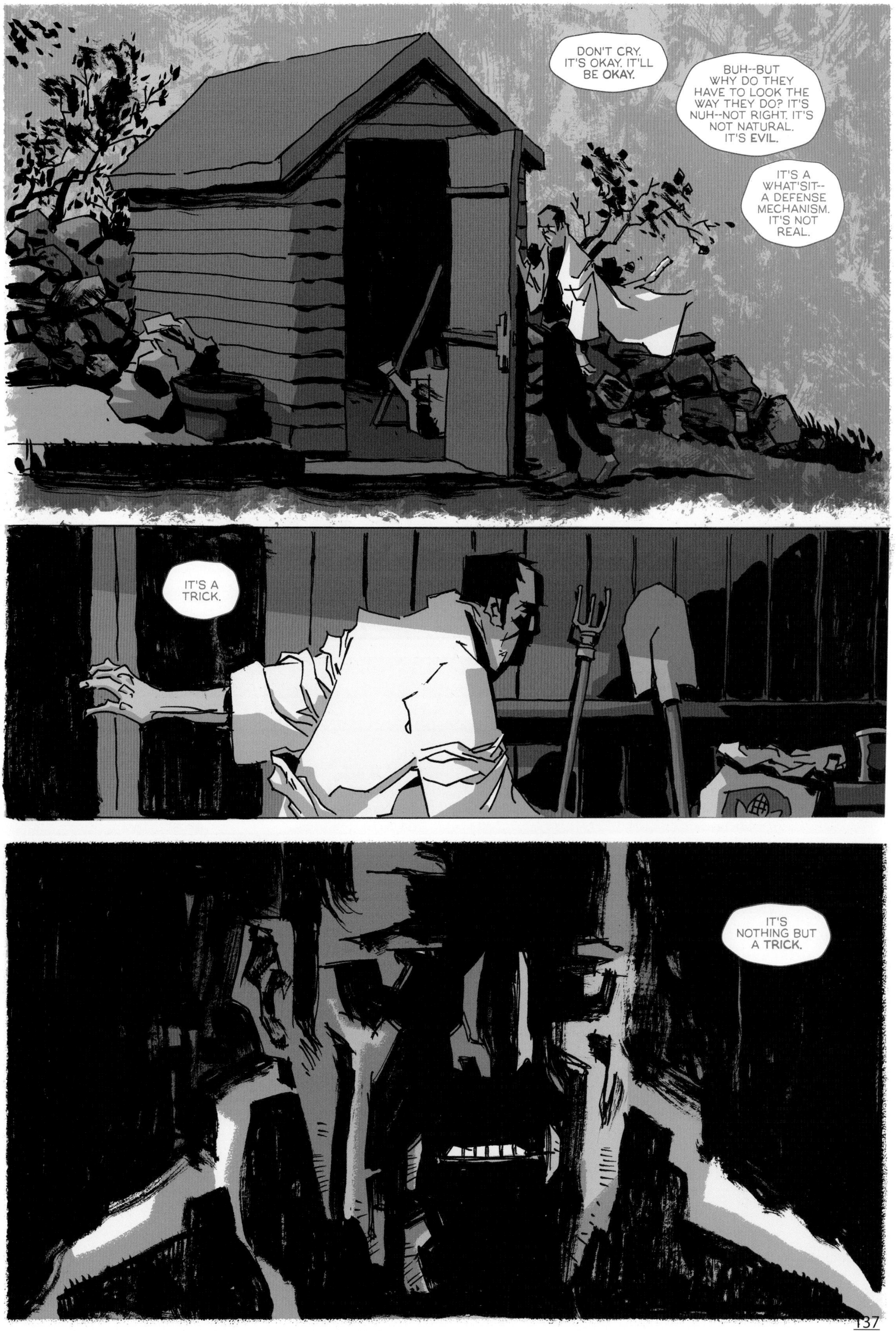
DON'T CRY. IT'S OKAY. IT'LL BE **OKAY.**
BUH--BUT WHY DO THEY HAVE TO LOOK THE WAY THEY DO? IT'S NUH--NOT RIGHT. IT'S NOT NATURAL. IT'S **EVIL.**
IT'S A WHAT'SIT-- A DEFENSE MECHANISM. IT'S NOT REAL.
IT'S A TRICK.
IT'S NOTHING BUT A **TRICK.**

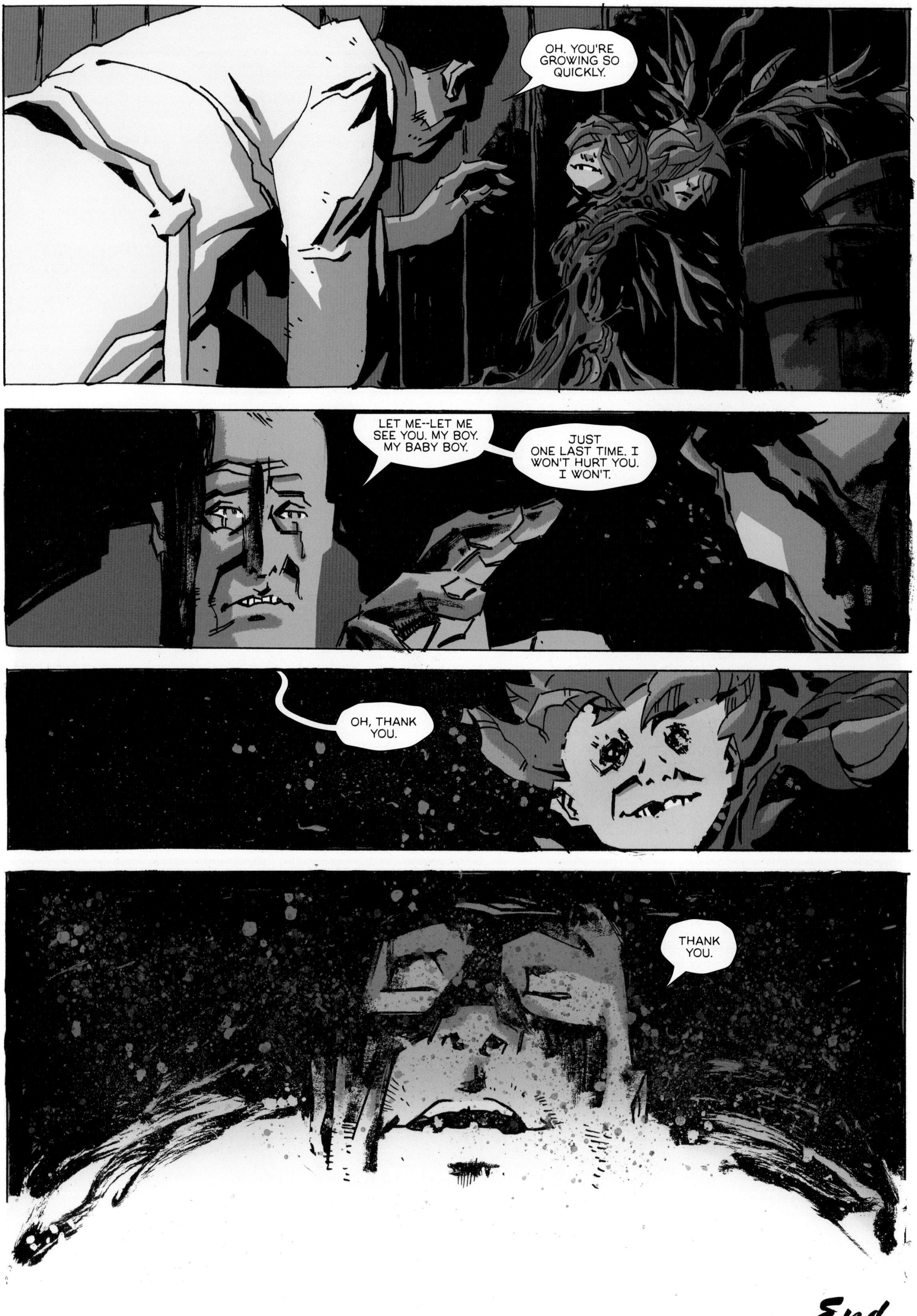
OH. YOU'RE GROWING SO QUICKLY.
LET ME--LET ME SEE YOU. MY BOY. MY BABY BOY.
JUST ONE LAST TIME. I WON'T HURT YOU. I WON'T.
OH, THANK YOU.
THANK YOU.

End.

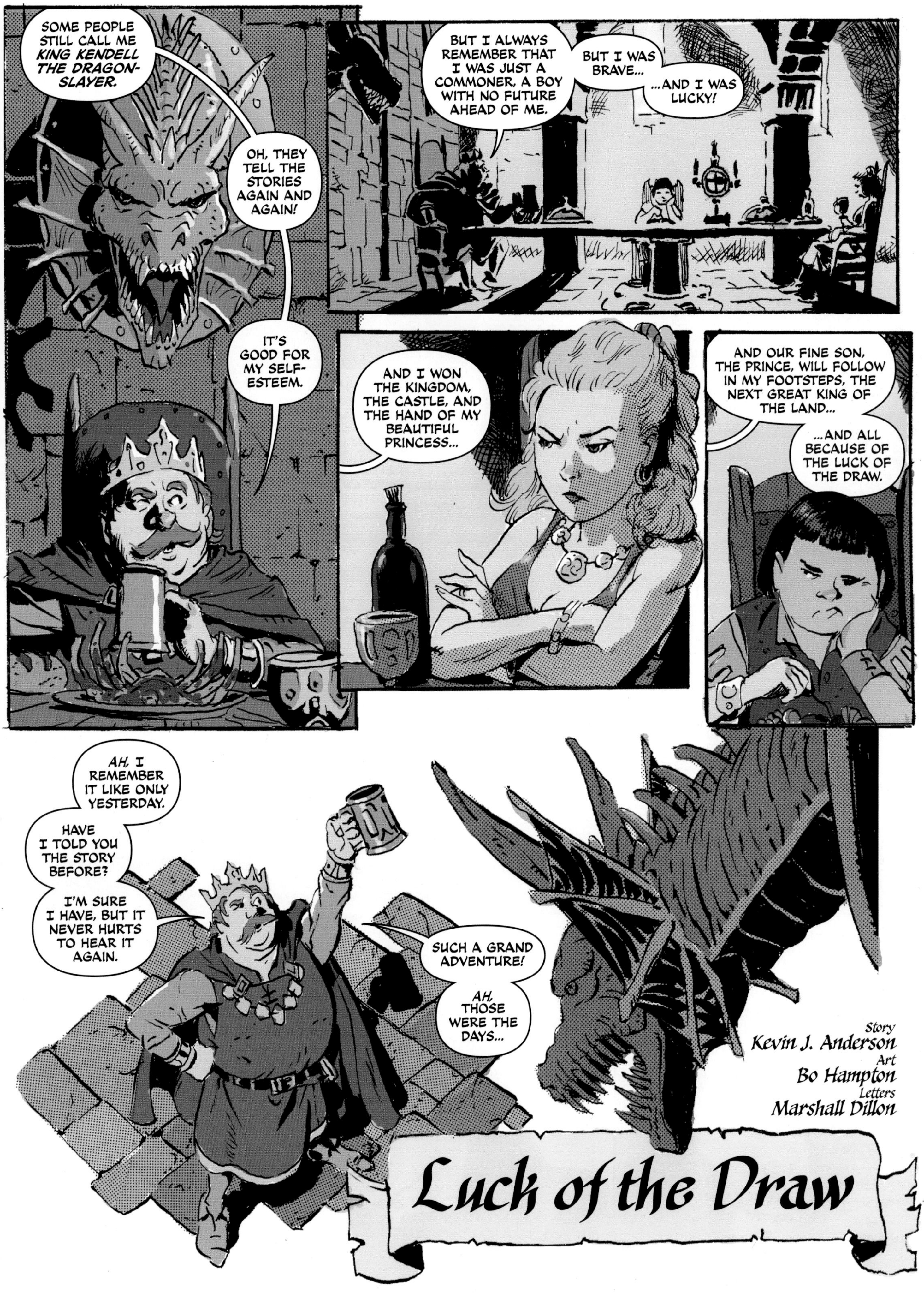
SOME PEOPLE STILL CALL ME *KING KENDELL THE DRAGON-SLAYER.*
OH, THEY TELL THE STORIES AGAIN AND AGAIN!
IT'S GOOD FOR MY SELF-ESTEEM.
BUT I ALWAYS REMEMBER THAT I WAS JUST A COMMONER, A BOY WITH NO FUTURE AHEAD OF ME.
BUT I WAS BRAVE...
...AND I WAS LUCKY!
AND I WON THE KINGDOM, THE CASTLE, AND THE HAND OF MY BEAUTIFUL PRINCESS...
AND OUR FINE SON, THE PRINCE, WILL FOLLOW IN MY FOOTSTEPS, THE NEXT GREAT KING OF THE LAND...
...AND ALL BECAUSE OF THE LUCK OF THE DRAW.
AH, I REMEMBER IT LIKE ONLY YESTERDAY.
HAVE I TOLD YOU THE STORY BEFORE?
I'M SURE I HAVE, BUT IT NEVER HURTS TO HEAR IT AGAIN.
SUCH A GRAND ADVENTURE!
AH, THOSE WERE THE DAYS...
Story
Kevin J. Anderson
Art
Bo Hampton
Letters
Marshall Dillon
Luck of the Draw

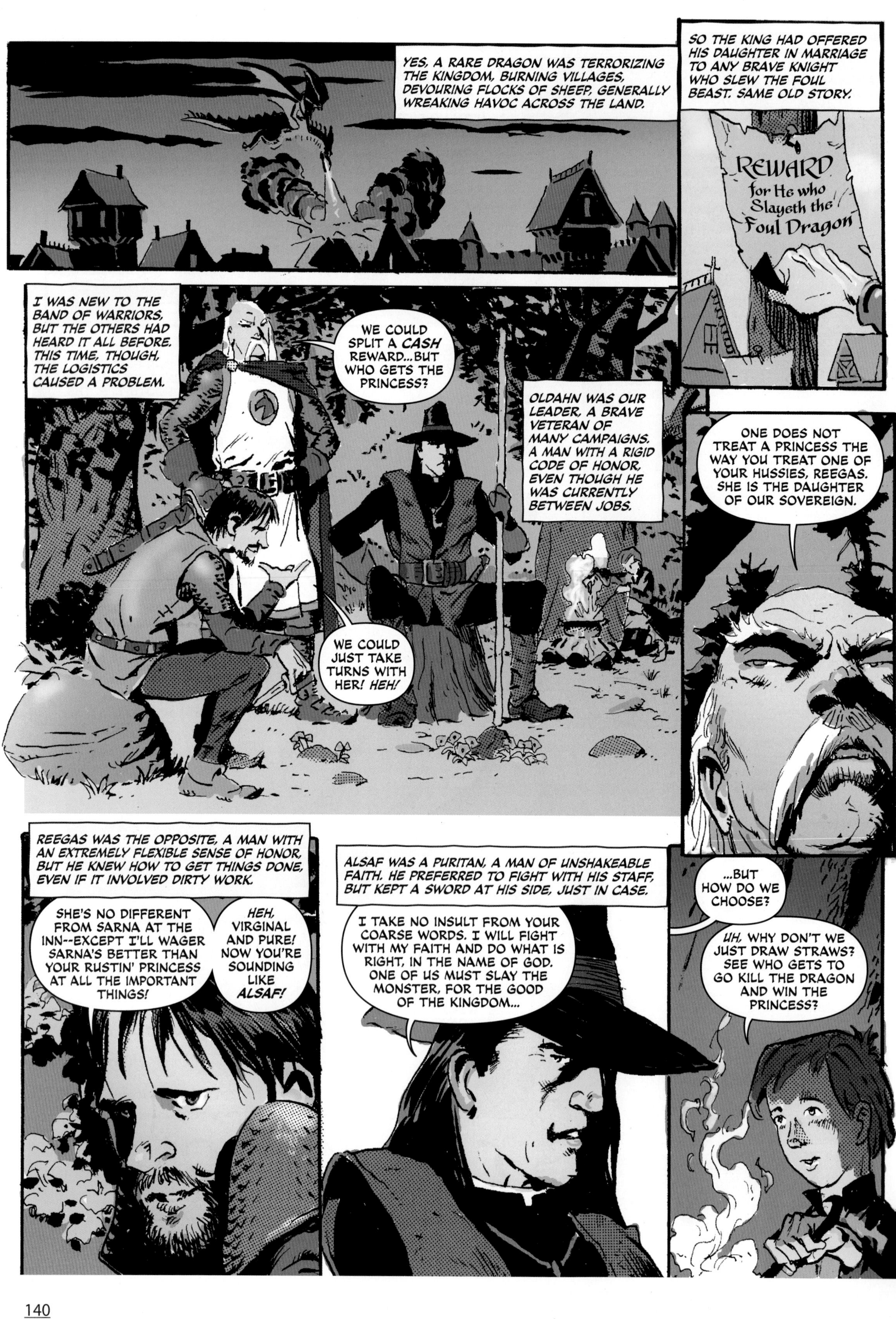
YES, A RARE DRAGON WAS TERRORIZING THE KINGDOM, BURNING VILLAGES, DEVOURING FLOCKS OF SHEEP, GENERALLY WREAKING HAVOC ACROSS THE LAND.
SO THE KING HAD OFFERED HIS DAUGHTER IN MARRIAGE TO ANY BRAVE KNIGHT WHO SLEW THE FOUL BEAST. SAME OLD STORY.
REWARD for He who Slayeth the Foul Dragon
I WAS NEW TO THE BAND OF WARRIORS, BUT THE OTHERS HAD HEARD IT ALL BEFORE. THIS TIME, THOUGH, THE LOGISTICS CAUSED A PROBLEM.
WE COULD SPLIT A CASH REWARD...BUT WHO GETS THE PRINCESS?
OLDAHN WAS OUR LEADER, A BRAVE VETERAN OF MANY CAMPAIGNS. A MAN WITH A RIGID CODE OF HONOR, EVEN THOUGH HE WAS CURRENTLY BETWEEN JOBS.
WE COULD JUST TAKE TURNS WITH HER! HEH!
ONE DOES NOT TREAT A PRINCESS THE WAY YOU TREAT ONE OF YOUR HUSSIES, REEGAS. SHE IS THE DAUGHTER OF OUR SOVEREIGN.
REEGAS WAS THE OPPOSITE, A MAN WITH AN EXTREMELY FLEXIBLE SENSE OF HONOR, BUT HE KNEW HOW TO GET THINGS DONE, EVEN IF IT INVOLVED DIRTY WORK.
SHE'S NO DIFFERENT FROM SARNA AT THE INN--EXCEPT I'LL WAGER SARNA'S BETTER THAN YOUR RUSTIN' PRINCESS AT ALL THE IMPORTANT THINGS!
HEH, VIRGINAL AND PURE! NOW YOU'RE SOUNDING LIKE ALSAF!
ALSAF WAS A PURITAN, A MAN OF UNSHAKEABLE FAITH. HE PREFERRED TO FIGHT WITH HIS STAFF, BUT KEPT A SWORD AT HIS SIDE, JUST IN CASE.
I TAKE NO INSULT FROM YOUR COARSE WORDS. I WILL FIGHT WITH MY FAITH AND DO WHAT IS RIGHT, IN THE NAME OF GOD. ONE OF US MUST SLAY THE MONSTER, FOR THE GOOD OF THE KINGDOM...
...BUT HOW DO WE CHOOSE?
UH, WHY DON'T WE JUST DRAW STRAWS? SEE WHO GETS TO GO KILL THE DRAGON AND WIN THE PRINCESS?

RUSTIN' GOOD IDEA, KENDELL!

AGREED.

THEN IT IS DECIDED. LUCK OF THE DRAW.

FOUR STRAWS, THREE LONG, ONE SHORT. HE WHO DRAWS THE SHORT STRAW SHALL GO FORTH AND SLAY THE DRAGON.

KENDELL, IT WAS YOUR IDEA. YOU DRAW FIRST.

THE IDEA HAD SOUNDED GOOD, BUT I WASN'T SURE I WANTED THE HONOR OF BATTLING THE DRAGON.

SURE, BEING WED TO A PRINCESS WOULD BE NICE, BUT I HAD BARELY BEGUN MY SWORDFIGHTING LESSONS AND, ACCORDING TO STORIES I HAD HEARD, DRAGONS WERE DANGEROUS.

LONG STRAW.

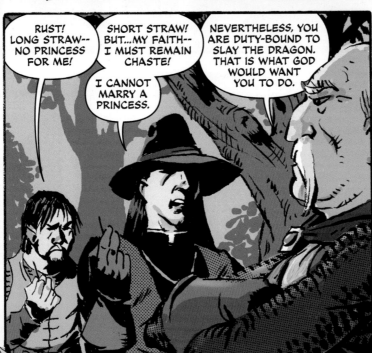

RUST! LONG STRAW-- NO PRINCESS FOR ME!

SHORT STRAW! BUT...MY FAITH-- I MUST REMAIN CHASTE!

I CANNOT MARRY A PRINCESS.

NEVERTHELESS, YOU ARE DUTY-BOUND TO SLAY THE DRAGON. THAT IS WHAT GOD WOULD WANT YOU TO DO.

WE KNEW WHERE THE DRAGON'S LAIR WAS, HAVING INVESTIGATED EVERY FOUL-SMELLING, BONE-CLUTTERED CAVE IN THE KINGDOM. AND NOW WE HAD CHOSEN OUR CHAMPION.

YOU ARE RIGHT, OLDAHN. MY PURPOSE IS TO DESTROY EVIL IN ALL ITS MANIFESTATIONS.

A DIVINE HAND HAS GUIDED MY SELECTION, AND I WILL SERVE HIS PURPOSE.

I SHALL BE PROTECTED BY MY UNQUENCHABLE FAITH.

MY STAFF WILL SEND THE DEMON BACK TO THE FIRES OF HELL!

I PROMISE I WILL RETURN.

IT WAS THE ONLY PROMISE ALSAF EVER BROKE.

FOR OUR HONOR, WE MUST CONTINUE. ALSAF HAS BEEN MURDERED BY THE BEAST. COME, REEGAS. DRAW FIRST. WE MUST AVENGE HIM!

AND WIN THE RUSTIN' PRINCESS.

NOT ME! LONG STRAW! NOT ME THIS TIME.

LONG STRAW FOR ME, TOO...

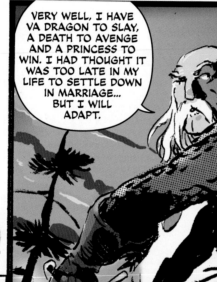

VERY WELL, I HAVE VA DRAGON TO SLAY, A DEATH TO AVENGE AND A PRINCESS TO WIN. I HAD THOUGHT IT WAS TOO LATE IN MY LIFE TO SETTLE DOWN IN MARRIAGE... BUT I WILL ADAPT.

MY BRAVE EXPLOITS SHALL BE SUNG BY MINSTRELS ALL ACROSS THE KINGDOM! I'LL BE BACK BY NIGHTFALL!

OLDAHN DIDN'T COME BACK BY NIGHTFALL, OR BY MIDNIGHT, OR IN THE DARK BEFORE DAWN.

WELL, NOW WHAT DO WE DO? OLDAHN WAS THE LEADER OF OUR BAND.

RUST! WITHOUT OLDAHN AND ALSAF, WE'RE NOT MUCH OF A BAND ANYMORE.

YOU KNOW WHAT WE HAVE TO DO. WE'VE GOT TO FINISH THIS. SOMEBODY HAS TO SLAY THE DRAGON AND WIN THE PRINCESS...

DRAW!

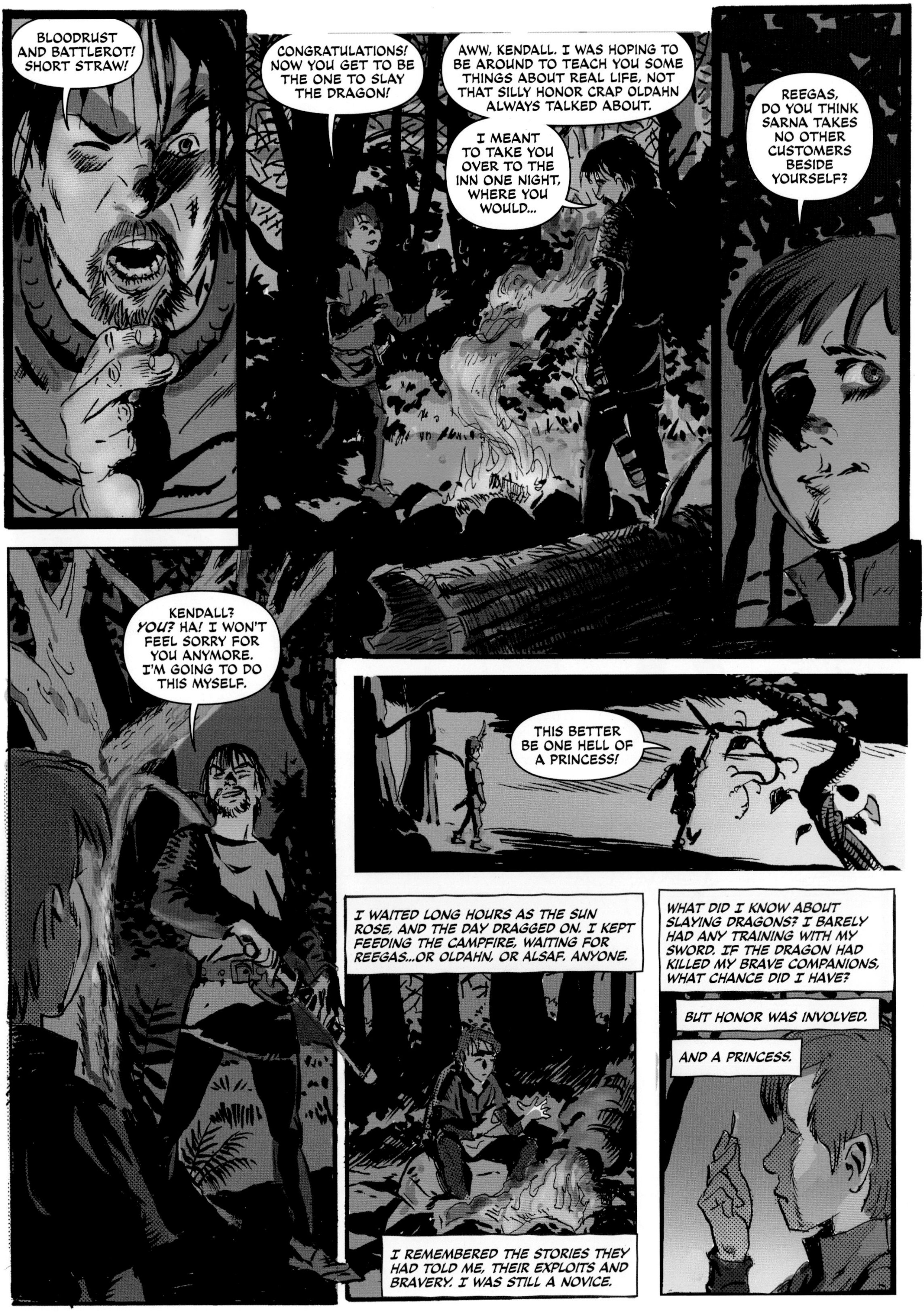
BLOODRUST AND BATTLEROT! SHORT STRAW!
CONGRATULATIONS! NOW YOU GET TO BE THE ONE TO SLAY THE DRAGON!
AWW, KENDALL. I WAS HOPING TO BE AROUND TO TEACH YOU SOME THINGS ABOUT REAL LIFE, NOT THAT SILLY HONOR CRAP OLDAHN ALWAYS TALKED ABOUT.
I MEANT TO TAKE YOU OVER TO THE INN ONE NIGHT, WHERE YOU WOULD...
REEGAS, DO YOU THINK SARNA TAKES NO OTHER CUSTOMERS BESIDE YOURSELF?
KENDALL? *YOU?* HA! I WON'T FEEL SORRY FOR YOU ANYMORE. I'M GOING TO DO THIS MYSELF.
THIS BETTER BE ONE HELL OF A PRINCESS!
I WAITED LONG HOURS AS THE SUN ROSE, AND THE DAY DRAGGED ON. I KEPT FEEDING THE CAMPFIRE, WAITING FOR REEGAS...OR OLDAHN, OR ALSAF. ANYONE.
I REMEMBERED THE STORIES THEY HAD TOLD ME, THEIR EXPLOITS AND BRAVERY. I WAS STILL A NOVICE.
WHAT DID I KNOW ABOUT SLAYING DRAGONS? I BARELY HAD ANY TRAINING WITH MY SWORD. IF THE DRAGON HAD KILLED MY BRAVE COMPANIONS, WHAT CHANCE DID I HAVE?
BUT HONOR WAS INVOLVED.
AND A PRINCESS.

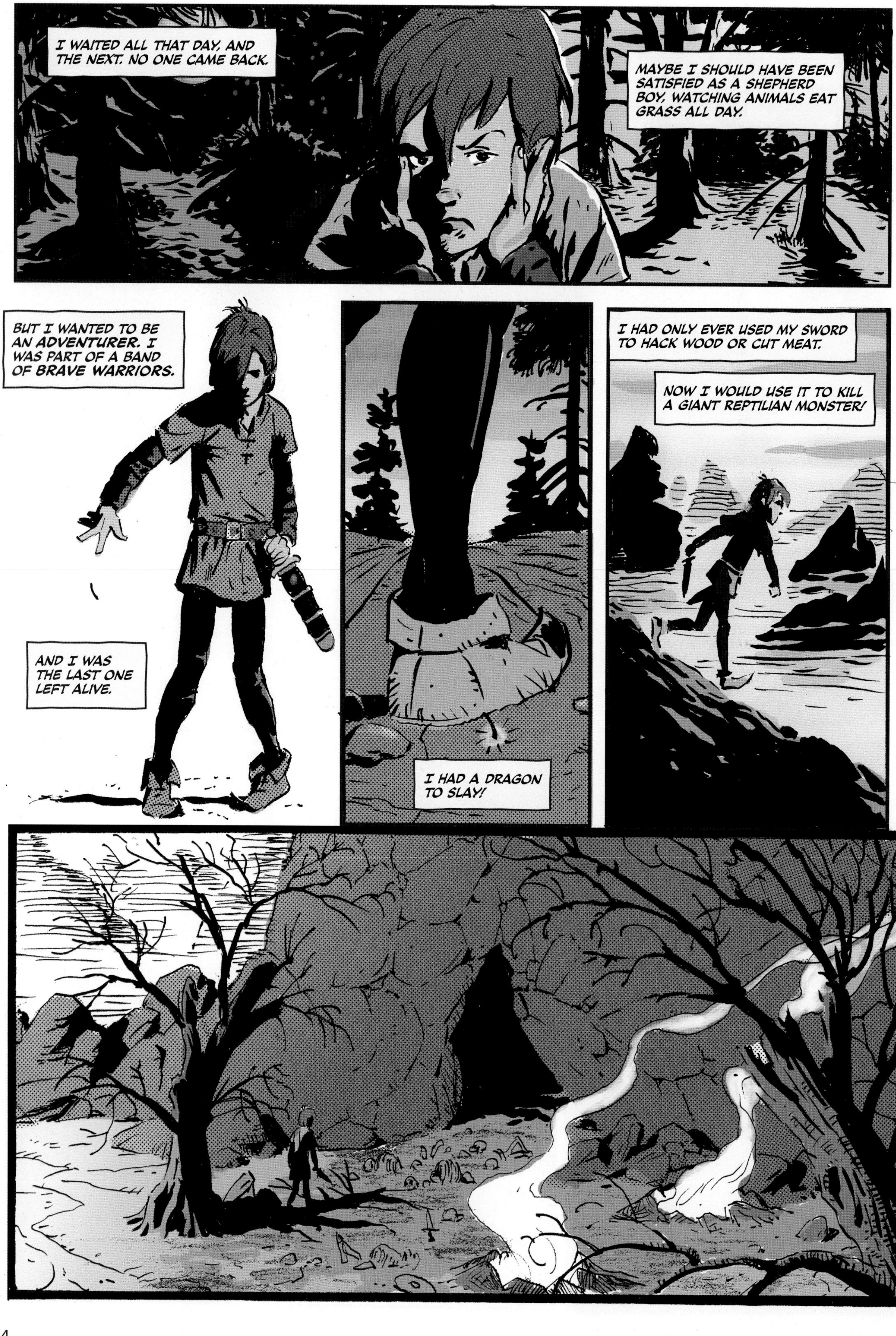
I WAITED ALL THAT DAY, AND THE NEXT. NO ONE CAME BACK.
MAYBE I SHOULD HAVE BEEN SATISFIED AS A SHEPHERD BOY, WATCHING ANIMALS EAT GRASS ALL DAY.
BUT I WANTED TO BE AN ADVENTURER. I WAS PART OF A BAND OF BRAVE WARRIORS.
AND I WAS THE LAST ONE LEFT ALIVE.
I HAD A DRAGON TO SLAY!
I HAD ONLY EVER USED MY SWORD TO HACK WOOD OR CUT MEAT.
NOW I WOULD USE IT TO KILL A GIANT REPTILIAN MONSTER!

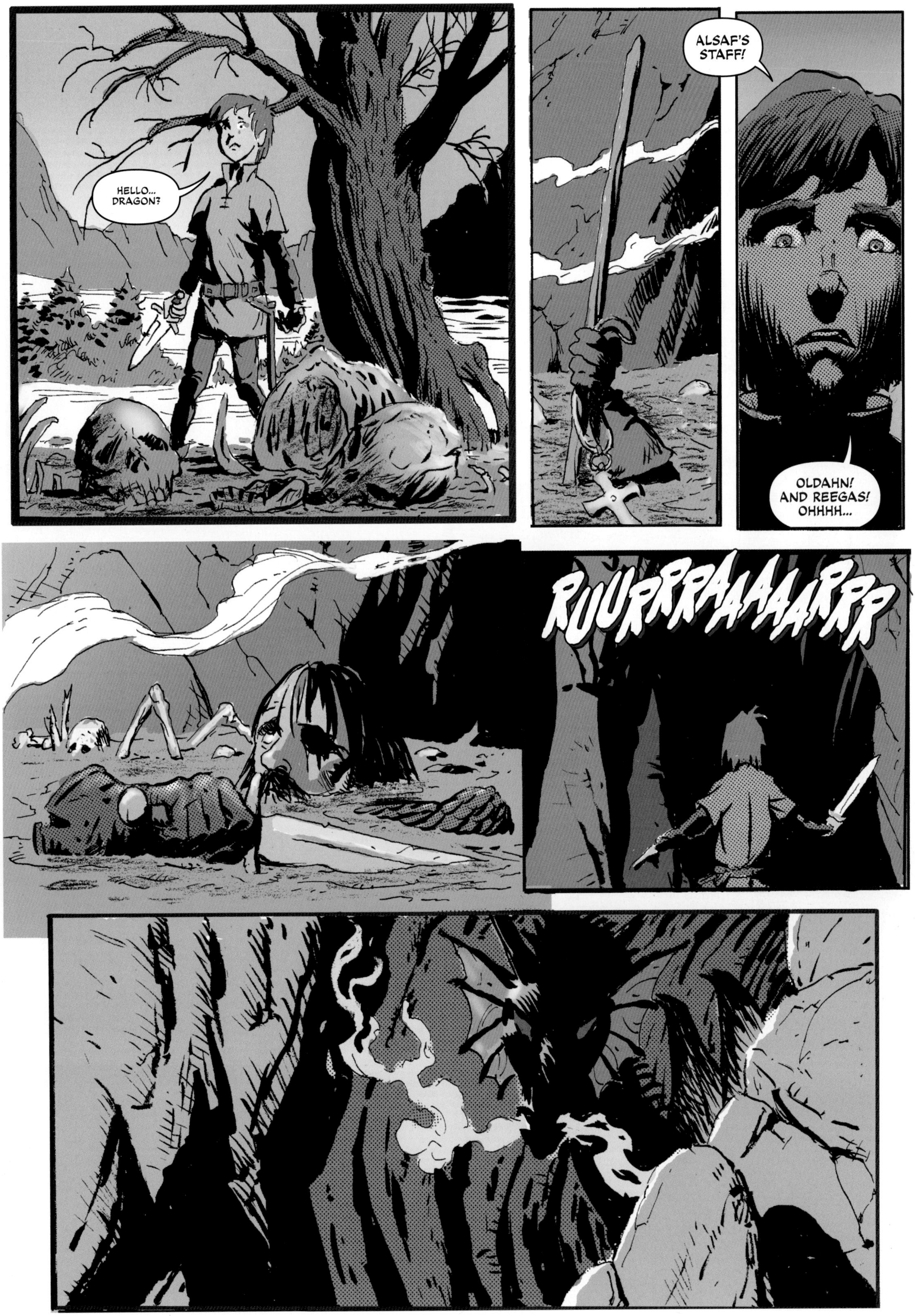
HELLO... DRAGON?
ALSAF'S STAFF!
OLDAHN! AND REEGAS! OHHHH...
RUURRRAAAAARRR

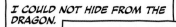

I COULD NOT HIDE FROM THE DRAGON.

NOR COULD THE DRAGON HIDE FROM ME. THIS MONSTER HAD KILLED MY FRIENDS. I WAS THE ONLY ONE LEFT!

I WANTED THE PRINCESS... AND I WANTED REVENGE!

LET ME DIGRESS A MOMENT. I'LL BET YOU DON'T KNOW HOW I GOT OUT OF THAT ONE, DO YOU, SON?

DRAGONS ARE NOT EXACTLY THE BEST-FED OF ALL CREATURES LIVING IN THE WILD. THEY HAVE LITTLE TO EAT, ESPECIALLY IN A SMALL KINGDOM LIKE OURS.

THIS DRAGON HAD FALLEN ON HARD TIMES. ONLY IMPENDING STARVATION HAD DRIVEN IT TO ATTACK THE PEASANTRY, FORCING THE KING TO OFFER HIS DAUGHTER AS A REWARD TO RID THE LAND OF THE BEAST.

AND THEN, WHEN MY COMPANIONS WENT OUT TO FIGHT IT, AN UNEXPECTED FEAST BEYOND THE DRAGON'S WILDEST DREAMS!

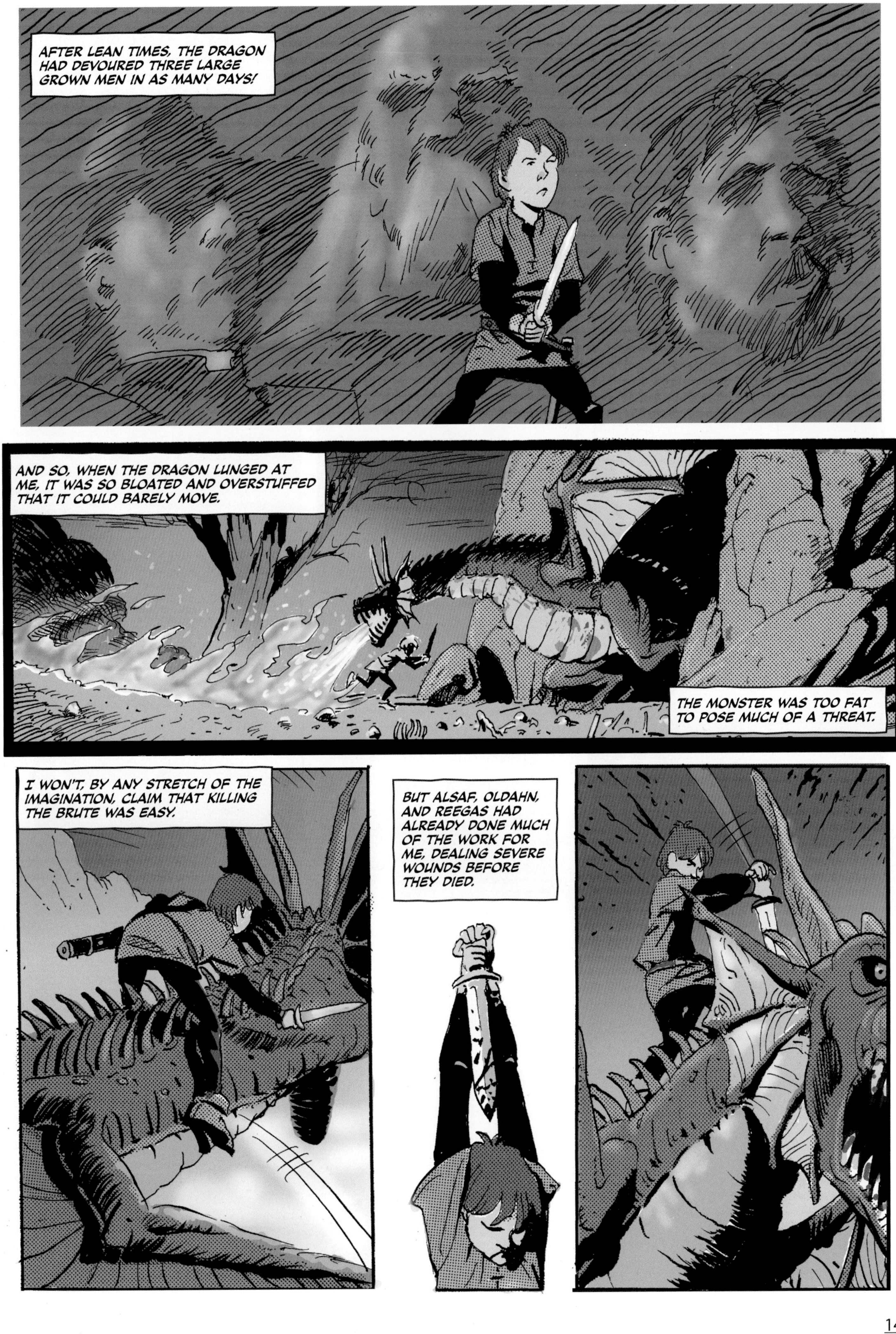
AFTER LEAN TIMES, THE DRAGON HAD DEVOURED THREE LARGE GROWN MEN IN AS MANY DAYS!
AND SO, WHEN THE DRAGON LUNGED AT ME, IT WAS SO BLOATED AND OVERSTUFFED THAT IT COULD BARELY MOVE.
THE MONSTER WAS TOO FAT TO POSE MUCH OF A THREAT.
I WON'T, BY ANY STRETCH OF THE IMAGINATION, CLAIM THAT KILLING THE BRUTE WAS EASY.
BUT ALSAF, OLDAHN, AND REEGAS HAD ALREADY DONE MUCH OF THE WORK FOR ME, DEALING SEVERE WOUNDS BEFORE THEY DIED.

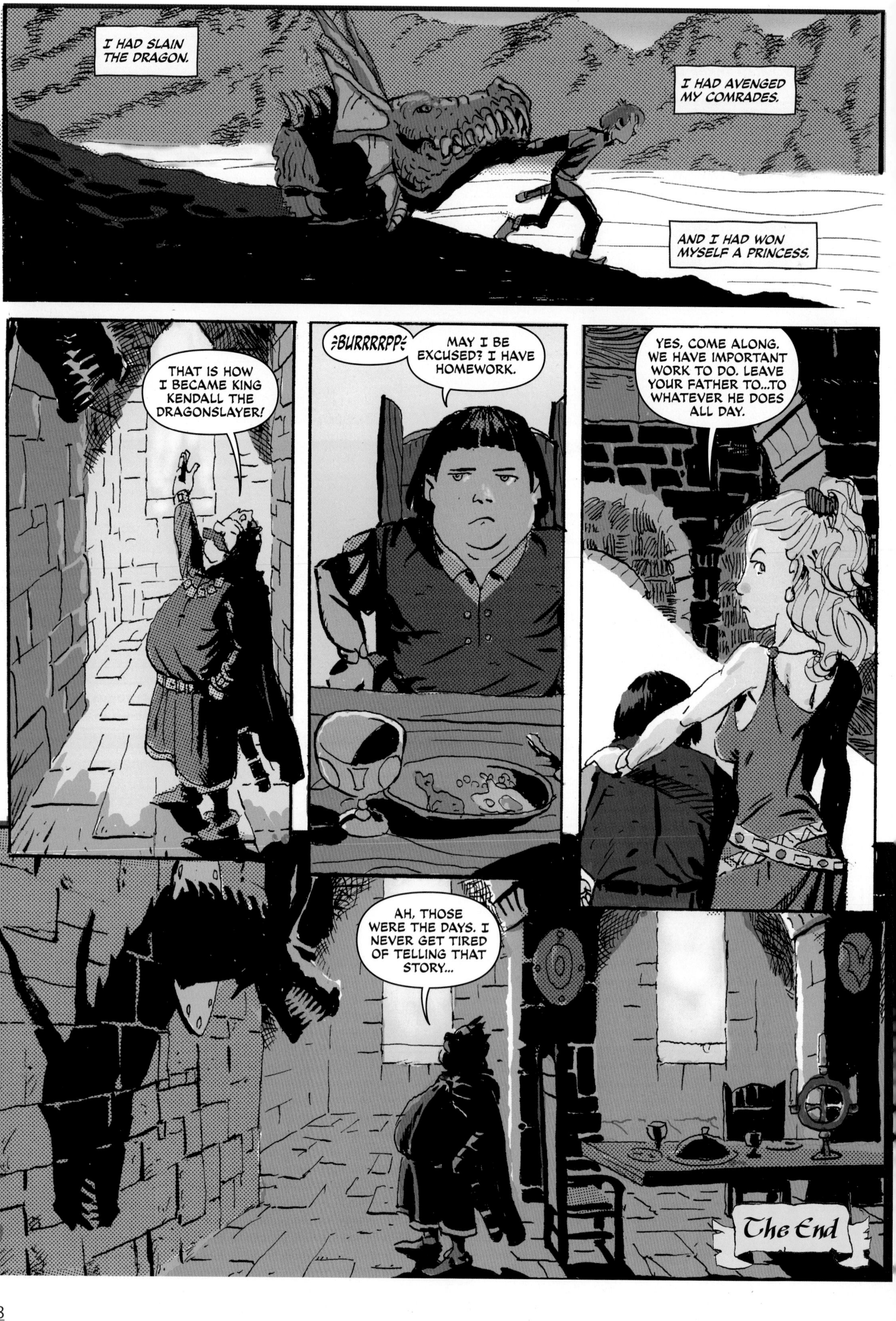
I HAD SLAIN THE DRAGON.
I HAD AVENGED MY COMRADES.
AND I HAD WON MYSELF A PRINCESS.
THAT IS HOW I BECAME KING KENDALL THE DRAGONSLAYER!
BURRRRPP
MAY I BE EXCUSED? I HAVE HOMEWORK.
YES, COME ALONG. WE HAVE IMPORTANT WORK TO DO. LEAVE YOUR FATHER TO...TO WHATEVER HE DOES ALL DAY.
AH, THOSE WERE THE DAYS. I NEVER GET TIRED OF TELLING THAT STORY...
The End

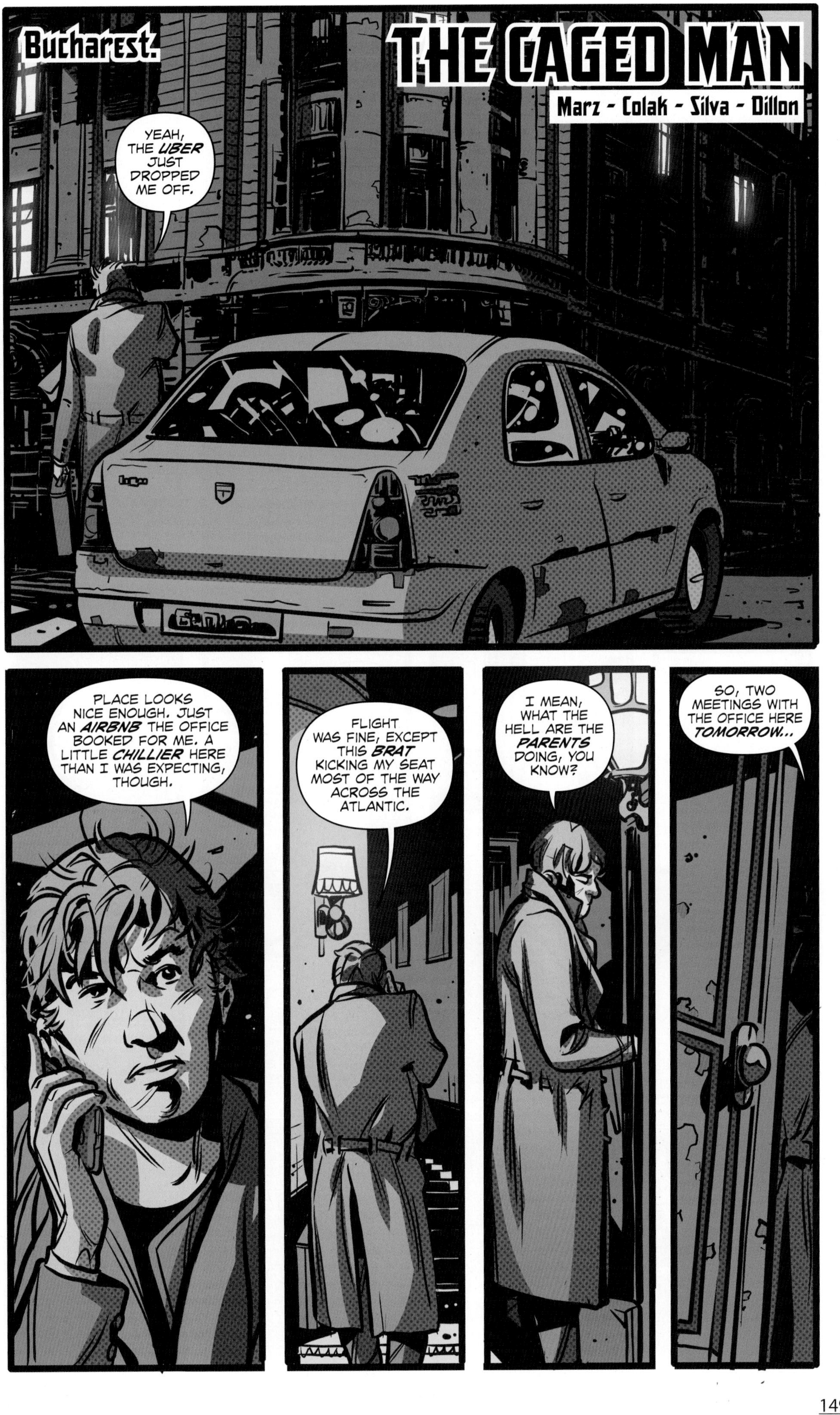
Bucharest.
THE CAGED MAN
Marz - Colak - Silva - Dillon
YEAH, THE UBER JUST DROPPED ME OFF.
PLACE LOOKS NICE ENOUGH. JUST AN AIRBNB THE OFFICE BOOKED FOR ME. A LITTLE CHILLIER HERE THAN I WAS EXPECTING, THOUGH.
FLIGHT WAS FINE, EXCEPT THIS BRAT KICKING MY SEAT MOST OF THE WAY ACROSS THE ATLANTIC.
I MEAN, WHAT THE HELL ARE THE PARENTS DOING, YOU KNOW?
SO, TWO MEETINGS WITH THE OFFICE HERE TOMORROW...

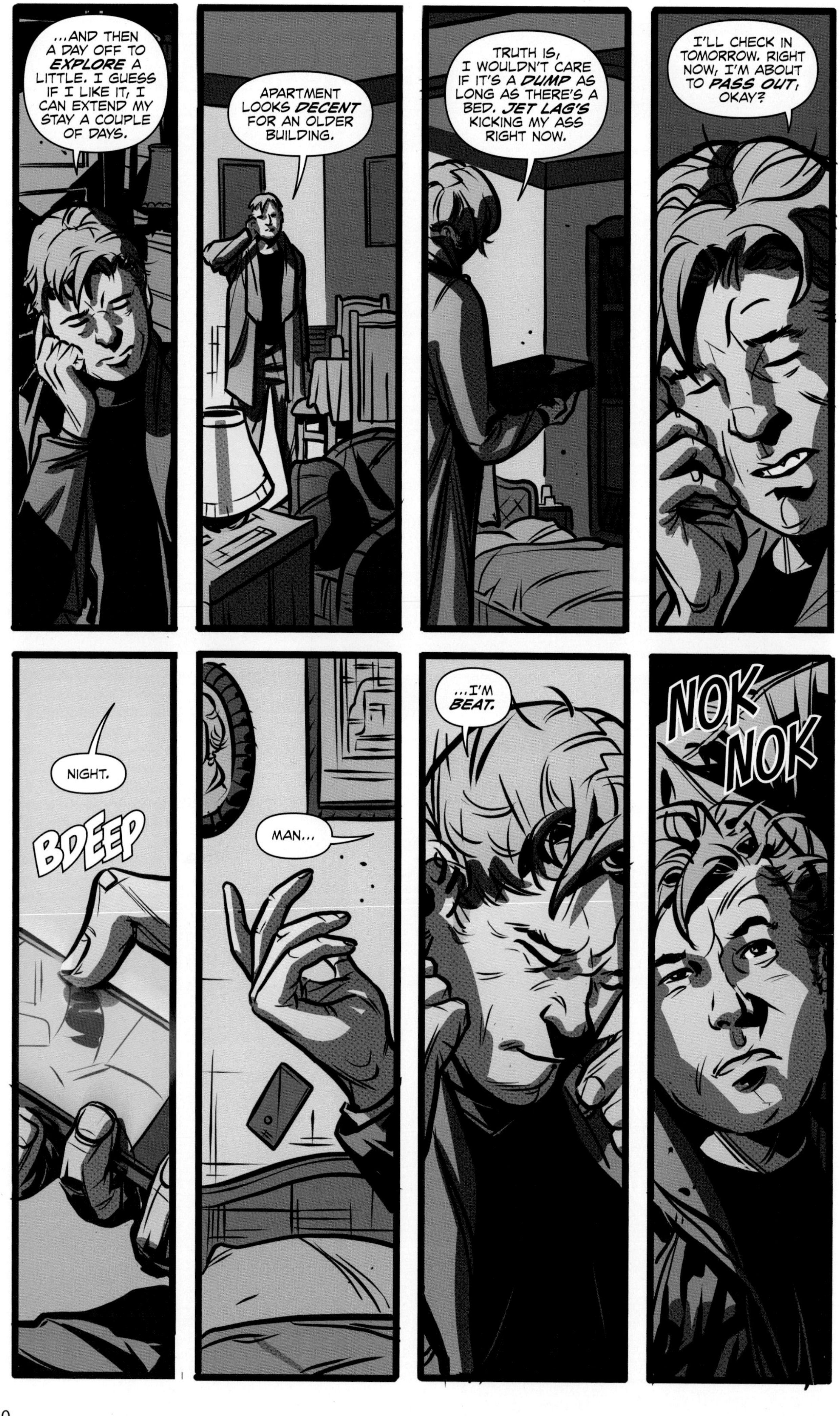
...AND THEN A DAY OFF TO EXPLORE A LITTLE. I GUESS IF I LIKE IT, I CAN EXTEND MY STAY A COUPLE OF DAYS.
APARTMENT LOOKS DECENT FOR AN OLDER BUILDING.
TRUTH IS, I WOULDN'T CARE IF IT'S A DUMP AS LONG AS THERE'S A BED. JET LAG'S KICKING MY ASS RIGHT NOW.
I'LL CHECK IN TOMORROW. RIGHT NOW, I'M ABOUT TO PASS OUT, OKAY?
NIGHT.
BDEEP
MAN...
...I'M BEAT.
NOK NOK

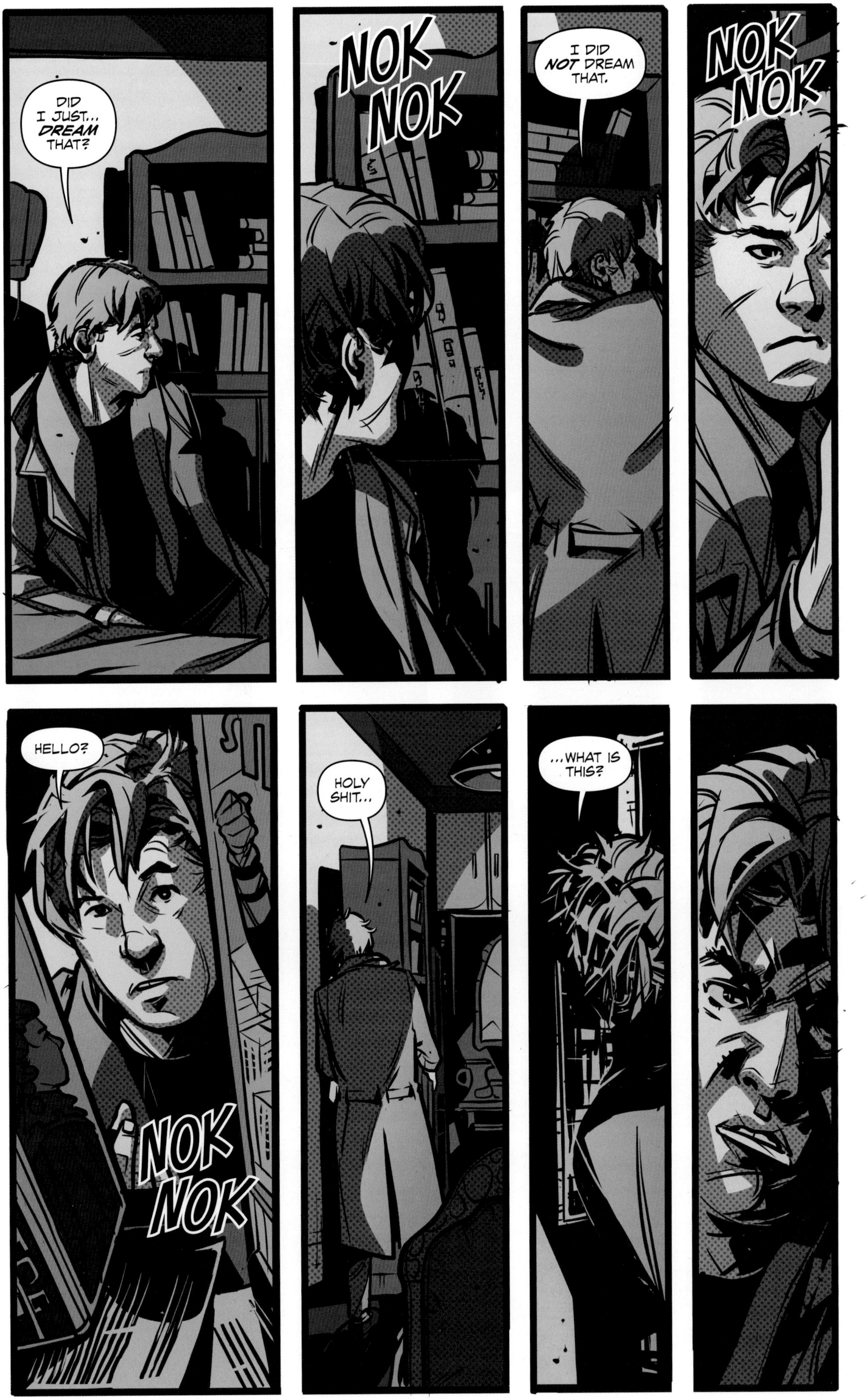
DID I JUST... DREAM THAT?
NOK NOK
I DID NOT DREAM THAT.
NOK NOK
HELLO?
NOK NOK
HOLY SHIT...
...WHAT IS THIS?

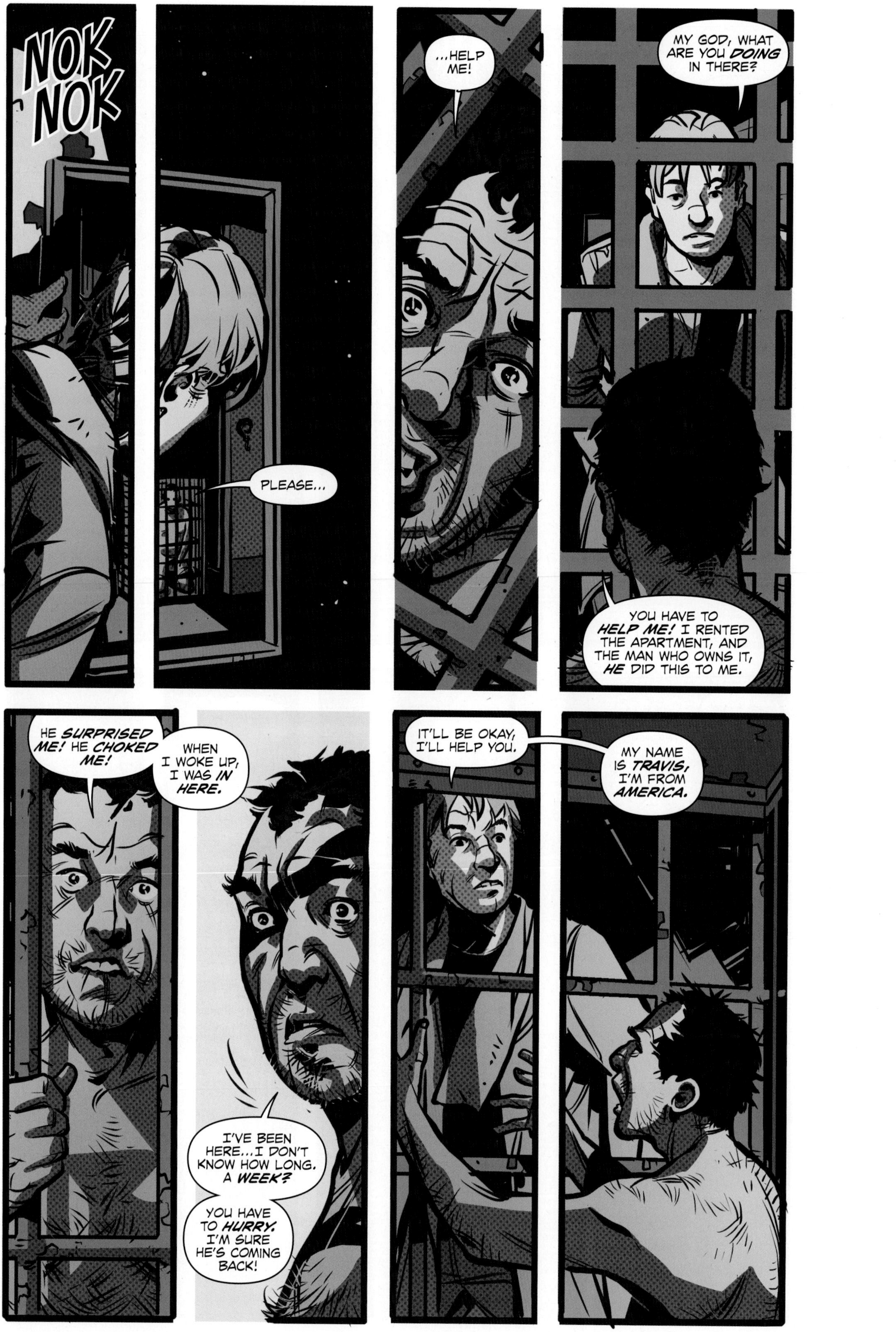
NOK NOK
PLEASE...
...HELP ME!
MY GOD, WHAT ARE YOU DOING IN THERE?
YOU HAVE TO HELP ME! I RENTED THE APARTMENT, AND THE MAN WHO OWNS IT, HE DID THIS TO ME.
HE SURPRISED ME! HE CHOKED ME!
WHEN I WOKE UP, I WAS IN HERE.
I'VE BEEN HERE...I DON'T KNOW HOW LONG. A WEEK?
YOU HAVE TO HURRY. I'M SURE HE'S COMING BACK!
IT'LL BE OKAY, I'LL HELP YOU.
MY NAME IS TRAVIS, I'M FROM AMERICA.

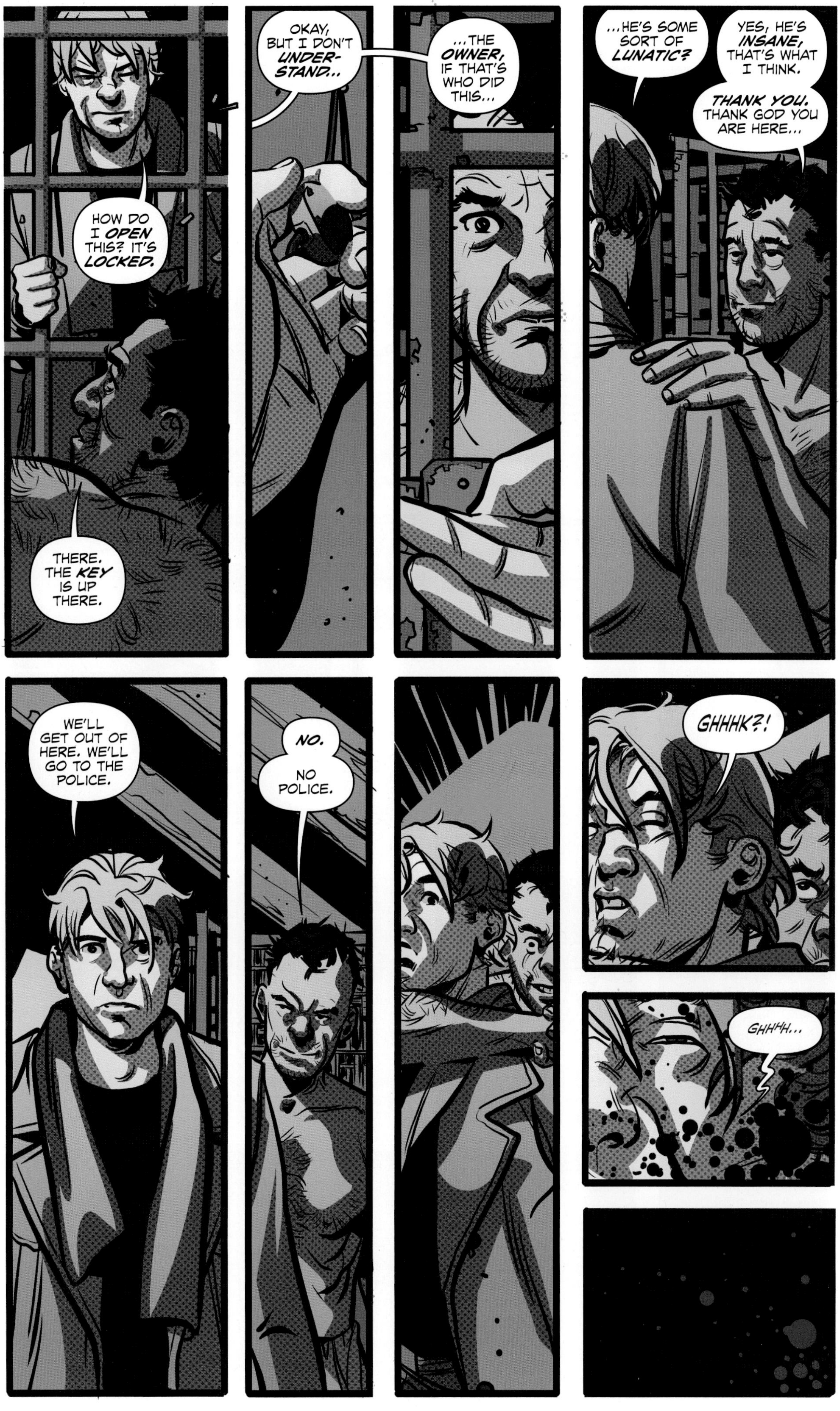

HOW DO I OPEN THIS? IT'S LOCKED.
THERE. THE KEY IS UP THERE.
OKAY, BUT I DON'T UNDER-STAND...
...THE OWNER, IF THAT'S WHO DID THIS...
...HE'S SOME SORT OF LUNATIC?
YES, HE'S INSANE, THAT'S WHAT I THINK.
THANK YOU. THANK GOD YOU ARE HERE...
WE'LL GET OUT OF HERE. WE'LL GO TO THE POLICE.
NO.
NO POLICE.
GHHHK?!
GHHHH...

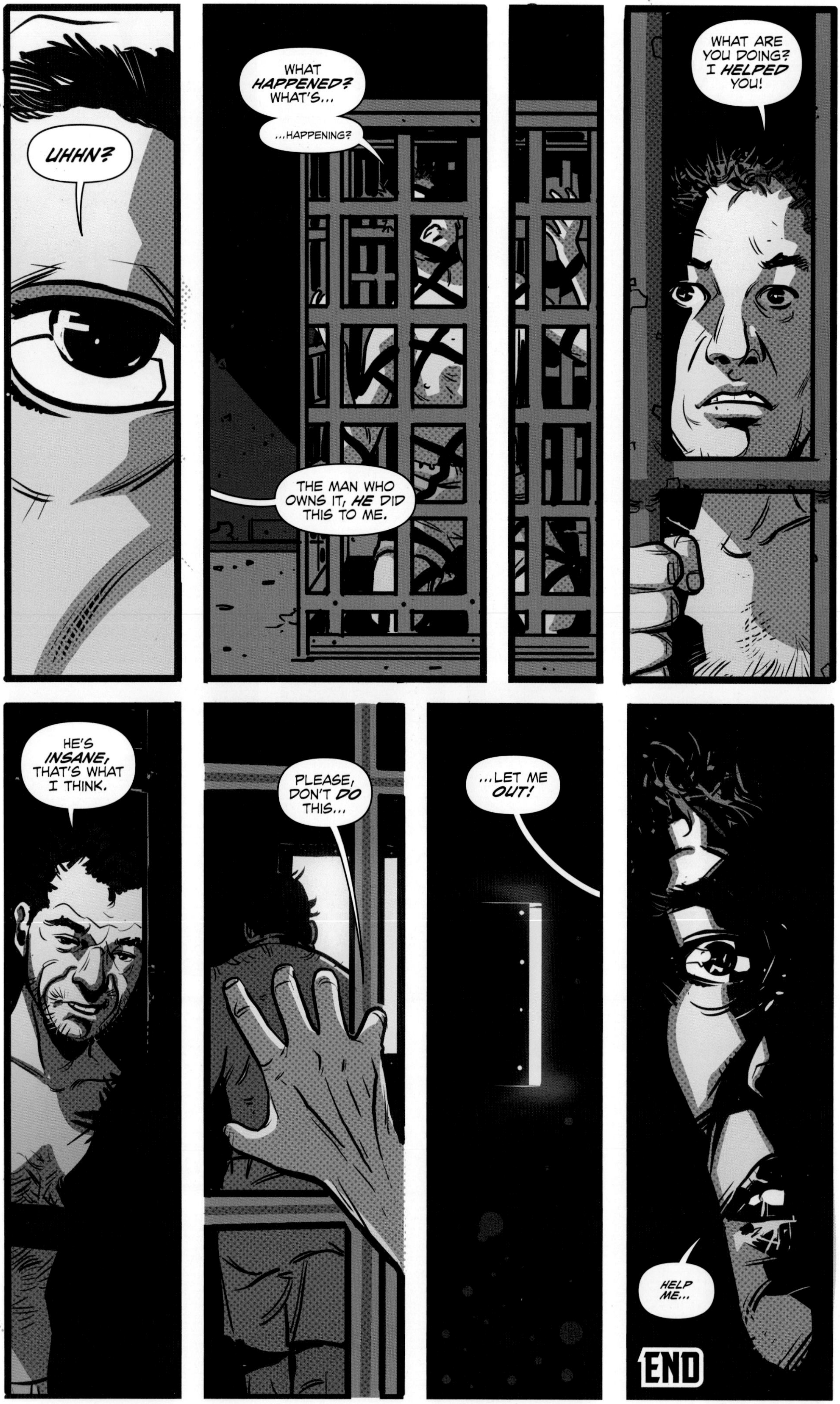
UHHN?
WHAT HAPPENED? WHAT'S...
...HAPPENING?
THE MAN WHO OWNS IT, HE DID THIS TO ME.
WHAT ARE YOU DOING? I HELPED YOU!
HE'S INSANE, THAT'S WHAT I THINK.
PLEASE, DON'T DO THIS...
...LET ME OUT!
HELP ME...
END

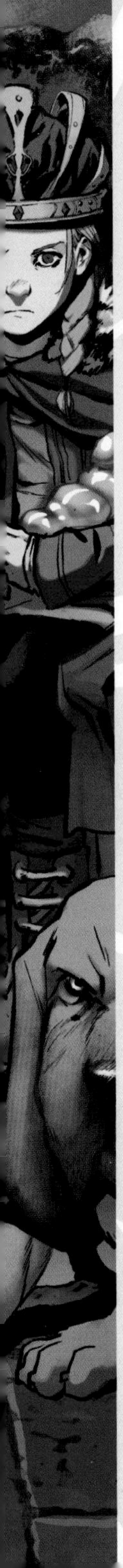

STOCK UP ON THESE GREAT AFTERSHOCK COLLECTIONS!

A WALK THROUGH HELL VOL 1
GARTH ENNIS / GORAN SUDZUKA
SEP181388

ALTERS VOL 1 & VOL 2
PAUL JENKINS / LEILA LEIZ
MAR171244 & APR181239

AMERICAN MONSTER VOL 1
BRIAN AZZARELLO / JUAN DOE
SEP161213

ANIMOSITY YEAR ONE, VOL 1, VOL 2 & VOL 3
MARGUERITE BENNETT / RAFAEL DE LATORRE
FEB181034, JAN171219, AUG171130 & MAY181314

ANIMOSITY: EVOLUTION VOL 1 & VOL 2
MARGUERITE BENNETT / ERIC GAPSTUR
MAR181079 & FEB188089

ANIMOSITY: THE RISE HARDCOVER
MARGUERITE BENNETT / JUAN DOE
AUG178324

ART OF JIM STARLIN HARDCOVER
JIM STARLIN
MAR181077

BABYTEETH YEAR ONE, VOL 1 & VOL 2
DONNY CATES / GARRY BROWN
OCT181328, OCT171087 & APR181225

BETROTHED VOL 1
SEAN LEWIS / STEVE UY
DEC181449161115

BEYONDERS VOL 1
PAUL JENKINS / WESLEY ST. CLAIRE
JAN191468

BLACK-EYED KIDS VOL 1, VOL 2 & VOL 3
JOE PRUETT / SZYMON KUDRANSKI
AUG161115, FEB171100 & JAN181152

BROTHERS DRACUL VOL 1
CULLEN BUNN / MIRKO COLAK
SEP181404

CAPTAIN KID VOL 1
MARK WAID / TOM PEYER / WILFREDO TORRES
APR171231

CLAN KILLERS VOL 1
SEAN LEWIS / ANTONIO FUSO
JAN191469

COLD WAR VOL 1
CHRISTOPHER SEBELA / HAYDEN SHERMAN
JUL181518

DARK ARK VOL 1 & VOL 2
CULLEN BUNN / JUAN DOE
FEB181035 & SEP181394

DREAMING EAGLES HARDCOVER
GARTH ENNIS / SIMON COLEBY
AUG161114

ELEANOR & THE EGRET VOL 1
JOHN LAYMAN / SAM KIETH
DEC171041

FU JITSU VOL 1
JAI NITZ / WESLEY ST. CLAIRE
APR181241

HER INFERNAL DESCENT VOL 1
LONNIE NADLER / ZAC THOMPSON /
KYLE CHARLES / EOIN MARRON
OCT181341

HOT LUNCH SPECIAL VOl 1
ELIOT RAHAL / JORGE FORNES
DEC181449

INSEXTS YEAR ONE, VOL 1 & VOL 2
MARGUERITE BENNETT / ARIELA KRISTANTINA
APR181228, JUN161072 & SEP171098

JIMMY'S BASTARDS VOL & VOL 2
GARTH ENNIS / RUSS BRAUN
DEC171040 & JUN181333

MONSTRO MECHANICA VOL 1
PAUL ALLOR / CHRIS EVENHUIS
JUL181517

OUT OF THE BLUE VOL 1
GARTH ENNIS / KEITH BURNS
JAN191460

PESTILENCE VOL 1 & VOL 2
FRANK TIERI / OLEG OKUNEV
NOV171154, OCT181340

REPLICA VOL 1
PAUL JENKINS / ANDY CLARKE
MAY161030

ROUGH RIDERS VOL 1, VOL 2 & VOL 3
ADAM GLASS / PATRICK OLLIFFE
OCT161101, SEP171097 & AUG181474

SECOND SIGHT VOL 1
DAVID HINE / ALBERTO PONTICELL
DEC161186

SHIPWRECK VOL 1
WARREN ELLIS / PHIL HESTER
MAR181078

SHOCK HARDCOVER
VARIOUS
JAN181139

SUPERZERO VOL 1
AMANDA CONNER / JIMMY PALMIOTTI / RAFAEL DE LATORRE
MAY161029

THE LOST CITY EXPLORERS VOL 1
ZACHARY KAPLAN / ALVARO SARRASECA
NOV181434

THE NORMALS VOL 1
ADAM GLASS / DENNIS CALERO
SEP181391

UNHOLY GRAIL VOL 1
CULLEN BUNN / MIRKO COLAK
JAN181151

WITCH HAMMER OGN
CULLEN BUNN / DALIBOR TALAJIC
SEP181387

WORLD READER VOL 1
JEFF LOVENESS / JUAN DOE
SEP171096

www.aftershockcomics.com/collections

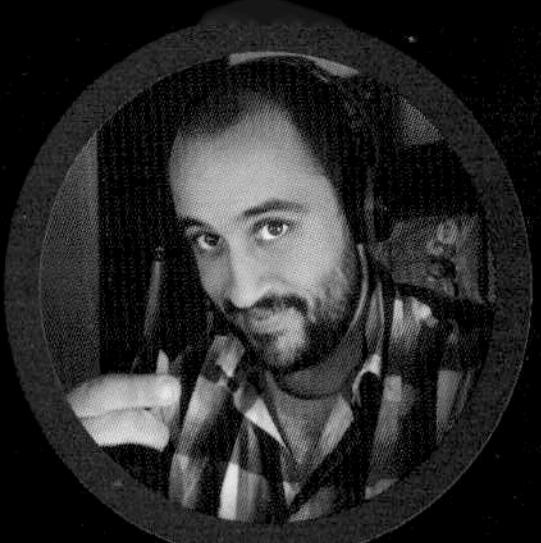

DC ALONSO

colorist

DC Alonso is passionate about classical art, especially painting. In his colors, he tries to capture things he's learned from great painters. Alonso has worked for companies like Blizzard, IDW, Lion Forge and AfterShock. To date, he's colored about 50 comics since he started working in the comic book industry three years ago.

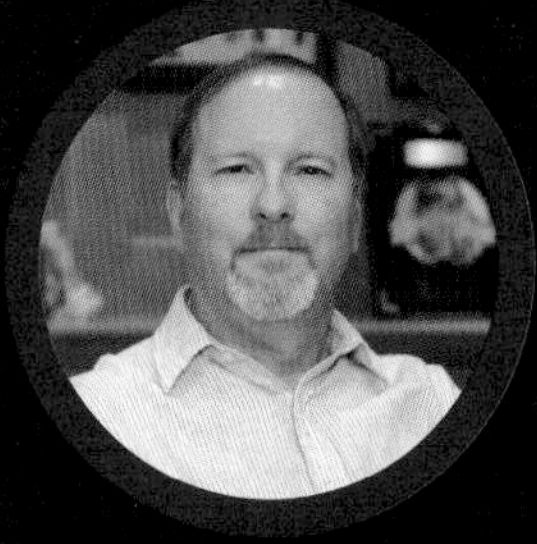

KEVIN J. ANDERSON

writer

One of the most prolific and successful authors currently working in the science-fiction and fantasy field, with over 150 books published—56 of them national or international bestsellers. He has written for *Star Wars*, *Star Trek*, *X-Files*, *Batman*, as well as every major comic book publisher and his own *Saga of Seven Suns*, and the *Dan Shamble, Zombie P.I.* series of novels.

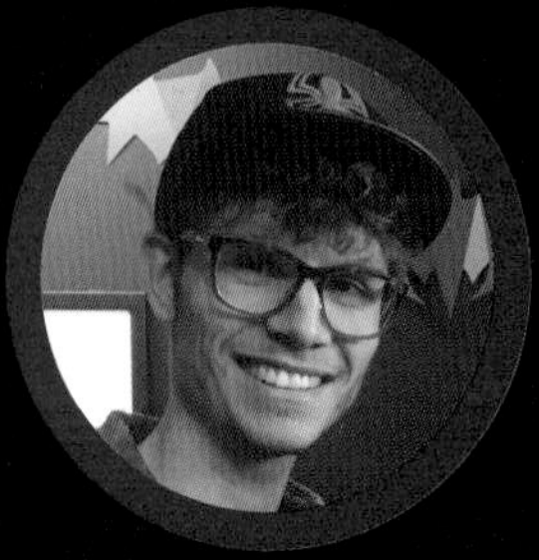

SYLVAIN BAUDURET

colorist

Sylvain Bauduret is a French comics author. After a higher degree in Mechanics and a first job in industry, he began his career in 2018 with the collective magazine *Tribute to Voltaire*. Now he works for the French editor Petit à Petit and he draws books for children.

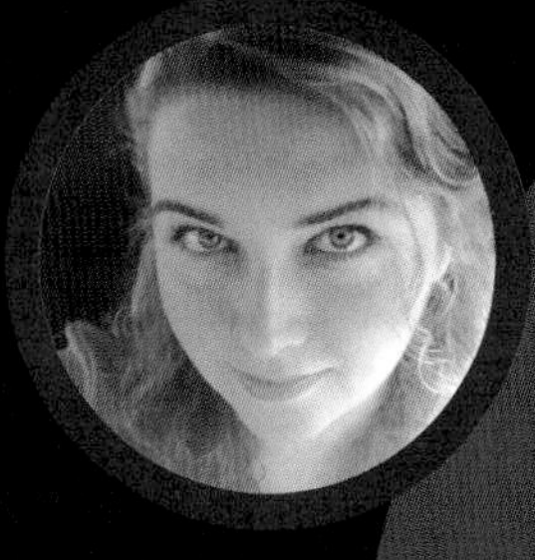

MARGUERITE BENNETT

writer

Marguerite received her MFA in Creative Writing from Sarah Lawrence College in 2013 and quickly went on to work for DC Comics, Marvel, BOOM! Studios, AfterShock Comics and IDW on projects ranging from *Batman*, *Bombshells*, and *A-Force* to INSEXTS and ANIMOSTIY, which has been optioned for development as a feature film with Legendary Pictures.

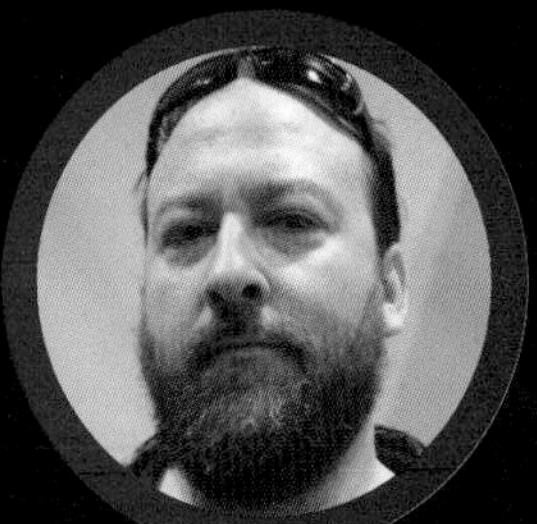

TIM BRADSTREET

artist

An Eisner Award-nominated illustrator whose work has spanned three decades in the fields of comic books, role-playing game art, trading cards and conceptional art for film and television, Tim enjoyed critically-received runs as the cover artist for Marvel's *Punisher* and DC's *Hellblazer* comic book series, garnering a fanatic fan-following that continues to this day.

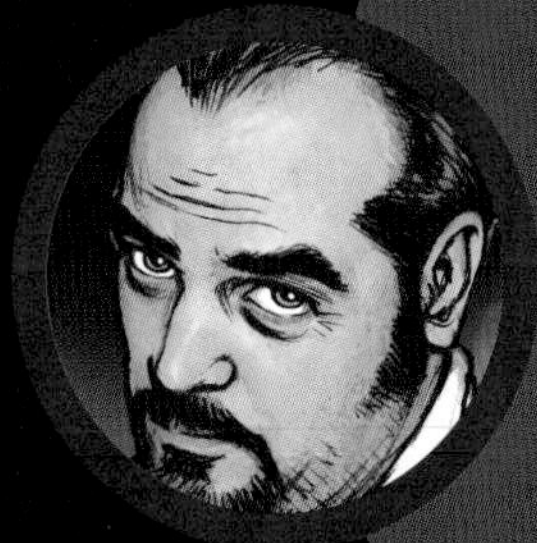

RUSS BRAUN

artist

Russ has been drawing comics for over 25 years, with a seven-year break for a stint with Disney Animation. Russ has worked on numerous titles, including *Batman*, *Animal Man* and *Swamp Thing* for DC. Russ is best-known for his frequent collaborations with Garth Ennis, including *The Boys*, *Battlefields* and, most recently, JIMMY'S BASTARDS at AfterShock Comics.

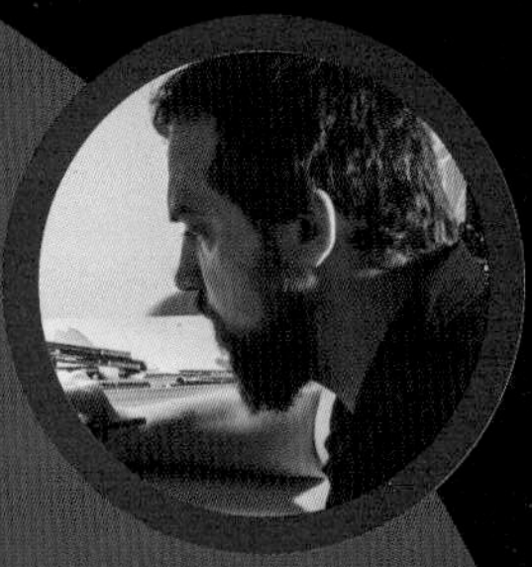

ANDREI BRESSAN

artist

Born in Piracicaba, São Paulo, Brazil, he is a penciller, inker and illustrator. He graduated in Advertising and Publicity, honing his skills at the Department of Fine Arts of University of Campinas, State of São Paulo, and at Quanta Academia de Artes. Active in the international market since 2009, he currently illustrates the series *Birthright*, published by Image/Skybound.

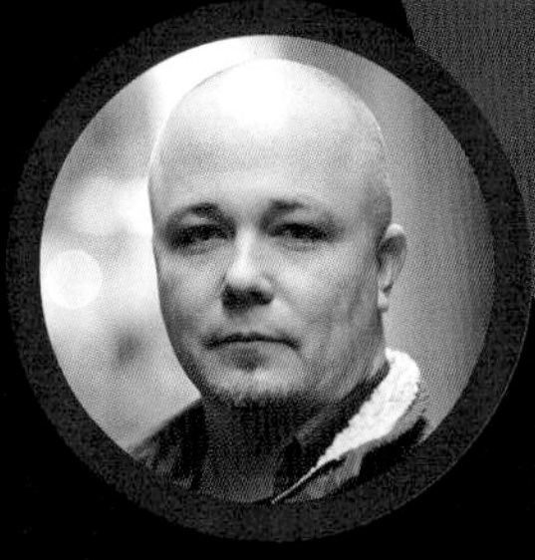

CULLEN BUNN

writer

Cullen is the writer of such creator-owned comics as *The Sixth Gun*, *The Damned*, *The Dark Man*, *Harrow County*, BROTHERS DRACUL and DARK ARK. In addition, he writes *X-Men Blue*, *Monsters Unleashed*, and numerous *Deadpool* comics for Marvel. A film adaption of *The Dark Man* is completed and *Harror County* is currently in development as a television series with the SyFy Channel.

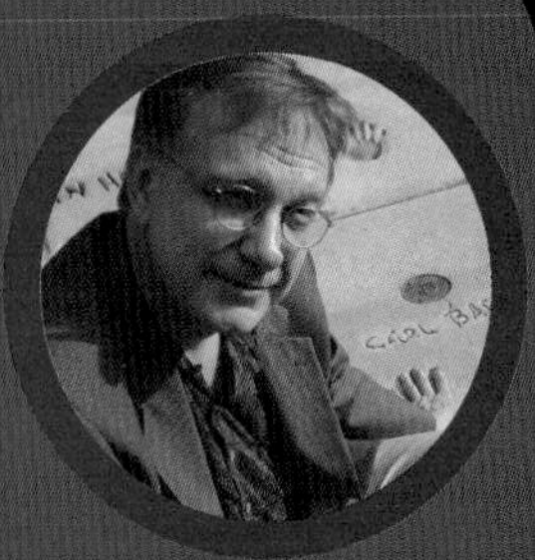

BOB BURDEN

writer / artist

As one of the founding members of the 80s comic book "New Wave" generation, Bob Burden's career in the field has been legendary. His Flaming Carrot has to be the most quixotic and outrageous character of the past few decades, continuing on today as the world's first surrealist superhero in a new series form Dark Horse later this year.

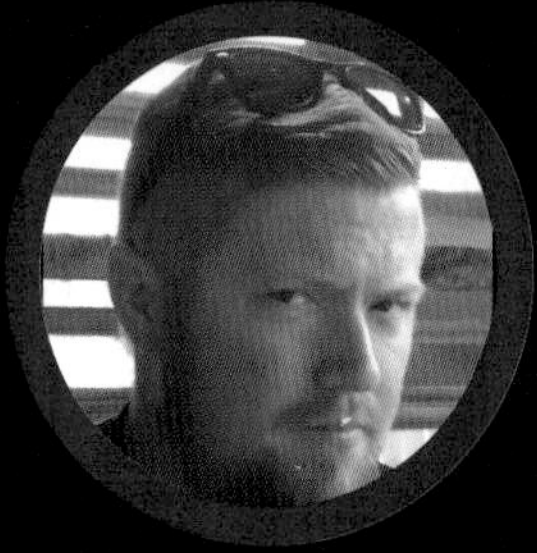

RYAN CODY

colorist

Ryan Cody is a comic book creator based in Northern Arizona. He has previously done work with Dark Horse Comics, Image Comics and Golden Apple Books, among others.

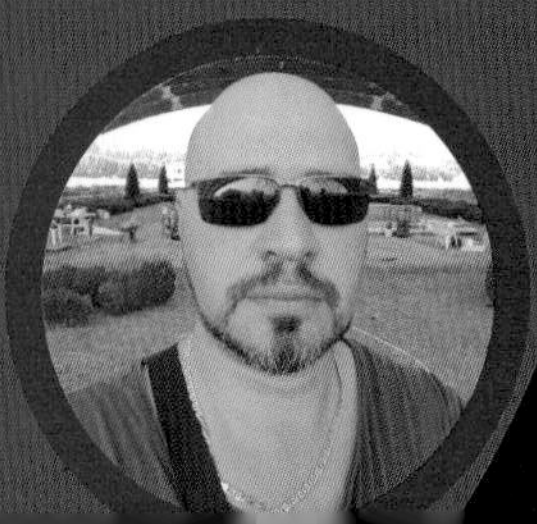

MIRKO COLAK

artist

European readers first had the pleasure of seeing Mirko's earlier artistic work in such Soliel publications as *Atlantide Experiment* and *Templier*. More recently, his intricate, masterful style has been seen in such comics as *Red Skull*, *Punisher*, *Spider-Man*, *The Avengers*, *Red Sonja*, *Deathstroke*, *Green Lantern*, *Turok*, UNHOLY GRAIL and

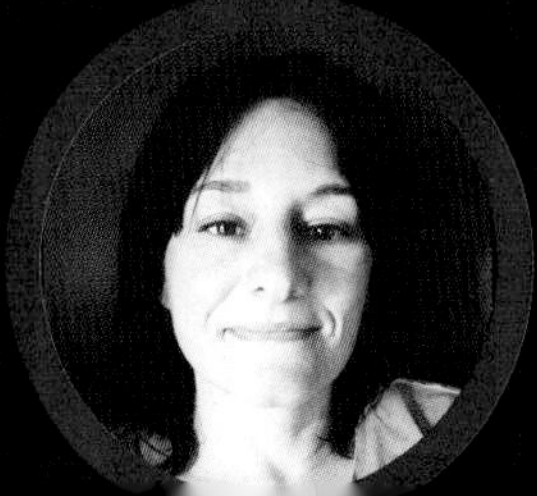

PATRIZIA COMINO

colorist

An Italian colorist, painter, illustrator, cartoonist and mother to two destructive Huns, Patrizia has drawn a graphic novel, as well as humor strips for numerous Italian publications. She also studies theatrical improvisation, so when she has to wait in line at the grocery store she can amuse the old ladies.

MARSHALL DILLON
letterer

Over the years, Marshall has been everything from an independent self-published writer to an associate publisher working on properties like *G.I. Joe*, *Voltron* and *Street Fighter*. He has worked for just about every publisher, except the "big two." Primarily a father and letterer these days, he also dabbles in old-school paper & dice RPG game design.

JUAN DOE
writer / artist

A professional illustrator and cover artist with over ten years experience in the comic book industry, Juan has produced work ranging from Marvel's *The Legion of Monsters* and the *Fantastic Four in Puerto Rico* trilogy, DC's *Joker's Asylum: Scarecrow*, and AfterShock's AMERICAN MONSTER, WORLD READER and DARK ARK series.

AARON DOUGLAS
writer

Aaron is a film and television actor best known for his portrayal of Chief Galen Tyrol on Syfy's *Battlestar Galactica*. With almost 100 screen credits on his creative resume, Aaron is excited to branch out into writing and get on the other side of the camera.

GARTH ENNIS
writer

A muliple Eisner Award-winner, Garth has been writing comics since 1989, and is considered one of the most successful writers of his generation. His credits include *Preacher* (recently picked up for its fouth season as a television series on AMC), *The Boys* (soon to debut as a series on Amazon) and A WALK THROUGH HELL.

RAY FAWKES
writer

A Toronto-based author and illustrator, Ray is an Eisner, Harvey, Shuster and Doug Wright Award nominee. He is also a YALSA award-winner for his *Possessions* series. His work for DC and Marvel includes such titles as *Batman: Eternal*, *Constantine*, *Justice League Dark*, and *Wolverines*. He also released the heist-thriller JACKPOT series with AfterShock Comics.

FRANCESCO FRANCAVILLA
writer / artist

Francesco, an Eisner Award-winner and *New York Times* best-selling creator, is best-known for bringing his signature style (Neo-Pulp) to the comics industry. In addition, he works on art for movie posters, DVD/BD, albums, concept and storyboards for film and television.

ANTONIO FUSO
artist

An Italian comic book artist based in Rome, Antonio has contributed to such titles as *Judge Dredd*, *Torchwood*, *James Bond 007* and the graphic novel adaption of Stieg Larsson's *Millennium Trilogy*. Antonio has also produced covers and illustrations for Valiant, IDW, Archie, Titan, Vertigo and the Belgian rock band *dEUS*. He is an interior design lover, as well a coffee addict.

BO HAMPTON
artist

Bo is a long-time comic artist known for projects that span the entire course of human events. His most recent Graphic Novel was published by Dark Horse Comics in 2018—*The Once and Future Tarzan*.

PHIL HESTER
artist

Phil has been writing and drawing comics for nearly three decades. He broke into the mainstream with a long run as artist of DC's *Swamp Thing*, with writer Mark Millar, and artist of Kevin Smith's revival of DC's *Green Arrow*. His work, as both artist and writer, has been featured in hundreds of comics from nearly every American publisher.

JAMAL IGLE
artist

Jamal Igle has been a writer and cartoonist for almost 30 years, working for nearly every major publisher in the comics field. The creator of the all-ages series *Molly Danger*, the co-creator of *Venture* (with Jay Faerber) and *The Wrong Earth* (with Tom Peyer). Jamal resides in New York City.

MILAN JOVANOVIC
artist

Milan was born in Koper, Slovenia, currently working and living in Zemun, Serbia. He is the artist behind *Ultimus*, *La Bete Noire*, *Jason Brice* and *Carthago*. He is currently working on a the series *Le Roi de Fer* for French publisher Soleil, as well as illustrations for galleries. He is a son, a brother an uncle a husband and a father

SAM KIETH
artist

Sam broke into comics by co-creating and illustrating DC Comics' *The Sandman* with Neil Gaiman. In 1993, Sam created *The Maxx* for Image Comics, which sold over a million-and-a-half copies and was later adapted in 1995 as an animated series for MTV. The series was honored with an Annecy Award for Best Animated series.

DRAZEN KOVACEVIC
artist

Drazen Kovacevic, born in 1974, is a Serbian comic book artist, storyboard artist and illustrator. Best-known for the comic book series *Walkyrie* for Soleil, he has created many comic book series for different French publishing houses, including Glenat, Humanoides Associes, Delcourt and Dargaud.

SZYMON KUDRANSKI
artist

Born in Poland, Szymon got his big break working with writer Steve Niles in 2004's *30 Days of Night Annual*. Since then, he has worked with DC, Marvel and Image Comics. Szymon also is credited with co-creating the AfterShock Comics series BLACK-EYED KIDS and is currently the artist for Marvel Comics' *Punisher* series.

LEE LOUGHRIDGE
colorist

Lee Loughridge is a devilishly handsome man, despite his low testosterone, who has been working primarily in the comics/animation industry for well over 20 years. He has worked on hundreds of titles for virtually every company in the business.

DARKO MACAN
writer

In the past three decades Darko Macan wrote SF stories, YA novels, computer games and comics ranging from *Mickey Mouse* to *Star Wars*, including fondly remembered runs on *Grendel Tales* and *Soldier X*. He is currently writing the well-received western series *Marshal Bass* for the French market.

GUY MAJOR
colorist

Guy Major is an artist and photographer who has been working in comics since 1995, when he responded to an ad looking for colorists for Wildstorm's *WildC.A.T.S.* series. When not working on comics or out with his camera, he is studying about, tasting, or drinking wine.

RON MARZ
writer

Ron has been writing comics for almost three decades, having worked for virtually every major publisher and compiled a long list of credits, including stints on *Thor* for Marvel, *Green Lantern* for DC, *Star Wars* for Dark Horse, and the landmark *Marvel vs. DC* crossover, among many others. He is also Editor-in-Chief for the revived Ominous Press. Twitter: @ronmarz

OLEG OKUNEV
artist

Oleg is a Ukrainian-born artist who got his start in comics after creating a humor strip for the digital newspaper *Regionline*. After that, he got involved in the creation of gaming projects such as *Space Rangers* and *Metropolis*. Later, he worked for the well-known Russian publishing house *Bubble*. These days, he illustrates AfterShock Comics series PESTILENCE.

CHARLES PRITCHETT
letterer

Brought up on the wrong side of the tracks in a bustling metropolis in Newfoundland, Canada, Charles enjoys a fine stew from time-to-time and hates to travel. He can be found currently living in Canada's smallest, but nicest province, outnumbered by powerful women in his own household.

JOE PRUETT
writer

Joe Pruett is an Eisner Award-winning comic book editor and writer. Best-known as the publisher for AfterShock Comics, and the writer of BLACK-EYED KIDS, he has also written for virtually every major comic publisher, including Image, Vertigo, IDW, DC, AfterShock and Marvel, where he wrote for *X-Men Unlimited*, *Cable*, *Domino*, *Wolverine* and *Magneto Rex*.

CLIFF RICHARDS
artist

Brazil-based comics veteran Cliff Richards has been a mainstay at DC Comics, where he has drawn Batman/Superman, Wonder Woman, Cyborg, and many others. For seven years, he drew Joss Whedon's *Buffy the Vampire Slayer*, *Angel*, and other related titles, along with such offbeat graphic novels as *Pride & Prejudice & Zombies*.

ZACHARIAH ROANE
artist

An illustrator who lives and works in Los Angeles, California, Zachariah has worked for WB Animation and Sideshow Collectables as a concept designer and storyboard artist. You can usually find him with his dog Brody hunched over his sketchbook immortalizing the legions of demons forever dancing and singing in

MARIA SANTAOLALLA
colorist

Born in Málaga, Spain, Maria initially studied tourism in college before realizing she wanted to be a comic book colorist. Being a dreamer and loving new challenges, Maria taught herself how to color, eventually earning professional work first at Fantasy Prone and later at IDW on *Back to the Future* and at AfterShock on

HOYT SILVA
colorist

Hoyt Silva is the most versatile storyteller to grace the pages of a comic. From pencils and inks to colors, he handles each with an unequivocal freshness the game just isn't ready for. Check out more of his work on Patreon at patreon.com/hoytsilva or on Instagram as @thehoyt.

ROXANNE STARR
letterer

Born in Paris, France, Roxanne came to New York City at the age of two. She took graphic design at the School of Visual Arts, taking two years off to work as a traffic editor at *The National Enquirer*. In 1980, she moved to Atlanta and worked as a freelancer in the graphic design field, before starting her lettering career in comics, initially with Bob Burden's *Flaming Carrot*.

R. L. STINE
writer

One of the best-selling children's authors in history, his *Goosebumps* and *Fear Street* series have sold more than 400 million copies and have been translated into 32 languages. Several TV series based on his work, and two feature films, *The Goosebumps Movie* and *Goosebumps 2*. Bob lives in New York City with his wife Jane, an editor and publisher.

LARRY STROMAN
artist

Larry is best-known for long runs on *Alien Legion*, *X-Factor*, various graphic novels featuring *Cloak & Dagger*, *Punisher* and *Black Widow*, as well as his creator-owned book, along with Todd Johnson, *Tribe*. Larry spends most of his time doing covers, pinups and various books for Valiant, Lion Forge, among others. A return of *Tribe* is also in development.

JILL THOMPSON
writer / artist

Jill Thompson is a 10-time Eisner Award-winning comic creator of titles such as *The Scary Godmother*, *Magic Trixie*, *Wonder Woman: the True Amazon*, *Beasts of Burden*, *Finals*, *Sandman*, *The Little Endless Storybook* and more! She lives in Chicago with her cats, her magical paints and her swords.

ALJOŠA TOMIĆ
colorist

Aljoša Tomić is a comic book colorist stationed in Novi Sad, Serbia. With more than 10 years of professional experience, he has had his work published by various publishers from around the globe, including Dark Horse, Markosia and Delcourt.

JIM STARLIN
writer

Best-known as the creator of Marvel Comics' Thanos, Gamora, and Drax the Destroyer—all of which play large roles in Marvel's movie universe in the *Guadians of the Galaxy* and *Avengers* franchises—Jim is the "father" of the cosmic soap-opera he made popular as a writer and artist on Marvel's *Warlock* and *Captain Marvel*, in addtion to his own *Dreadstar* series.

ROB STEEN
letterer

Rob is the illustrator of the *Flanimals* series of children's books written by Ricky Gervais and the Garth Ennis children's book *Erf*. He is also the colorist of David Hine's graphic novel *Strange Embrace* and letterer of comic books for AfterShock, Marvel, Dynamite, Image and First Second.

MARKO STOJANOVIĆ
writer

Marko is a writer, editor and translator. He has published his comics in 12 countries, including Great Britain, Belgium, France and Uruguay. He's also the winner of lifetime achievement awards for his contribution to comics in three different countries: Serbia, Macedonia and Bulgaria.

STEVE RASNIC TEM
writer

Steve Rasnic Tem, author of over 400 short stories, is a past winner of the World Fantasy, British Fantasy, and Bram Stoker Awards. His most recent novel is *UBO* (Solaris Books).

FRANK TIERI
writer

Frank is an award-winning writer and creator working in comics, video games, animation and television. Best-known to comic readers for his three-year run on *Wolverine*, he has also worked on some of the biggest franchises in the industry for Marvel, DC, Dynamite, Top Cow and Archie. He lives in Brooklyn, like three million other people.

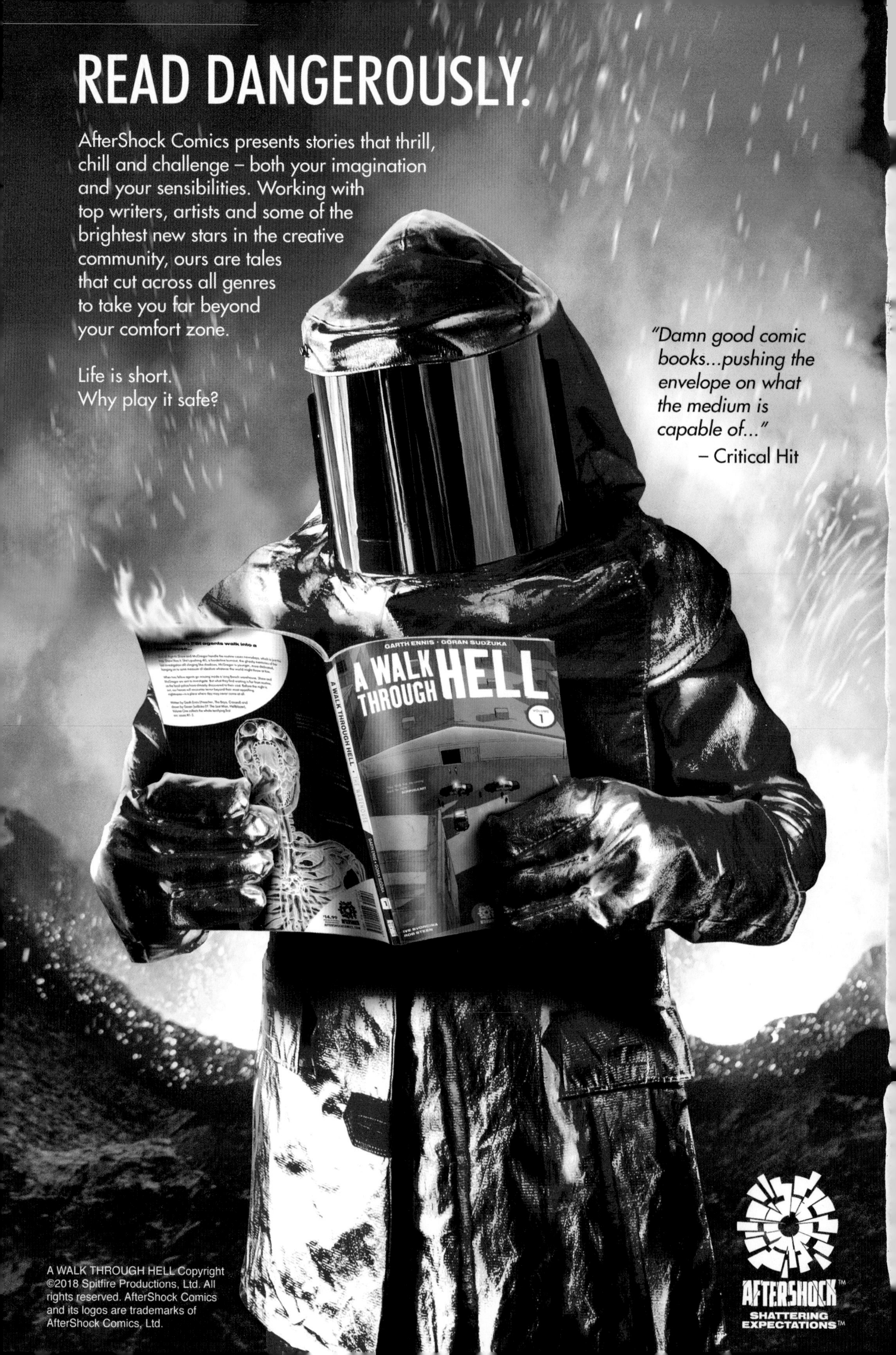
READ DANGEROUSLY.
AfterShock Comics presents stories that thrill, chill and challenge – both your imagination and your sensibilities. Working with top writers, artists and some of the brightest new stars in the creative community, ours are tales that cut across all genres to take you far beyond your comfort zone.
Life is short.
Why play it safe?
"Damn good comic books...pushing the envelope on what the medium is capable of..."
– Critical Hit
GARTH ENNIS · GORAN SUDŽUKA
A WALK THROUGH HELL
A WALK THROUGH HELL
A WALK THROUGH HELL Copyright ©2018 Spitfire Productions, Ltd. All rights reserved. AfterShock Comics and its logos are trademarks of AfterShock Comics, Ltd.
AFTERSHOCK™
SHATTERING EXPECTATIONS™

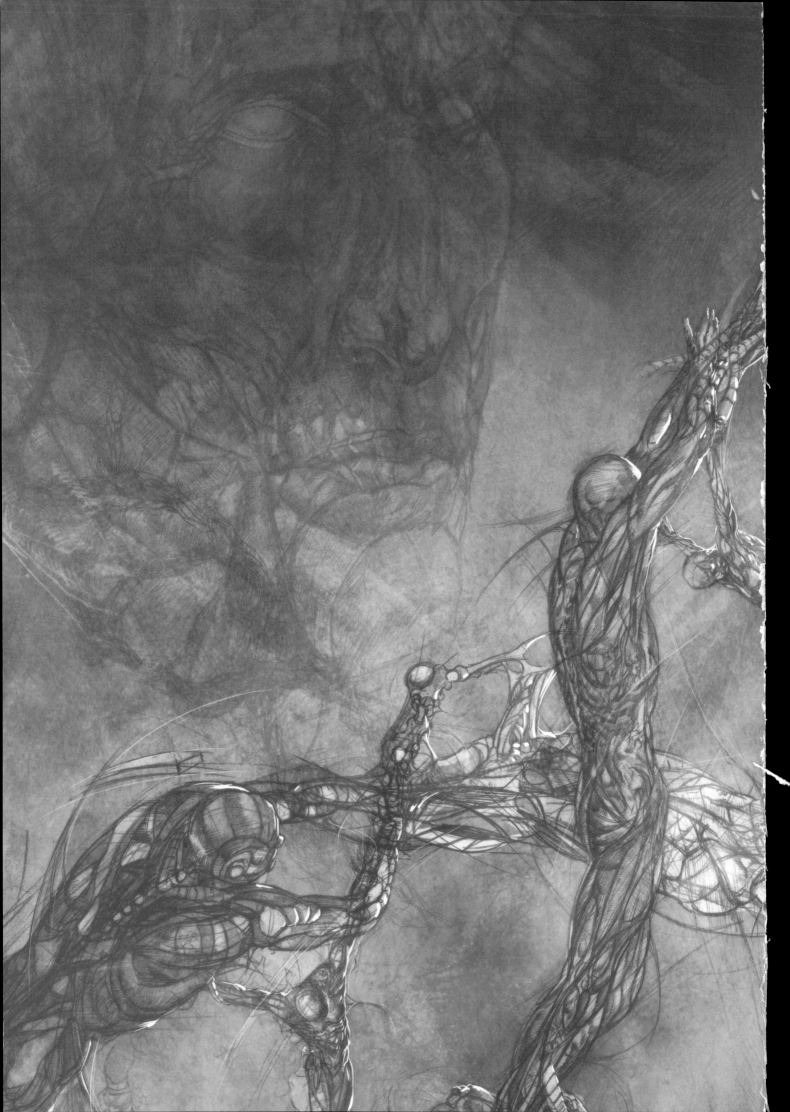